# RIVERBY INN

A 1930's Portrait of the Blanks Family in the
Swannanoa Valley

# RIVERBY INN

## A 1930's Portrait of the Blanks Family in the Swannanoa Valley

Betty Hedges Barritt & Francis Fields Leake

Addendum by M. Miriam Hedges

KwestWorks

Cover Image: Artistic rendering of Riverby Inn by Sarah Maynard © 2019

Published by: KwestWorks LLC
Bountiful, Utah

Edited by: Christine Lee Richards

Please send comments or questions about this work to: support@KwestWorks.com

Printed on Demand in the United States

Library of Congress Control Number: 2019957098

Hardcover ISBN 13: 978-1-7343818-0-1
Paperback ISBN 13: 978-1-7343818-1-8
e-Book ISBN 13: 978-1-7343818-3-2

*For Leon the first of the Trundle-Bed Trash to "walk the Big Pipe"*

Homer Leon Banks, September 1960[1]

# Table of Contents

# List of figures

*Figure 1: Riverby Inn circa 1930 (Photo Courtesy of Martha Lee Blanks Nickless)*

# Riverby Inn

Riverby Inn was a prominent two-story structure that dominated the Blue-Ridge encircled Swannanoa Valley from the early 1900's until it was destroyed by fire in the 1950's. But Riverby Inn was much more than a place. Its story is the story of its family, the Frank and Jeffie Blanks clan. Like a Norman Rockwell painting with unspoiled goodness captured in rich colors and caricatures, the Blanks' story is an uplifting reflection of human relationships, childhood adventure, and life in the 1930's American South.

In January of 1964, the authors sent out letters to all surviving members of the Blanks Family. One by one as memories were jogged, they returned their contributions. From these, the authors were able to reconstruct one long summer of happy childhood memories. Through their story, Riverby Inn has opened once again for both family and guests.

Book your reservation for the entire summer. The welcome rug is out by the front door. Take a rocker on the front porch of the Riverby Inn and join the Blanks family.

# Preface

## My Turning Point – "The Pipe Walker"

In 1922 a doctor built the place for a sanitarium. He died before it was completed and my grandparents, Mam-maw and Grandy, bought it at public auction. It was too large for one family to live in but it certainly wasn't Grand Hotel size.

The Inn dominated the Swannanoa Valley. It sat solidly on a hill surrounded by the Blue Ridge Mountains. The mountains sat all around the Valley like elegant, well-bred ladies around a tea party. In the summer they were at their best. . . groomed to perfection with their dark green leafy skirts overlapping one another. Like the Inn, they looked solid, strong, attractive and comfortable.

The beet view of the place was the long approach from Asheville. An unsuspecting motorist rounding the big curve a mile away and coming upon this sudden vista had a full and complete view of the whole scene. The Inn was huge and rambling and many-winged. It was painted white with green gables and shutters. Its several red chimneys pushed up from the roof and emitted curling plumes of smoke from open fireplaces and the Royal Oak coal stove in the kitchen. Long porches, or galleries, hugged three sides of the house and were shaded by wisteria vines that clung to the upright post supporting the porch roof. The vines not only climbed the posts but crawled over onto the roof and felt so rewarded they bore huge clusters of dark blue flowers up there. American boxwood nestled up against the porch and tulip trees suitable for our tree houses were scattered throughout the yard.

A circular driveway led the weary traveler through the tall rock pillars at the bottom of the hill and up around the house. In the spring the dogwood and cherry trees lining the driveway looked like young ballet dancers in bright tutus joining hands. The acres of yards were kept in strong and springy grass. At the foot of the yard, a low wall separated the lawn from the vegetable and flower gardens.

The Swannanoa River ran just down the hill in back of the property and though its origin was deep in the hearts of the mountains and that water was pure and crystal clear, the river was dirty and dangerous and usually a rainbow of colors from the dyes from the local mill. We all lived in the river from sunrise to sunset.

And that is where the name came from. Riverby Inn. The Inn by the River. But a name as magical and powerful as abracadabra, Hosanna and Excelsior!

The family who owned the Inn was just as attractive and comfortable and unique as the Inn, itself.

Francis Marion Blanks (or Grandy) was born before the Civil War and was named for the Swamp Fox. He lived his name to the hilt and by the time he was in his late seventies and had been made a grandfather fourteen times, he was still pretty foxy and more than a little swampy. He was strong as an oak and straight as a pine. He had the bearing and carriage of a West Point Plebe and his voice had the authority of a god. He was the father-figure supreme back in the days when no one had ever heard of Freud.

Mam-maw was christened Jeffie Lee Gill. She was born during the Civil War and was named for Jefferson Davis and Robert E. Lee. Her home, heart and arms were lovingly open to all mankind.

She was loving to the unlovely and found only the very best in each person and situation and she did it without being sickening. It was a natural talent. She represented Motherhood and Mother Earth. At the same time, she was earthy and down to earth.

In the season between Memorial Day and Labor Day, their four children arrived with all their children. The Inn on the hill was a fascinating collage of the union of Mam-maw and Grandy.

All hands heaved to clean, paint and staff and stock the Inn for the summer influx of tourists. By the first week in June the old place was beginning to wink and smile and shine as it beckoned to vacationers. All summer long, Old Hickory Mountain across the way watched with age-old stoic calm the screams and shouts of pain and hilarity of the antics over at Riverby Inn. He must surely have looked with respect and admiration at Mam-maw when she would throw open the big front doors in the early morning sunlight and looked back at him as she said, "I will lift up mine eyes unto the hills from whence cometh my strength".

For many years now Riverby Inn has been no more. Throughout all these years members of the family and summer guests have said, "Those years must be remembered. They must be written down. The years of that Camelot were too precious and special to too many people and it must not be forgotten."

But the task was too great. There was too much to say. Personalities were as many and as varied as the people who came there and left their footprints on the welcome rug that lay just over the threshold of the big double front doors.

And that is how a Turning Point in my life came for me. A cousin arrived in town for a visit and together we determined to get it all down. She has a background of Journalism while I had only a huge willingness to try my best. There were many talented people in the family who were better equipped to undertake writing up of this book. But for reasons of their own they declined.

I had much to ponder: would I be able to 'write'? In fact, would I be able to learn how to develop a technique for writing a lengthy manuscript? Would I have the sustaining power and interest for at least a year? How could I possibly collaborate with someone I saw but rarely and who lived many states away? I was always the quiet one. The timid one. The whole idea seemed absurd for me to even try it. My natural reticence and timidity and the fear of looking the fool made the whole idea even more implausible.

We knew the whole story must be told. As in most every family there was a skeleton or two in the closet. How could I live with myself if even one member of the family was upset or unhappy with the outcome?

Even as I was pondering all these intangibles in my conscience and heart there were some very real concrete problems to deal with. How could I possibly co-author with my cousin who lived a thousand miles away? We would be writing together and separately. Would it all mesh? And where would I find the time to write? The role of a suburban housewife and mother is legend in this country. Surely, I would allow nothing to interfere with even one segment of my duties and interests. It would be easy to bow out of the venture with all these excuses.

Then I remembered The Pipe. And the symbolism of learning to become a Pipe Walker. At Riverby Inn, a large water pipe lay exposed across the Swannanoa River. It led from the property of the Inn across still waters and deep channels and on across dangerous rapids and currents. At the other end of the pipe lay an island as enchanting to children as any island Tom Sawyer ever discovered. Every summer one or two small children were left weeping and sobbing at the Riverby side as they watched the older children walk or even run across to the island. Each of us in turn knew the frustration of not being able to follow the leader to the island to swing on the grapevine swings or climb to the crow's nest of the big pine tree. Or to eat the wild grapes that grew in profusion over there. Or to spend the night camping out with the older ones. Then gradually our fears would leave us as the desire to accomplish the seeming impossible overwhelmed us. Suddenly, another pipe walker would appear in the family on a particular glorious and wonderful summer day. It was not only an adventure and a real accomplishment but also a sort of coming of age.

It became symbolic to us all and even in later years when we could all walk the pipe without falling off, and one of us had overcome a fearful and terrifying problem in life, we would say, "Yes, he has accomplished the impossible. He has walked the pipe."

I, too, determined to walk the pipe and help write this story.

That moment was my turning point. Even as I had fears and worries and many unanswered questions running through my mind, I WAS WRITING ON THE BOOK FROM NINE IN THE MORNING UNTIL THREE IN THE AFTERNOON. It was the most thrilling experience of my life. It was an adventure into love and life. And it was very hard to do.

It took months of research in getting facts straight. It meant drawing up a separate biographical sketch on each person in order to get an objective view. Since we decided to lay the scene in the summer of 1934, it meant we had to be very careful in projecting ourselves back into that era. What were the newspaper headlines? What were the songs of that time? Who were the movie stars? What did the women wear? Watch out! Don't put a Mixmaster on the kitchen counter.

There were family historical facts to check. We felt the book should certainly be quite accurate but read like a novel. Some members of the big family had become prominent, even a bit famous, in their communities... how would they feel about certain disclosures? One of Mam-maw's favorite Bible quotations was: "A good name is to be chosen rather than great riches; and loving favor is better than silver and gold". How best to keep the family's good name and loving favor at the same time?

The work was long and arduous and tiring. Spring went into summer and then school started and very soon snow fell and still we wrote and wrote for hours every day and loved every minute of it. Some chapters were so funny we nearly fell off our chairs laughing over them. Some parts were so poignant we wept unashamedly. We fought and wrangled between ourselves via the United States Mail. But the story shaped up and one compelling thought and our driving force was that it was at long last all written down for our family. What had been our book was now their book.

As we progressed on the manuscript and delved more deeply into each personality, we realized we were head over heels in love with each person all over again and each character was appearing, in spite of his faults, as a real hero in his own right. With God's help, the book turned into a lovely work of love and honesty and happiness and gratitude and compassion and plain old home made fun and good times. This is the way we felt when we wrote The End to the story.

Once again, I had walked the pipe. When another Turning Point had appeared in my life I was proud and pleased that I had taken on a difficult task and not only triumphed over all my fears and difficulties but realized once again how wonderful it is to attempt something new and different and bold and reach a symbolic island of childhood dreams instead of being left behind sobbing in frustration.

I think with great pride and satisfaction that I, too, had 'looked and lifted up mine eyes unto the hills... and had found great riches... and loving favor'.

*Elizabeth "Betts" Barritt*

*Figure 2: Frank and Jeffie Blanks*

# ❧ *Frank and Jeffie Blanks* ❧

# Family Trees

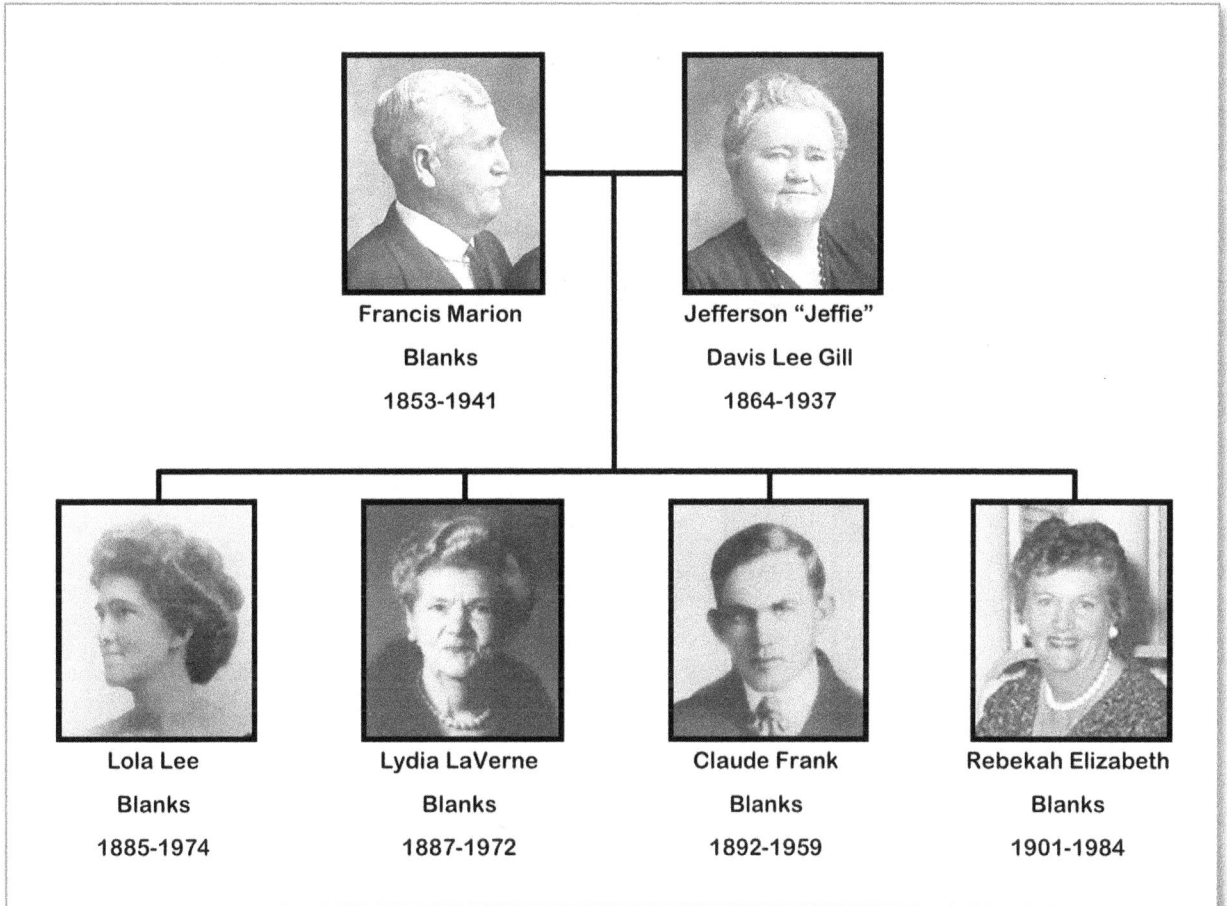

*Figure 3: Frank and Jeffie Blanks Family Tree*

| Francis Marion Blanks 1853-1941 | Jefferson "Jeffie" Davis Lee Gill 1864-1937 |

| Lola Lee Blanks 1885-1974 | Lydia LaVerne Blanks 1887-1972 | Claude Frank Blanks 1892-1959 | Rebekah Elizabeth Blanks 1901-1984 |

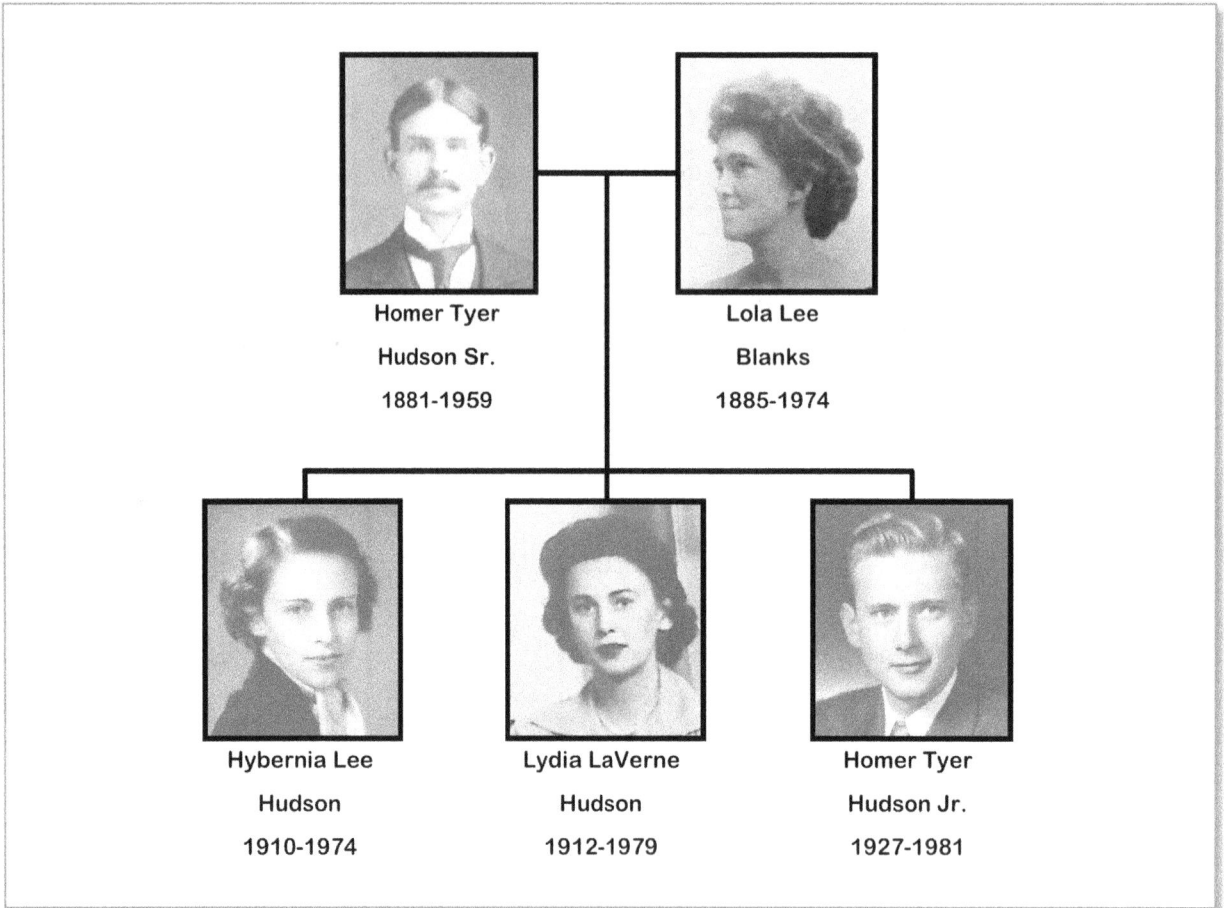

*Figure 4: Homer and Lola Hudson Family Tree*

**Nicknames Used in Story**

Hybernia – "Hy"

LaVerne – "La"

Homer – "Sonny"

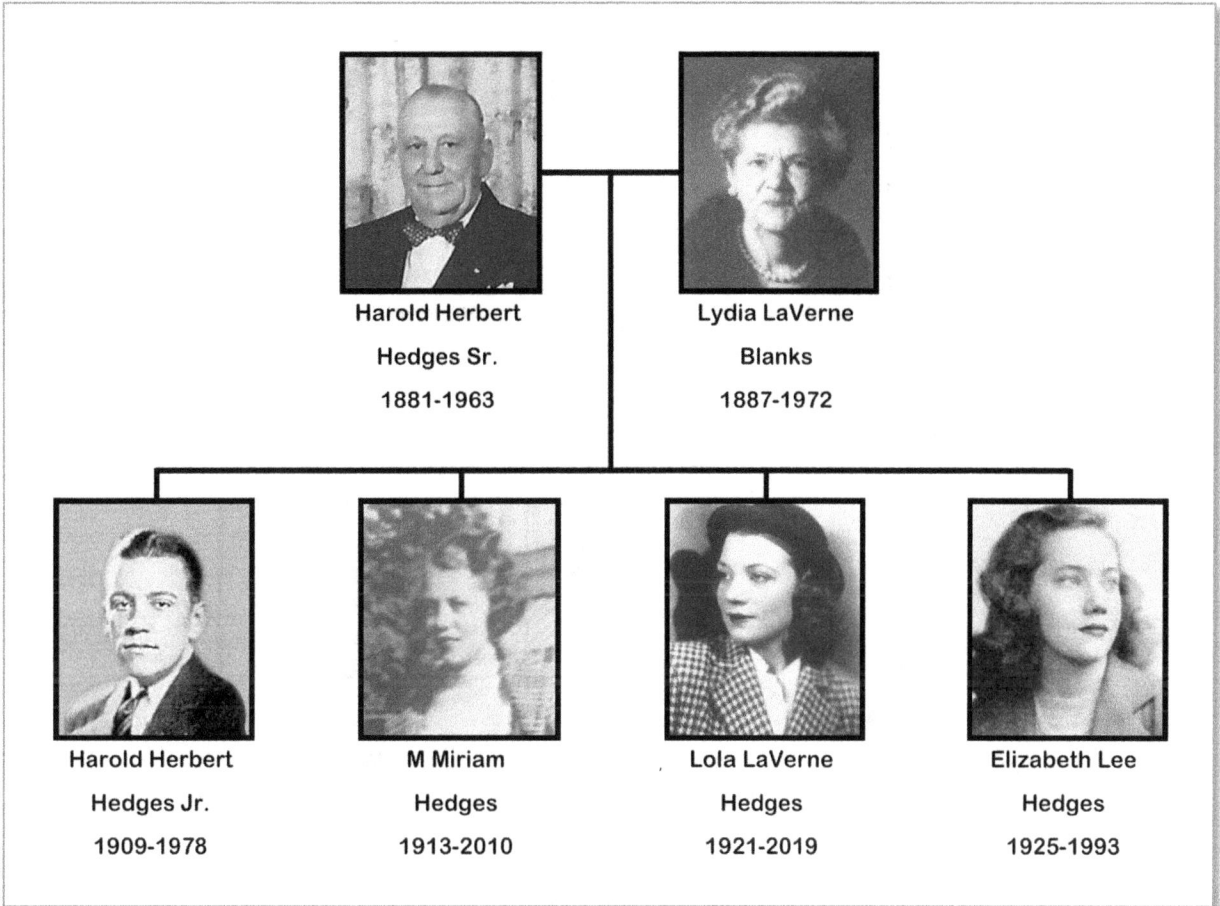

*Figure 5: Harold and Lydia Hedges Family Tree*

**Nicknames Used in Story**
Miriam – "Mabes"
Lola LaVerne – "Bobbie"
Elizabeth – "Betts"

*Figure 6: Claude and Norma Blanks Family Tree*

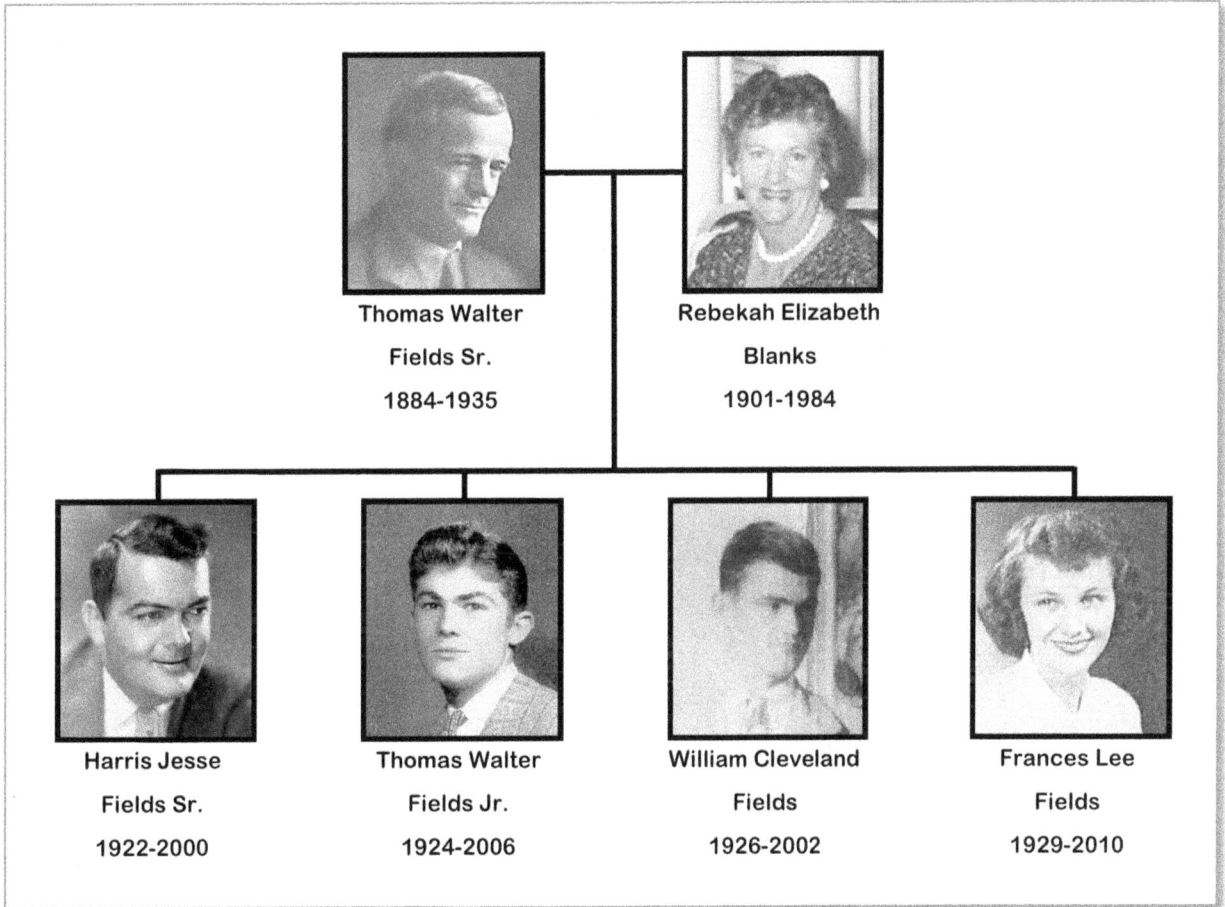

*Figure 7: Tom and Rebekah Fields Family Tree*

**Nicknames Used in Story**

Harris – "Jaybo"

Thomas – "Tom Jr."

William – "Bill"

Francis – "Sis"

Bee Tree Road

Frank  Jeffie

Johnson Farm

Lola's Cottage

Riverby Inn

RIVERWOOD ROAD

PIPE

Swannanoa

NEW 70

OLD 70

Asheville

Swannanoa

Bee Tree Reservoir

Burnett Reservoir

"North Fork"

OLD 70

OLD 70

River

Factory Housing

PARK St

WHITSON AVE

Beacon Blanket Factory

Black Mountain

Carolyn Hudson Vail

# The Gathering of the Clan

LaVerne sat bare headed on the rope tied trunk at the entrance gate of Riverby Inn and composed her travel worn spirits as the bus ground its gears and started off toward Black Mountain. Tears of joy and relief lowed from her blue eyes as the feeling of sweet security surged through her tired body.

"We're here!!! We're here!!!" Harold Jr., Mabel, Bobbie, and Betts vocalized their arrival to the whole valley. The oversized two-story frame house on the hill, with its green tipped gables and inviting porches echoed back to them in welcome. They ran up the long driveway, piercing the mountain air again and again.

"We're here! Mam-maw, Grandy, we're here! Are we the first to arrive?"

A shimmering sun winked over Ole Hickory mountain mirrored LaVerne on the black patent leather of her bandbox. She pushed back her disheveled blonde hair, wispy from-three days on the train and studied her parched face. Suddenly she remembered.

"Stop! Stop! Oh, driver," she tried vainly to hail the Trailways coach that had brought them out from Asheville.

"Yoo Hoo! You, stop! Just a minute. Please! I left my hat. My new blue straw…. it's on the overhead rack." The bus continued over the Swannanoa River bridge and around the bend out of sight.

"Oh Dear! It's gone. He didn't even hear me." She spoke to her mute image in the useless bandbox, bent down, picked it up then gathered the empty lunch hamper in her other hand and started up the deep rocky ruts behind her children.

Up the hill in front of her were her parents. By now, with the broadcasting of her flock, she knew the old couple were standing, arms outstretched on their front porch. Behind her lay hell! Fort Smith, Arkansas, already scalded with the midwestern heat and Harold, her husband still waving farewell in her memory.

The day after school was out, he had loaded the trunks on the luggage rack of the old Studebaker touring car and slowly drove them to the train depot. His free passes as agent of the Railway Express even now were tucked in her brassiere.

"Well, the Hedges contingent is here."

———————— ❧ ❦ ————————

*June 1, 1934*
*Mrs. T. W. Fields.......... Anguilla, Mississippi..............*

Rebekah Fields signed the first check in the navy-blue folder of American Express tender, ripped it out of the end tabs and handed it to the manager behind the desk. Half turning to conceal her movements from the elderly gentleman, she secreted the folder once more inside her bosom.

"Don't forget to take out for the hams," she reminded him of the four Tennessee hams she had purchased from the Hotel at breakfast.

"I declare, Mr. Burrows, The Poinsettia Hotel serves the most delicious home cured ham in Tennessee... I wouldn't think of going home to Swannanoa without passing through Dixon. I've had my mouth set for that ham for weeks."

"Oh Mrs. Fields, we look for you to come. Wouldn't be June without your stopping in for a night. How are Mr. and Mrs. Blanks? We sure miss them in these parts since they moved over to North Carolina. Your mother was a sight for sore eyes when she came through here on her way to see you. Let's see now.... Thanksgiving time, wasn't it?"

Rebekah dropped her eyes, drawing Mr. Burrows attention to her black attire.

"Mrs. Fields, we were so distressed to hear about Mr. Fields. Our condolences. So sudden wasn't it? Such a young man."

Beck's eyes clouded and she bit her lower lip to stop its quiver. Sis ran across the lobby and pulled at her mother's skirt for attention.

"Thank you, Mr. Burrows. Yes, it was sudden. Tom was eighteen years older than me ... but...but...Well, mamma was with me almost a month." She reached down to pat her youngest child on the head.

"Mamma, Mamma! The boys...Bill...Jaybo...Tom...they..."

"Shhhhhhhhhhhh child!" Beck pushed Sis away from her hoping to quiet her sudden outburst. Mr. Burrows nervously counted out her change.

"20...30...40...50...60...70...80..."

"Mamma, I'm trying to tell you sunpin," Sis raised her voice excitedly. "Jaybo and.... those boys stole a towel from the bathroom. I saw it. Bill has it in his pocket now.... It says Poinsettia Hotel right down the middle in green...See...It's in his pocket...See it?" Sis pointed across the lobby to where her three brothers stood sheepishly under a giant potted palm. Bill poked his tongue out at her and chanted, "Tattle tale.... tattle tale....... Sis is a tattle tale...."

Beck receiving the money in the palm of her hand, counted along to herself.

"60...70...80...90...100...Hush up! Sis. Can't you see I'm busy?" Beck didn't catch the story, the confusion intruded on her.

"But Mamma listen! They stole it!"

Beck popped Sis across the side of her cheek without raising her eyes from the pile of money accumulated in her hand.

"Shut up! This minute! Go get in the car. I'm coming."

The red imprint of Beck's hand stung the side of Sis's cheek and burned all the way down to her deep-seated sense of right and wrong. Determined not to cry, she gathered her hurt seven-year-old emotions together, turned on her heel, gave her brothers a look of disgust, and sped from the lobby.

Beck looked up in time to see her coat-tails round the corner of the doorway and out of sight. She addressed Mr. Burrows.

"Don't pay any attention to her. These children have literally tried themselves on this trip. Sometimes I think…"

"I had the boy put the hams on the floor of the back seat." Mr. Burrows interrupted Beck's excuse. She reached into the box of candy on the desk and picked up a 25¢ sized Hershey bar.

"Here, this will quiet her down." Beck gave him a quarter from her change and covered her quick remorse by turning gayly to her three sons who were still hesitating under the palm.

"Let's go, Riverby Inn, next stop. Hurry up! Your Mam-maw is probably baking each of you a pie right this minute." The boys relaxed under her change of mood and ran to the new green La Salle parked by the front entrance.

"Bye, Mr. Burrows. See you in September. We'll be back just after Labor Day. And, well thanks again. That ham was just delicious."

—————————————— ❧ ❧ ——————————————

"Homer Hudson, keep in the ruts now and sound your klaxon. I want to be the first one home but I don't care to arrive with flower girls beside the coffin." Lola pleaded.

The highway from Highpoint was narrow but two-laned until it reached Old Fort, there the paved road stopped and a crooked narrow trail weaved in corkscrew turns up and down the last mountainous fourteen miles to Riverby Inn.

"Why on earth are you stopping? Just sound your klaxon and keep in the ruts." Lola urged him to steer the Franklin on.

"Got to let the motor cool off. Its air cooled but no car was built to take this nature trail. If the North Carolina road commission doesn't pave this road soon, I'm not going to come back." Hudson found a cigarette and fumbled in his plus-fours pockets for his silver lighter.

La and Hy hungrily watched him inhale the Lucky Strike and exchanged knowing looks. La poked through the space between the buttons on her blouse and exposed for her sisters benefit the rumpled green package secreted in her bosom.

"Aw shucks! Dad" Sonny addressed the driver. "Let's hurry up. I wanna get there in time to go up the mountain with Leon and Charles to bring down the cow for the evening milking."

"Mom, do you think Mabel and Harold and them will get there today?" Hy wondered.

"Well, I certainly hope so. We have that whole house to spring clean and I'm certainly not going to do it by myself." Lola answered her daughter then turned to continue her thoughts to her husband.

"You just watch, I bet Rebekah, times her arrival just right. Probably won't show up till the last bed is made and the pantry is laden with food. She forgets that she's just family and not one of the paying guests."

"Oh boy, just wait till I show Bill Fields my new lead soldier set. Bet they don't have anything like that down in the country." Sonny boasted.

"Well don't start a fight before either one of you even get there. You two beat all." Homer chuckled at the thoughts of bloody noses and blackened eyes. Inside he smiled secretly. He would not be around Riverby Inn but for one short night.

———————— ❧ ❧ ————————

Mam-maw and Grandy waited, rocking on the wide front porch. Martha, Leon and Charles sat on the steps.

"Oh, Mam-maw won't it be wonderful having everyone back for the summer?" Martha speculated. "I hope Betts hasn't outgrown me. Everyone says we're just like twins."

Jeffie Gill Blanks looked at her son's children and noted that indeed, they all wore a year's growth. Leon had almost caught up with the older Charles and both were nearing manhood.

"When's Norma coming? I thought she said she'd be a little earlier home from the mill today. Starting her vacation, bless your mother's soul, taking her vacation to help us ready the Inn for the first summer boarders." Mam-maw mused aloud. No one answered.

"Reckon Lola'll beat Verne again. You can sure depend on that one. If she says she's coming this afternoon at four, she'll turn in that drive exactly at four."

Francis Marion Blanks took out his long gold watch chain, plopped the old watch in his palm, fingering it to flip open the front.

"Well, it's going on four. You boys better skedaddle up to the orchard and bring down ole Sally Kate. Lola will want everything to be running right on schedule." He concluded his timetable.

"Yes, Sir, Grandy." His grandsons began to move.

"We're here, we're here!" The voices of Harold Jr, Mabes, Bobbie, and Betts penetrated the quiet scene on the front porch. The Trailways Coach had gone unnoticed.

Grandy leaned forward in his rocker near the highway end of the porch, peeked through the wisteria vines and exclaimed.

"Well now, it's Verne and her four. Don't that beat all? She's beat Lola. I'll bet Homer gets all the blame when she comes in second."

"Yeah, you're first." Martha darted from the steps and down the drive. The three Blanks grandchildren joined forces with the Hedges foursome and exchanged excited greetings while LaVerne huffed and puffed up the hill.

"Here, Mamma, let me take those things. I was gonna go back and bring everything up at once." Harold Jr. relieved his mother of the burdensome traveling equipment. LaVerne caught her breath and agreed.

"Oh, yes, son. Get Leon and Charles and go fetch our valises. Wouldn't do to have someone take them. By accident of course." She added.

"Aunt Boom." The Blanks boys grabbed their Aunt LaVerne up off her bunion sore feet and twirled all her poundage around.

"Well the Hedges contingent is here." She laughed as her parents came down the steps. Martha just clung to her blue knit suit, speechless with joy and was carried along to the parental reunion. Betts had collapsed in giggles and hiccups; her car sick stomach was at last settling.

"Hello Verne." Grandy spoke with some little embarrassment overcoming his usual tongue-tied reaction to arrivals and departures.

"You beat Lola. They ain't here yet." He shook his head with puzzled concern.

Figure 8: A gathering of many family members circa 1925

Adults pictured left to right back to front:
2 neighbors, Norma, LaVerne holding Bobbie, Jeffie, Frank
Lola, Rebekah, Tom Fields
Children left to right: Mabes, Neighbor boy (sitting back row), Hy, La, Leon
(standing), Charles (sitting in front)

"Mamma" LaVerne choked," I'm home."

Mam-maw stood, waiting her turn to get at LaVerne. Her arms opened wide and closed around her middle daughter. LaVerne buried her face in her mother's breast and drank deep of her familiar smells of snuff, candied orange peel and yeast.

"Marth! Marth! Is the river still here? And the stream?" Betty, quickly untying her brown school oxfords, looked up at Martha who stood nodding in reply. Betty tore off her shoes and socks and wiggled her hot feet in the dust and cinders of the driveway.

Mam-maw disengaged herself softly from LaVerne's embrace and turned to the children.

"Now, why don't you girls go do a little wading in the stream. Mabes, you run upstairs and pick out the room you want for yourself and the Hudson girls. We can spread out as much as we want to before the house is put in order for the paying guest. Did you bring your water colors and some art work?" She spoke directly to Mabel.

"Yes'sum, I brought a lot of sketches and some still lifes. And I'm real interested in Gilbert and Sullivan. We put on the MIKADO in Fort Smith this spring and I was the stage director. I designed all the sets too."

Mam-maw interrupted. "LaVerne, I have the most talented grand-children. Harold, I want to see your Eagle Scout badge. Bobbie, you're grown, all of a sudden, sixteen years old and just as pretty as a picture. Are you too old to go wading with Martha Lee and Betts or do you want to help Mabes unpack and make up the beds?"

"That river? Ugh! I want to go on up and claim that little pink room right across from the bathroom. I want to have a bath and shampoo right now. I smell like that stinky train and Betts even had the nerve to get some throw-up on my new shoe. and I can still smell it. Phew!!!!"

Mam-maw ignored Bobbie and continued, "I'm taking your mother in the house so she can wash her face. Just leave these valises, LaVerne, let the boys take care of them."

LaVerne followed her mother gratefully through the wide double doors of Riverby and down the long wide hallway which served the Inn as a lobby, through the hotel sized dining room and into the big country kitchen.

"Boys. You Charles, Leon, Harold." Grandy's thundering voice brought a halt to the good-natured scuffling among the three boys.

"Git them grips upstairs and go on up to the pasture and bring back Sally Kate. If her bag gets too full, she'll be gettin' rising udder. Git going! Where's my paper? I'm waitin' here til' Lola comes. Mark my words, she'll be wheeling in soon and somebody oughta be on the porch to meet her."

Grandy returned to his seat in the end rocker facing the highway. He pushed back his brown felt hat and before taking up the Asheville Citizen, he removed his spectacles. He polished them with his crumpled handkerchief. First the right lens with the clear glass in it and then he gave a swift wipe to the left lens that had the smoked glass. He replaced them over the bridge of his nose and around his ears, the smoked glass did not quite hide his deformed eye. Before returning the handkerchief to his pocket, he wiped the tobacco spittle from his mouth and brushed his moustache which he kept trimmed to a cat's eyebrow.

"Now let me see what them yellow-bellied Republicans is up to," he muttered as he shook open the paper.

———————————— ❧ ❧ ————————————

"LaVerne, go on over to the sink and wash off your face. I'll pour you a glass of cold buttermilk. You look tuckered out." Mam-maw remarked as she headed for the ice box.

"I'm thankful for the new indoor plumbing but I'd rather go out on the back porch and pump up some water from the well. I've been thinking about that cold well water since day before yesterday." LaVerne gave several pumps on the old handle before the cold, clear water began to spill over her hands and into the enamel catch basin. She cupped her hands and let the water overflow them and repeatedly buried her face in the refreshment. Finally, when her thirst was satiated and her face felt clean, she patted it dry with the soft huck towel her mother handed to her.

"You look better already," Mam-maw said as she looked at her daughter with keen eyes. "Here's some buttermilk, compliments of Sally Kate."

LaVerne closed her eyes as she tilted the tall jelly glass to her lips. The creamy milk was liberally dotted with blobs of butter and its sweet acrid coldness seemed to have an immediate effect.

"Mama, there's nothing better in the whole world than cold buttermilk…… and being home with you…and Papa."

"Well, tell me, how did you leave Harold? Will he be coming?"

"I…I don't know yet. We'll have to wait and see." LaVerne rushed her words. "Mama there's so much I want to talk to you about. Harold…. well…. then Harold Jr will be ready for college this fall and we have to make plans about him. Mabel needs special art classes; she won all the honors in art this year and her teacher says she does have great talent. And Bobbie, I must talk to you about Bobbie. And Betts, poor little thing, she has these heart seizures, you know. I don't know which way to turn." LaVerne seemed on the verge of tears, her mother knew the symptoms only too well.

"Now daughter, we've all week for a heart to heart. Now isn't the time to go into all these things. You're exhausted and unstrung from the long trip. Rest up, relax, you're home with your people and everything will work itself out we'll see to that. Remember what the good book says, 'Trust in the Lord, with all thine heart; and lean not unto thine own understanding.'" Mam-maw refilled the empty glass from the ironstone pitcher of buttermilk and smiled confidence to her second born.

"There's a horn honking. Must be Lola and Homer and the children." LaVerne put down her glass and the two women hurriedly retraced their steps to the front porch. Their heavy frames made the old oak floor squeak and sigh.

Grandy was on his feet with his newspaper rolled up in one hand, he shook it as he greeted his eldest daughter. "Yore off'n your schedule, Lola. It's past four o'clock going on four-thirty."

"Blame it on the Franklin, Papa. Homer had to let the engine cool off coming over Old Fort Mountain. Mama, how good it is to see you. Are you here all ready?" She saw her sister behind Mam-maw.

"Her dust has hardly settled," Mam-maw offered her cheek to her first-born child and stood back to note her strait-laced figure.

"Come on you two girls. Give Mam-maw a big Riverby Inn kiss. I want to hear all about your beaus. What's this I hear about a debut?" She gathered Hy and La under each wing and squeezed them hard.

"You'll have to talk to mother about that," they said squeezing their grandmother back.

"Is Mabes here? Harold too? We want to show them how to do the Highpoint Stomp."

"Mam-maw? Mam-maw? Love me too?" Sonny Hudson stood with his hands on his hips, his fierce blue eyes showing out from under his shaggy white-blond hair.

He was swept up almost off his feet as Mam-maw smothered him with her hugs and kisses. "You run fast now, and you'll catch up with the big boys. Yonder they go down the lane toward the Bishops…going after Sally Kate. Scoot fast you'll catch them."

"Good Granny Alive!" Exploded Grandy. "I never heard so much female chicken cluckin' in all my born days. Get out of the way, let Homer out of the car. Been waitin' or you Hudson, how's business?"

"Won't have any, if I don't hurry and get back to Anvil Brand. The government is breathing down the factory's neck for that contract we made on CCC overalls. I told Lola, this is the last year I can just take off and drive her and the girls up here to the mountains. I've never seen such roads in my life. My digestion is acting up. Must have an ulcer or something. Can't even have quietude around home with all those beaus hanging around the house after my girls. Lola? Where is my albumen water?"

"Now, Homer, I just this minute got here. Girls, Mam-maw says Mabes is upstairs, run on and get settled. LaVerne you look peaked, was the trip as bad as usual? Mam-maw, do you have some good fresh eggs? I better go fix Homer's albumen water."

"Yes, Lola the hens are laying well right now. But how about an N.R. tablet? I have one right here in my pocket. Let Homer try it. Nothing beats Nature's Remedy pills."

Homer waved the offered tablet aside and headed for a rocker. He took off his plaid golfing cap and sat down weakly. His hand shook slightly as he pulled out a clean Irish linen handkerchief with the monogram HTH in one corner and laid it against his forehead.

"Looks like this fellow Roosevelt is a goin' to git things done. What'd ya know about him? He seems awful Yankee-fied. But I can't deny he's a helpin' the south git over the gall-darned depression."

"Papa don't talk politics to Homer. It upsets his ulcer." Lola shook her head at her father.

"Ulcer? What's that? Just another one of them dad-blamed things the doctors have thought up to make money off of. Look what happened when they thought up germs. That's all they can talk about. Them germs has made those doctors a mint of money, you can bet your life on it. All you need is some pure well water Homer, and some greens and cornbread with maybe a touch of pot licker."

Homer moved his handkerchief from his forehead to his mouth and stifled the result of a stomach spasm.

"Lola. My albumen water, PLEASE!" He pleaded.

---

"Norma, your coffee, how delicious it is. I had almost forgotten." LaVerne complimented as she held out her cup to her sister in-law for a refill.

"Do come and sit down, let's visit here on the porch. Nothing on earth rests my spirits more than sitting here looking up at the mountains in the twilight." She drew her shawl around her against the chill night air.

The younger children had disappeared, hopefully to bed. The four teenage girls were upstairs in their bedroom talking girl talk. Grandy had talked politics to Homer until Homer decided to put his ulcer to bed. In the parlor room Grandy now held the floor with his grandsons.

"Your mammy says you aim to go to college, Harold. Education is a good thing, but if you change your mind, you could go way on west. Texas maybe, or Kansas or Nebrasky, you could take up calving. Get yourself a big herd of beef. Turn 'em out to pasture, cows'll graze and grow whilst you're sleeping. Yes siree, a man's got to have a cow."

"Charles and Leon may want to go into logging. Did I ever tell you boys about my logging days in Arkansas with Brother Bill? Well sir, me and Bill…."

Norma chuckled as she set the empty coffee pot down on the floor near the door and with her steaming cup in hand, she took her seat in one of the rockers beside Mam-maw.

"Grandy's back in Arkansas with Brother Bill, his logging days, again. Those boys have heard his stories a million times. But they know better than to let on. LaVerne, speaking of Arkansas, tell me about Harold. Is he coming up here? You know we Blanks in-laws have to stick together. I don't feel quite so surrounded by Blanks, when Tom Fields, Homer Hudson and Harold Hedges are here to back me up. Oh Dear, I keep forgetting, sweet Tom, I can't believe he's gone. "

LaVerne was glad the darkness concealed her face. "I don't know……just now…... Tell about yourself. I hear you've taught yourself shorthand and typing down at the mill office. Norma I've always said you are the most mechanical woman I know. Imagine! Learning to peck one of those machines."

"I had to. Looks like I'll have to be the bread winner…. with Claude…. Well, you certainly know how your own brother is."

The Blanks women caught their breaths and swallowed hard.

"Anyway," Norma continued," When I heard Mr. McFadden was looking for a secretary, I just marched myself into his office and told him straight out that I wanted the job and would he give me a chance. Well, as Mam-maw says, necessity is the mother of invention and I sure invented my own brand of shorthand. He seems satisfied so far and I can certainly use the raise in pay. Leon and Charles seem to grow a foot a week and Martha is going into junior high school this fall."

"I wish Rebekah was here tonight." Mam-maw broke in. "They were to stop in Dixon and stay the night with the Burrows at the Poinsettia Hotel last night, but I don't know where she is tonight. I worry about her alone with all those children in some strange hotel."

Lola stopped rocking and shrugged a laugh. 'Why on earth would you worry about Beck? Even though she is your baby, there's one woman who can more than take care of herself. She'll try to out drive, out maneuver every man on the highway. She knows all the roads like the back of her fat hand. She's the only woman I ever saw who can drive with a wad of chewing gum in her mouth; eat an apple; slap at the children and keep the car in the middle of the road, all at the same time. I just don't want her stopping off in Trezevant, Tennessee and every other wide place in the road visiting all our kith and kin. She knows good and well that we have mountains of work to do here. Mark my words…. she'll turn in through those posts, bearing down on the horn with all her might, just in time to sit herself down to dinner."

Norma smiled and nodded, "That's Beck all right."

"Now Lola," LaVerne protested, "Beck is a wonderful sister. She wrote me she's bringing a navy-blue polka-dotted dress."

"Unless she's lost a hundred pounds, you'll never cut it down to fit your 'figger'." Lola put in. "It's so good to sit here quietly in the country," Lola changed the subject abruptly to avoid further protest from her sister.

"Hy and La have just about driven me crazy this spring with those silly boys. I can't begin to sit on my corner terrace without horns honking, brakes squeaking and girls giggling. I tell you; it has been awful. Those boys have made cars… Yes, that's what I said, been making cars. They take the fenders from one kind of car, the engine from another kind and then they add a blasting horn They are dreadful looking things and of course they are completely unsafe. All the girls think of is boys, boys, boys and cars. I had to force them to pack to come up here. And don't think they didn't make our trip miserable. Poor Homer! He threatened once to just put them out, right on the side of the road. Peace at last. Just listen to those crickets, heavenly music to my ears."

"If Beck pulls in for dinner tomorrow, I think I'll have some of that ham we cured last fall, with grits and red gravy. She loves home-cured ham, and hot biscuits. I'll make some in the morning." Mam-maw decided. She stood up, adjusted her crocheted shall around her shoulders and started for the door into the house.

"You gals can stay up as late as you like, I'm going to bed. It's been a big day for a grandmother. It's so good to have you all home." She turned one last time to the mountains which framed her porch and slipped quietly into the house.

"We'll all go to bed," Lola spoke to her mother's retreating figure. "Tomorrow will be a busy, busy day. Norma, we'll have to go up on Negro Hill and get Mose and Annie lined up to come and help us. Delilah was sure a welcome sight behind the stove tonight. We have mattresses to air, linens to go over, windows to wash, floors to scrub and when I think of the painting…...! Everywhere I look I see something that needs a fresh coat of paint.

# Chapter 2

# Combustible

"Pick it up! Up, Up, off the floor. You children are ruining that freshly waxed floor. For heaven's sake! Mabes, put that paint brush and those water colors down. I left you in charge here. The minute I turn my back, everything goes wrong. Can't I depend on anybody around here?"

Beck came from across the hall, her step ladder draped over her diamond watch band.

"Lola, let's hurry. I've simply got to have a coca cola and stretch out for a rest. After all, I drove over 800 miles by my lone self and I deserve some respite."

Lola stopped her fussing and turned to look at her younger sister. For the first time since Beck had arrived, Lola was able to study her. Beck's over-indulged body spread the seams of her size 40 black dress. LaVerne's right, Lola thought, we must get Beck out of those widow's reeds. Only thirty-four years old and though she is terribly fat, she really is a handsome woman. I must talk to Mama and see if she can't do something with Beck. If she would only give up all of those Coca Cola's she would lose a few pounds and any little bit would be a help.

"A coke?" Lola answered her sister, "Really, Rebekah, you ought to be ashamed. You just ate half a Tennessee ham for lunch. Can't you get your mind off your stomach long enough to do a little work? The exercise might do some good."

"Oh you, you'd think cokes were alcoholic, the way you carry on about them. Always bragging…. 'I wouldn't let a coca cola touch my lips'…. What's wrong with cokes? Besides you know I have a thyroid problem and that just makes me more nervous. The children make me nervous. Just look at the load of responsibility I have to carry… and by my lone self."

"I know Beck", Lola felt badly that she had touched the open wound of sorrow within her sister, sixteen years her junior. "But you must not give in. Tom left you well fixed, and for that, we can all be thankful. You're young….and well…. you're pretty….and….and…. maybe…Well the children need a father."

"Lola!" Beck stopped her sister from saying more. "You know I'd never do that! Remarry?? Never!!! Oh, come on. Let's stop. I want a coke and I'm going to get one this minute…"

"There's a car turning in the drive. Car turning in! Car coming!" The rug beaters who had been flexing their sixteen-year-old muscles under the cherry trees on the other side of the house, came stampeding across the front porch. They darted back and forth between the bedsteads of the redbird, grandfather Hopper, calico, pink and double-wedding ring rooms.

LaVerne called to her sisters from the foot of the stairs, "Beck, Lola? There is a car coming. Our first guest isn't due for a week. A car just turned off the highway, right through the gate, though. What are we going to do?"

LaVerne had been putting fresh paper on the shelves she had scrubbed all morning in the pantry. The health inspector was due any day and she knew that the antiquated kitchen would have to wink and smile for a good rating.

Lola and Beck ran to the window and saw a car pulling into the parking area in front. LaVerne came up the stairs to find her sisters. The children half-heartedly hid themselves in the tearoom, peering from the windows and doorway, waiting. Fourteen in all, the youngsters were encouraged to stay in the background when prospective guests arrived to inquire about accommodations, lest they dispel the peaceful setting of Riverby Inn,

In the car, settled now under the giant tulip trees, two men passed a Mason jar between them. One of the passengers threw back his unkempt blond head and let out a raucous laugh.

"Go ahead. Knock on the door and say what I told you. I want to see their faces." He spurred his buddy under the wheel into action.

Norma heard the rapping on the outside of the front door. The house had suddenly become deathly still. Closed up in the parlor dusting the shelves and waxing the books she had been so engrossed in her industry that she had not heard the children's signal. The knock came again.

"Now, I wonder where everyone is? "Norma said to herself as she climbed down from the kitchen stool. She opened the door into the hall and went directly to the front door, several books still clasped in her hands.

"Beg your pardon, Mam." The man spoke thickly, his strong breath filtered through the screen door into her face.

"My friend over there in the car, says ask you, is this the place what's having a rummage sale?" He waved his arms over the. furniture on the porch and directed Norma's gaze to the bed clothing flapping on the side lawn and back to the front lawn where the mattresses lay in the sun. Norma realized that the whole beautiful hillside was a mass of bedclothes, half painted, half scraped furniture and the old house must stare with gaping clean windows down on the scene.

The strange man left in the car, roared with laughter and half rolled from the car. His feet on the solid grass lawn at last, he bent over double with convulsive mirth, and stumbled toward the porch where his buddy, catching the joke began to giggle. Like a silly school girl, he pointed one hand toward Norma and held the other over his mouth. The man coming from the car was no stranger. Norma recognized him instantly.

Norma's back arched and stiffened like a cat's. Her face turned white with rage. She sucked in her breath. Slowly, deliberately like and old-time organ puffing its bellows, Norma worked into a full crescendo. "Claude Blanks! You get out of here!"

"Leon? What does combustible mean?" Sonny Hudson asked. Leon smiled from ear to ear. He didn't hear Sonny; he wasn't even aware that anyone spoke at all. He had just witnessed from the tea room screen door, the scene his mother and father acted out in the front of the big house.

Lola, LaVerne and Beck, the three sisters, descended the steps from the second floor. They came down into the main hall, breathless from bringing their over-weighted bodies down the long steps at unaccustomed speed.

Norma slammed the screen door violently.

"Whhhhhho…" Lola gasped for enough breach to continue. "Who on earth was that?" She addressed her sister-in law who stood defeated but for the tears which aggressively filled her eyes.

"It was Claude! Your brother! I ran him off. One of these days he's going to get himself killed, horsing around like a school boy playing hookey."

"Leon! I says, what's combustible mean?" Sonny tried vainly to start a conversation among the painters in the tearoom.

Preoccupied with his filial thoughts, Leon did not reply immediately. He knew. It was about now, at this time of summer at Riverby, that Claude put in his first appearance of the season. Absent for weeks, even months, maybe, the warm sun of late May and early June, told Claude that the whole family was in residence. Somewhere along his way, he noted that children were on the sidewalks or playing on country roads. He knew then, that school was out.

Out of state license plates along the highways and byways came to his fuzzy attention. He realized that one of these might belong to a sister enroute home. Home! On a hill in the Swannanoa Valley, Mammaw, and Grandy embraced their family one by one as they gathered for the summer. Home! They were all home!

And Leon knew, Claude could not take part in it.

He was unacceptable. Norma, his wife. Charles, Leon and Martha his children, what could he say? What could he do?

All summer he would think of ways, things to do, things to say, to bring him in contact with all of this. None of it really worked out right ever, but he would try anyway. Today he had made his first foray.

"Doesn't anyone know what that C-O-M-B–U-S-T-I-B-L-E means? It's written right here on the gasoline can." Sonny spelled out his question once more and broke, finally into Leon thoughts.

Leon gave a half-hearted reply. "Oh! Sonny. It's hard to explain. Someday, I'll show you."

# Chapter 3

# Walking The Pipe

Grandy was in his glory the next morning when he routed out the sleepy heads at five.

"Suns up. Work to do. Vern, Lola, Becky, Jeffie, everybody up."

The children quickly crawled into their clothes, donned heavy sweaters and ran to the coal range, burning hot in the kitchen. Mose, Delilah, and Annie grinned at the sleepy heads as they served up steaming cups of coffee and cocoa, with sausage and eggs.

"Annie, you clear up the breakfast things and then report to me in the parlor. Leon, Charles, Mose, Will…get all the mattresses from the family rooms out on the front lawn. Mother, get all of the rugs you've hooked and braided this winter and check on the linens. We'll go to Asheville one day soon to restock the towels and sheets. Girls you get your buckets of suds, mops and rags and start on the back-wing upstairs…sister, don't you think you better start on the kitchen? Have you made a list of the staples needed?" Lola was at her best early in the morning.

"Just like Grandy," Beck though to herself. "She's just like Grandy. Early to bed, early to rise…blah…blah…blah…" Early rising just didn't fit Beck's daily routine.

The old house after a long winter's nap was beginning to wake up and yawn.

———— & & ————

Sis sat on the bottom step by the river. The pipe stretched across in front of her.[2] Her sobs were lost in the sound of the tinkling water as it flowed over the rocks and made rapids. The tears ran down her chubby cheeks and bumped over her protruding bottom lip which was set in a pout.

"Goooooood granny alive! What ails you?" Sis jumped off the bottom step as Leon's teenage baritone reached her. She hadn't heard his soft footsteps as he approached around the hillside. He came by the edge of the river by the barn. An empty milk pail swung over his arm.

"I could ride to Black Mountain on your bottom lip and if you don't stop popping those tears from your big brown eyes, you're going to flood the Swannanoa."

He lowered his long willowy body to the damp stone step next to sis. He sat the empty pail in front of him.

Remnant of pipe that once crossed the Swannanoa river. In later years it was encased in concrete.

Figure 9: The pipe

"That fool Sally Kate kicked over this whole bucket of milk. Boy! Am I going to catch it? You won't be the only one crying when Aunt Boom here's we weren't got any morning's milk."

Sis stopped her sobs and stared at the empty bucket, then at Leon, with brimming eyes.

"Wwwwwhat happened?"

Leon turned the bucket around to show the dent in one side as explanation.

"Come on now, tell old Leon, what ails you?"

"It's that dag-gummed pipe! I can't walk it." Sis boo-hooed out loud. "I've fallen in three times already this morning and I haven't made the first rib. I'm soaking wet and Aunt Lola said not to dare change my clothes again, cause I mess everything up and they are trying to get everything straightened up. And everybody has something to do but me! They won't let me do nothing to help! They all tell me to shoo and get out of the way. I'm probably just going to fall in that river and drown. They don't care. Sides, I don't neither care! Can't walk the pipe, can't do nothing like nobody else in the family does…"

"Whooooa, there." Leon stopped her onrushing words. "I can't make head nor tail of your misery. Calm yourself down, sos' we can talk this thing over man to man."

He soothed her babbling while brushing a string of yellow hair back from her eyes.

He turned to the pipe which lay challengingly at Sis' feet. The steps came, one-hundred and fifty, down from the house to the River. Down to the pipe which ran across the river from Riverby land to nobody knew whose land.

The pipe was about a foot in diameter and presented a constant obstacle as a bridge to the other side of the water. Walking the pipe took guts. Whatever flowed through it (and if one stopped long enough to speculate, they almost preferred a dunking to walking on it) was warmer than the water that flowed all around it.

It was sticky wet with condensation and slimy to the barefoot. The pipe was treacherous for the running adolescent but almost impassable for little ones moving hesitatingly along at a snail's pace, forgetting to look straight ahead and never down.

Walking the pipe had become among the Blanks clan, both for those who had mastered it and for those whose dream it was to "walk on water." The river rarely covered it except during flash flooding thunderstorms but during normal conditions, it was one-fourth above the water level. So, from a distance the pipe was hardly visible and children scurrying across on bare feet truly looked as though they were walking right on the water.

Mastering the pipe had sort of separated the men from the boys and being a little girl was no comfort to Sis. Leon knew she could jump fast moving trains through McLain's' cornfields in front of the Inn. She could climb higher in a tree than anyone of the older kids. She smoked grapevines like a veteran nicotinic, but, she had not mastered the pipe.

"Dag Nab it! I'm gonna walk that pipe right this minute. Just you watch me." Sis stood up, stamped her little bare feet in determination and set one cautiously forward on the pipe. Leon watched in silence holding his breath as she teetered. With both feet on the pipe, one behind the other, her outstretched hands moved in windmill fashion as she struggled like a tightrope walker to keep her balance and keep her eyes straight ahead.

Leon knew that everyone had learned to walk the pipe last summer, except Sis. When the gang made for the island, she was left at the foot of the steps, furious with herself and screaming mad at the retreating backs of her cousins who teased, "Sis is a sissy!"

"You are doing…" Leon never got the "fine" out. Sis had looked down at the fast-running water and had dumped herself once more into the cold mountain water. Leon ran out onto the pipe and fished her out, gasping and sputtering with indignation. He sat her soaked batiste covered seat on the pipe in front of him.

"Now, put one leg on each side of the pipe and scooch along. You're too hard on yourself little gal. You may not be able to walk the pipe yet, but you can sure crawl over it." Blocking any retreat on her part, by holding his ground behind her, he made her advance laboriously to the other side.

"See there, you got to the island under your own steam. Now anytime the gang leaves you, just cross over the best way you can. Don't be ashamed to crawl. We all crawled before we learned to walk over."

He swung her potty black legs and damp bottom over his shoulder got a visor like grip on her midsection, let her head bob over his chest and walked back across the pipe. He took the steps two at a time hesitating only to recover the abandoned milk bucket, and arrived at the back-porch door, hardly out of breath.

"Now, get up those back steps and change your clothes, I'll go face up to Aunt Boom with an empty bucket and we'll get a job that both of us can do." Leon slapped her rear and sent her up the steps. With her proud little head high, she left him, contemplating her new feat. She drawled over her shoulder as she mounted the steps, "Just think, now I can do anything!"

———————————— ❧ ❦ ————————————

Leon found his Aunt LaVerne in the kitchen pantry. Hibernia was at her side, making notes in pencil on a small pad.

"One barrel of sugar…One barrel of flour…One sack of salt…Two twenty-pound bags of corn meal…Three twenty-pounds cans of lard…One can of grapefruit juice…One case of sliced pineapple…Fifty pounds of course ground coffee." LaVerne called off the list of needed items.

"Make a note…white corn meal! Preferably home ground. That wholesale grocer is always mixing me up by sending that Yankee yellow meal! In fact, I think I'll ask Lola to drive me up to see if I can get some freshly ground meal from Alexander's Farm." LaVerne continued thinking out loud.

"Have you got all of that Hy?"

"Yessum."

"Well read it back to me and let me check."

Hy winked at Leon who stood in the doorway between the kitchen and pantry. He waited an opportune moment to inform his aunt that there would be no morning milk. Hy began to reread the list with a sly little grin.

"Sugar…Salt…Flour…Corn meal…Remind you to stop by that Yankee Alexander's Farm and pick up some yellow-bellied republican corn meal and tell the wholesale grocer to grist your mill and not mix you up." Hy giggled to the end. LaVerne, her mind racing along the empty pantry shelves, hadn't paid any attention to Hy's rattling off the list until she heard the word yankee teamed up with Alexander. Her dander flew.

"Now, listen here young lady, that's not in the least bit funny. The very idea of a yankee Alexander, makes my blood run cold. You know very well that Mr. Alexanders grandfather almost got scalped by the Cherokees."

Hy interrupted, "Cherokees? I never knew that. What happened?"

LaVerne, eager to tell a good tale, continued into the story. "Well, Miss Priss, I guess there's a lot you don't know. Poor man's ancestors were wiped out one night by a scalping party, right here in the Swannanoa Valley. Isn't that the irony of fate? Swannanoa meaning 'beautiful' in Cherokee and then those savages doing an ugly thing like that? Mr. Alexanders grandfather was about six-months old when they came over the Blue Ridge from Virginia to settle here. They scalped the poor man, but his wife grabbed the infant and walked all the way to Old Fort right along the Ridge. That brave southern woman saved her Alexander baby and when he was a fair-sized boy, they came back here and settled right on the spot. Built the log house and used it as a stage coach stop for years. First family of Swannanoa. Yes sir, the Alexanders have a real pioneer southern heritage."

Before she could continue, Leon decided now was the time. He came between his aunt and his cousin, the empty bucket in hand. LaVerne saw immediately that there was no milk in it.

"What did you do with the milk? Did Mama strain it already?"

"No'un, that fool Sally Kate kicked over the bucket and spilled every drop."

LaVerne crossed her hands over the front of her apron and clinched them together so hard, the knuckles turned white.

"Well that settles that! She's got to be disposed of."

"LaVerne? Oh LaVerne!" Mam-maw called from the dining room. She was sitting in the big room. The morning sun lit her lap as she sewed by the window. On many tables there were stacked in piles, bath, table and bed linens. Mam-maw had spent the morning in counting and sorting them from table to table. She had weeded out all that needed repair and was at this moment applying her needle to the new rips and old worn places.

"Yes, Mama?" LaVerne called as she swung through the door from the kitchen.

"See, if you can thread this needle for me? This darning thread is so heavy, I can't get it through the eye."

Mam-maw had pushed her glasses back over her forehead and they rested in the snow-white pouf of her topknot.

"Hy, thread your grandmother's needle for her." LaVerne directed her niece and then addressed her mother.

"Mama, that jersey jezebel has simply got to be disposed of, she's got something wrong with her bag and she just kicked the whole gallon of mornings milk all over Leon and the barn. Now we'll have to go to Miss Lou's for milk. "

"Now LaVerne, don't get upset, as your papa would say. You know Frank takes real pride in Sally Kate and you'll sure stir up a hornet's nest if he hears another word against that cow." Mama turned from her daughter to her grandson in the doorway.

"Leon, my dear, go up in the music parlor room and ask your mother to come here a minute."

"LaVerne, I'm going to have Norma make a nice neat list of these things and then we'll all sit down and figure out what we need to replace in the way of linens. When you go into Asheville you can shop for some new ones.

"Mama, we'll have to mend as many as possible and make do with mostly what we have. Since Beck didn't bring much linen with her, I guess we'll have to go to Penny's and get a few sheets to fill in with. We can take some of the more torn sheets here and cut them up and make pillow cases. We have to buy some sugar sacks for kitchen toweling, The Health Inspector warned us last year about the manner in which we dry the dishes, said there was some new regulation about steam or something. Anyway, I want plenty of towels in evidence when he comes."

Norma had polished the old piano to a soft patina and was arranging the box of games Lola had brought down from Highpoint to add to the old dog-eared cards Beck had contributed from Mississippi.

"Ma." Leon broke into her precise straightening, cleaning waxing, washing neat little mind.

"Mam-maw wants you in the dining room."

Norma gave the sticky pile of cards one final pat and moved backwards toward the hallway, admiring the overall effect of her mornings labor.

"Son, go out and check on the painting crew in the tearoom. They ought to get those porch rockers finished this morning."

Leon grunted a yes and turned to go.

"Oh, Son. You better get Harold Jr. and Charles lined up to start on the porch floor. Your Aunt Beck and Lola went to the hardware store to get the paint and soon as they get back, I want you all to get started. Beck and Lola are chafing at the bit to get started cleaning up the yard. But I want that porch painted first, TODAY! The yard can wait till tomorrow."

"Aw Mom, do we have to?" We painted it last year and we're sick and tired of slaving over this ole barn."

"Now, don't you argue with me, young man. This ole barn, as you call it, puts food in our mouths twelve months out of the year and it's not asking too much for you boys to help out over the summer. Just what do you think we'd do, if it wasn't for our summer paying guests? Money doesn't grow on trees you know!"

"Shucks, Norm." Leon knew she hated him to call her by her first name. "We need to have some fun. Just let us go swimming this afternoon and we'll paint that old porch first thing in the morning."

"No, the answer is N-O, no! Now get." Leon slammed the front screen in disgust as he went out and Norma went down the hall to the dining room saying as she entered, "Lola had better get a hold of that piano tuner this afternoon. The music parlor room is all finished except for that. It's so out of tune it would make a buzz saw-sound like a Chickering by comparison."

"Make a note of that Hy." LaVerne called to her niece secretary.

"Oh, Norma, would you mind going through those piles of linens and counting them? Hy will make a list as you go," Mam-maw said as she rummaged in her sewing basket in search of her glasses. Unrewarded, she began to fumble with the deep creases in her lap where her dress strained and puffed over her fat stomach.

"Now where do you suppose I put my glasses? I know I had them in my hands not five minutes ago."

"Mam-maw. My goodness, they're right here where you pushed them." Hy reached up to her grandmother's head and pulled the glasses down over her eyes.

"Here now! Here's four needles all threaded and ready to go." She extended the armed weapons up from her place on the floor at her grandmother's feet. She had been spitting and twisting on the darning yarn and at last had gotten it through the four different needle eyes.

Hy rose and joined forces with Norma. LaVerne turned to go back through the door into the kitchen. She gave the swinging door a hefty push. It swung forward and stopped six inches from her hand with a crash, then came swinging back to smack her in the right hip. The door swung crazily in its small orbit between two immovable objects. LaVerne on one side, her father on the other. Stitching, counting and itemizing stopped as Mam-maw, Norma and Hy followed the commotion like spectators at a tennis match.

Grandy finally caught sight of his daughters skirt on the dining-room side and warned, "Vern! Vern! Stop that infernal banging on the door. I got a wash stand wedged in on this side and I'm coming through. With that announcement, LaVerne stepped aside just in time to miss being laid-low as her father pushed and shoved a weather-beaten old piece through the door.

Baby Sis came down the back steps wearing her third dress of the day. She caught sight of Leon as he came around from the front door and hailed him, "Did'ja get us a chore, Lee?"

"Yeh! Come on little bit, you and I are gonna show Sonny Hudson what combustible means. It's time somebody around here had some fun."

In the dining room, Francis Marion Blanks gave a piece of furniture one final push and let the door swing back in place. All save the Lord and Master of Riverby Inn, who speechlessly examined the object of his grunts and groans. He looked straight at his wife with manly pride and announced.

"Jeffie. I brung you a fine antique for the parlor room. Found it up in the loft of the barn, hid under some hay. No telling how old it is, probably been a sittin' up there for fifty years."

"Papa? That old piece of junk in OUR parlor?" LaVerne was thunderstruck at the thought.

"Yep. A genuine antique, you gals been talking about searching the hillsides for one ever since you got here. Well, here's one right under your nose. Purrty, ain't it?"

LaVerne moved closer in to observe the wreck. "Papa why that's, that old atrocity that used to be out in the tearoom. Why, I threw that out two or three summers ago. I told Samson to haul it off with all the trash when we closed the tearoom."

"Tain't no sech thing! This here's been a settin' in the barn, I told ya."

"It's been there since you pulled it off of Samsons truck and hid it out. You beat all! Dredging through junk plies and garbage heaps resurrecting dead ole refuse from long overdue graves."

"Now you just hush up LaVerne Blanks! That ain't no way to talk to your Pappy. Hard as I work around here trying to save money and keep you gals from spending every last cent we got."

Norma regained her tongue in an effort to forestall the further advent of the cobwebby, molded, termite ridden oak veneer monstrosity. "Well, I don't care where it came from. Get it back out on the kitchen porch before you mess up our clean house with it. I'll scrub it up and we'll see if something can be done with it."

"I'm not moving this washstand one inch! Y'all been nagging around for a real nice table to put the lamp on in the parlor and this is it. Move out of the way cause I'm coming through. I'm not wasting no more time or money on fixing up this here Inn."

Jeffie Gill Blanks had quietly monitored the whole debate. She weighed both sides of the argument and was ready to throw her weight to the opposing team. "Now Frank, just calm down and take that thing out before you get wood lice all over the bed linens. We'll do what Norma says and see." "I'm not moving an inch, I tell you." His moustache was bristling. "A man's got to run his household and I'm not gonna have any petticoats ruling around here. This washstand stays, cause I say so and I'm the BOSS."

Mam-maw daintily lifted her 250 pounds from the chair. She walked deliberately up to her husband, hoisted one leg up and sat on top of the controversial furniture, bottom first. "Alright, Frank Blanks, MOVE IT! Go right ahead on into the parlor with it, and with me too. I've got a full day sewing to do and I'd just as well do it sitting up here as in that chair."

"I brought you a present and now you want to throw it out? I says it stays! It must be solid if it'll hold you. All it needs is a dab of paint and it'll serve us good for years to come. Perch all ye want to on it Jeffie, but it stays." Grandy turned and left the same way he had entered.

"Mam-maw," Hy whispered, "what are you going to do? Grandy is mad."

"I'm mad, too! Just because he was named for the Swamp Fox, he thinks he can get everyone to jump to his orders. I wasn't named for Jefferson Davis and Robert E. Lee for nothing. I say it goes! When Leon comes back, I'LL have him chop it up for firewood. Grandy'll never know the difference." Mam-maw descended from her throne.

---

"Leon, what does combustible mean? Tell me first. Tell me fore you tell Sonny Hudson. He's such a smarty Tell me PLEASE!" Sis had joined Leon in front of the tearoom and held him under fire with her questions.

Inside the little one room-house, formerly used by the owners of Riverby as an out patients clinic for nervous complaints, all the children of the family were painting. In season, there were thirty-odd rockers used on the wide front porch of the Inn. Often there were not enough to go around. Each child had painted at least one rocker. Many were now working on a second. Jampacked with little sweaty bodies, the tearoom was close and hot. The atmosphere was heavy with mingled gases, A can of gasoline which was used to clean brushes and remove spatters from arms and legs stood open. The air was leaded.

"Where did you get that match from Lee?"

Leon stood to one side of the open screen door, he motioned Sis to join him. Cautiously she crept up to where he stood. Leon's finger was over his lips in age old gesture of silence.

"Lee", Sis whispered, close to his ear. Leon bent down to reach her level of height. "You're up to something, I can tell. I'm not sure about this. I've been in trouble all day so please don't make Aunt Lola mad at me again. Sides I'm out of clean dresses and mother's gonna be hot about that."

"Shhhhhhhhhhhh!" Leon blew into her ear. It tickled and Sis squirmed to keep from giggling. "Now when I toss this match, run for your life. Hide! There's gonna be a terrible racket so don't be scared, that's gonna be the combustion." Leon prepared to light the match and sure that his warning was an understatement, Sis clasped her little hands over her ears.

The first match fizzled out before it reached the door. Leon took careful aim and lit another one. Sis started to run before it left his hands and crawled under the side porch behind a big boxwood bush. The second match went all the way. It landed unobserved with dead reckoning, about three feet from the open gasoline can.

The explosion was deafening! It rattled the sagging windows in the little house and blew the wooden door shut, trapping the painters inside.

LaVerne Hedges, in the dining room looking over Hy's lists, threw the papers in the air and screamed. The others in the dining room, sat stunned, waiting for the very roof to cave in on them.

"That gol-durned water heater on the second floor has blowed. Vern, I told you not to let that Earl come on this place. He's done gone and hooked something up bass-ackwards." Grandy fussed at LaVerne in vain.

She was in complete shock. Loud noises turned her into a raving, jabbering idiot and momentarily she became completely irresponsible. A slammed door, raised her from her chair; a dropped tray in the kitchen set her to throwing anything in reach; and this unexpected jolt on the hillside had her doing the St. Vidus dance.

Grandy, receiving no satisfaction from her, ran into the hall and up the steps. Norma, assured that the roof wasn't coming down began to hear muffled screams from outside. Hy's adolescent mind picked up an immediate warning and she ran to Mam-maw in distress, "Mam-maw, Mam-maw, somebody must have lighted a match, the tearoom. . . they're all in the tearoom…"

Mam-maw was on her feet. She too heard the screams and this time they were loud and clear. Fearing that Hy was right, she and Norma ran to the rescue.

Bill Fields got the door of the tearoom open and was yelling at the top of his lungs. "Help! Somebody. Help! We've been bombed. We's 'sploded up. He was knocked flat to the ground by the scrambling, half blinded, frightened mob of Blanks grandchildren, as they clawed their way to safety from the awful smoke and fumes.

Norma reached the scene first and began shaking each child as he came through the door, Mam-maw stood on the porch counting limbs as each one emerged with singed hair and smoked faces.

Grandy, realizing that the noise had come from without the house, had made for the front door and galloped onto the scene. One of his suspenders had come undone in the haste of his movements and his trousers dropped and dragged on the gravel deterring his agility. Only the bitter thoughts of his grandchildren caught in an inferno kept him coming. With only one good eye, he was unable to ascertain that the entire group of youngsters was already safe outside. He dashed headlong through the smoke belching doorway. He was greeted there by clouds of low hanging smoke and the strangling odor of raw gaseous fumes, but there were no flames, not a sign of fire anywhere.

He stumbled out of the door, tears streaming from his good eye and running down his nostrils. "Tain't a soul left in thar, and they's no fire, Thank the Lord!" The aged man collapsed into a porch rocker, sticky wet with paint, which had been set out front to dry.

One by one, Norma checked the children. Everyone was whole and in reasonably good health. Mam-maw wandered back and forth between the stunned refugees, checking and rechecking arms and legs and counting heads. "Everyone's here except Sis and Leon, Norma." She called to her daughter in-law who had corralled her eldest son and little daughter to her.

"Martha, Your eyebrows. They're gone!" Norma shrieked.

All eyes turned to Martha Lee. Her poor little blackened face was denuded. She presented a comic picture. Her minstrel like face, all black save the white line where her eyebrows had been, white spots where her tears had washed off the soot and round her mouth there was a great white circle where her tongue had made a wide circuit to moisten her lips.

LaVerne stumbled down the back steps and surveyed the scene, half dazed. A loud masculine whistle pierced through the hub bub and announced the arrival of Leon, hands in pockets, a faraway look in his eye, Leon rounded the side of the front porch and sauntered up to the mob.

"What in heavens name happened here? You all look like a lynching mob." Leon appeared innocent.

"As if you didn't know," Bill Fields challenged him. Sis squirmed in the rocky soil under the porch.

Uncomfortable in her hiding place, she wanted to give herself up, but she wasn't sure just when she should make her entrance.

"Leon, the tearoom exploded and we got blown up." Sonny missing Bills insinuation, was anxious to spread the exciting news.

"O K, Buddy, come on fess up. You did it, I know you did. I saw you and Sis sashaying around out here, just before it happened. Now don't tell me a fib, you did it, didn't you?" Bill pursued the subject.

Sis figured it was time for her to give herself up. She crawled out from under the porch, threaded her way through the lower branches of the boxwood and crawled right out into the middle of the ensuing court session.

She took the witness stand. "Now, I ain't no tattletale…….." she stopped and looked with genuine appeal at Leon. He caught her SOS and took up in the middle of her sentence. "Alright! Alright!" He shrugged his broad shoulders. "That was C-O-M-B-U-S-T-I-B-L-E ! ! ! I promised Sonny, I'd show him what it meant. Now you know Sonny." Leon turned to Sonny and broke into laughter. With his head thrown back and his blue eyes swimming in tears he enjoyed his joke.

LaVerne at last regained herself and marched straight up to Leon, "Young man, do you realize, you could have blown Riverby Inn to bits?" She gave Norma a curling look that said, 'If that were my child, I'd beat his backsides.' She marched herself back to the kitchen porch.

"Leon", his mother began to scold.

Leon's laughing had become contagious and others caught it. They pointed to each other and passed the joke along. Norma was too convulsed herself to go on with her scolding.

"Toooooooooooooooooooot……Honk……Honk……Honk!"

Becks La Salle nosed around the house, horn going full blast and slammed to a stop just in the nick of time. She almost ran down Sis and Leon who still stood out in front of the mob, waiting for their final sentence. Lola jumped from the other side of the car seat, left the door ajar and advanced on the group, waving a letter in her hand.

"Mama, Mama! You got a letter. It's from the University of Chicago. A doctor. It's from a Dr. Taylor of the University of Chicago. Quick open it, Beck and I are dying of curiosity. Maybe they want to have summer school at Riverby Inn, Ha!... Ha!... Ha!..." Lola chuckled at her little joke and handed the envelope, which had obviously been pinched, squeezed and half unsealed, into Mam-maws waiting hands

# Out Moo-nipulated

Jeffie Blanks settled herself comfortably on the sofa in the now spotless parlor room. Lola and Beck sat on either side of her. LaVerne was left the fat overstuffed arm. Grandy and Norma stood awkwardly with their elbows supporting their weary heads on the mantle of the fireplace. Mam-maw read aloud.

```
May 28, 1934
Mrs. Francis Marion Blanks
Riverby Inn
Swannanoa, North Carolina

Dear Mrs. Blanks,
     A patient of mine has referred me to you regarding your Inn
in the Swannanoa Valley. I wonder if you would be so kind as to
give me some first-hand information about it. My wife and I would
like to spend several weeks in the Blue Ridge area and are looking
for a comfortable family type guest house.
     I am a doctor of Psychology, I was active as a consultant
on the Leopold-Leob Murder case some years ago, here in Chicago.
I am now on sabbatical from the University and am writing a
treatise on adolescent behavior. My wife and I feel that a
complete change of scene and pace is in order.
     I would appreciate an immediate answer as we are anxious to
get away from Chicago before the extreme heat of summer.

Kindest regards,

Dr. Benjamin B. Taylor
```

Jeffie gently let her strong hands come to rest on her lap still holding the letter intact.

"Isn't that exciting," LaVerne let her quick mind do hand springs at the thought of such an intellectual addition to the Inn. "Just think, a real doctor of psychology here at Riverby. He will certainly add prestige to our guest list this summer."

"I don't know sister," Lola was immediately on the defensive. "That's an awful sordid mess, that murder case. He may be a very famous man but he's certainly gotten in with an infamous bunch of criminals and it's bound to have rubbed off on him. I know Homer wouldn't approve of us having that kind of celebrity around here."

"Now, Lola, don't open your mouth and let your brains fall out like that! You've got better sense. He's a doctor of psychology. Probably was THE expert witness in the case using his genius to help those poor mixed up young men. Certainly, a man of his rank is above mixing with criminals except in an intellectual manner."

"What do you think Beck?" Lola sought her baby sister as an ally.

"Well, I think it's up to Mama. After all this is her home." Beck hedged.

"I don't know what all those high fangled terms are that you girls are tossing around, but as for me; I'd be dang well sure he could pay his bill. You know how doctors are, absent minded, fumbling around with the good Lords creation. Likely as not, he don't aim to pay for his bed and vittles with anything more than his fancy titles." Grandy put in his two cents worth.

"You all hush! It seems that all we've done this whole day is to fuss among ourselves. What on earth have we come to? Let's not forget that the Good Lord in his infinite wisdom had provided for us to be together here in our home in the mountains. Now, let's not abuse his grace." Mam-maw spoke to her flock.

"AMEN!" Norma reverently added her Baptist blessing to Mam-maw's sermon. She was eternally grateful for her place in the family.

"Now", Mam-maw seemed to come into action with renewed strength, "If you gals will get on with your chores, Norma and I will get down to answering this kind gentleman right now. Skedaddle all of you. Norma and I have work to do."

Hurt at Mam-maws rebuke, her daughters filed out of the room. The disappointment showed openly for they were loath to be left out of this exciting new development. Grandy left saying, "I'm a going down to my garden now Jeffie."

Norma looked through damp eyes at Mam-maw, her rock of Gibraltar, resting among the cushions on the household's best sofa. "Mam-maw, you're a caution." Norma managed a smile. "But you're the best friend a girl ever had." She seated herself next to Mam-maw in the warm valley of down which Lola had just vacated. She self-consciously reached over and touched Mam-maw's chubby workworn hand.

"Now, daughter let's get busy and answer that letter." Mam-maw couldn't have pleased Norma more in all the world than by calling her daughter and she meant to warm Norma with this affectionate gesture.

"Now you just sit here a minute thinking what you want to say and I'll run get my note pad." Norma hurried from the enchanted circle of Mam-maw's love, eager to return, her secretarial talent to give.

Beck's La Salle pulled out of the driveway right past the front door with all three sisters crowded into the front seat. Norma caught a glimpse of them as they passed and asked her eldest son Charles "Now where have they gone off to?"

"Said they were going to see a man about a cow, or some such thing." Charles continued down the hall to the dining room.

"Hmmmmmmmmmmmmmmmm!" Norma wondered aloud. She returned to the parlor room.

"What day is it?" Mam-maw was about to begin her dictation.

"June 4 "

"Alright! June 4, 1934, Dr. Benjamin Taylor and so forth. Make it business like. Dear Dr. Taylor. Is that the way you do it Norma?"

"Un Huh," Norma replied, "Go on, that's perfect"

"Thank you for your letter of inquiry dated May 28. Let me welcome you to Riverby Inn and hope that you will accept this invitation to come and be with us for as long as you can. How's that sound?"

"You're doing fine, professional sounding, yet folksy too."

Jeffie Blanks looked at her daughter-in-law, so neat, so tidy. A willing hard worker, Norma certainly carried her weight in the family. As the children would say, 'Norma can sure walk the pipe.' It isn't easy for her, Mam-maw thought. Poor thing! I tried to warn her about Claude. My son. My son. She was so in love with him, but even then, yes even then, he was gone. But the Lord works in strange ways. He sent me Norma as a comfort for lost son. And those precious children of his, such a joy to my old tired heart.

"Mam-maw………. Are you cat napping on me?" Norma broke into Mam-maw's thoughts.

"Oh, yes. Where was I?" Norma read the first paragraph of her dictation back and her mother-in-law quickly resumed.

"Riverby Inn is a large two-story frame house. My husband and I have enjoyed sharing it with our four children and fourteen grandchildren for fourteen summers. We have also had the privilege of having as our guests many prominent southern families."

Norma's thoughts raced as the old woman said the words. Having as our guests……. yes, we have guests…we have to! But she is really sweet to put it that way in the letter…

Dr. Taylor, you're just another pair of shoes…another way to pay the doctor bills through the winter…another week of meals… you see… we couldn't manage… least they couldn't manage, Grandy and Mam-maw with me and the children here if it wasn't for you…a guest… another guest.

"Riverby, with its commodious size, remains a family type Inn and all who come here are treated as one of the family. We feature home cooked meals of vegetables and meats grown on the grounds. Our specialty is bread and pastry from our own ovens. Do you think I ought to say that?" Mam-maw asked.

"Certainly, you're the best bread maker left in the old south. Any yankee from Chicago ought to eat that up with a spoon."

"Well, I'm not sure… you know the Lord says…'Pride goeth before a mighty fall…and I am sure bragging in that paragraph." Norma chuckled and encourage the proud one to continue.

"We are in the country surrounded by the beautiful Blue Ridge and enjoy the finest climate this side of heaven. There is a little village a mile from us but for the most part, Riverby creates its own entertainment. We offer croquet, swimming in the Swannanoa River, hiking, bridge tourneys, occasional square dances and we are treated frequently to the home grown shows of our grandchildren…. There now I think that about covers it. Don't you?"

"One thing Mam-maw. Maybe you had better mention that we don't have any phone here. It might be important for him to know that. In case somebody had to get in touch with him in a hurry or something."

"Certainly, you're right. We really must tell him that, it's only fair. Be sure and tell him though that he can be reached through central in Swannanoa. You know fix it up some way in a paragraph and say central can always get a message out here to the house. Then after that, let's see, say…. I hope you will come and be with us and May God Bless you. Sign it yours truly, Jeffie Gill Blanks."

"Have you got all that down? Well, while we're about it, let's get out the guest book and make a check. We open the Inn on Monday and I forget from day to day who's reserved what, when and for how long."

Norma crossed the t's and dotted the i's, crossed to the desk in the corner of the room and took the wooden backed guest book from the top drawer. She read from it as she walked about the room.

"James Bodkin, Boston, Mass. (Mr. and Mrs.) expected June 9. Emma Mullen, school teacher; Mobile Ala. expected the tenth. Isn't she the one who wrote the funny mixed-up letter? Something about going to an S.P.C.A. convention? Andre Bouquet, New Orleans, La.; second week in June. Margaret and Mrs. Tate are coming back again. Poor woman. Imagine having a grandchild like Margaret. She's so sweet and kind to that poor pathetic child. Mrs. Tate wrote that she'd let us know exactly when they'd come as soon as Margaret's mother gets back from Europe. Mrs. White and her son. Birmingham, Ala. expected June 12. The Haile family, Baltimore, Md.; Third week in June. There's a note here, they will be down as soon as girl's scouts camp is over. What a dear family. I can hardly wait to see them all. You know Leon was quite taken with that oldest girl of theirs last summer. Four girls, imagine! I guess I can count my blessings that I only have Martha Lee to rear."

Mam-maw interrupted Norma's accounting. "Don't forget Mrs. Peake's daughter and niece. Remember? She said something about them taking a room here. Now I wonder what's wrong there. Does seem like Mrs. Peake would keep them up on the hill with her. I tell you, Norma, she's a good neighbor but she's a puzzlement to me. Living up on Little Hickory all by herself in that log cabin. Does look like she'd welcome some of her own family for comfort. Oh, well, she must have some good reason. Anyway, she said she'd let us know definitely by the last of the week."

Norma continued. "Well that's all for this month. Course we can add the Taylors now, or do you think that would be premature?"

"Best not count our chickens till they hatch. Now after the fourth of July we will just about be full up with the old regulars…Tommy and Mary Ann Thompson…Gloria and Joe Parkerson…Birdie and her children…Jewel Barnett… Twelve children among them. We'll sure have to double-up if anybody else shows up." Mam-maw clucked her tongue on her teeth, satisfied that so far, the roster was filling up well.

"This is a pretty good start. Always good to know in advance but I sure hope we can attract some highway trade. We have some empty rooms scattered over the summer. LaVerne and her children and us, we'll gladly give up our beds if we can rent them out. We just have to make a little extra this summer. Our three boys are almost ready for college and goodness knows how she and I are going to manage on what little we can make."

"Don't worry Norma, the Lord will provide. You'll see. LaVerne can always pick up a little extra on the passing dining room trade. She works hard in that kitchen and feeding a few more mouths isn't much more trouble, when you're already preparing food in such quantity. We'll send Mose down on the road in his white coat and dark pants and with the big dinner bell. We're sure to attract some cars, Mose has a smile as big as the Grand Canyon, who could pass him by?"

"I sure hope Mr. Mc Fadden will welcome me back with a little raise. Here my vacation is almost over and I spent all my advance pay on clothes. I had to have something to go to work in and Martha Lee needed a Sunday School dress. I don't mind though; it's been a good vacation. We almost have the Inn ready to open and it's been so gay having all the family back in the house. I'll hate to leave them every day for work but it's just as well. Looks like things are going to be really crowded."

There was a loud knock on the front door. Roy, the valley plumber, stood waiting on the threshold. Norma went to the door.

"Miz Norma, my old lady she say Miz Hedge come by and tole me to come back by here. She musta forgot sumthin' when I was here the other day a fixin' that new hot water heater."

"NO, Roy, it's those new handles you put on in the bath at the top of the stairs. You seem to have gotten them backwards. The hot water handle is on the cold and the cold-water handle is on the hot."

"Well, Miz Norma y'all ain't a gonna let a little thing like that bother you, is you? Them guesties of yourn'll git hit figgered out in time. Theys'll ketch on."

"They'll no such thing. You get up those steps and get those handles changed right this minute. Be just our luck to have someone scald themselves. Then where would we be? Sued for our eyeballs, that's where. No siree. We'll take no chances. Now get busy." Norma dismissed the inexperienced mountaineer on whom the valley depended to do their plumbing work.

"Mam-maw…Mam-maw" Norma called to the parlor. She stood gazing down at the blank space in front of the front door. "Where on earth is the WELCOME rug? Heaven knows we can't open Riverby without your work of art at the front door."

— — — — — — — — — — 🙠 🙢 — — — — — — — — — —

Down in the garden, Grandy chopped at his beans and grumbled. Chopped and grumbled. He was right put out over having to take in a doctor. He just naturally didn't trust them. But worse than that, he was highly suspicious that his women folk had been getting around him all day.

Head down, hoe down, Grandy didn't see the passing form of Sally Kate as she wandered loose over the front lawn across lover's lane and into Mr. McLain's cornfield.

"Petticoats! Bunch of feisty petticoats! That's all I got around this house." Grandy spoke out load to the empty garden, his private domain. "Well, they ain't seen no house cleaning till they see what I'm gonna do around here."

Sally Kate ate her way along the first row of Mr. McLain's corn, chomping and stomping, she set her usual course toward the interior of the field. This was the third time in as many weeks, that the cow had escaped into the young green stalks not yet high enough to hide her glossy burnt orange jersey hide.

Charles, Leon and Harold had started painting the front porch. They began the big job by taking the side nearest the highway. From there they would move to the tearoom side and just before the end of the day they would finish up on the front side. In this way the family could move in and out of the front door all afternoon without stepping on the wet paint.

"Hey Y'all, look yonder," Charles directed the attention of his helpmates to Sally Kate in the cornfield.

"Darn fool cow, wish she'd eat herself to death, so I wouldn't have to milk her anymore." Leon thought out loud wishfully.

"Hey, see over there." Harold Jr. pointed toward the lane that ran between the cornfield and Mrs. Bishop's property. "It's Mr. McClain and he's got his shotgun. He warned Grandy last week, said he was gonna shoot that cow if it got in his corn again. Uh, Oh! Watch out Sally Kate you're about to get your fanny full of buckshot."

The resounding echo of a shot, brought Grandy back to reality and he jerked around till he saw Sally Kate, then Mr. McClain "Looka here, Jonas McClain, you stop that shooting at my cow!" Grandy yelled to the man with the gun. A violent yelling, gun waving, hoe waving argument ensued as the men each tried to protect their own property.

Becks La Salle zoomed down the highway from the direction of Asheville and careened into the gates of Riverby. The sight of Grandy waving his hoe and screaming caused Beck to screech to a dusty stop right by the garden. All three sisters got the full picture of the two men screaming it out. They chuckled at Grandy's expense.

"This is absolutely the final straw. It's the same summer in and summer out, Sally Kate is a nuisance. She doesn't give enough milk to supply the family much less the guests. Papa is just sentimental about having his own cow and we can't afford either." Lola commented.

"I almost wish Jonas McClain would shoot her," LaVerne added, "Anything would be better than arguing with Papa about it."

"Oh, NO! Sister. We can get fifty dollars for that mangy jersey. I know. I talked with Miss Lou while we were buying butter. She told me about a man who lives back near Piney Grove whose been looking for a milk cow. She told me how to find him and tomorrow I'm going back out there and talk him into buying Sally Kate, if it's the last thing I do. Like Mama says, 'be sure you're right then go ahead, and I know I'm right."

"Papa will have a conniption fit. He'll never part with his cow." Beck warned Lola.

"Well, there's a fifty-fifty chance he will!" Lola smiled secretly and closed the subject. Grandy had gone to round up Sally Kate so Beck eased out on the brake and the car moved forward up the driveway.

Lola continued, "While I'm doing that, Beck you get started on the yard. Sister you can go along with me. We'll set out early tomorrow morning, I'll get a crew started cleaning my cottage. You know Hudson. He won't come up here if I don't set it opened. He just can't rest up at the big house with all the children running around."

That night since no one could sit on the porch due to the wet paint, the kids assembled in the game room while the adults sat across the hall around the open fire in the parlor.

"Wish we had a fourth for bridge, don't you Mama "Beck asked giving her non-card playing sisters a reprimanding look.

"A waste of time, cards!" Lola rebutted. "I'd much rather spend my free moments keeping up with my piano. It's much more worthwhile to belong to the MUSIC STUDY CLUB than is to be a party BRIDGE CLUBBER."

Beck popped a stick of Doublemint into her mouth and rewrapped the thread around her crocheting index finger.

"Sister, why don't you learn to play?" Beck spoke to LaVerne.

"I'm just too tired. Too busy all day and too tired by night." Beck rather regretted that she had put LaVerne in the position of having to make such a pitiful answer. She laughed a little nervously and tried to cover up her foray. "Oh, I forgot, you belong to the Delphiniums. I know that takes much of your energy. The classics, isn't that what you all study?" LaVerne let Becks question drop unanswered. Mam-maw rose from her cushioned rocker by the fire and announced, "It's time for me to go through the children's contributions to the Riverby Beautification Program. They're waiting across the hall." She crossed to the Music Parlor room.

Each year toward the end of spring-cleaning Mam-maw sat down with the children and one by one they displayed their works of art. Created through the school year and carefully saved to bring with them to Riverby, the objects were lovingly brought before Mam-maw.

Leon sat on top of the piano. When Mam-maw entered the room, he strained to get the heavy antlers lifted above his head. Charles sat down with his potted mountain fern before him. Their sister Martha closed her fingers over her palm. Her collection of colored broken glass and rusty old buttons shrunk in her hand.

"What have we here?" Mam-maw carefully studied her grandchildren who were forming a semi-circle around the room except Leon who maintained his high spot on the piano. "Is everybody ready? Mam-maw can hardly wait to see your treasures."

She was cut short by the chorus of "me first's" which beckoned her in all directions. Baby Sis pulled at her black Cretan skirt. "Me Mam-maw. See what I brought you?"

"What has my little fairy princess brought to her Mam-maw?" Sis placed a Gulf oil can full of Mississippi Delta sandy loam in Mam-maws hands "It's a cotton plant, Mam-maw all the way from the Delta. See there it is." Sis pointed to a droopy three leaf plant which had no intention of standing up even for Mam-maw. "It'll bloom next month, just like the cotton does at home. You can plant it in your wild flower garden and watch the blooms turn from yellow to red, every day."

"Sis, Baby, what a lovely addition to my garden this will make. You run give it a good watering, just leave it in my bathroom sink. Tomorrow you and I will set it in the ground."

Martha Lee gathered her courage and came forward before anyone else had a chance to break in." And these are for your garden too, Mam-maw." She opened her little scared hand and displayed the broken bits of glass and buttons. "We can make another fancy bird bath like last year. Like the one that busted when the water froze in it this January. These will look pretty when they are set in cement." She held the colored bottle glass up to the light and the reflected colors danced across her face.

"How thoughtful you are, Martha Lee. Of course, we must make another bird bath. Everyone can help. We'll do it first thing Monday before the guests come."

Bill dropped one of the horseshoes he was holding on to his right foot. "Oooouch! Dad-gum-it, Mam-maw take these ole things before I make a hole in the floor."

"Bill, Bill," Mam-maw chuckled, "here let me have them. What fun you can have playing horseshoes on the front lawn. Did these come off the plantation?"

"Yasssum." Bill hung his head, embarrassed that Mam-maw had tried to give him a hug.

"Well I made a clay ash tray for your parlor room. See! Everybody can enjoy using it, can't they?" Sonny advanced on Bills heels, pushed him aside from Mam-maws embrace and vied for her attention.

"Indeed, they can, Sonny. Even I like a puff every now and then, but we'll tell your mother that I am going to use it as a pin dish."

"Mabes," Mam-maw called her artist grand-daughter forward, "All of these for me?"

Mabes had come forward with a stack of water colors, each one more excellent than the other." l tried to do one for each bedroom. I hope the guests will like them too."

"Oh, my dear." Mam-maw hugged the water colors to her full bosom. "First thing tomorrow you must show me where to hang each one. We'll go from room to room. I can't wait to see them and hear how you did everyone."

"Here." La tenderly draped the shawl she had hand-knitted around Mam-maw's shoulders. "Why, La isn't this beautiful? Don't tell me you did this all by yourself after that one lesson I gave you last summer." La was to overcome with her generosity to answer.

"Where's my Big Scout" Mam-maw called for Harold Jr. He had carefully framed his Boy Scout medals, all except for his Eagle Scout Badge. That he had owed to his mother and she cherished it as her own. "Oh, son, I am so proud of you. Just look at all these impressive honors. Now tomorrow you must explain how you got each one of them."

"I thought you might like to hang them in your room. Mama said you'd like that. Harold prayed that she would not display them in one of the public rooms of the house.

Charles shyly placed the potted fern while Mam-maw was talking to Harold Jr. He placed it at her feet and returned to the circle without saying a word. "Now who do you suppose brought me this lovely fern?" She winked at all the children and blew Charles a kiss.

"And Betts. Where's my Betts." Mam-maw pretended she did not see her. "Here I am Mam-maw. How could you miss me? I had a place on the front row. Oh, here," She extended her skinny arm bearing two raffia mats to her grandmother. "I know there are only two and that isn't enough for the Inn but I thought you and Grandy might use them. Just you two. The teacher got sick and we never got to make anymore."

"Why how very special. Just for Grandy and me." Betts interrupted her again, "Maybe I can make some more. If the teacher gets well, I'll bring lots back next summer."

Hy came forward hesitating to show her handiwork, Mam-maw took the little felt pin cushion from Hy. "How dear this is. It's made just like a pumpkin. It even has a green stem. Did you do this in your home-ec class, Hy?"

"Uh Huh. But it isn't very good. The teacher says I'll go naked if I have to make my own clothes."
Bobbie jumped out of line,

Bobby jumped out of line an organdy apron waving in her outstretched hands. "Here, Hy. We can't have you running around naked." She tied the apron over each of Hy's shoulder blades. "Sorry Mam-maw. you just lost your apron to Sally Rand." Bobbie flipped as she giggled her way back into the everchanging line of cousins.

Tom Jr, spoke from his place, "There's mine over there. He pointed to a linoleum covered brick bat which he had already put to use as the door stop by the hall door, "Tom Jr, you're an angel. You remembered. Didn't you? I said last summer that we needed doorstops so badly." Tom ducked his head and toed the worn rug. "Yassum" he replied.

Leon, tired of holding the antlers and jealous that Mam-maw hadn't sought him out in his place atop the mass, came down from his perch. He bent over and rode the antlers on his backsides "Heavens, Leon. Is that you? Couldn't be anyone else. Stop prancing around and let me see. What beautiful antlers. Where on earth did you find those?"

"Find 'em? Mam-maw I didn't find 'em. I shot them myself during the winter season. I tried to bring down one before Christmas for your present, but it wasn't till January that this bugger came along. Eight points, just count 'em. I bet Pa never got one any bigger."

"Leon, did you really?" Mam-maw could hardly believe that her grandson had been man enough to bring down such a prize at his tender age. "They simply will be perfect over the mantel in the hall. Come, let's hang them right now."

"But Mam-maw. What about me?" Jaybo came forth at last, his hands hiding something behind his back. "Oh Jay, I got so excited, I lost count of grandchildren. What do you have for Mam-maw?" Jaybo brought forth in his hands a polished pine medallion. On the face of it, he had burned with his electric wood burning needle, his grandmother's favorite hymn.

"Others, Lord, yes, others,
Let this my motto be,
Help me to live for other,
That I may live like Thee."

Tears sprang to Mam-maws eyes. She encircled Jaybo with her arms and squeezed him especially tight. "Yes, Lord," she thought, "Others. I pray that others might be so blessed."

"You precious children, see, you've made Mam-maw cry."

"How can I thank you for all these wonderful gifts you've brought to Riverby, to me? Jay, darling, we'll share this lovely poem with all the others. We'll put it right in the front hall by the door so that everyone who comes across the welcome rug can see our Motto." She hugged him again. All the children came forward to embrace her, their hearts touched to see their Mam-maw so happy and so happy to be once more within her reach, within her loving shadow.

———————— ✿ ✿ ————————

The restful night was passing over the mountains and day was about to break in the valley. Everyone at Riverby was fast asleep. The deep draught of predawn slumber hung over each bed. Mam-maw's blinders, as Grandy called her eye shade, were in place against the intruding rays of early daylight. By her side, Grandy sawed logs under his felt hat.

The quietude was interrupted by the family dogs, Queen and Binx. They barked loudly and backed from the yard onto the new paint job on the porch. They got right under Mam-maw's and Grandy's window and set up a howling, scratching fight. Mam-maw awakened to their din. She rose from bed, raised her blinders and looked out of the window. Unable to see the stir going on, she eased open the door to the porch for a better view. The smell of dirty fur greeted her nostrils and she realized that some unusual beast had upset the dogs. In fact, she had that eerie feeling that whatever it was, it was too close for comfort.

"Frank! Frank! Wake up! There's something after the dogs." She tried to stir her husband, but his snores drowned her pleas. She returned to the big double bed and shook the sleeping form of her loved one.

"Huh! Huh! What's ailing you Jeffie?" Grandy fought her off and tried to pull the covers back up around his chin.

"Get up and come here. There's something on the porch!"

Grandy was on his feet in no time, adjusting the hat on his head. He grabbed his shotgun from its place in the corner of his closet and joined Jeffie by the door. She gently let the door swing open. Grandy could see the hulking shape outlined against the horizon. The sun was peaking its topside over the rim. Grandy fumbled for the trigger and let go a load of buck-shot, right through the screen door.

The dogs barked and cried out in fear as they scrambled off the porch and onto the yard. The animal who had tormented them was in hot pursuit. Down the steps crunched the huge paws. Grandy followed out onto the porch and let go another load of shot.

*The porch on the left of the picture is outside Grandy's bedroom and is where the bear was shot. The bear ran down to the river through the trees to the left*

Figure 10: Riverby Inn From the Northwest

Mam-maw caught sight of the creature as it went over the hill and down toward the river. A six-foot black bear had left his calling card all over the sticky paint on the porch floor. Grandy ran blasting his gun after the animal.

The whole household was a stir with the commotion and soon the girls gathered in their parent's room on the first floor. Many of the children, also disturbed, had followed their mothers to the room of their grandparents. Grandy returned to take the floor.

"Never seen such a big critter before in all my born days. Not even in my days at the logging camp of brother Bill out in Arkansas has there ever been such a bear. Why standing long side of Jeffie, that varmint would make her look like a baby-doll." Grandy's exaggerated comparison fascinated the audience of sleepy heads. "I'm most near sure I got some buckshot into him. Probably find him lying dead near the river's edge when I goes out. Why, Jeffie I believe that if them dogs hadn't of waked you up, that wild beastie would have come right through the door."

"Now Frank! You know better," Mam-maw cajoled, "Why I bet, if I was a bettin' lady, that that bear was as scared of you as you were of it."

"Scared? Me? Why Jeffie Blanks, you ain't ever seen the day that Francis Marion Blanks was scared. Here I am up at the break of dawn protecting you all. "He let his hand sweep the air, pointing toward his family." Protecting you and my chillun's, them Trundle-Bed-Trash, there." He pointed directly at the staring grandchildren. "Protecting you all from the wild hungry critters off of the mountain and you say I'm scared. Next time, I'm a gonna just roll over and go back to sleep. That'll fix you, Miss Jeffie Gill. You can do your own bear hunting from now on."

48    *Riverby Inn*

Grandy's offspring were speechless in the face of his outburst. His Trundle-Bed-Trash were shocked to see him fire back at Mam-maw

"Aw, Frank, I didn't mean to hurt your feelings, you know I didn't mean you were really scared. I was just using an example." Mam-maw tried to soothe his hurt pride.

"Well that's more like it! You owed me an apology. You all's been flapping your underskirts around here all week and I'm not going to have it, No siree!" He shook his fist at all the faces of this women folk. "And that goes for you gals too! There ain't going to be any Petticoat Government around my house." The Lord and Master of Riverby had laid down the LAW.

——————————— ✺ ✺ ———————————

That morning LaVerne reached up over the kitchen sink and tore the day off the calendar, leaving Friday, June 2 1934 staring back at her. She rolled up her sleeves and went to work on the stacks of dishes left from the family breakfast. She hurried as much as she dared in favor of the imminent departure she and Lola were to make for Piney Grove.

Aunt Lola came out of her cottage at the bottom of the hill. She had recruited the seventeen and eighteen-year-olds along with Mose and Annie. She was leaving them with scouring pads and pails of soapsuds to start the restoration of her cottage, while she and LaVerne went to see the man about Sally Kate. "Mose. Annie, I'm leaving you in charge here till I get back, Miss Rebekah will check on you all from time to time." Lola charged each one with their duties then added for inspiration.

"Now if you children do a good job, I promise I'll take you to North Fork this afternoon."

It was Lola's cottage. She built it and furnished it herself. Grandy had given her a plot of ground just down the back hill from the big house. It rested on a sturdy foundation of rocks from the river and every room was pine paneled. It had a small porch, ample sized living room, kitchen with small coal range and three bedrooms on the first floor. One bedroom was just off the kitchen and this was where Delilah slept.

Steps led up from the living room to a large sleeping balcony. Any number of cots and pallets could be spread out up there to accommodate the family overflow when necessary. It was early American throughout; Braided rugs, mountain furniture of hand rubbed pine and mohk's cloth curtains framed each window. A flag-stone walk lead from the front door out through two white wagon wheels to the driveway. Marigolds and petunias nodded their heads at all who came and went down the walk.

Lola nodded her approval as she passed the children raking leaves under the cherry trees.

"Do a nice neat job now. Be sure to get all the leaves piled up by the road here. Samson will pass later on in his truck and haul them off. Let's walk the Pipe around here this morning and I'll treat you all to a trip to North Fork this afternoon,

She mounted the steps of the side porch and the children squealed with anticipation at thoughts of a trip to North Fork." LaVerne? Are you ready "She called?

LaVerne stood on the front steps, forewarned by Lola's little speech in the side yard, she was ready and waiting.

Beck was in the kitchen preserving some late May pears. As she pulled the sterilized jars from the oven she spoke to her mother.

"These will be delicious with Delilah's hot biscuits. We can fill in with them when the jam runs low. What do you think of making some pear relish too? Mam-maw was stretching some crochet luncheon mats on a wooden pegged board and the gelatinous like starch ran down her fingers in globs as she struggled and pulled on the lacy Loops? "Are there anymore pears left?" She answered without looking up.

Norma and Hy had returned to the dining room where they had been interrupted the afternoon before. In the melee of the previous day's happenings, they had abandoned their work.

"Guess Beck and Lola will take all of you girls tomorrow." Norma spoke to Hy.

"Is it definite? Are we going tomorrow?"

"Yes, your mother talked to Beck and LaVerne at breakfast about it. We have to have these things from Asheville. We're expecting guests on Monday you know."

"Aw nuts! That soon? I hate waitin' on tables and making up other people's beds."

"Well right now you better be thinking about this list. Let's see, sit down and let's go over it all. Did LaVerne finish the kitchen list? She's going to Asheville too, and will need to get all the staples for the pantry."

---

The morning passed quickly. There were no idle minutes spent in counting the passing hours. Each one applied themselves eager to finish and be first to greet Lola. "We're finished, ready to go to North Fork!"

With their bathing suits on under their overalls and Khaki shorts and shirts and one thread bare towel to each car, the kids leaned out and banged on the sides of the cars with the flat of their hands. "C 'mon Mama, c'mon Aunt Beck let's go."

Beck and Lola formed a two-car caravan and left for North Fork. The children cried back and forth to each other, "Look out North Fork here we come.", And to each other they recalled. "Man, that water is cold. This time I aim to pick up a stone off the bottom."

As the cars of his two daughters passed by him in the garden, Grandy raised his hat. He watched it pass from view over the bridge above the Swannanoa River and around the bend in the highway which led to Black mountain. He lifted his hoe, placed it over his shoulder and started up the hill toward the house. When he reached the neatly piled up rows of leaves which the children had finished, he stopped. He pushed the old felt hat back from his eyes and looked first at the house then around the hillside. Satisfied that no one was in view, he quickly lowered the hoe and in moments scattered all the leaves. The afternoon breeze from Ole Hickory picked up his motion and swayed the debris gently but effectively. Once again there were leaves all over the hillside.

"Tain't no use paying Samson to haul off these leaves. It's a sinful waste of money. The Lord above done caused them to fall and I reckon as how he meant for them to stay where they was." Grandy spoke his miserly peace to the empty yard

"Wheeeeeeee hooooooo eeeaeeeee! I keep forgetting how cold the water is." Bobbie screamed as she dove in.

North Fork was a very large upper tributary of the Swannanoa River, it ran much swifter but more shallow at the foot of Riverby. At North Fork, the river went into a lazy curve and formed a large lake. The water was crystal clear and small mountain trout swam underneath the surface swimmers. The mountains marched right down to the banks and poured their frigid streams into the river. Rhododendron and laurel grew as high as two story houses and their flowers sent out aromatic perfumes into the mountain air. Bee Balm, and Bitter Bloom and Toad Flax tried to choke out the Indian Paint Brush, Golden Rod and Shooting Star.

"Swim fast and you'll keep warm." Martha yelled to Betts.

"What are you talking about? Your lips are bluer than mine, I bet." Betts ducked under the water.

"Look at Charles and Leon way down below us. Bet they'll bring up a pebble off the bottom". Tom Jr. said to Jay.

"Nobody had ever touched bottom here. Some folks say its forty feet deep in the deepest part." Martha imparted her native knowledge.

"Let's go over there where Sis is. It's more shallow. I want to learn to stand on my hands." Betts invited the boys to follow her.

"Water fight! Water fight! Look out! You boys are going to drown Sis." Beck cautioned the rougher boys.

"Alright, young'uns, everybody out. Time to go home for supper". Lola was right on her schedule.

"Aw shucks, I was just beginning to learn to walk on my hands." Sis begged for more time in the water.

"You mean we've been here two hours? Seems we just got here. Will you bring us back tomorrow? We just love it here!" All the children chorused.

"We'll see. Get dried off and get your clothes on. I don't want my upholstery all wet." Lola warned.

"Last one out's a rotten eeeeggggggggggggggg!" Leon teased.

"I bet a hundred people have dried off on this towel. It's so wet I can wring it out." Bobbie was fretful.

"Aw hurry up and get your clothes on, Bobbie. I need the towel. The boys can't see you from behind this laurel bush." La nagged back at Bobbie.

"They're starting the cars. Come on." Martha hurried the female swimmers.

"Hang your suits on the door handles, they'll dry in the breeze on the way home. Beck suggested.

"Gosh, I'm starved. Hope Aunt Boom has plenty of biscuits and gravy for supper." Jaybo was licking his lips.

"Goood......... Bye, ole North Fork. We love you and we'll be back reeeeeeeeeeal soon." All joined Betts in her fond farewell.

# To Buy A Fat Pig

Lola pushed open the double screen doors and let them slam behind her as she began to address her mother on the front porch.

"Mama, we're going to take both cars. Rebekah will drive the LaSalle and I'll take my Franklin. We'll combine business with pleasure. We're going to take as many of the children as we can and run our errands and do a little shopping and take the children to the S and W for lunch. It might be as late as four o'clock before we get back. Penney's is having a sale on linens and I want to see if we can get some bargains in sheets and towels and then, of course, we will have to go to the wholesale grocers and order kitchen supplies. But everything is lined up in the kitchen for lunch and Delilah can be depended on to start supper in case we're not back in time."

"Oh yes, LaVerne is making up the Red Bird room. If anyone turns in you can rent it out for a night or two but the Taylors will arrive on Monday and of course that is to be their room for some weeks. So, have that clearly understood with the people if they want to take it temporarily." Lola was talking a mile a minute as she put on her driving gloves. No matter what her costume was or how hot the day, she donned brown pig skin gloves to handle the big steering wheel of the Franklin.

"You take the rag off the bush, Lola" Mam-maw exploded as she stopped rocking. "You act like I don't have a brain in my head. I was renting out rooms and seeing to meals before you were born. Now go on with you. The place will be here when you get back. Send LaVerne out here before you go. I want a word with her."

Lola stepped back inside the hallway and called, "LaVerne! You-hoo. Where are you? Aren't you about ready to go? Oh, there you are and you look very nice. You did a nice alteration job on that polka dot dress of Beck's. It looks very neat on you. By the way, Mama wants a word with you on the porch before we go. Just don't you two talk all day, I want to get to Asheville sometime before 10:30." Lola announced as she went out to warm up her motor.

"Daughter, here is some money. I want you to do something special for me," Mam-maw said. "Here is a swatch of material. Please get me a spool of Clark's O & T thread, No. 60 in this lavender shade. If you get near that corner drug store on Pack's Square, I'd love to have a large can of Rose O'Sharon snuff. Now, now, don't look at me that way, I dip and I'm not ashamed of it. I know you girls think it's messy and not becoming to a lady but I learned to dip when I went to finishing school. All young ladles of my time used it. This Bruton's I get from Mr. Veazy's store in the village is all right in between time but I want a can of Rose…."

"All right, Mama. You can depend on me. You know how we feel about it but since it means so much to you, I'll get it. Just please use discretion." LaVerne put the swatch in her old black pocket book and handed the money back to her mother. "I think the profits from Riverby can stand you to a spool of thread and a can of snuff," she laughed. "Try to rent that Red Bird room while we're gone. We need to pick up any extra we can."

Beep, beep, beep went the Franklin's horn.

"Sister, come on here or I'm going to leave without you. You are as pokey as Aunt Lil. Beck's been gone twenty minutes with her crew." Lola roared the engine and began to back off the section of the yard used for a parking lot. LaVerne folded herself into the front seat and slammed the door just in time. She turned and waved goodbye to her mother. Mam-maw noticed a triangle of polka dots resting on the running board. She waved back to her daughters and made motions about the dress but her signaling went unnoticed "Oh, pshaw, they didn't pay me any attention."

Beck was some miles down the road, in fact, she was approaching Oteen. Home of the United States Government Veterans Hospital for Tubercular Patients, when Lola and LaVerne left the Riverby property.

The car was in Free Wheeling and the big tires of the LaSalle hummed on the hot pavement as Beck hummed a little tune. Her diamond dinner ring sent out colored sparks of fireworks as she clutched the steering wheel. The large brilliant-cut engagement ring sent out regular little S O S messages when she used her left hand to signal. Tom's tenth anniversary present to her couldn't be seen. The handsome diamond bar pin was pinned inside her brassiere along with two one hundred-dollar bills. Her jaws were working overtime on a piece of Juicy Fruit gum. Rebekah's thoughts were already in Asheville as she thought out her itinerary for the day. Where she would go, what she would buy and what she would have for lunch. From time to time she would reach out her sturdy arm and slap at a whining child or break up a small fracas in progress on the back seat. When the LaSalle came to the railroad tracks, Rebekah quickly checked both ways and eased the car on across with hardly a jostle as they passed over the rails.

Actually the car load of children she had was behaving very well. Asheville was a big treat and it was fun just to think about what adventures might lie ahead.

Lola didn't drive as fast as Rebekah and the car had a tendency to sway dangerously near the center line in the highway. But she kept a steady speed up and made good time. When the Franklin approached the railroad tracks, Lola brought he car to a full stop, honked the horn three times, and without looking to see if a train was approaching, she slammed her foot on the accelerator and the car leapt across like a gazelle.

Rebekah had made one stop at a filling station just outside Asheville. Several of the children had to go to the bathroom and she drank a Coca-Cola. Since Lola didn't permit stopping along the roadside for anything ("Just hold it until we get where we're going.") both cars were riding in tandem when they reached the Asheville tunnel.

The tunnel was blasted from rock under Beaucatcher Mountain.[3] Without a word or a signal from anyone, all the talking, wrestling and restless children sat up straight and held their breaths and made their private wishes. If they held their breath all the way through the tunnel their wish would come true. Sometimes the older children could do it but usually they were all red in the face and flopping their arms wildly to regain their correct amount of oxygen when the cars shot through the opening on the other side of the mountain.

"Well, I would have had my wish if Martha hadn't crossed her eyes and made me laugh." complained Betty.

"That's nothing," said Bobbie who had joined in the childish game, "Tom Jr. tickled my ribs and I couldn't hold on any longer. Darn you! I had very important wish."

"Bobbie, don't use those swear words." corrected her mother.

The two cars pulled into the parking lot of the Bon Marche Department Store and the occupants began to pile out.[4]

"We're going to "Sit Up and Rare Books" and look at all those keen boats and golf clubs and tents. Where are you all going?" asked Bill.

*Figure 11: Beaucatcher Tunnel*

*Figure 12: Bon Marche Department Store*

"I'm not going to Sears Roebuck today We'll meet you at the S & W at twelve noon sharp. Right now, we are going to Ivy's across the street. Don't be late for lunch. We'll save table for everybody," Lola said as she removed her driving gloves.

Beck worked methodically. In Sears Roebuck's she bought eight green hammocks with yellow and orange stripes, a new hoe for Grandy and an electric iron for Riverby use. In Bon Marche's she bought a bag of peanut brittle which she began to munch, ordered a 48-piece set of breakfast pottery made by the mountain people and had it mailed to Mississippi. Finding herself in the dress department, she suddenly decided to treat herself to a colored dress. "After all, I have been in mourning almost a year. Sister is right, I shouldn't wear black all the time." Rebekah bought three batiste dresses made just alike but in different colors pink, green and blue.

Since the Sewing Department was nearby, she bought herself a new knitting bag. To put in the bag, she bought two whole boxes of baby soft perishable white yarn and four sets of knitting needles in different sizes. While in the Sewing Department she purchased a dozen different spools of thread for Mam-maw in every color but lavender.

In the Shoe Department she bought each of her children a new pair of reds and two dozen pairs of socks for the gang. Just before noon she was working her way into the Notions Department.

Lola was in J.C. Penney's getting some sugar sacking for kitchen use. She gave the clerk a ten-dollar bill and waited for her change. The clerk put the money and the order blank in a little brass tube and turned to wrap up the purchase. The children watched in wonderment as the tube shot up into an open network of cages and whisked along the tracks to the office in the rear balcony of the store. In a few minutes the change and receipt were sent back the way it had come.

"Which way to the bargain counter, Miss?" Lola quickly moved in the direction of the clerks pointed finger.

LaVerne, with Martha and Betty at her side, went to the drug store and purchased Mam-maw's snuff. "We won't say anything about this to the others," she cautioned.

When they walked into Kresses ten cent store. The beauty of it! The wonder of it! Each of the girls had earned a dime for not giggling all the way into the city and they ran excitedly from counter to counter fingering the ribbons, smelling the perfume and playing with the toys. LaVerne matched up Mam-maw's lavender thread with the swatch and waited for the girls to make their purchases.

Martha bought a paperback song book with the words of all the latest popular songs in it. They knew how to play the songs by ear and now they could sing them.

*Figure 13: S&W Cafeteria*

Betty bought a ten-carat diamond ring that could be adjusted to fit her finger. "You can wear it any time you want to, Marth," she said, holding out her thin hand and admiring the brilliance of the sparkler. When the Court House clock began to chime all groups of people from were making their way to the S & W.[5]

"Hello Jesus "

"Good morning, Jesus."

"Jesus you're looking swell."

The Riverby children gravely acknowledged Jesus every time they passed the S&W.

"Come on children," Lola ordered briskly. "Go on in. Don't block the door. I don't know why the authorities don't lock up that wretched man. It's indecent for that imposter to be loose in the city."

"He doesn't hurt anyone and I feel sorry for him. I know for a fact that the Presbyterians at Montreat have tried to take him under their wing and do something about him. That was last summer, right after the Baptists at Ridgecrest gave up over him. Maybe this summer the Methodists will do something," LaVerne wished she had a dime to hand him.

"I was hoping the Baptists would give him a good dunkin'…. long hair, long whiskers, flowing robes and all," said Lola, "he could sure use it."

Bobble spoke up. "Who knows? Maybe he really IS Jesus. I'm always careful to speak to him…. just in case."

"Bobbie don't be sacrilegious," her mother scolded as she stole a grin at Rebekah.

A more or less orderly line formed to get trays. The attendants behind the steam table worked efficiently but a little frantically to serve the Riverby influx. It took six tables to hold everyone and their good food. Jaybo had a side of roast beef. Tom Jr. had five slices of pie. Three slices had meringue that stood up like a top hat. Bill had four chocolate milks and two iced teas and half a fried chicken. Rebekah had a tray filled with watermelon and cantaloupe halves. Some trays held hard rolls and cornbread while others had chicken pot pies and fruit salads.

The three sisters looked around at the trays, laughed dryly and busily went about dividing all foods up among themselves and their children until each person had a well-balanced lunch.

"Jay, you just eat what I've given you. If you're still hungry you can go back for seconds. You cannot eat a whole steer by yourself. It's not good for you." Beck brought the argument to a close.

"Sonny, don't put so much sugar in your tea. Your glass is already half-filled with sugar. I can't even see the lemon." Lola was worried about diabetes.

"Bobbie, I just found a mushroom cap in my chicken pie. Wouldn't you like to have it? Bobbie? Where did Bobbie go?" LaVerne began to look about her from table to table.

"There's Sarah Bernhardt going into her act now," Bill spoke up with his mouth full of lemon pie and pointing across the room with his fork.

Bobbie was bending her blond head down toward the gray hair of a most distinguished looking gentleman who was deeply engrossed in his business man's lunch. Snatches of her conversation drifted back to the Riverby lunchers. "Oops, terribly sorry, sir…..those dreadful people over there want me to eat at their table…... don't really know them…… I feel faint….."

LaVerne almost upset her chair in her haste to reach her daughter's side. "Pardon the histrionics of this young woman. I'm terribly sorry if she has inconvenienced you in any way. Get your tray, young lady. Take your limp hand from your brow and come with me. If you faint, I'll bring you around with this pitcher of ice water."

Sarah Bernhardt quickly picked up her tray and laughing at her mother's confusion and the gentleman's uncertainty she took her seat at an empty table next to the Riverby group and daintily began to eat her fruit cocktail.

"Just wait until I get her home. I'll have a good long talk with her." LaVerne's face was flushed as she rejoined her sisters.

"Just don't pay any attention to her. She just loves to attract attention. I saw her one time go into a play faint in a priest's lap. Never so mortified in my life," Beck said.

"She put on a good show that time she crossed her eyes and said her mother and father were cousins," Martha giggled.

*To Buy A Fat Pig*   57

"Aw, leave her alone. I'm glad she won't associate with us. I don't want anybody to know she's kin to me," Jaybo said as he went back to get seconds.

"All those in favor of seeing Carole Lombard at the picture show say aye," sang out Beck.

"Aye!"

"Yeah"

"Yes Mam"

"Whoopee"

The children quickly placed their wadded-up napkins on the tables and pushed back their chairs. Even Sarah Bernhardt drank down her large glass of iced tea in one swallow and stood.

"Beck, that's foolishness," Lola said, "A pure waste of money and I don't think we have time.

"Don't be an old Grandy, Lola. The children have only been to the movie once this summer and it'll only take an hour or two. We'll meet you at Ivy's at two thirty or three o clock." Looking like the Pied Piper, Rebekah eagerly took her charges in tow and marched right up to the ticket window and bought seats for everybody in the balcony.

"I have never seen anybody throw money away like Rebekah," Lola said hotly. Tom should have put her on a strict allowance years ago to curtail her gross spending."

"But Lola, she is so good and generous with her money," LaVerne offered.

"Mark my words, her auditor will have to plow under her Georgian Colonial house and put it in a paying crop to pay for all the things she has bought today. I saw a new knitting bag and some white wool. She was already casting on stitches at the S & W. No telling what all she has bought."

While Rebekah and the gang were at the movie and Lola and LaVerne were at the Wholesale Grocer's ordering stocks of lard, flour and sugar, salt and coffee, a gray Dodge turned into the driveway of Riverby.

---

Mam-maw was dozing in her rocker on the front porch.

When the car door slammed, Mam-maw jerked her head up and cleared her throat. As she adjusted her glasses, a rotund dark-haired man swam into view.

"Good afternoon, madam. My wife and I wonder if we could have a room for the rest of the afternoon and for the night. You see, we've come from Pennsylvania and we have an eight-month-old baby. He has been so fretful because we have been on the road for several days and my wife says we just must let him have a long quiet afternoon nap and restful full night sleep before we continue. The Asheville Chamber of Commerce recommended your place to us. My name is Zimmerman. Nathan Zimmerman and this is my wife Esther."

As Mam-maw made her way to the steps she was thinking fast. What a stroke of luck to rent out the Red Bird room. This man is charming. Such courteous manners and all the way from Pennsylvania. They must be Pennsylvania Dutch. I'll have to ask them if they know that Schlimmer couple who made pretzels and spoke that charming patois.

"Welcome to Riverby Inn, Mr. and Mrs. Zimmerman. I'm Mrs. Blanks and I'll be delighted to show you a room that should just suit you. Now you give me that fussy baby. I can see that your arms are ready to break holding that fat baby while he's twisting around that way. You just let me sit here and rock him on my shoulder while you go up and look at the room. It'll be the room to the right at the top of the stairs. It has cardinals on the paper. Come here to Mam-maw, Big Boy."

The Zimmermans couldn't believe their good fortune and their eyes.

Most southern resort hotels didn't take Jewish families. Time after time they were told politely that the rooms had all been taken but to 'try on down the road'. Some of the places had seemed like Sodom and Gomorrah but this place was Sinai.

Mam-maw's girls had followed the practice of 'try on down the road' since these people are just different and the other guests might resent it. But Nathan and Esther didn't know this, Mam-maw thought they were Pennsylvania Dutch. Mam-maw's girls were having a good time in Asheville. So, the Zimmerman's moved in.

Mam-maw told Esther, "While you take your bags up and get settled, you give me the baby and a clean diaper and fresh jumper and I'll give him a good bath for you and he can take a nice quiet nap. He and I have already gotten acquainted and he's taken to me. You know, I had four of my own and have fourteen grandchildren."

Esther was ready to cry from weariness and relief.

Nathan was very busy. He unstrapped the bags from the luggage rack on the running board and brought in a crib, mattress, rubber sheet and pad. He opened the trunk of the car and brought in a play pen and baby buggy. Next came the baby's bottles and cans of formula, baby foods, zwieback, and tote bags of diapers and clothes. Then he carried up his and Esther's luggage and brought up the camera and its tripod. The room was beginning to look pretty crowded but Esther said not to worry she'd straighten it up after a little nap.

"Ho-hum, darling go down and bring little Sammy up for his nap. Do you think they operate a Kosher kitchen? Better not ask, though, it doesn't really matter and we'll find out soon enough anyway. We could just as easily spend the next three weeks here."

———————————— ❧ ❧ ————————————

"I just love Carole Lombard's nose," Beck said. "She has a wonderful profile. And she's just plain cute. And that leading man...... so handsome."

The forces had just joined up at Ivy's Department Store.

"Sister, I'm going to take Martha and Betty and buy them some Sunday School shoes. Now, now, don't protest like that. I'm just going to get them some white sandals they were admiring in the window." Beck couldn't bear to have LaVerne look at her that way. LaVerne's soft blue eyes so quickly swam in tears over a grateful gesture.

"Beck, you and Lola are the best sisters in the world. Lola is going to buy them each a petticoat and a blouse for Bobbie."

Beck bought them each a pair of sandals and then she bought them some sturdy oxfords for school. The girls took turns standing at the x-ray machine. Poking their feet into the little slot on the floor, they could look down into the box and see their feet inside their shoes. The clerk took a pointer and said, "Observe the bones are well formed and have plenty of space to move inside these Parrot shoes. No fear of them not fitting properly in this day and age with our modern equipment."

Martha and Betty were speechless. Two pair of shoes in one day. Lunch at the S & W and Carole Lombard and the song book and the ring! Would wonders never cease? They hugged each other and gave shy kisses to Beck. They kept the oxfords on and hugged the packages containing the sandals to their twelve-year-old bosoms.

Esther had had a wonderful nap. Little Sammy was still asleep in his crib and only the occasional noise of sleepy thumb sucking interrupted the quietness.

"I wonder where Nathan is?" Esther mused as she gathered up the soiled diapers and baby clothes and went to the kitchen. Ora obligingly helped her set up laundry on the back porch and brought her a glass of iced tea.

As Esther was hanging up her laundry on a string line outside the kitchen window facing the highway, she looked down toward the barn and saw Nathan talking to a man in a brown felt hat with glasses on and a man dressed in overalls. The center of attention was a cow. The man in overalls was standing to one side with his hands on his hips and his head cocked to one side. The man in the hat was pointing to the cow's full bag and nodding his head. Nathan was patting the cow's side and gesturing with his right hand and his head.

"Wonder what they're talking about," Esther said to herself as she shook out another diaper and pinned it in place on the clothes line. "It must be a business transaction. When Nathan uses his hands and his head at the same time, he means business. Just like his father."

"Mam-maw was rocking to and fro on the porch. A smile played around her mouth as her needle darted in and out of the Snowball pattern cotton quilt pieces. She was very pleased with herself about renting the room and anticipating her after dinner dip of Rose O'Sharon. It was getting on to four thirty and the cars should be turning in at any moment.

The cavalcade of cars had pulled away from the parking lot of the Bon Marche at four. The children held their breaths going back through Beaucatcher Mountain tunnel. Since their wishes had been realized in Asheville, they had had a hard time thinking up new ones. Passing the Recreation Park, they gave a cheer, "Hey there Rec Park. We'll be back to see you real soon," they called hopefully. They eased off their new shoes and wriggled their toes on the floor of the back seat and brought out their newly-bought treasures and admired and compared them.

Rebekah's car looked like a traveling delicatessen. Draped on the front fender on the left-hand side was a new bag of Texas onions. "So sweet, just like eating an apple," she had remarked to the children in her car.

The trunk of the LaSalle and the front and back seats were laden with her purchases. Riding on the seat beside her were two large butcher wrapped packages of calf's liver. "The most succulent and delicious calf's liver in the world is to be had in Asheville," she commented.

As the LaSalle whipped down the highway, a large red balloon flapped in the jet stream. Sis was letting it out on a long string to see how far she could trail it without its being exploded.

The Franklin was in the lead this time since Lola had no intention of going to the butchers or anywhere else after their necessary shopping was attended to.

"If you don't mind looking like a bunch of Okies you can travel with Rebekah. I have never seen such a glutton. She can't stand to pass by anything for sale without touching it, tasting it and buying it. Would you please tell me why she bought that $2.00 bunch of delphiniums? We have a flower garden and the whole range of mountains covered with flowers but, no, she has to go to a florist." Lola gave an elaborate hand signal to the empty highway as she suddenly decided to put the car into second gear.

LaVerne was scarcely listening to Lola. Her mind was already on the dinner. How tired she was. After being up since 5:30 and getting all that work done so she could go into the city for shopping, it hardly seemed worth it. It seems I never have a decent outfit to wear. She voiced her silent conversation to the patient mountains. Here I am a grown woman and I have on a navy-blue polka dot dress, brown shoes and a black pocket book. She looked down at the coarse leather shoes on her feet and compared them with the artificial alligator purse in her lap. The snap fastener wouldn't stay closed and she had to grasp it, by the top when she carried it so it wouldn't fly open and spill out the contents. The cheap alligator grain made her flinch to look at it. She noted more cracks in the carrying strap. If I don't do another thing at the end of the summer, I'm going to buy myself one outfit that matches up. The mountains didn't answer.

"It looks like somebody had a baby while we were gone," announced Lola as she spied the diapers on the line. "You don't think the stork has added to our population since this morning, do you?" She roared at the idea of it. "Remember last summer when the children saw that big crane down at the river and thought it was the stork? Beck said, 'Get the gun, Papa, and kill it.' After putting up with all our Riverby children and the guest's children and that bus load of singing orphans at the tail end of last summer, all we need is for the stork to start hovering overhead." Lola pulled the Franklin into its parking place.

"Look! There's a car with Pennsylvania tags on it," one of the boys said. "Wonder if they have any kids our age."

Lola gave her horn a blast to announce their arrival and the children began to jump out of the car. Rebekah had just turned in the driveway and was bearing down on her horn.

"We're home everybody." Bill called.

"Mam-maw where are you? I want to show you my new road racer," Sonny pleaded.

"Let me play her a tune on my harmonica first." Jaybo elbowed his way through the crowd.

"Mam-maw, see my ring? Look at the way it sparkles. "Betty held her hand up to Mam-Maw's face.

The children tumbled out of the cars and surrounded Mam-maw. She admired each present and said how glad she was they were home. The hill had been too quiet.

The presents were handed out. The Rose O'Sharon was discretely hidden in a little brown paper with the spool of lavender thread. Grandy strolled up from the garden and ran his finger over the edge of the new hoe to see how sharp it was. Lola handed him a plug of Bull Durham and a can of Prince Albert, crimp-cut.

In the midst of the confusion, Mam-maw told LaVerne about the lovely young couple who were Pennsylvania Dutch.

Beck sent her packs of liver back to Ora by Martha and Betty. "Tell her I'm cooking the meal tonight and I want her to put out a pound of Miss Lou's butter to soften."

Turning to LaVerne, Rebekah said, "Sister, I've already planned dinner. We'll have broiled liver and onions, baby carrots, new potatoes and English peas cooked with a little mint. Hot biscuits and blueberry cobbler for dessert. If you will supervise the dining room getting set up and make one of your good salads, I'll handle everything else."

It wasn't too often that Rebekah took over the cooking of a whole meal but when she did it was a night to remember. Delilah stood by like a nurse assisting a famous surgeon. Butter, salt, pepper, dash of rosemary, butter, cream, A-1 Sauce, butter, squeeze of lemon, more butter. As Beck called out what she required, Delilah produced it. The dishwashers worked hard all during the preparations and after Rebekah sailed out of the kitchen to eat her dinner, the groans could be heard all the way to Black Mountain. More dishes and pots and pans and ladles and silverware were used than during a whole week of cooking.

———————— ❧ ❦ ————————

By sundown on Saturday nights, Grandy considered the Lord's Day had arrived, and Mam-maw helped him prepare for it.

After supper they disappeared into their downstairs bedroom and closed the door. Mam-maw went to the large old mahogany dresser, opened the top drawer and took out a clean pair of long underwear. This she laid carefully on Grandy's side of the big double bed.

As she was doing this, Grandy sat at the foot of the bed and removed his brown work shoes that came up high over the ankles. Working at the lacings in the hooks at the tops and unwinding them from the crisscross pattern they made, he eased them off with a sigh and wiggled his toes. Next, he removed the once white cotton ribbed socks that he had worn all week and dumped them into a heap next to the shoes.

Pulling at the spotted and stained necktie which bore the traces of his meals since last Sunday, he flicked it from around his neck and proceeded to unbutton his shirt. Adding those items to the sock pile on the floor, he un-fastened his galoshes and began to remove his belt. Lola had given him the leather belt one Christmas and he wore it but he never felt his pants would stay up with just a belt on, so he still continued to wear his suspenders, too. Dancing a little, first on one foot and then on the other, he managed to divest himself of his trousers.

Standing there in the bedroom with his long-johns on and his brown felt hat on his head, he slipped his bare feet back into the dusty work shoes. Mam-maw handed him a clean 'wash rag' and towel and he collected his straight-edged razor and shaving mug with a ragged shaving brush inside. The bristles were embedded in the shaving soap which lay dried out and cracked looking in the bottom of the mug.

Mam-maw opened the bedroom door for him and he went out into the great central hallway of Riverby. Nodding to the foursome of his teenage grand-daughters playing bridge in the hallway, he went out the side door, down the short porch with its view of the highway on one side and the dining room on the other and entered the bathroom.

Setting down his shaving equipment on the washstand, he inserted the rubber plug into the drain of the tub and turned both faucets on full blast. Draping his clean long-johns and towel over the back of the little three-legged stool, he unbuttoned his underwear and slipped out of it and gave it a swift kick to one side. Pushing his brown felt hat back a little from his face, he stepped into the tub and settled back to soak.

When the water was nearing the very top of the tub and beginning to overflow onto the linoleum floor, he turned each tap off with a violent wrench.

Lathering up with the Octagon soap he casually slapped the wash rag over his body and wrenched off. Lifting out the plug, and leaning over to get his towel to dry off, his clean long-johns fell onto the floor and his hat almost fell off his head. The water sluggishly and reluctantly went down the drain and into the Swannanoa River. Garden dirt, honest sweat, small sticks and stones and broken chicken bones swirled and swished in a little whirlpool at the throat of the drain.

With his clean underwear on, Grandy ran hot water into the sturdy shaving mug. Sloshing the matted brush around and around, he lathered up his face and picked up the straight-edged razor. Like a dueler using his own face for an opponent he worked quickly and with fancy gestures lunging and swerving and with great sweeping motions of his arms, he attacked his face time after time with the long sharp blade. He kept his eye glasses on and only used caution when the razor approached his deformed eye.

Dabbing wet toilet paper at the bleeding scratches on his face, he then removed his hat and set it gently upon the stool. Running warm water over the bar of Octagon soap, he used the whole bar as a comb and brush and hair tonic. Slicking back his gray-white hair with the bar of soap, he admired the finished product in the mirror.

Settling his hat back on his head, he gathered up his razor and shaving mug and slipped his feet back into the work shoes. Flinging wide open the bathroom door, he strode back onto the side porch, in through the door into the central hallway and nodded again to the young girls who giggled and seemed unusually intent on their cards.

Bobbie said, "Well Grandy, I see you're ready for church tomorrow."

Grandy slammed back into the bedroom.

Bobbie turned to Hy, La and Mabes and said, "if cleanliness is next to godliness, Grandy is all set."

After his bath, Grandy got dressed in the clean clothes Mam-maw had left laid out on the bed. He adjusted his tie and inserted a small amber stick pin in it and picked up his buckskin snap purse. He checked inside it to see for certain it held its treasure. Reassured, he put the purse into his coat pocket next to his heart and headed for the front porch.

"I might as well put up my knitting. It's getting too dark to do close work." Beck carefully pushed the thirty-two cast on white stitches well to the back of the steel needles and dropped the bundle back into the new knitting bag.

"Beck, I don't see where you get all your stamina," LaVerne sighed. "I just want to sit here peacefully and rock. I feel so contented after our fruitful day in Asheville and that delicious liver. Gazing out over those wonderful mountains gives me renewed energy and peace."

Mam-maw, Rebekah, Lola, LaVerne and Norma were enjoying themselves. They sat quietly rocking and talking about the trip into Asheville and the unexpected new guests and talking about the summer to come. The teenage girls had broken up their bridge game and all the children were playing out on the big lawn.

"Oh, Papa, I thought you had gone to bed," Lola was the first to notice Grandy coming through the double doors onto the porch.

"Thought I'd try out that new t'baccie you brought me." Grandy stood facing his women folk and brought out his pipe and the can of Prince Albert. He shook some of the crimp-cut tobacco into the bowl of the pipe and tamped it down. He struck a kitchen match on the sole of one shoe and began to light up. He pulled on the pipe stem until blue smoke wafted in the breeze.

"I wish Homer would take up a pipe. Maybe it would relax him. He has business on his mind all the time." Lola said aloud.

"There's a time for business and a time for relaxing. I made a good little business deal today." Grandy reached into his coat pocket and withdrew his snap purse and handed it to Lola. "Go on, Open 'er up."

"Why, Papa, there's a fifty-dollar bill in here!"

The women stopped their rocking and mocked astonishment.

"Frank where did you get a fifty-dollar bill?" Jeffie demanded to know.

"Whilst you gals were cavortin' in town today, I was in my garden tendin' to my corn and I looked up and there was this stranger standin' there wantin' to know about buying a cow. Well, sir, I tell him right off the bat that Sally Kate is the best heifer I ever owned. In spite of that risen udder she had, she gave good quality milk and plenty of it. We ambled over to the barn and that new boarder fellow joined us and we stood there admiring Sally Kate's coat and large hips and her clear eyes and this fellow in the overalls wants to know how much I'd take for her. I told him right off I wouldn't take less than...... well, I was going to say forty dollars….. but something told me not to name a price. Then he pulls out this fitty-dollar bill and we shook hands on it. Not bad, I'd say, for half hours bargaining." Grandy couldn't conceal his pride.

In the growing darkness, LaVerne nudged Lola and they resumed their rocking.

"I never dreamed that cow was worth $50," LaVerne cooed.

"You sure know human nature and how to deal with a man in a business transaction," Lola complimented.

Beck said, "That was a good deal since you only paid $35 for her and she served the family well."

Norma laughed, "Leon will be glad to know he doesn't have to milk her anymore and get kicked. She was a mean cow."

"Frank, that was handled very well "Mam-maw turned to her daughters and said, "Mountain people are hard to handle in a trade."

"Yep. It's all in knowing your man and how to handle him." Grandy collected his money and went to bed.

"His last statement was priceless," Rebekah threw back her head and laughed until the tears came. "If he only knew how we knew a certain man and how we handled him "

"Hush girls, he might hear you. Don't ever let him know or he'll put on his fighting clothes and declare war on petticoat government," Mam-maw cautioned.

---

Out on the lawn the children were restless. After supper the Kick the Can game seemed to start out all right but somehow it palled after not more than half an hour. A Crack the Whip game was started but it seemed to require too much running and soon disbanded. The Riverby children were milling around the big yard and the smaller ones were catching lightning bugs and tearing off the little green lights to wear for rings.

"Oh! Look at that beautiful moon," Mabes shouted.

"WOW---------weeeeeee!" Bobbie answered.

"Man is it big and close. I bet if we was on Ole Hickory, we could near bout touch it." Bill felt quite certain of it.

"I see the Man in the Moon. See his big round cheeks and eyes? He's bald-headed," Sis pointed.

The full moon had risen just as quickly as the sun had set. In the mountains one minute the sun would be kissing the top of a mountain on its way to bed and the next minute it would be gone. The same was true of the moon. One minute you could see it shyly peak over the top of the mountain and hocus-pocus the next time you looked, there it was shining big and round and bright. As if by a signal, the stars appeared in gigantic clusters against the back drop of the royal blue sky.

"Tell us about the stars and the moon, Harold," urged Jaybo.

"Come on Leon, you know something about the stars, too," Martha encouraged.

They all lay back on the springy grass on the lawn and looked up at the sky.

"Well," started out Leon, "do you see that star next to the moon? Yes, that's the one just to the right-hand side. You don't actually notice it, but every single night it gets closer and closer and closer to the moon. When they meet, the world will come to an end. Yep, it's already much closer than it was last night. Guess it won't be long now." He announced with satisfaction.

He was properly rewarded with oohs and ah's from the younger children.

"That's just an old wives' tale," corrected Harold. "What I'm really interested in is what is beyond the Milky Way and the Big Dipper and the Little Dipper and," he lowered his voice, "those constellations."

"Why, nothing's beyond them…..just sky. I can see it. Plain blue sky." Tom Jr. was most emphatic.

"Wrong! Our eyes aren't strong enough to see beyond those constellations. There are billions and billions and billions of stars and planets and even……galaxies with their suns and moons and stars stretching waaaaay off into SOMEWHERE."

There was quietness as each imagination tried desperately to comprehend this bit of news.

"Now, where do they all go? Where do they end? Are there people out there in that SOMEWHERE?" Harold had a most appreciative audience.

Jaybo didn't want to think about lt. The loss of his father had been too recent. The conversation was getting into the realms marching right up to the Pearly Gates and he didn't want to go that far tonight. "Aw, I'm not interested in all that stuff. I just want to know how many stars there are that we can see right here from Riverby? Maybe a million?"

"Closer to a million billion zillion, I reckon," said Sonny. He desperately needed to go to the bathroom. He was beginning to feel nervous and uneasy.

"If I was Buck Rogers," volunteered Bill, "I would put on my space suit with that automatic gas gun on my back and I'd just take myself a little trip and find out. I'd sure like to have myself one of those silver space overalls. They're keen. Wonder if Uncle Huddy's factory could make me some. And you know the way Buck Rogers takes off with those flames shooting out behind…… man, that's something."

"I like the way they shine," said Mabel. "Stars are very hard to paint. The moon, too. To make them look real, I mean. When I first started to paint and draw small pictures, I'd just take an Indian Head penny and draw around it for a moon. Next time you're in the Music Parlor Room take a good look at that painting somebody gave Mam-maw. You know, that one of the girl in the canoe with the long hair? I'd like to be that girl in that boat with the big full moon shining through the willow tree. I like the way she trails her hand in the water through the water lilies. Does that painting have anything to do with moon madness, do you suppose?"

"I don't know anything about moon madness," said Bobbie, 'but I saw a picture of a queen one time with a tiara on and the diamonds around the top looked just like little stars. I could sure use one of those to wear with my pink formal."

"How does God get those little points on the stars?" Betty wanted to know.

"They're not really pointed," said the Great Sage Harold, "it's your eyes that make them pointed. Stars are round.

"Look! Everybody! A falling star! A falling star! Make a wish, quick," Martha shouted.

"Make all the wishes you want to make," Leon advised, "but it really means somebody just died. Listen to old Queen, she's howling because she just smelled somebody dying."

Jaybo flinched, "Aw she's just howling at the full moon. She always does that."

"Beyond the beyond," Harold announced again," Our sun, moon, stars are but just a drop in the bucket when you think of the REAL galaxies and constellations and all the other THINGS we don't even know about extending on and on into e……..tern……..i….. ty." His voice dropped low.

"I think I hear my mother calling me," Sonny said and ran to the porch.

"It gives me the creeps to think about all that stuff. It's worse than ghost stories and cold-blooded murder. Let's don't talk about it anymore," Tom Jr, said.

Martha agreed," You all make it sound spooky and it isn't like that at all. God made the sky and the earth and the moon and stars and if He made them, there's nothing to be afraid of. It's like that hymn we sing at church. "he began singing in her clear young soprano voice,

*'I sing the might-y power of God, That made the mountains rise,*
*That spread the flowing seas a-broad, And built the lofty skies.*
*I sing the Wisdom that ordained, The sun to rule the day,*
*The moon shines full at His command, and all the stars obey."*

"Time for bed," their mothers called. "Everybody's going to sleep on the sleeping porch tonight."

Before the family children could say their 'Now I lay me down to sleep' prayer, they first had to find a place on the sleeping porch to lay their heads.

Since they had first arrived at Riverby, they had been able to pick out their room-mates and their room but with the season upon them, all the rooms had now become cleaned and decorated for the guests. Lola's children would continue to sleep at the cottage.

The children filed out onto the big sleeping porch and turned their backs on one another while they slid out of their overalls and khaki shorts and shirts. Lining up at the washstands, they splashed cold water out of the big pitchers into the basing and washed their faces and hands and brushed their teeth. The soap, towel and often the same tooth brush was community property.

"This cot is sure rickety. Bet it won't stand up all night." Jaybo jiggled it to show off its antiquated condition.

"Better to have a cot than a bed roll with heaven only knows who." Tom Jr. didn't like a bed fellow.

"You all get quiet; I want to get some sleep. Church tomorrow. You know we all have to go with Grandy and he leaves early." Martha cautioned.

"Why can't Aunt Beck and Aunt Lola drive us over? It's three or four miles over there," Bobbie was thinking about her silk stockings.

"He says it's part of religion. Working a little hard to get it," Martha said. "Don't forget to listen to the text…. sure as anything, he'll ask us later on in the day about the text. If you don't know it, he'll give you a thump on your head…. like that." She reached out and thumped Jaybo on his head. He reached out to thump her back and his cot collapsed.

Amidst yells and catcalls, he got it propped up again and the children's voices became quieter.

Martha whispered to Betty, "Tomorrow night let's get another pallet. Wouldn't you know it? We got one made up with those checkered table cloths. Ugh, I hate to sleep between table cloths."

"Yeah," Betty replied quietly, "we'll come up early and get dibbles on a pallet with real sheets."

A mountain breeze began to rustle the leaves on the old oak trees outside and the river chortled along just down the hill. The stars spread a protective covering over the roof of the porch and over all of Riverby Inn.

———————————— ❧ ❧ ————————————

Grandy sat on the front row of the little red brick Presbyterian Church on the hill.[6] His grandchildren sat with him and were lined up on the pew according to age. They over flowed onto the pew behind him. As the Reverend Coffin began to intone the Apostle's Creed, Grandy was the first one on his feet and the children imitated his perfect posture as they joined in reciting:

"I believe in God the Father almighty Maker of heaven and earth; And in Jesus Christ, His only Son, our Lord….

*Figure 14: Frank's Presbyterian Church*

When church was over, the children began to straggle back toward Riverby. Their stomachs were rumbling with hunger and there was quite a bit of grumbling among them.

"Well, he did it again, if this keeps up, I'm not going to sit with Grandy again," La was plainly embarrassed. I've just gotten so I refuse to look when the collection plate is passed. But even though I don't look, I can still see in my mind Grandy putting a copper penny in the plate."

"La, it won't do you any good to sit in the back of the church. Everybody knows you're one of the tribe."

"And to think', He has $50 in his snap purse. He should be ashamed of himself." Mabes shook her head sadly.

"I think Grandy must have some kind of agreement with the Lord," Leon put in, "he's been doing that for years. Maybe he thinks the Lord doesn't see him, Well, it's his business and far be it from me to try to get that old skin flint to part with any of his money."

"I'm glad Reverend Coffin turned us out early today. I'm hungry." Jaybo hurried on ahead of the gang.

──────────── ❧ ❦ ────────────

"But I hate to turn them out on a Sunday!" LaVerne bent her head over the salad bowl.

"Oh, you're not turning them out on a Sunday. Just tell them today they have to leave by tomorrow morning and bright and early. They've known all along the Season starts tomorrow and our rooms are all taken. Anyway, they've just about driven us crazy, I can't believe they've only been here less than twenty-four hours. The play pen is in the middle of the parlor room and that baby buggy is everywhere you step." Lola was helping Delilah flour the chicken for frying.

"Yasum and that Miz Esther is always in the kitchen in my way. She say she got to coddle an egg or braise a piece of steak or strain some orange juice for the baby. She all time in my way steralatin' bottles and boiling diapers on the stove. Ah don' know how much longer ah can stand this interference."

"Just be glad you don't have to play Mr. Zimmerman's games, Delilah. He knows a hundred silly games and they all have the most complicated rules I've ever seen. The children were beginning to make rude remarks and that's not all, Sister, the older girls don't want to clean up their room. You simply must tell them plain out today that they have to leave tomorrow. Frankly, I wash my hands of the whole affair." Lola shook the flour from a drum stick vigorously.

Beck said, "That's the last time we leave Mama in charge."

"I know you girls are right but I still feel unchristian about it somehow." LaVerne paused and looked out the kitchen window. "There he is now. He's lifting the baby up in the boughs of that dogwood tree….. he's such a sweet father. Yoo-hoo! Mr. Zimmerman! May I have a word with you?"

LaVerne removed her apron and resolutely went outside to the laughing father and the cooing baby.

# Chapter 6

# Mam-maw's Satchel

The dust was flying in the Red Bird room. Right after the Zimmerman's had driven out of the rock pillars and on to the main highway, LaVerne had sent Hy, La, Mabes and Mose upstairs to clean up the room and get it into order. The Taylors would arrive at any moment.

"Mose if you'll take the laundry down to the kitchen and come back later on and take out this trash, we'll finish up in here." Hy tied the sheets and towels into a buddle and handed them to Mose.

"Yassum, ah's sho tired. I musta made twenty trips up and down, up and down, helping Mr. Zimmerman getting loaded up. Dey sho had a heap of belongings." Mose staggered out of the Red Bird room and headed for the back steps where he tossed the laundry down to the porch below.

"I already miss little Sammy," La said. "I just adore babies. In fact, I miss the Zimmerman's. I thought they were kind of fun. "

"I'm anxious for this Dr. Taylor and his wife to arrive. They sound so interesting. Do you think he'll talk about his dealings with Leopold and Loeb? I was too young to know about the case back in the 20's but I thought I'd do some research on it so I could talk to Dr. Taylor about it intelligently."

"You know he won't talk about it. Against medical ethics."

"Well as soon as Mose comes back for the trash, this room will be in shape. We'd better report back to the kitchen for the next assignment. Something tells me this is going to be one of those days when they'll keep us jumping every minute."

Hy gave an extra pat to the pillows on the bed and began gathering up the dust rag and mop.

Down in the kitchen the Royal Oak was stuffed full with kindling and lumps of coal. The range was eight feet long and over three feet wide and the top of it was hot enough to fry an egg. Pushed to the back of the stove was a large lard can with a big hunk of solid tar in it. Slowly it was beginning to melt down. The melted mixture would be used to plug up leaks in the Tearoom roof.

In the old tin wash tub, a dozen jars of cherries were being processed for canning, Norma had also added many small jars of something new. She was experimenting with pickling cherries.

"You can pickle peaches and I don't see why not cherries. We can use them along with olives and pickles and they'll be tasty and pretty to add to cold meat dishes."

"As soon as that oven cools down some, I want to put in my pans of salt rising bread and some coffee cakes and rolls." Mam-maw spoke to the busy workers.

"Mama, you make the best salt rising bread. Go over that recipe once more for me. Somehow mine doesn't turn out as well as yours, "LaVerne commented.

"You can't rush it. Now listen carefully and follow my directions and you'll have the Staff of Life fit for a king. Yesterday I let one cup of sweet milk fresh from the cow come to a boil, then thickened it to the consistency of mush with cornmeal. Place mush in a small glass jar, then place in a vessel of warm water closely covered and set in a warm place over night. Now this morning the mush had risen and was very light, so I took one pint of fresh sweet milk and added enough warm water to make one quart of mixture…..have it a little more than lukewarm. Then you pour it into a gallon stone jar and add a small pinch of soda, tablespoon of salt, two heaping teaspoons of the mush and enough flour to make a batter stiff enough to drop from a spoon. Heat well and set the jar in a pot of warm water, as warm as the hand can bear comfortably. Keep it an even temperature and it should rise to top of jar in two or three hours. When it has risen to the top of the jar, pour into a pan with sifted flour into which has been put the soda, salt -and a handful of sugar and one- and one-half cups of lard. Work it into a soft dough… knead well, daughter, and make into six loaves. Keep it about the same temperature as the yeast and the loaves should rise to the top of the pans in two hours. They're just about ready now. Then bake them off in a moderate oven for not quite an hour. Oh yes, use one pound of flour to a loaf. That's all there is to it." Mam-maw lined up the pans on the counter and checked the oven, "I think I can put them in now," she decided.

"Maybe my stone crock isn't big enough," LaVerne sighed, "Oh, girls, are you sure the Red Bird room is in good order? You can start on those dishes in the sink. "

A groan went up to the ceiling of the old kitchen as the teenagers looked in the sink. It held four pots, six pans, two cups, three jars, lid, five spoons and one-quart stone jar.

"Mabes, you'd better get that big stick and stir these vats of dye. I just added some cypress bark to that vat of forest green and it needs to be stirred," Mam-maw directed.

Mabes took the wooden paddle and moved to the far side of the stove. There was dark green brewing in one vat and old rose in another one. Smaller pots and pans held indigo, yellow, pale green and a light cobalt blue.

"Mam-maw, I'm sure these are ready for the rags and stocking clips."

Mam-maw raised her eyeshade and studied the mixtures. Nodding in agreement, she and her grand-daughter began to dump in the strips of clean rags and the cotton stocking tops Lola weaseled out of her good friend who was in the hosiery business.

"Beautiful. Just beautiful, "Mam-maw remarked as she stirred. Mabes held up the dripping rags for a test of color.

"Don't drip that violet color in my shampoo," Bobbie warned. She had a small enamel pan into which she had shaved Castile soap slivers and then had added water. This mixture was slowly melting down into a shampoo base.

"When it cools, I'll add the yolk of an egg, "Bobbie announced. "It will bring out the lights in my hair and give it some body."

"You'd do better to eat an egg once in a while," her mother said, lifting a hot sad iron off the stove to continue her ironing. Rebekah had forgotten about the new electric iron she had purchased in Asheville.

Beck said, "Oh, yes, everyone should have an egg for breakfast. Look out, Bobbie, don't knock over my sugar starch."

Beck had a blue pan on the center burner with a heavy mixture of sugar and water in it.

"I'm going to try this out for starching my pink crocheted table mats. Look out, I'm taking it off the fire." She quickly dipped her finger in it and tasted it, "I just wanted to see if it is thick enough." Beck glared back at Bobbie. "Here, Miss Priss, stir that kettle of apple butter and Lola's pan of cleanser."

Bobbie took the offered spoon and leaned over the coffee can on the back of the stove.

"Ugh, what's in this?"

"New recipe for cleaning and scouring and polishing copper, silver, pewter and brass. It has salt, vinegar, soda, and ammonia and some borax in it. When it all boils down, I want you and the other girls to get started on all those accessories on the big dining room table. I want to see my face in them." Lola quickly checked the bubbling pots and pans on the range.

"What in the world is this smelly brew?" Lola drew back her pug nose and wiped the water from her eyes,

"Oh, how is it coming along? I forgot all about it," Mam-maw grabbed a pot holder and removed the pan from the stove, "It's some medicine I'm brewing up to send to the mountaineer who bought Sally Kate. He can use it on her in case she gets the risen udder again. It has beeswax, mutton suet and gum camphor in it and a tablespoon of linseed oil. Best thing in the world for risen breasts---or udders, if taken in time."

"Too bad you Blank's gals didn't use some of that years ago. I've never seen so many risen breasts in my life," Hy commented as she and the other girls went giggling into the dining room.

"Coming through! Hot stuff coming through!" Delilah cautioned. "I got to add these vegetables to my soup pot. Look out!"

Placed on the largest dining room table and two of the smaller ones were all manner of copper, brass, pewter, silver and gold colored accessories.

"I'll set this devil's brew in the middle where we can all reach it. It's still a little hot." Hy warned.

The girls picked up some soft rags and began to tackle the items.

Give me the brass candle sticks and the Riverby Inn bell and that big brass apple bucket. I don't mind doing the brass things," decided Bobbie. "Wish I had a nickel every time this bell has been rung. But golly it's loud. You can hear it all over the valley...even if you're on Little Hickory."

"Why do you think they have Mose ring it out on the highway? Every car from Maine to Florida knows dinner is served at Riverby when they hear that bell and see Mose in his white coat and sandwich board." Mabes began to tackle the pewter vases, pitchers, trays and the big pewter cornucopia.

Hy and La had divided up the rest of the articles and reluctantly began the tedious job of cleaning and polishing.

"Is that the Welcome Rug, Aunt Norma?" Mabes noted her aunt walking hurriedly through to the kitchen.

"Yes, I unearthed it and it is so worn and dusty I don't know whether we can use it or not. I'm going to get the boys to beat it good." She didn't stop to chat but talked as she clipped along. Her tiny feet carried her through the kitchen door and out onto the porch. "Boys!" She called.

Lola and Rebekah hardly noticed Norma as she passed them by. They were sorting out their scissors and garden shears.

Lola chose her favorite shears and took her stance by the family dining table on the porch. Facing her on this battlefield of mealtimes, were several dozen vases. All shapes, all sizes, all colors. Some were antiques and some were of mountain made pottery. Many of them had been made by the children of Riverby.

These receptacles came from every room in the Inn to be invaded with stems of thirty odd varieties of flowers which lay alongside on a bench. The major general was planning her battle attack. Inserting first one long stemmed zinnia, retreating…. one gladiola…. retreating. Somehow her line of battle strategy conflicted with her artistic line.

Lola took great pride in her flower design. She religiously attended her garden club classes on flower arranging and showed great perfection in her art. A stickler for the rules of symmetry, it mattered not that a lowly daisy became her focal point or that her background consisted of Indian Paintbrush, wild from the hillsides. Each arrangement would have the care of a true-blue ribbon show winner.

Nearby Lola, across the porch, Beck feverishly filled stone churns with mountain greenery. Her complete abandonment stood out in sharp contrast to Lola's precise movements. Beck's theory of arranging seemed to stem from the massive abundance of greenery laying all around her feet. A shame to waste one pine needle, she thought, as she stuffed and gorged the containers. By late evening, every dark corner of the Inn would have sprouted forth with one of Beck's jungle arrangements. The sheer magnitude of which would attract each new guest as they passed from reception hall to parlors to dining room.

Every so often, first one and then the other sister would stand back to admire their handiwork, registering aloud the pleasure they took from their live still life. Occasional criticisms were voiced between the two, neither of whom paid heed to the other's comment but continued in wild pursuit to capture nature in a jar or vase.

"Lola, you take up too much time with each arrangement. Just pitch in and make a bouquet," Beck criticized.

"It's more important to be artistic than to cram a vase full of flowers and have it done. Why, the Japanese take all day making an arrangement. They choose a vase or dish, put in a pussy willow bough and pray over it. Then they come back later and add a spray of cherry blossoms. Their arrangements are a real work of art." Lola secretly decided even she'd never take as long as the Japanese over an arrangement.

The conversation was briefly broken by the giggling of Martha Lee and Betty coming in with arms laden. They had been sent first up the hillside to gather wild flowers and then to the garden to gather vegetables.

After Beck finished with the pine trees she was building, she launched into a vegetable arrangement. With a huge basket of vegetables over her arm, she sailed into the dining room and snatched up the metal cornucopia Mabes had just finished polishing.

This being the standard decoration for the center table in the dining room, Beck used the cornucopia for this master piece and gorged it beyond the brimming point with Grandy's colorful home produce. She worked directly on the table so the tide of vegetables would roll over the white cloth. Cabbage, yellow neck squash, early beets, yellow tomatoes, purple eggplant, white turnips, red radishes, dried golden ears of corn, white onions, green cucumbers and bell peppers all spilled forth like a promise from the kitchen. The vegetables that the early garden couldn't produce had been secretly bought by Beck in a specialty market in Asheville.

Beck paused in her arranging and looked up at Lola as she backed through the swinging doors into the dining room with a vase of flowers in each hand.

"Lola, do you think those people will pay papa for the damage they caused in the garden this morning?"

"Not if I know anything about human nature, my dear." Lola set down her flowers in the center of two of the tables and gave a last-minute touch to the arrangements. "At least once every year, some fool man fails to make that curve in the highway and ends up in Grandy's garden. He hasn't collected a cent for damages yet."

———————— 🙦 🙤 ————————

Early that morning, the children had arisen with Grandy and swigged down forbidden coffee with him. The younger ones trailed him to his garden. They marched Indian fashion behind him and mocked his stance. Bodies straight as arrows and with their hands clasped behind them, they measured their steps with his.

As they neared the garden, they saw a young woman sitting on the edge of his plow which rested in the corn row from yesterday's work. By the early mornings light, she was powdering her face and adding lipstick. As they entered the garden, they discovered in the fence corner a small run about car which had failed to make the big curve in the high way. It had broken through the fence where the lima beans grew, landing topside up in Grandy's corn bed.

Grandy shook his head in disbelief as he watched a man, the owner of the car, struggle to get it back on its all fours. The pretty young lady crossed her legs, leaving her kneecaps well without her skirt line and gave Grandy a provocative shrug of her shoulders. Her young man had by now gathered up some of the loose fence boards and was prying the car upright, using a see-saw type motion to jack the car up.

Grandy, speechless with this intrusion into his domain, approached the young woman. The children giggled in anticipation of hearing his ire directed elsewhere. He walked briskly up to the long-legged girl, grabbed her skirt and yanked it down over her knees.

"Young woman, have you no shame? Sittin' up here in my garden, half naked!"

Bill exploded in laughter and whispered around the huddled group, "Watch out for the serpent, gang. Eve's in Grandy's Eden."

By this time, the young man had the motor going and had ascertained that though damaged, it would still run. His young lady, somewhat shaken by Grandy's onslaught, had made a beeline for her side of the front seat. The young man popped in beside her, gunned the motor and said, "Don't worry about the damage, old farmer, I'll take care of everything."

Zoom! Off they went in a cloud of dust and lima beans. Grandy's mouth hung loose from the lower jaw. He rolled up his fist and shook it at the departing couple

"Why you low, livered, yellow bellied scoundrel. You come back here and fix my fence, my lima beans….my garden." He turned toward the children and continued; "My beans are ruined. Why they've stirred up all my corn plants. I'll sue him. I'll sue that rascal!"

The children cringed from his anger only to feel a flow of sympathy from deep within, to see their Grandy so upset. Slowly, one by one they crossed to the fence and began to replace the boards. Jay and Tom ran up to the house for hammer and nails. The girls carefully lifted the vines, heavy with beans and began to replace them tenderly.

Sis and Betty and Martha even got down and smoothed by hand the deep ruts made by the car's tires. Afraid to pat Grandy, they petted the ground trying hard to find a way to say they were sorry.

———————— 🙦 🙤 ————————

While Lola finished placing the vases of flowers through-out the house, LaVerne went upstairs to check over the rooms. By nightfall, most all of the rooms would be filled with guests and she wanted to make sure everything was in readiness.

The doors of all the rooms stood open in welcome. The floors and windows were shining clean. Crisp organdy curtains greeted the sun and breezes were invited inside. The old-fashioned spool beds .and newly painted washstands were ready. Fresh sheets and towels looked inviting. The covers were turned back over the tufted bedspreads. At the foot of each bed was a folded quilt, made by Mam-maw. Her braided and hooked rugs lay on the floors.

LaVerne went from the Red Bird room to the Grandfather Hopper room. From there she checked the pink and blue checkered wallpaper rooms of the Morrison's. They would arrive after the Fourth of July. The little pink room and the green room looked eager for occupants. On and on LaVerne went and was satisfied with the appearance all twenty bedrooms. It was a satisfying feeling.

Coming back down the front stairs, she saw Norma and a group of children huddled at the front door. She was startled at first until she heard the conversations of the youngsters.

"See that yellow strip with the red dots? That used to be my school dress."

"Here a piece of my old Sunday School dress. I just loved that blue dress.

"This orange flowered material was my sisters evening dress."

"Now I know we're ready for business with the Welcome Rug down," LaVerne laughed as she joined Norma.

"It cleaned up very well, but it's beginning to show wear. Do you think it'll last through another summer with all the feet pounding across it?" Norma was worried.

LaVerne studied the fan shaped hooked rug with the word "Welcome" spelled out in old rose across the center of it.

"It looks fine to me. Just fine."

"Lift it higher, Harold. I got to set the bolts in straight." Charles was calling down from his precarious perch on top of the rock pillar at the entrance way to Riverby.

Leon and Harold, below, strained again and sent out a shout when the bolts locked home. Charles jumped down and stood back with the other boys to admire the sign.

A black frame held in place the white sign with the words neatly lettered in black across the face of it GUESTS.

The sign was homemade but professional looking. Mabel had carefully drawn a coach and horses on plywood and Charles had whittled them out and attached them to the top of the board. Leon painted the sign and Harold Jr. had carefully printed the word GUESTS across the white expanse

"Come one, come all. We're ready for business," Harold remarked as they went back to the house to report their mission was accomplished.

"Hey, a car is turning in!" Leon shouted.

"Car nothing. Look what it says on the side," Harold stood stock still.

"North Carolina State Board of Health," Charles read as the car shot past them up the driveway and rounded the house to the kitchen door.

———————————— ❧ ❧ ————————————

"Sorry lady, Grade B is the best I can do." The Health Inspector was emphatic.

"Your ice box is too small and there's a new regulation that says you have to scald the dishes with steam. Live automatic steam."

"But we do use steam and scalding water!" LaVerne was getting frantic. "Our dishes are clean through and through."

"I'll have you know, young man, that I washed those dishes myself. I used Octagon soap on them and poured scalding water from the tea kettle over theme. If that's not live steam, then I don't know what is." Mam-maw dried her hands on a towel and waved the towel toward the lined-up china.

Lola spoke up. "It seems to me that the North Carolina State Government could find something better to do than quibble over dirty dishes. Are politics going to take over the American home?" She quoted Homer.

"Those cracked cups harbor dangerous germs," the Inspector added.

"What will our guests say?" Beck wanted to know, "Does this Grade B card have to be prominently displayed?"

"It has to be tacked to a wall and available to anyone wanting to see it." The inspector quoted the rule book.

"We're ruined! No one will want to stay in a second-rate hotel." LaVerne was stunned, "I've worked so hard. "

"Get rid of the cracked dishes and get a larger ice box and I'll see on my next visit." The Inspector signed the Grade B card and prepared to leave. "Thanks for the coffee cake, Mrs. Blanks. I'll see you in August." He slammed the kitchen door.

"When the government starts telling me how to wash dishes after fifty-five years of practice.......words fail me." Mam-maw was worked up over the injustice. "Wish I'd put some hellebore or at least a dash of hartshorn in that coffee I gave him. Don't worry daughters, we'll make up in good food and good conversation what we lack in a big ice box and live automatic steam."

LaVerne nailed up the Grade B card in the back panty and placed a big cracker box in front of it.

"Well, I've hung up the card on a wall, just like he said to do."

———————————— ❧ ❧ ————————————

"I'm going off kitchen duty for a while," Mam-maw said as she started for the door. "When I get tired of grown-ups, I know it's time for me to go play with my grandchildren. And I'm more than worn out with adults at this point. The children and I have a project going on down on the lower lawn near the fish pond."

"I don't want any unsightly messes made in the yard, Mama," Lola cautioned.

"The children are beautifying, not messing up. You girls leave us alone." Mam-maw headed for the yard.

"Here she comes, everybody!" Sonny sent out a warning shout. "Here comes Mam-maw. Look at your pretty garden we made for you."

"I know I have the most original and talented grandchildren in the whole wide world. I am certainly a lucky woman to have a whole garden of loveliness made just for me." Mam-maw looked about her.... at the garden and the grinning children.

"Show me around. I want to see each thing."

The garden was about half the size of the parlor room at the big house but it was choked full. The four corners were heavily anchored with huge concrete vases or urns. Studded with bits of bright pieces of broken glass and unusual buttons, they appeared as a matched foursome. In the center of the garden was a tall bird bath which matched the decorated urns. The children had worked hard to make the garden beautiful. It was certainly eye-catching. The sun rays bounced off the broken bits of glass and bounced right back again. In the four large urns, mountain ferns had been transplanted in two of them and the other two held a hodgepodge of geraniums and petunias. Baskets and buckets of cinders and gravel had been raked over the little walkways and edged right up to the dozens of wildflowers that had been brought down from the mountains and planted with tender care. White Snakeroot and Monkshood and Trout Lilies were in querulous riot. Hens and chickens nestled together for protection from the Fuchsia Swamp-Thistle and Coreopsis. Mam-maw continued to inspect each item and praise the children. She also made a mental note to prepare her three daughters for the surprise. *They'll think it is horrible but there's not a thing they can do about it. This is my yard and these young'uns are wonderful to want to please their old Mam-maw.* She felt deeply touched by their present to her.

"Is the concrete in the birdbath still wet? Maybe we can work in a few more of these pieces of green and lavender glass." She bent her head low and forced the broken glass into the solidifying concrete and smiled to herself. "Good," she announced, "it's almost hard." *Her daughters were going to be furious.*

"They're turning in! A car's turning in. Look Mam-maw, here comes a blue Oldsmobile with Illinois tags." Tom Jr. sent up the alarm and the children and Mam-maw stopped what they were doing and watched the car slowly turning in between the rock pillars at the entrance of Riverby.

"You children finish up here. Don't forget to put some water in the bird bath. Old Mr. Woodpecker and Miss Wren will be looking for a drink of water. I'd better go in and take off my apron to greet the new guests. It must be Dr. and Mrs. Taylor all the way from Chicago."

--------------------------- ❧ ❧ ---------------------------

"Guess I'd better change to second gear to make this incline, Beth." Dr. Taylor followed through with his suggestion.

"Ben! This place is charming. What a lovely setting. This big old house on the hill completely surrounded by the beautiful mountains! Such a relief to get away from Chicago. Look at that large woman with that big old-fashioned Mother Hubbard apron on. I haven't seen one of those since my grandmother died."

"Beth, look at the children in that garden. Those outfits! Are we in Munchkin Country or is that a miniature Cox's Army?"

The Taylor's couldn't keep from smiling at the Riverby children. Some wore overalls. Some wore khaki shorts and shirts. Some of the older girls wore tunics with the hems fringed and they had brushed wool beanies on their heads. Most of the children were barefooted but some wore homemade thong sandals made from strips of leather. Some wore sandals which the Taylors would later learn were made from inner tubes.

"Beth, I'm delighted with what I see. These children will be perfect for me to study and perhaps use in my paper I'm writing on juveniles." Dr. Ben Taylor applied the brakes at the front door.

The three ladies on the front porch wore soft dresses of lawn and batiste and were obviously sisters. One of them came forward with her hand extended in greeting. Under her breath Beth murmured, "These ladies don't look like the mothers of Cox's Army."

That afternoon after the Taylors and several other car loads of guests had checked in, Mam-maw pulled her rocker down to the end of the porch where Ben and Beth were resting and talking quietly. Clasped tightly in Mam-maw's lap was her satchel, as her grandchildren called it. It was a tremendously weather beaten, black leather carry-all. In this tired old worn bag, she kept all of her children, grandchildren and loved ones' pictures.

Beck and Lola who were sitting near the main door doing some needle work said to her, "Mama, don't bother Dr. Taylor with those old pictures. He's busy working on his paper." Beck and Lola were very impressed to have such a renowned guest at the Inn and wanted to be sure they were well settled in before they themselves would bend his ear.

Mam-maw paid no attention to either of them but just kept rocking away by the Taylors just out of hearing distance of her daughters.

"Here comes another car turning in, Lola. If you'll check in this bunch of new arrivals I'll try to eavesdrop on Mama." Beck was dying to hear the conversation.

The Taylors were introduced one by one to the pictures as Mam-maw unashamedly told of the talents of each one of her grandbabies.

"Now you won't recognize Harold Jr. from this. Why, he grown to be a man. He was made an Eagle Scout last year. I'm so proud of him. He's my oldest grandchild. He's the one who carried your grips upstairs." Mam-maw took the picture back from Mrs. Taylor and caressed it in the palm of her fat hand before she returned it to the bag.

"Now this is Miriam, his sister. We call her Mabel. Looks just like her daddy, doesn't she?" Mam-maw absent-mindedly forgot that the Taylors never having seen either Mabes or her daddy could make no reply.

"She paints the loveliest pictures. Why I believe that you have one of her paintings in your room. The one of wild flowers in the crockery churn?"

"Yes, we do." Mrs. Taylor acknowledged. "It's so lovely."

Dressed in a plain black silk print dress with her black carpet slippers on her feet, Mam-maw brushed off a dab of flour from her bosom and continued.

"Here's the family beauty, Bobbie. She's surely the prettiest of the lot, all those blond ringlets and the bluest eyes you ever looked into. Sort of an Alice Blue. But," Mam-maw leaned toward Dr. Taylor and cupped one hand round her mouth to guard her whisper, "she's a Holy Terror when she gets mad. Now don't tell her Mama I said that but she does throw tantrums. LaVerne says she's temperamental and tries to reason with her, but my, I'd give her a swat on the rear she pulled one of her fits on me."

Mam-maw withdrew the next photograph and studied it. "And this is the youngest one of the Hedges group, Elizabeth Lee. The Lee is after me, my name is Jeffie Lee. Not only is Betts the smallest in age but the smallest in size. Poor thing she just hasn't gotten a good hold on life yet. Kinda sickly, you know? But she keeps up with the rest of the gang."

"Here's my son, Claude. Wonder how on earth his picture got in with all the children," Mam-maw mused as she admired her son's image. "Well, he's never quite grown up himself. Guess he belongs in with the Trundle Bed Trash. That's what Frank calls his grandchildren."

She quickly replaced Claude's picture and pulled out several more from the satchel.

"Oh! Look here are Claude's two sons, Charles and Leon, aren't they fine? Mighty fine boys. Why both of them can shoot the eye out of a squirrel at fifty feet. They are a real help to us oldsters. They live here all year long. They roam the mountains and bring us squirrel, rabbit and venison. Just wait till you taste some of our squirrel stew."

Mr. Taylor noted with his keen sense of human beings that Mam-maw took on a special glow and pride as she fondled the next picture from within the bag.

"My Martha Lee. Bless her sweet heart, just look, isn't she an angel? Claude's baby girl. How she has warmed our old hearts with her beaming smile and soft ways. Why this little girl has made pets of every animal in the valley. And just wait until you hear her sing. You have a real treat in store for yourselves."

LaVerne came to the front door in search of her mother. She looked down the porch since her chair was not in its usual place by the door and discovered Beck and Lola with their sewing.

"Where's Mama?" She inquired.

"Down there boring poor Dr. Taylor with her satchel," Beck replied mentally counting the chain of stitches hanging down from her crochet hook.

"Oh, Beck, leave her alone," Lola reprimanded as her needle flashed in and out of the Flower Garden quilt she was piecing. He says he came here because of Mama. Now just leave them alone, both of you," she addressed LaVerne as well.

"Well, if you say so," LaVerne replied, "but you don't suppose he is psychoanalyzing her, do you?"

"Heaven forbid," Lola butted in, "he would come out second best if he tried to rework Mama. He'll think the Blanks are a crazy quilt, though, soon enough."

"Here comes another car, Sister. You check these people in," Beck reported as she continued with her Water Lily square.

"My oldest daughter, Lola, has these two fine girls and one little boy born late, you know, mid-life baby. The girls are called Hy and La but their real names are Hybernia and LaVerne. They have so many beaus in High Point but they left them to come see their old Mam-maw and Grandy. Here's Sonny. Another terror. Lola spoils him rotten. You'll see when they come in to dinner."

Sis Fields had quietly come up on the porch from the fish pond and when Mam-maw broke her conversation, she slipped up on her big lap as if seeking protection.

"Here's my baby," Mam-maw introduced the child, pushing back a lock of straight blond hair from Sis' eyes. "Our baby grandchild and the baby of her family. She's my salt rising bread gal. Always helps me taste it right out of the oven, don't you, Sis?"

"Sis is a sneaky…. Sis is a sneaky," chorused Bill, Tom and Jaybo as they pounced over the edge of the porch towards Mam-maw.

"Mam-maw, make her give 'em back. She's a snitcher. She stole 'em."

"Let me get my hands on her," Bill threatened.

"Now, now boys, what's the matter?" Mam-maw asked.

"She snuck up and took all our marbles, while we were swimming and she won't give them back," Jay explained.

"Boys, I want you to meet Dr. and Mrs. Taylor, our new guests. Turning to the Taylors she said, "These are Sis's three older brothers. They are pretty hard on their little sister but I know that she's going to give them back their marbles."

The boys acknowledged the introduction while Sis reached deep into the satchel and pulled out a slightly damp bag of marbles.

"Well bless my soul," Mam-maw said. "Wonder how those got in there." She winked slyly at the Taylors and gave Sis a tap on her buttocks. Sis rose and so did Mam-maw.

"Well, guess I've taken up enough of your time with my children. Better go check on my rolls." She turned to go down the porch toward the front door.

"Oh, Mrs. Blanks, don't leave us," Mrs. Taylor recalled her. "We think your family is just lovely and we want to know all about them. We can hardly wait to meet each and every one."

"Well, when that dinner bell rings, watch out, you might get trampled by all the children." Mam-maw threw back her head with its wispy white hair piled high on top and gave a good laugh that shook her all the way down to her round stomach.

Beck stopped her as she passed, "Mama, what on earth have you been telling those people? Why, you've been talking their ears off for an hour."

"Never mind what I've been doing Miss Rebekah. You and Lola put up your sewing and come to the kitchen and start shelling peas. It's getting onto dinner time."

"What a charming person," Mrs. Taylor remarked after they had gone through the big front door.

"Yes, Beth, I think we've found ourselves a real family. Mrs. Blanks is so wholesome, she has really made us feel at home and we've hardly unpacked our bags. I can't wait to meet the rest of the family." Dr. Taylor reached over and patted Mrs. Taylors hand.

The Taylors didn't have long to wait. Beck and Lola got behind the children and got them all cleaned and slicked up for dinner. A rare occurrence at Riverby except on Sundays, but both mothers sought to impress the new guests. Leon and Charles balked at taking a bath but were persuaded to lean their heads under the back-porch pump and a little of their dust was settled in the act. They even combed their hair, slicked back. Not without giving their aunts unmerciful teasing, to the accompaniment of blowing through their combs.

The children paraded through the dining room, stopping by the Taylors table to introduce themselves and proceeded from table to table repeating the introductions to the other guests before seating themselves at the family table. Tomorrow night they would begin eating on the back porch.

Leon sat down at the head place. He bowed his head low in mock reverence and said a lengthy confused blessing which he obviously created as he went along and followed by a loud AMEN!

Leon looked down the table at the plate of steaming rolls, with his fork and speared one head on. "Told you to pass the rolls," he said.

The Taylors and guests had met the gang.

# Chapter 7

# One Fuss Pot

LaVerne was more than pleased with how well the 1934 resort season was going. During the past week, the old house had begun to absorb more and more guests. In the evenings, lights showed in almost every room. All the family members were pressed into service. Grandy manned his garden and LaVerne directed the kitchen activities and saw to renting the rooms. Lola and Beck scurried around where ever they were needed or wanted to be at the moment. The children had certain chores they had to perform in the mornings and during meal times. It was understood that after their duties had been executed, they could spend the rest of the day in play.

The morning sun brazenly peaked through the dining room windows and made the colored glassware on the window shelves wink back in return.

The breakfast dishes were being cleared away. Bobbie and Martha Lee and Betty brought their large trays to the tables. They skillfully stacked the empty plates, placed them on the trays and Mose the valet, waiter, busboy and red cap, carried the over-loaded trays to the kitchen. His bow legs formed parenthesis as he swung his five feet two-inch frame through the swinging door of the kitchen.

Back again into the dining room with his black face split into a half-moon smile, he sang out, "Miss Bobbie, Miz LouVun say, she say that las' load was a lazy man load and to be keerful not to pile them plates soooo high. We done already gots three broken saucers from yestiddy evenin's meal. Mr.Grandy's already seed 'em and warned Miz LouVun nots to put dem in de riber lak she done las' time."

Grandy had learned from his mother during the Civil War that 'to waste not is to want not' and he and LaVerne had a continual kitchen argument over broken crockery.

"Papa, things just get broken and we can't help it. You know yourself you fired Annie, the only professional waitress we've ever had and while she was here not one thing was broken. If we use the children to wait tables and clean up, we're going to have broken dishes. I won't allow the girls to wait tables in their bare feet and those inner tube sandals are against the regulations of the North Carolina State Board of Health. Those thong sandals slip and slide on the waxed floor. Just yesterday at dinnertime Hy's feet went clear out from under her when she passed the cornbread and that's why we're having spoon bread at noon today," LaVerne scolded.

"Good granny alive! If the handles come off, you can still use them cups. They'll still hold the coffee. Those girls are so busy sashaying they don't keep their minds on their business. They better mind they don't spill my vittles."

——————————— ✌ ✌ ———————————

Everyone had finished breakfast and gone on their way pursuing the morning activities. LaVerne and Lola were having a final cup (with handles) of coffee on the back porch going over the noon menu with Delilah.

"We'll have fried ham and spoon breed. Just take all those broken up pieces of corn bread that Miss Hy fell on yesterday and use that for your basic ingredient and go on from there with the recipe. Then make up some of that good succotash. You know, fresh early corn cut off the cob, okra, butter beans, onions, tomatoes and celery. Instead of salad today we'll have some homemade apple sauce from those June apples. Tell the boys to go down to the barn and gather some apples from that no-name apple tree. I wish someone could identify that tree for us. Anyway, use plenty of brown sugar and cinnamon and nutmeg, the way you do, and for dessert, I guess, rhubarb pie. Lola, I'll declare that rhubarb is just gorgeous."

Delilah nodded in agreement and shuffled back into the kitchen. She was in her usual uniform. A man's white hand kerchief tied about her head with stray ends of kinky hair jutting off over the top of the handkerchief. A large white butcher's apron was worn over a wash dress. It was so long on her that it swept the top of her slides as she shuffled along. Slides were her favorite shoes. She took hand-me-down high heel shoes, axed off the high heels then split the sides for her bunions to ease through. The back seam was split and there were her slides.

"Come on LaVerne, let's get moving. We've got to go to Miss Lou's for butter. Beck is overseeing the housework this morning. Mama's on the porch with her Carolina Rose quilt pieces. She'll watch the children and keep an eye on everyone turning in. We'll take Sonny and Bill with us. With everyone busy we don't want those two left up to their own devices. Girls! Have you finished up with cleaning the tables?"

Bobbie appeared on the porch in answer to Lola's call.

"Everyone but Margaret and Mrs. Tate," Bobbie said as she bit down on a piece of left-over toast. "I'll be darned if I'll clean off that table. The mess Margaret makes. Ugh,"

"Don't swear, young lady, and furthermore I want you to be courteous to those less fortunate than ourselves," LaVerne answered.

In the dining room at the table next to the window over-looking the highway sat a grandmother and grand-daughter.

"Come on, Margaret, dear, finish your lovely egg. Soooo good for you," Mrs. Tate urged adding a dash of salt to the cold yolk.

Margaret relaxed languidly in an arm chair. Her obese and stunted body filled the chair completely and her tiny fat feet swayed inches from the floor. Her round moon face was paled as she contemplated the open window with her vacant brown eyes. Her lower lip hung slack and revealed the drool that threatened to overflow the miniature dam. Her thin stringy hair rested in uneven strands atop the round collar of her yellow frock. Margaret must have been in her early teens but her mother passed her off as an eight-year-old. Mrs. Tate the grandmother, looked after this poor child with devoted and patient care.

"Margaret, Margaret……look at Grandmother. Here, finish your milk and you can get down from the table and we'll take a walk," she encouraged.

"Tuk tumming, Bililigggg tuk the tumming, Ganmuddeh."

"Why, Margaret, I do believe you're right. Yes sir, it's a big red truck coming right up the driveway and stopping at the front door, Come, child, let's go see what it wants."

The truck stopped with a jolt as the driver, Samson, forced the brake to the floor with his big foot. Beck came dashing out the front door,

"Samson. We've told you a million times, no deliveries at the front door."

"But Miz Fields, ah's got…"

"Samson, never mind what you've got. Everything you bring in your truck goes to the kitchen door."

"Yas'um, but ah's got a…."

Beck strode down the front steps to have it out once and for all.

Samson weighed 300 pounds and wore especially made overalls that Homer Hudson brought him from the factory. Because of his size and having the biggest truck in town, he did all the heavy hauling. Coming toward the truck, Beck decided to make it just as plain to him as possible and for the last time.

"You're to pick up that load of leaves and trash around on the side yard so drive on back. It may look all scattered around, Mr. Blanks does that sometimes, but get it all up anyway and haul it off."

As she got closer she saw Samson had a passenger. He was a middle-aged man in a beige linen suit and Panama straw hat. Perspiration poured down the cheeks of his porcine face. Upon seeing Beck, his round green eyes showed interest and he tipped his hat.

"Why, Samson…."

"Yas'um, ah tried to tell you, Ah brought this genimn out. He got off the morning train out of Statesville, He's got a heap of valises."

"Good morning, sir, I'm Mrs. Fields and welcome to Riverby Inn."

"Name's Bouquet. Andre Bouquet. I trust my room is in readiness. Something quiet. I must have quietude. Watch my baggage, boy, handle it with care. Easy, easy, I said EASY," replied green eyes.

Samson was tossing bag after bag to the ground. Mr. Bouquet jumped down out of the cab of the Dodge and ran to the rear.

The after-breakfast rockers momentarily stilled their motion and turned their faces to study the new guest.

They saw a short, heavy man wiping his thinning hair and perspiring face with a large handkerchief. His tiny feet shod in two-tone shoes were cutting capers on the cinder driveway as he hurriedly lined his suitcases and grip in a neat row on the bottom step.

"Don't let this man carry my luggage to my room! Call your houseman at once! These bags contain my valuables and must be handled with care. Watch out there, Overalls. Careful! Easy!"

"Don't worry, Mr. Bouquet, we haven't lost a suitcase yet. "I'm Mrs. Blanks," said Mam-maw putting aside her quilt pieces and stepping forward, Mose our houseboy or my grandson Harold will take them to your room and I'll personally be responsible for their safety. Harold Jr.! Come at once!"

The younger children who had been playing on the hillside were attracted by Samson's truck and came running to see if he would give them a ride.

"Hey, Samson! How about a ride? Huh, Samson? Just down to the highway," Jaybo shouted.

Sonny was already climbing into the cab and with his thin white arms on the large steering wheel he was 'driving fast'.

"Not so fast, Buddy," yelled Bill as he beeped the horn and attempted to push Sonny to one side.

"Tickle lock. I told you tickle lock on my side. Any way you all have to go with Aunt Lola and Aunt Boom to Miss Lou's. Now get out of here," Tom Jr. attempted to keep out the three kids piling in on his side.

Mr. Bouquet was kept busy lining up his luggage and securing the leather straps that kept the bulging bags from bursting open.

"What's your name, Mister?" Piped up Sis. "Are you going to have the green room with the long crack in the ceiling? That's a good room. It's not too far from mine and I'll come visit you all the time." She sat down on a suitcase and crossed her skinned-up legs.

"Off, off, little girl, You, boy, with that smoldering grapevine stick in your mouth….. get off my Gladstone. You can't ride it like a horse! Madam, I implore you. Call off these children! "

Mr. Bouquet straightened up and looked beseechingly at Mam-maw. For the first time he was aware of the vast number of children. They were swarming on the truck, climbing over the luggage and hanging onto Samson. It was fortunate that in his confusion he didn't count heads. There were twenty-two children surrounding this fuss pot. Number twenty-three was waddling through the front door.

"Hey deah mit-tah mi name 'e Mar-gaaa," the child grinned as she grabbed Mr. Bouquet's hand and gave it a very wet kiss.

"Oh, my stars and garters. My reservations are for a month," he moaned as he sank down on the bottom step, "I just want quietude," he whimpered.

"Now, now Mr. Bouquet, you shall have quietude. Your room is delightful and has a lovely tranquil view of Ole Hickory. Children! The excitement is over, Samson will give you all a ride to the village, Everybody on board! All aboard…. Jaybo, help the little ones up. Hold tight everybody. Drive slowly Samson."

Samson eased his 300 pounds behind the wheel, adjusted the side mirror, smiled a man-sized smile at Mam-maw and started up the engine. As the big red truck rounded the corner of the house, Mam-maw waved both her hands in a goodbye gesture at the grinning faces disappearing from view.

"bod-----den, boden, boden, boden, "some of the younger children imitated the sound of changing gears. Beck laughingly joined the ladies rocking on the porch as they, too, waved and shouted instructions to the children.

"Well, back to flower arranging," Beck said to the ladies.

In the great void of stillness, Mam-maw took Mr. Bouquet by his arm and speaking soothingly to him, escorted him up the stairs. As she went past Margaret, she leaned down and gave her a kiss on her cheek and with her large soft hand she caressed the unlovely little face.

"I'm going to bring you a lemon drop in a minute. You sit here and rock in my big chair and wait for me. I'll be back."

"But my valuables," protested Mr. Bouquet.

"My grandson is an Eagle Scout and is trustworthy. Now see, he's already bringing them up the stairs. See how strong he is and how careful. I can just tell you are the kind of man who loves the out of doors," she said diverting his attention.

"Oh yes," he brightened, "indeed, yes. Tell me about these mountains, Are the trails well marked? I am interested in geology and pre-historic man."

"Then you've come to the right place, sir. To my knowledge we've never been fortunate enough to have an archeologist here and it would be splendid if you would make a study of the rock formation on

Little Hickory. The children often find Indian arrowheads and relics with interesting markings on them in Mr. Patton's cornfield. But a man with your knowledge will want to go after bigger things."

What a stroke of luck, Mam-maw thought. I can get him so interested in this study that he'll be content to spend all his mornings on the mountains away from the children. They are usually in the river in the afternoons and he won't be disturbed. She estimated it would take an hour before the children returned from the village.

"Why don't you lie down and relax for half an hour or go and change to your walking clothes, I'll point out the way up Little Hickory. Oh, that's fine, Harold, Jr. put them here. Nine pieces of luggage correct? Good, they're all here, safe and sound. You'll find me on the porch later."

"Mam-maw, Mam-maw," whispered Harold as they started back down the stairs," what on earth do you suppose he has in those grips? They were awkward to carry but light. I could hear a soft swishy sound inside."

"Hush, child, he'll hear you. There's nothing mysterious in those bags. He's a dapper dresser and I'm sure he just has a lot of fancy clothes packed along with his hiking things."

"Well, I don't know. He sure acts funny to me."

"He's just not used to children. Oh, run look in my top drawer and bring me that little bag of lemon drops. I promised one to Margaret."

Harold Jr., still thinking about the funny old fuss pot, went into Mam-maws room and began to rummage in her top dresser drawer. Her fine-toothed comb with teeth on both sides of it lay well to the left side. Bits of laces, tatting, horehound, candied lemon, orange and grapefruit peel, a small can of Bruton's snuff and linen hankies intermingled. He was just about ready to give up on the hard candy when he moved back the bars of yellow soap shaped like large lemons, he spied the striped pink bag of candy.

He delivered them to Mam-maw on the front porch and she carefully opened the bag and gave Margaret one in each hand.

"Mabes, Hy and La are looking for you, son, "she said as she smoothed Margaret's bib down. "They're out yonder in Grandy's hammock."

"Here we are, good Scout," they teased.

"Oh, cut it out, will you?"

"Well, come here, we want to ask you about that old fuss pot," Hy hissed.

"You can't tell ME there's not something fishy about him and his mountain of luggage. He said and I quote: 'No one, absolutely, no one is to touch these satchels when my room is cleaned' and I unquote."

"Maybe he is an eccentric millionaire and carries his money around with him in cold hard cash," Mabes suggested.

"I saw him give Samson a five-dollar bill. Just for bringing him out here from the station."

"Well, he didn't give me anything for lugging all those bags upstairs. But you do have a point there. I just feel sure he has a fortune with him"

"There's one way to find out," purred La." Search his suitcases."

"Do we dare?" Mabes put in. "Mother would be furious!"

"Who needs to know? We aren't going to take anything. Just satisfy our curiosities," La continued.

"Well, he does plan to be on the mountains a lot," Harold said, "and if you all clean his room, you'll HAVE to move some of that stuff."

"Let's think about it for a while. Mam-maw says he will be here a month. The whole idea sounds unethical to me," Mabes already felt guilty. "Anyway, I'm going to get my net and go after some of those little green butter flies down at the far end of the yard. I don't have any of those in my collection. See you later."

When the big brass dinner bell rang, the guests flowed into the dining room and the family poured onto the back porch and grabbed their seats around the pine table.

"Too bad you all didn't get to go to Miss Lou's with us. We opened the big cattle gate and rode on the running board all the way up to her house." Sonny said in a 'too bad for you' voice.

"Who cares about that? We rode down the highway in Samson's truck," hooted several of the other children, "Man whatta ride."

"Don't hog the ham down there," punned Jaybo, "pass it up here to me."

"……. and then I heard old fuss pot say to Mam-maw…. 'Madam, I found a fossil'…..he's killing, just killing," laughed Hy.

"I found something better than that," Mabes declared as she took off her brushed wool beanie and searched inside it.

--------------------------------- ❧ ❧ ---------------------------------

"I'll just declare, this meal will never end and the day gets worse as it goes on," sighed LaVerne appearing on the porch lugging two large water buckets of peaches. "Lola, do you know what Rebekah did with the gorgeous rhubarb from the garden? Grandy brought up arm loads of that beautiful pink rhubarb with a whole umbrella of foliage on the end. Delilah says she never got to use it for pies. Miss Beck used them for flower arrangements in the big gray crocks in the hall. MY rhubarb. MY dessert for today. Furthermore, all the guests are simply raving over the effectiveness of it, Such color, Such genius! And such an inconvenience for me. It seems I can't leave this kitchen for more than a minute without something going wrong."

"Sister, you'd better think of something quick. Miss Mullen is almost through with her meal," Lola was ready to shake Beck good.

"I'm thinking fast. Quick, help me peel these nice peaches we got from Miss Lou. We'll simply peel them, slice them in individual bowls and serve with cream. Delilah baked off a big batch of sugar cookies, thank goodness, and we'll serve them alongside."

"Here, family, we don't have time to peel for you all. So, you just take your peaches on outside and eat them plain. And don't throw those pits at each other," Lola warned.

With several helpers pitching in to peel the peaches, the guests were soon served and compliments were sent back to the cook.

Bobbie appeared on the back porch and announced everyone had been served.

"Well, that's good," her mother replied, "because there are just two or three left and they are decidedly greenish."

Martha came bounding onto the porch. "Quick, Margaret is setting up a fuss for her dessert. She hasn't had her dessert yet."

With a glare at Bobbie, LaVerne said, "I'll just have to peel her one of these green-looking ones. Poor child, she won't know the difference, thank goodness. Give her all the cookies she wants. That'll help make up for it."

As the guests were folding their napkins and talking about taking a nap, a high piercing voice interrupted all conversation. It was Margaret.

"Whet Hedness, I ike peatnies but I DON'T IKE DREEEEEN PEATNIES."

LaVerne rushed into the dining room with a plate of cookies.

"Here, dear, have another one of Delilah delicious sugar cookies," LaVerne shoved one gently into the open mouth that still had traces of 'dreeen peatnies' in it.

"Don't tell me you're still sucking your thumb, Norma," Lola chided as she saw Norma standing over the basin in the bathroom with her fingers in her mouth. "No, gave that up forty years ago. I misplaced my tooth brush and I'm trying to brush my teeth with my fingers."

"Pardon me, my dear, if I come in while you go about your toiletries," Lola said as she put out some clean towels on the racks and glanced around the bathroom to see if it was in tidy condition. "We've got to get a new toilet seat in this bathroom. This one has a crack in it. The guests are going to want a better place to sit."

Beck poked her head in the door. "Your loud mouth is echoing up and down the hall. Don't you have any sense of delicacy?"

"Mind your own business while I mind mine, Miss Sassy mouth."

"By the way," said Beck as she started to close the door, "have you all seen my pink tooth brush?"

Lola unwrapped a new bar of Ivory soap and placed it in the soap dish. "What are those children up to now? "This is the second lost tooth brush this morning."

Norma had finished with her teeth and now had her small pot of lip rouge open. She took the little finger of her right hand and dabbed it across the surface of the shell pink Tangee. She carefully outlined her lips with her little finger and blotted her lips together. Studying the effect in the mirror she said, "Miss Mullen was complaining something disappearing yesterday. I think It was a blue tooth brush."

"Well," Lola remarked, "I'm going to put a stop to this foolishness right now." She dried her hands.

Looking out of the bathroom window she saw numerous Trundle Bed Trash playing under the large oak trees between Riverby and the little cottage.

"They're making play houses down the back hill there and I'll bet that's where we find the culprits and the toothbrushes. I'll just go investigate. Beck have the girls started making beds? Cheek on them."

As Lola vanished down the stairs Beck complained to Norma, "That bossy major general. She thinks I don't have anything better to do than check on bed making."

Norma was scouring the tub and basin. As she stood up, she straightened the hand towels neatly and said, "Well, I'm off to the mill. See you at noon. And Beck, thank you so very much for the shoes you bought Martha in Ashville the other day. They're wonderful. She and Betts feel so gorgeous in their identical shoes. It's so nice of you and such a help to me."

Beck, caught in her generosity, said, "It was nothing. The school things will be in later on and I want to get each of them a school dress, too, before the summer's over. Now I'll bet Hy, Mabes and La are holed up in that back room. I hear them whispering. I'll just go eavesdrop. See you later."

——————————— ꝏ ꝏ ———————————

The back room was a small room and was once used as an over-sized linen closet. But now it was called the Medallion room. Claude had arrived gloriously drunk one early spring day and had brought a peace token with him, rolls of wallpaper. The background was dove gray with a large design in gold that looked like a medallion placed at irregular intervals. Small fleur-de-lis designs also in gold marched up and down next to the medallions. He didn't remember just how this wallpaper came into his possession.

Norma had been so furious with her intoxicated husband that she had grabbed several of the rolls from Claude and with her tiny fists clutched around the rolls had lambasted him across the shoulders.

"I'll medallion you…., you irresponsible child. Now I'll show you where you and your gold wallpaper can go……right where you both belong."

She gathered up as many rolls as possible in her shaking arms and in her delirium ran down the back hill to the pig pen and threw them onto the mire of the pigsty. The frightened pigs squealed and ran. Their sharp cloven hooves cut and sliced the paper to bits.

"Don't make peace with me with this stuff," she shouted, pay bills and buy clothes. Your children need a good father they can depend on." The tears choked her throat and the smell of the sty made her sick.

"Claude, the wallpaper was a nice thought", consoled Mam-maw. "Look, here are some rolls left on the floor. We'll paper that little store room upstairs and my how it will brighten it up. Oh Claude! How good to have you home. Sit down, my son, beside me and let's talk."

"Mama, oh Mama, I love you so." His anguish was very great, "Where are my children? And Papa?"

So, the old store room had been papered in the Medallion paper and Norma could never enter it without feeling a turn in her stomach.

Beck tiptoed cautiously to the closed door and quietly put her hand on the knob. Then she threw open the door.

From behind the haze of cigarette smoke she could see three startled teenage faces peeking at her through the smoke screen. She quickly stepped inside and closed the door.

"Why you ingrates. How dare you smoke in this house? Or any place else for that matter! I'll tell your mothers," she threatened.

"I could care less," was Hy's standard reply. La's answer was a deep inhalation and a string of skillful smoke rings blown in Beck's face.

Mabel was terrified. "Oh, please don't tell mother. She'd be so disappointed in me, I'm sorry…. really I am."

"We'll see young ladies. I'm not going to say yes or no. Just don't let it happen again. Ever! Just because I'm younger than your mothers doesn't mean that I'll side with you. Now get on with those beds. Make haste to make up for time used smoking cigarettes." She flounced out and slammed the door.

"Whew," said Mabel "that was close. It could have been mother or Aunt Lola or even Grandy."

———————————— ❧ ❦ ————————————

"All right, everybody, give me your attention. Put down those cars and sticks and listen to me," Lola commanded.

The children hadn't heard her approach. Around the bases of numerous oak trees, the summer storms had eroded the earth around their roots. The exposed roots formed natural play houses. The children brushed away the debris and made rooms, garages and driveways. Small blocks of wood and a few of Sonny's Dinky-Toy cars were to be seen parked in the small roadways. Homemade corn shuck dolls presided over each tree root domain. Tom Jr. was lolling against a tree with an acorn pipe in his mouth.

The gang looked up in surprise at the sound of a grown-up voice. They had been completely absorbed in their play.

"Where are the toothbrushes? Several have been missing and I strongly suspect you've used them to clear away your little front yards."

"Tooth brushes?" They repeated in obvious bewilderment, "We don't have any toothbrushes. Who brushes their teeth?" Martha truthfully answered

"Several are missing and I just thought I'd warn you that tooth brushes are private property and are to be left strictly alone," Lola patted Martha's head and turned to leave. "Don't forget to brush your teeth, everybody."

The children returned to their play grumbling about being falsely accused and reminded to brush their teeth. The ways of grown-ups were curious, indeed.

———————————— ❧ ❧ ————————————

"Pssssst, psssst, psssssst. "Mabel was just leaving the Red Bird room when she heard the hiss. Harold Jr, and Hy and La were motioning to her from just inside Mr. Bouquet's door.

"Harold escorted Mr. Bouquet across the railroad tracks to the trail to Ole Hickory. He has a bag lunch with him and some old maps. He'll be gone for hours and now's our chance." Hy whispered excitedly.

Mabel hesitated for just a moment. Two sins in one day were almost more than she cared to commit. That had been a pretty close thing with Beck and the cigarettes. And she still didn't feel sure in her own mind that Beck wouldn't tell on her. But if I chicken out on this escapade, they'll tease me about it for the rest of the summer. Who knows? Maybe he has a chopped-up body in those bags and if they find it out and report it to the police, they might even get a reward. That decided her.

"All right, but let's hurry. He might turn back you know and catch us in the act. Or Beck might come back to check on how we're doing with the cleaning. I'm all through. How about your rooms?"

"We've finished all but Mam-maw and Grandy's room and we thought we'd save that for last so all of us could pitch in on it. Then too, we figured out we might need their room to count the loot in," Hy suggested.

Harold said, "Let's don't stand here all-day gassing about it or we'll be sure to get caught. Pull those satchels out here and start opening them. I'll tackle this Gladstone."

They were disappointed. Out of the nine bags Mr. Bouquet had checked in with, four had been found empty and the contents were neatly arranged in the drawers and were hanging behind the curtained off area that served for a closet. Three others contained additional clothing and some pulp novels.

"He's not much for the classics, that's for sure," La commented. "Outlaws on the Range, The Bell Tolled, Midnight, Love life of the Watusi, Trails West and Other Stories," she read.

"I know he had two more bags. One of artificial alligator and a nice looking one in simulated Morocco," Harold was positive. "Look. Here they are under the bed. Watch out, I'm going to pull them out. Yep, these are the funny ones I told you about the day he arrived."

They cleared a space on the floor and quickly unbuckled the straps. The locks proved to be a little sticky but both lids were thrown open at the same time. The little room with the long crack in the ceiling resounded with their gasps. Tooth brushes! Both bags contained dozens and dozens of tooth brushes! Red ones, green ones, pink ones, blue ones, orange ones, white ones. Some had short bristles and some had long bristles. Some were used and some were new.

"It's a toothbrush graveyard!" Harold whistled between his teeth.

"I'm getting out of here," squealed La slamming down the lid of the alligator bag and hastily buckling the straps. Hy was just as quickly attending to the Morocco case. They shoved them back under the bed, smoothed the spread, straightened the throw rug and one by one slipped out and closed the door. They beat a. hasty retreat to Mam-Maw and Grandy's room and slammed the door behind them.

"Well, I never! Did you ever? That silly old fool! Do you think we should tell mother or Mam-maw? Maybe just Aunt Beck." Mabel was standing limp against the closed door.

"You want to tell your mother everything, you silly goose," La said opening up her pocket and extracting the pack of Chesterfields. "I need a smoke, how about you all?"

"No thanks, I've been caught once today and riffled through private property and that's enough for me," Mabes winced. She had been stung by La saying she tattled everything to her mother. Well, it wasn't true and she'd show them. She'd never tell about the tooth brushes. She turned and left the room to get her cleaning equipment.

Harold said, "We've all had a shock. Put out your cigarette, La. You girls go on, I'll spread out the bed and straighten up this room. Not a word about this to anyone…. yet."

"I'm willing to not say anything," Hy said, "I could care less what the old buzzard collects."

--- ❧ *Chapter 8* ❧ ---

# Show Night

Mam-maw and Mabes closeted themselves in Mam-maws room right after breakfast. From time to time they called Leon for a fitting or Harold Jr, to speak about the staging or Charles to consult on the lighting. For everyone else, the room was forbidden ground.

Beth Taylor tapped lightly on the closed door and called, "Mrs. Blanks, I'm sorry to disturb you but could I please have a few words with you?"

Mabes opened the door, Mam-maw looked up from the mass of tangled black cotton rug yarn in her lap. She removed her eyeshade and rubbed her eyes.

"Hello, Beth. Come into our inter-sanctum. Big secrets are going on in here, but we'll let you in."

"I don't mean to intrude, but, Ben and I are so excited over the Show Night. Ever since we received your answer to our letter and you mentioned your grandchildren put on homegrown talent nights for entertainment, we have looked forward to watching the children perform. We wondered if there was anything we could do to help out? Ben has simply fallen in love with your grandchildren and would monopolize them completely if he could. When he publishes his paper on juveniles, I'm going to send you a copy. I wouldn't be a bit surprised if you don't recognize some of the youngsters mentioned in his chapter on How to Develop The Best In Children.

"We promise we won't be in the way. Maybe he could sit on the sidelines and observe."

"Bless your hearts! You may feel free to watch all you want to. The children have been excused from their duties for the day so they might rehearse their numbers. No telling where you'll find them all. I am the only grown-up allowed to help them. The rest is entirely up to them."

"Mabes here is in charge of the over-all production. She sees to the make-up and auditions and sets. I help out as I can with the costumes. But Mabes is our creative genius, the director and boss of the show."

"Thank you very much, Mrs. Taylor. We'd be honored to have you and Dr. Taylor observe," Mabes spoke up.

"She's such a dear person," Mam-maw observed as Beth withdrew from the room. "They have both been such pleasant guests, I hate to see them leave next week. Just between you and me, I think you children have been a great revelation to Dr. Taylor. You know in his work, he sees so many, well, less fortunate, unhealthy children from all walks of life. Some are from poor families with no fathers and mothers and, well, I just think it's been a help to him to see normal children like you all…. living in a happy, normal home."

"But Mam-maw, you were an orphan and you seemed to have turned out alright and Grandy, he didn't have any daddy, after he was four years old, and he, well, he's cranky and stingy, but he turned out alright too."

"Daughter, that was different. We were people of genteel background…. after all we came from the rolling hill country of Tennessee. Those poor souls Dr. Taylor sees, for the most part, live like animals in the glums of a big city."

"I guess I understand but tell me about you and Grandy."

Mam-maw chuckled to herself and slyly thought with pride of her grand-daughter's interest.

"Mabes, there's usually a reason why people turn out the way they do, just like the Rock on which the church was built, you know the story. Well, take Grandy, for instance. You say he's stingy and cranky. There's a reason for that. His father was killed in the Civil War and Granny, poor soul, was left to raise all those little children by herself. She was in a strange country. You know they had moved over to Arkansas away from their people and when the war came, she was left alone among foreigners. They had nothing and what little they were able to come by, they hung on to. That's why Grandy is close with his money. Even after Granny sought aid from the Masons, like her husband had taught her to do in case of emergency, and they got back home to Tennessee with their family, Grandy couldn't forget the days when they were so poor. He never will, I don't guess. Even now, as you say, he's tight because he still remembers those hard times and times are still hard.

"But he's good and kind and Christian to the core, don't forget that. Then, too, being born with that awful eye growth made him feel ugly and unwanted. He's suffered all his life with it and it's made him shy and self-conscious. That's why he appears cranky to you. Just think how you'd feel if you had some awful scar like that. Lord only knows how many sacrifices he's made in his life for others. He couldn't go to school and get an education like I did. He had to go to work and help support his family. He's a very good man. Most people don't know that he gives a lot of his vegetables to widows."

"Mam-maw, I feel so badly that I said those things about Grandy, I didn't mean them, really I didn't. I love him but somehow, I never quite know how to tell him so!"

"Don't ever feel sorry for him, child, that would hurt him. He knows you love him and, remember, you Trundle Bedders, as he calls you, mean a great deal to him. He bought this home place because of you. When he retired, he said to me, "Jeffie, let's go up in the Blue Ridge and find a place big enough for all our children to come home to every summer. Some place with a healthful atmosphere. This old house was built by a doctor for a sanitorium, as you know, but it was only used for a few months as a place for people to gain their strength back after a serious illness. Grandy got it because no one else wanted such a big house. We fill it up though, don't we?" Mam-maw loved speaking in confidence to Mabel.

"How did you and Grandy ever meet?"

"My goodness, you're full of questions today! Now let's see, where to begin. You know that when my parents died, Grandfather Hopper took me and reared me. Well, his brother had built a girl school over in Arkansas and naturally they sent me there for my schooling. When I was on my way back home to Tennessee, Grandy's aunt escorted me home on the train. Grandy met us at the station and, well, the rest, is history." Mam-maw chuckled at the pleasant thoughts of her girlhood. "Not very romantic by today's standards, I know, but we had our fun in those days, too and don't ever think we didn't."

"Speaking of fun, young lady, we'd better get busy here and get this wig made or we are gonna spoil a lot of folks fun tonight."

Mam-maw tried the black wig she had made from the yarn on Mabes' head. "There, that's not too bad! Look in the mirror and then go call Martha Lee to try it on. Did you get that cape hemmed for her?"

"Yessum, I think it will do nicely. After all she will be sitting down and she's supposed to look a little prim you know, like in the picture." Mabes referred to the Moon Madness painting in the Music Parlor room.

"Your idea for her song is very clever. Everyone is fascinated by that painting. Funny thing, you know we were talking about Grandy's aunt introducing Grandy and me? Well, Aunt Kizzie, that was her name, was the one who painted it. She was really a very talented artist; I just know that's where you get your talent from. Poor dear, had to be sent out to Arkansas because some young man had given her a love potion and her family were worried to death. She was so in love and I have often wondered if that picture wasn't a self-portrait."

Mabes was so amused by this story that she hurried out onto the porch to giggle and call Martha. "Aunt Kizzie was Moon Madness, how funny." She didn't let Mam-maw hear her laughing.

All day long the password was Show Night. The sliding doors of the music parlor room remained closed all day long and props were slipped into the room from the back windows that opened out onto the side porch.

The old costume bags were ransacked repeatedly. The only thing the guests could hear were the repeated choruses of:

Oh! we all came 'round Ole Hickory weeks ago!

Oh! we all came 'round Ole Hickory rarin' to go!

Yes, we all came 'round Ole Hickory with our appetites and trickery,

Oh! we all came 'round Ole Hickory with a HO! HO! HO! "

"Beth, these children are really very talented. I have been a regular spy all day long and they have really done it all by themselves. Mabel tells me that usually they have a variety show, like vaudeville with singing and dancing and magic acts and juggling and comedy routines but their custom is to have the first Show Night of the season one in which the guests are introduced to the children, and get to know one family group from another. They didn't need much rehearsal today because they like to use the same skits for the first show of the summer. All the words are original but they have fitted them to the tunes of nursery rhymes and old stand-by-songs."

"Ben, I hope it goes well. Some of the women guests with children want their youngsters to participate, I explained to them the way Mrs. Blanks explained to me that this one is entirely made up of family children but if the guest's children have talent good enough to offer, they can audition with Mabel in the following weeks and get a chance to perform, too."

"Some of the men have said they flatly refuse to have any parts of sitting through an hour of home-grown entertainment put on by children. But I imagine their wives will get them to sit down. I hope they do, because there are one or two surprises tonight they'll enjoy." Dr. Taylor pushed back his dessert plate and rose from the table. "Let's go help move the chairs in front of the sliding doors in the hallway. The show will start in about half an hour and I want a front row seat when the curtain, er… the sliding doors open."

Just before the time for the show to begin, the women guests took their seats in the audience and the guests, children sat in front of the chairs on the floor. The men were determined they would have no part in being hoodwinked into sitting through an hour of torture of childish entertainment. They lounged near the front door and smoked their pipes and cigars, only dousing them when their wives hissed to them to come take their seats. The show was about to begin.

Grandy walked with his hands behind his poker straight back out onto the front porch and selected a rocker near the door where he could see without being seen. He pulled on his pipe with apparent unconcern.

Mam-maw took her reserved seat front row center. She turned left and right saying, "You have a rare treat in store for you. It's really going to be good. We'll start as soon as my daughters get through in the kitchen. They are the piano players."

Behind the scenes, all was confusion and nervous giggling. Mabel had set up her make-up table out on the porch and had her costume rack near at hand. The windows were open to provide an entrance and exit for the performers.

"Quit shoving, Bill, you knocked my wig off," Martha adjusted her wig for the third time. "Oh well, I can't wear it now because all the girls do the Lee Dynasty song first. Here, Mabes, keep it on your table until my big production number." All the performers were on the porch but the MC.

Harold hissed for attention. "Mother and Aunt Lola are hidden in the shadows of the room at the piano. Line up out there in orders for your number girls. Remember, after I do the opening, and you all sing the background music for me, you come on. All right! Lights out! Turn on the spot light, Charles. Open the doors, boys.... come on, mother, start the music."

When the doors parted, Harold Jr. was on stage in his dark blue Sunday suit. He had Mam-maw's walking cane in one hand and one of Grandy's old derbies in the other. He was doing a cake walk while the chorus of children on the porch backed him up in singing to the tune of Hello, My Baby.

"Hello, our boarders, hello our boarders, hello our paying guests

Happy to have you here! We hope to make you cheer.

If you don't know us, don't fume and fuss;

We're going to tell you now.

We'll tell you why and how,

Relax and sit back.... now that you're unpacked,

Make yourself right at home.

To rhymes we are prone and our talent is home grown!"

Before the applause could begin, Harold Jr. spoke out. "Good evening friends, benevolent family and paying guests. The Riverby Inn Players wish to welcome you to the first Show Night of the summer season. We, here on stage, want to identify ourselves to you, so you will get to know what child belongs to which branch of the family tree. I am Harold Herbert Hedges Jr. and I am your host for the evening. Before we sing our next number, we want to present our family album. They will appear according to the ages of their Blank's parent. First, the Hudsons from High Point, North Carolina "

Hy, La and Sonny stepped from the shadows and stood in the spotlight. They sang their patter song about their parentage and introduced themselves. Hy ended the act by saying, "Don't think that everyone you see in Anvil Brand Overalls belongs just to the Hudsons.... everybody wears them on the hill. We are wearing them tonight to let you know that our daddy is the one who makes them and keeps the Quartermaster suppled."

"Thank you, thank you. Later on, in the summer, Hy and La will show us all how to do the High Point Stomp. Next in line is the Hedges family. Mother, how about a little Arkansas Traveler music?"

Harold took his place with his three sisters, lined up according to age. Mabel stood next to Harold followed by Bobbie and Betty. They did a fast jig to the music while the children in the background strummed washboards, twanged jews harps and blew into jugs.

As the boisterous music and dancing stopped and the Hedges family retired to the porch, Harold announced, "next in line should come the Blanks tribe; Charles, Leon and Martha Lee. But since we are saving Martha for our big production number, you'll get a chance to see them later. But now let's bring on the Fields from Mississippi!"

As soon as the Fields boys and Sis heard their introduction from the piano, they came forward marching and stamping their feet and singing boisterously their own original words to Dixie. Sis, being on the tail end behind Jaybo, Tom Jr. and Bill were vigorously waving a Confederate flag.

"Thank you! Thank you!" The M. C shouted above the applause, "we have a little surprise for a special person in this room tonight and without further ado, we will now dedicate our next song to Mam-maw!"

Before Mam-maw could protest, the grandchildren had launched into their own version of Shorten' Bread.

> *"Fire up the Royal Oak, till it is red,*
> *Mam-maw's gonna make a little salt risin' bread.*
> *That ain't all, she's gonna do,*
> *Mam-maws gonna make a little squirrel stew.*
> *Mam-maw's little trundle Bedders like salt risin', salt risin',*
> *Mam-maws little Trundle Bedders love salt rising bread.*
> *Fourteen little babes a-swimmin' in the river,*
> *They was porely with torpid liver,*
> *"Don't get the doctor," Grandy said,*
> *"Feed them Trundle Bedders on salt risin' bread.*
> *(Chorus)*
> *Came to the kitchen, answered the bell,*
> *Overall pockets stuffed good and well,*
> *Hugged that cook till she was near dead,*
> *Kissed Mam-maw makin' salt risin' bread.*
> *(Chorus )*
> *Found in our overalls, one little shred,*
> *Found out we ate all the salt risin' bread.*
> *The Blanks gals caught us and said,*
> *"Whatcha mean eatin' the guest's salt risin' bread?"*
> *(Chorus)*

Mam-maw stood up and blew kisses to the performers amidst the applause.

"Thank you, Mam-maw, for the best salt rising bread in the whole country. Next, we have a little act coming up called the Lee Dynasty "All the seven grand-daughters lay claim to the Lee, so we proudly introduce, The Singing Lees.

Hy, Mabes, La, Bobble, Martha and Betty and Sis formed a chorus line and began to sing:

> *"It all began with the Confederacy*
> *With Jefferson Davis and Robert E,*
> *Mam-maw's pappy off' to war*

Instructed that the babe must be a boy, in which case the name should be the heroic combination of Jefferson Lee.

> *"But, alas, the babe came a Tennessee Belle*
> *and to her the name Jeffie Lee fell.*
> *So, when each one of us arrived*
> *our mothers together contrived*
> *that we should inherit the name of Lee,*
> *And so it is noted on the family tree."*

As the chorus line began to move off to one side, the audience broke into screaming laughter. Baby Sis had insisted on getting up her own costume and her retreating back gave her costume away. From the front all the audience could see was a little blond girl with deep brown eyes wearing a pinafore and sweater. When she turned to go to her seat, it became apparent that she had dancing tights on where the pinafore stopped in the rear. Falling to her knees in the front, the pinafore covered her like a dress. Behind, she was in arrears, clothes-wise. In the skit with her brothers, she had been able to hid this incompleteness but singing with the big girls, she had completely forgotten her costume and had grandly made her exit.

The men guests had long since forgotten they might have been bored. They were the most persistent hand clappers and when they saw the seven grandsons coming forward, they leaned forward and listened to every word the boys sang about their grandfather.

"Do you know Francis Marion? Do you know Francis Marion?

Our Grandy is Francis Marion. He's the LAW of Riverby Inn.

The audience was most enthusiastic as the verses unfolded the facts that grandy was a tight wad, walked like a ramrod, grew corn, smoked t'baccies and used his grandsons for lackies…. they even brought in how he'd been named for the Swamp Fox.

As the boys were taking their bows, Grandy decided it was time to go to bed. He wasn't sure if he had liked that last song or not. As he knocked the ashes from his pipe, he scrapped the rocking chair loudly and went noisily through the screen doors into the hallway.

At a pre-arranged signal from the M.C. the girls rushed forward and joined the boys and they all sang lustily with gestures:

*"Behold the Lord Head Thumpity…. thumper*
*A personage of noble rank and title!*
*A dignified and potent punisher,*
*Whose functions are particularly vittlessss!*
*Bow down! Bow-down, To the Lord High thumpity thumper*
*Bow down……bow down…….*
*To the crankity crank…….to the blankety blank*
*To the Lord Head Thumpity…. thumper!"*

The applause was deafening, Grandy continued his way to his room and slammed his door. In the darkness of his room, Grandy was smiling.

"I'll tell, you, Beth…. that was wonderful!"

"I knew Mabel had staged the Mikado for her high school class this past year…. she must have thought that up," Beth replied to her husband.

"Mabes, are you going to put rouge and lipstick on me?" Martha wanted to know as she and Mabes had quickly exited onto the porch 'dressing room' while the applause continued. Martha was already tying the ribbons of her blue cape and was sticking her blond hair up under the wig.

"Hold still. Just a touch. You're supposed to look kind of pale, remember. Don't forget that you are in love and sad," Mabes replied as she blotted Martha's lips and began helping her back through the window.

The lights had been temporarily doused while props were being set up for the production number. LaVerne had exchanged places with Lola and now Lola was playing some chords on the piano in hopes of drowning out the sounds of scenery and props being prepared.

In a moment all was quiet and dark, save for a spot light shining on the picture of Moon Madness on the wall above the piano. Another spotlight was on Martha Lee as she sat in a cardboard boat that resembled the one in the picture. Reeds and cattails had been gathered in abundance from the river and held in place around her by Charles and Leon, who were partially and hopefully hidden from sight. She sang "Pale Hands I love beside the Shalimar" in her lovely high soprano voice to Lola's expert accompaniment. From time to time Leon slapped his hands in a tub of water to make it sound authentic and Charles went through his repertoire of bird calls and a dog baying at the moon. His dog imitations were so good that out on the lawn Queen and Binx caught the plaintive plea in his voice and joined in with steady howls. Martha was able to finish her song without breaking up into giggles. As her last pure notes lingered in the stillness of the rooms, the spotlights were turned off. Only darkness remained. For a moment there wasn't a sound to be heard. Then thunderous applause.

All the lights were turned on and the performers took their bows again and again.

"Beth, I wish they'd turn right around and do it all over again!"

# Chapter 9

# Leon

Leon had had enough! Riverby was bursting at the seams with boarders and family. Hysterical aunts and gripping guests cramped his style. So it was then that he decided to go up into the mountains for a few days.

He crept into Norma's room and told her. "Norma, I gotta go up on the mountains for a few days. There isn't a bed left to sleep in around here. I'll do a little hunting maybe bring back some rabbits and squirrels for the stew pot."

Norma understood this free soul, her nature boy who just had to make a retreat into his mountains every so often. She replied. "Alright, Leon, but do promise me you will be careful. Don't walk around with that shotgun loaded. Take a blanket for cover and be sure and carry along some provisions in case you don't get any game."

Leon chuckled softly and teased." Alright Norm, I'll be careful. But I'm so mean, the devil himself wouldn't bother me. I'll bring you some fresh dew-berries if I can find any up there." Leon knew his mother's penchant for dew berries.

"That's real thoughtful of you son. You be back day after tomorrow though. You hear? By nightfall at the latest."

He agreed and returned to share the bed with Charles and Harold. Dreamily he plotted his course of the morrow.

Wednesday dawned with a veiled face. There were low hanging clouds and the atmosphere was gray and heavy. Leon slipped from the bed quietly, careful not to disturb his bedfellows. The house was still sleeping except for the kitchen. There a live flame glowed in the Royal Oak Stove. The figures of Grandy and Norma were silhouetted on the dining room wall. The bubbling coffee pot made the sole noise except for the turning pages of the Asheville Citizen, split between Norma and Grandy.

Leon pulled on his overalls just above them in the Medallion room. He took the khaki colored blanket from the end of the cot. Claude's cot was always kept empty. He spread the blanket on the floor. Stealthily he fumbled over the door frame for the key. His fingers groped along the ledge and found it in its secret hiding place. Only Leon knew where his father hid the key. With this combination to the lock in his hands he moved back to the bed and checked to be sure his brother and cousin were sound asleep.

Assured, he returned to the end of the empty cot and bent over the wooden locker, the type sailors store in the hold of their ships. He deftly turned the key in its lock and raised the lid slowly lest the rusty hinges cry out and alert the two sleeping figures in bed. The lusty male odor of tobacco, sweat and whiskey filled his nostrils as he bent over the cache.

He removed the top tray. He rummaged through old jackets, sweat shirts and scarves and found the box of rifle shells.

He removed a dozen and put them in the pockets of the faded yellow hunting jacket which lay on top of the heap. They clinked against glass and he reached into the deep pocket on the left side and removed a half-filled bottle of whiskey.

"I don't expect any bites," he mused and buried the bottle at the bottom of the locker. "Wonder if it's Claude's," Leon thought. "We haven't seen hide nor hair of him in most near a month, except for the other day when Norma ran him off."

Leon replaced the tray. Then he searched through it for the canteen. He put it in the blanket, He found the hunting knife, some fishing line and hooks, the hatchet, the tin box of matches, a tin cup and a six foot tenth of rope. Claude was careful about these things like he was careful about nothing else, Leon knew. He kept all of the essentials necessary for camping out in the mountains, neatly locked away, Always there in case. He gave use of them only to his youngest son. Leon took care to always return them, after he used them; safely to the hiding place.

He hung the knife and cup from his belt. The hatchet, tin box and rope went into the blanket with the canteen. He locked the locker, replaced the key and made one last check to be sure the other boys hadn't observed his actions.

He picked up his pair of heavy boots, the jacket and the blanket and stole from the room. He passed through the sleeping porch carefully weaving in and out of the maize of beds. Sleeping two to a cot, his female cousins lay half clothed, half covered, half on and half off their beds and half dreamed they saw Leon descending the back stairs in the pre-dawn light, his camping equipment slung over his shoulder.

"Good morning son," Norma dropped her half of the paper.

"Where you think, you're going?" Grandy assessed his attire.

"He's going up the mountain Grandy," Norma answered for Leon. She rose from the table and got Leon a mug of coffee. While he sipped that, she prepared a skillet of fried salt meat, ran some left-over biscuits in the oven and went to the porch for some fresh eggs.

Grandy sat munching away on several varieties of left-over pie, Cherry from Sunday; apple from Monday; Bread pudding from Saturday and blackberry cobbler from last night's supper. He poured his hot coffee into the saucer and began to cool it by blowing loudly over it.

"Shhhhhhhhhhh, Grandy," Leon cautioned, "You'll wake up the whole house, I want to get out of here before I have half of the gang trailing after me."

While the meat cooked, Norma took the blanket from Leon. She opened it up and took out the canteen, she never questioned his possession of all this mysterious equipment. They had a silent pact. Both knew of its origin. No explanation, no excuse was necessary.

Norma cradled the big old World War I canteen in her left arm and went to the back porch to fill it from the pump. She returned it lovingly to the blanket. She checked on the supply of matches in the box and satisfied they were sufficient in number; she returned the tin box to the blanket. She rewound the rope into a neat circle, tied it with a sting from her apron pocket and set it on the blanket.

She returned to the stove. There she dished up the meat onto a plate and cracked four eggs into the grease. A spoon of steaming grits went next to the meat and then the eggs on top. Norma served the plate to Leon and returned to the stove for the biscuits.

While the hungry hunter dived into his breakfast, Norma wiped her hands on her apron and admired the back of her son's blond head. She moved silently to the pantry at the other end of the kitchen. Earlier she had laid out some provisions for him. She had taken some of Mam-maws empty metal NR tablet boxes and had filled them with salt, pepper and sugar. Next to those she had put out cans of sardines, a loaf of Mam-maws homemade bread; some salt pork wrapped in a clean cloth; a hunk of cheese, two green apples and a sack of cookies. Wild fruit grew abundantly on the mountain and she knew Leon would catch some fish if not shoot some game.

Suddenly she remembered the old coffee pot and she hurriedly got it down from the shelf and put some coffee in some of the cloth and placed it in the inside of the pot. She took the provisions into the kitchen and rolled them neatly in the blanket. She dug some more string from her pocket and neatly tied each end with loops which would slip up his arms and anchor the pack to his back.

A low rumble started on top of Ole Hickory and gathered speed and violence as it tumbled down becoming thunder as it echoed from one peak to another. Norma looked uneasily toward the back door which opened onto the screen porch and moved toward the opening. Lightening cracked somewhere in the distance. She passed out of the door onto the open porch and looked up at the ominous sky which promised rain. Above her, little bodies turned in their beds and she heard a small voice say. "Move over! Want me to get rained on?"

Leon came up behind his mother, his pack on his back, his shoes on his feet and an old hat in his hand. He had grabbed the head covering from the hooks by the kitchen door as an afterthought. Without turning Norma said.

"Looks like a nasty storm brewing behind Ole Hickory. Might rain all day. Feel it coming in the air?" She clasped her arms about her breast and shivered with the coolness of the air suddenly growing with humidity.

"Yep. Think you're right but doubt that it will rain long. Hope it lasts till I get some fishing done. Always have good luck in the rain." He leaned down and brushed his lips across the nape of his mother's neck. She knew it was useless to argue. Rain would not dampen his compulsion to retreat to the mountain. Not today. As the mountain people would say, 'he had a complement to go'. When she turned, he had gone.

Grandy came out onto the porch, searched the sky and announced. "I best go pick them tomatoes before it rains. They're so ripe, the rain is sure to bruise them." He got down his hat and left by the back door, Norma sighed, weary before the day began.

She returned to the kitchen for one more cup of coffee before she walked up the lane. She was on the early shift at the Beacon plant this month. Her day there began at 7 a.m. but she was home by 4 p.m. She liked getting home early. She could sit on the porch with the guests and knit and talk for a spell before supper.

———————————— ❧ ❧ ————————————

Leon had crossed the highway and was passing the Petersen's on the brief incline of the mountain by the time Norma left Riverby for work. There was little light from the sun which had risen gloomily two hours before. In fact, it was nearly dark, like a January morning, Leon mused.

He had started to whistle the minute he approached the land mass which projected above its surroundings. Happiness lay in the mountains. He loved every inch of their rocky, tree laden slopes. To crest the topmost point, breathe deep of the untouched air and survey the surroundings made this boy of seventeen feel like he was ten feet tall. His best friends lived here, in these mountains. He gathered their news and gossip as his feet crinkled over the pine needles and twigs. Some even ran to greet him, shyly peeking up from the rhododendron bushes. Others gave hearty greeting from low hanging limbs of balsam fir trees. As he climbed through the thicket and scrub of the lower region, searching out his usual path, he noted how overgrown the way had become since last he had travelled there. This indication of his neglect for his love of late caused him to ponder the recent activities which had kept him away from her.

The past few weeks had been busy, hectic full days at the Inn. That meant that everyone had chores to keep them away from their haunts. Every room was filled and still cars sought out the driveway and inquired for accommodations. Folks from all over the south, depressed from the first heat of summer, climbed to the Smokies, the Blue Ridge and the Pisgah for relief.

A full house at Riverby meant hard labor for Leon, his brother Charles and for Harold his cousin. The big boys, as they were called, were asked to do big jobs around the big old house. Bringing in firewood; setting up cots for the family, hauling groceries from the village, turning the crank on the old washing machine, gathering the fruit in the side yard and from the orchard on the mountain side. These were regular chores. Everyone "walked the pipe".

So, for weeks, Leon's life had been organized, his masculine pride had been bossed around and his time just wasn't his own. The past few days his subconscious desire to be free had rebelled and with his mother's consent he had escaped. If only for two days, he would live free, be his own boss and make his home here with his friends on the mountain.

Leon heard it before he found it, the small brook which bubbled from the lake on top of the mountain and trickled all the way down to the valley. It grew smaller and smaller near the bottom at this time of the year but if the dark clouds above released their stock of rain, it would become a rushing force of water in minutes. He walked swiftly in the direction of the sound and once finding its banks he followed it along up the steep grade. A bob-white sounded his old refrain in the distance and Leon whistled back. Over and over again the two males performed their feat of communication, sometimes very close to each other and again they repeated across the distance. A white tail wagged atop a rhododendron along the bank and Leon knew that a young doe was licking water from the stream on the other side confident of her speed if his presence became too threatening.

Leon cupped his hands and leaned over the stream for a drink of the cool clear water. He righted himself, returned for the gun and pack and started up the stream. The doe splashed on the other side keeping the water between herself and the wicked weapon. Leon never turned back but as he left, he softly told her goodbye. He knew that the crackling twigs meant that she was following along on the other side.

About a half hour later, Leon noticed that the water flowed more gently. In fact, the stream seemed calm. He knew that somewhere up ahead there was a beaver dam. His pace quickened as thoughts of fishing from the pool urged him upwards. He saw traces of the beaver's work before he got to the dam. The shore was sprinkled with foot high stumps of young saplings. Each stump had been shaved to a point like a new pencil.

He hid his gun and blanket in a hollow log nearby and searched the bank for a suitable pole. This he strung with line and hook from his pocket. He returned to the hollow log, opened the blanket, found the salt pork and with his pocket knife he cut up several small pieces for bait. He situated himself on a rock by the water's edge, dropped in his line and prepared to wait for the inevitable tug on his line. In minutes he had caught four fish, all mountain trout. He knew that this was all he could consume for lunch so he unrigged the makeshift pole, cleaned the fish on the rock by the water and strung them on the line. He got his pack and gun and started again for the top of the mountain.

He felt a few drops of rain just as he spotted the wild berries growing in a thicket across the stream. He skipped across some rocks jutting up from the water and made the other side, much to the surprise of the young doe who felt safety lay in the width of the flowing water. She darted into the woods as he thrashed through the thicket. As Leon examined the bushes the rain began to fall in large drops. He was pleased to find that the berries were ripe and luscious and grew in abundance. Wild dew-berries began to ripen in early June and by mid-month they reached their peak of production. Sometimes the same bush could be picked twice a week. The rain came in heavy sheets now and Leon decided to make a dash for the shelter he knew lay ahead. He carefully marked the spot by the stream where the berries were. He slashed two marks into a tree trunk and determined to return this way tomorrow and collect some of the fruit for his mother.

Leon ran up the few remaining yards to the top of the mountain. He knew of a place near the top where he could seek shelter. His father had brought him and Charles here the first time he had ever taken them hunting. There was an old fire tower right on the northern edge of the top. Occupied only when forest fires threatened the area so the tower was seldom used. Leon couldn't remember in recent years that it had even been necessary for a ranger to occupy this lookout. The tower had been built close by the stream and alongside there stood a decaying wooden shelter building which was provided to give cover if an emergency demanded the manning of the tower. It was nothing more than a lean-to with three open sides and a slanting roof from one standing wall. It was big enough for two rangers to sleep and prepare food in during a three-man shift, the usual operation under fire conditions. Leon and Glover were the only house guests the rangers ever had and were entertained in absentia. These two close friends kept their shelter a secret and so far as they knew they were the only people in the valley to have used it. Charles preferred hunting on Ole Hickory. The two frequently spent weekends here in the early spring and fall when little else stirred in the valley. The valley slept peacefully from Labor Day till Memorial Day, waking to outside activity only during the summer months.

Leon darted into the shelter, drenched to the skin by the driving rain storm. The ground was dry under the roof and he stretched head long out of breath on the red clay floor. His breath came so fast after running the steep mountain side that for several moments the blood pumping from his lungs to his brain, blinded his eye sight and made him dizzy.

His outstretched palms felt the cool ground. His fingers touched the smooth texture of the clay and reminded him of soft skin, the pores of which were filled with bits of mica and occasionally a small rock. He dug his fingers into the fleshy earth, eager to feel the fatty grains of sand which made up the cell structure of this mountainous mother earth. The drops of water on his hands ran down into the open wounds his fingers had made and he felt the anemic red blood of clay and water. Leon raised his head and looked out beyond the shelter at the clearing where rivulets of water gouged into the soft soil and formed open running arteries flowing in all directions seeking water level.

His breath came in short normal spasms now and his nose picked out familiar scents. The blooms of mountain Laurel shattered in the rain and fell to the ground sending out sickening over-ripe sweetness. The heavy aromatic pine and fir needles half in decay on the floor of the shelter fertilized the air with pungency. Even the unseen furry friends hovering nearby in the cover of trees and roots gave off a glandular scent. The heavy rain and dusty particles falling from the cooling cumulus through the waxy leaves above, tingled the olfactory nerves with heavenly aromas.

Leon stood up, stretched his limbs and felt for the clouds he knew hung suspended overhead. His knuckles contacted the raw pine boards which made the roof of the shelter and hurled his soaring soul back to earth with reality. His nose singled out the odor of freshly burned wood and he searched with his eyes for the stone fireplace in the closed end of the structure. His passing glance automatically checked the wood supply, close by, which he and Glover always replenished before they left this special place just as Claude had taught him to do.

That's funny, Leon thought, I know Glover hasn't been up here in more than a month, yet there was a fresh fire built here recently, maybe even today. The supply of wood was dangerously low. Glover must have passed here yesterday on a squirrel hunt. He gathered up several logs and twigs left by the pit and began to build a fire. "Darn that Glover. He snuck off up here without me. Wonder why he didn't come by for me before he came up?" Leon talked to himself.

As he banked the ashes and laid on the new wood, the ground beneath was warm, too warm. "Yep Ole Glover was here yesterday. I can feel the left-over fire." Leon concluded. The rain continued to fall and now was a steady patter. Leon ducked from the shelter in search of some young green branches with which to make a spit. In his haste to be out of the rain, he startled the doe once again. The small deer had pursued his course and lurked near the shelter, under the spreading canopy of a giant gum tree. The glistening black nose sniffed the odor of food.

Leon made a run back to the shelter, rigged up a make shift spit and stuck the fish on one long stick. The fire by this time was smoking merrily in the fireplace. He reached in the blanket for the salt and pepper and seasoned the aquatic game sparingly. He opened the blanket and spread it out on the carpet of pine needles making himself a resting place. He drew out his knife, cut a hunk of bread and cheese and munched along while the fish cooked over the fire. While he ate, the rain seemed to slacken and the fish toasted to a white doneness. He ate it with relish, thinking to himself that nothing ever tasted so good as fresh smoked fish.

He banked the fire again and noted that the rain was now only a drizzle. Braving the dampness, he darted from the shelter to the tower and began to climb the long ladder of steps up the side. It was an arduous task. The steel rungs were slippery and with care he made his way up into the little room on top. The cloud layer was gradually lifting just as he predicted this morning. "Doesn't look like it will rain all day." The deserted tower was dusty and musty smelling and though the glass sides were stained from the elements he could see that the storm was passing over and moving off toward Mt. Mitchell. The valley to his left was curtained in by the passing downpour and he could see nothing of the houses and fields that lay below the thick woods on the mountain side.

To his right the sun was breaking through the clouds and in the distance toward Asheville it beamed down on the highway which twisted and turned through Bee Tree Gap. Suspended between two fronts, Leon watched with interest. From his elevated perch he could see the storm move in giant strides from Old Hickory across the valley, up his mountain and on to the range behind. Like looking into a clouded pool of water, the landscape below slowly came into focus as the rain stopped and the sun brightened the reflection. He was able to pick out the Bishop's house first as the storm passed from the foot of Hickory. Then the rain crossed the highway and he was able to discern the buildings which made up Riverby Inn. He was able to see cars on the yard, but he couldn't tell an Oldsmobile from a Ford.

Bored with his game of seek and find he began to look for likely places where he might find rabbits and squirrels. "Sure would like to have a roasted rabbit for supper tonight," he said to the empty tower room. He came down the steel ladder like an elevator. Holding on to the side rails he was able to slip down the two runways, still wet with rain. His feet touched the ground and he heard a movement in the brush, Leon caught sight of the doe again and for the first time he noticed that she had one different furry foot. Like her bushy tail, the foot was snow white, supporting the cloven black hoof.

He rolled the blanket up, banked the fire and shouldering his gun, he set off in search of rabbit and squirrel. Leon spent the afternoon away from the clearing and shelter. The sun came out brightly lighting up the forest on the mountain and he bagged a couple of rabbits, found more dew berries some of which he picked and ate for dessert. Then ultimately, he found his way back to the beaver's pool. Warmed by his long walk and afternoon activities he decided to go for a swim where earlier he had caught the trout. He stripped off his overalls and undergarments and slipped into the icy water. He swam and played there. Curiously he examined the beavers dam and swam underwater checking the intricate structure. Marveling at the animals' accomplishment, he flushed them up from their watery stronghold and gave them mute approval of their handy-work.

The sun slipped behind the mountain and Leon became aware of the first bluish tinges of twilight. He donned his overalls and made his way back to the clearing. He gathered dry wood to replenish the wood pile and gave new fuel to the fire. He tidied up the shelter, unfurled the blanket and set up housekeeping for the night. He put the rabbits which he had cleaned by the stream on the spit and sat back to gather his thoughts as they cooked.

Darkness was descending and the light of the fire flickered in the half light of the sun, ready to dip below the horizon. Leon's head bobbed drowsily. The warmth of the fire on his freshly bathed skin relaxed him. The rabbit began to sizzle, spit and send out drafts of flavorful broiling dark meat.

The doe darted from the nearby bushes and glided across the clearing in five great long leaps. Leon's head bobbed up, startled by the deer, his keen sense of the woods told him something threatened beyond the circle of light made by the fire. He fumbled for his gun and froze over it waiting for the wild creature which was preying on the deer. Twigs snapped, bushes moved their branches and squirrels scurried up the flakey pine bark. Suddenly the dark growth around the clearing became alive. Leon moved his trained eyes back and forth around the clearing watching each new movement.

A dim figure emerged from behind the laurel bush at the opposite end of the clearing. Lurching forward it was impossible for Leon to tell whether it was man or beast. As it stumbled forward, weaving into the firelight, Leon could tell that it was a grown male. A week's stubble of beard covered the round face. Premature gray hairs stood straight up on his head and grew down into the collar of a badly soiled shirt. Dirty hands held a jug. Unsure feet carried a puffy unhealthy torso across the clearing.

On the verge of shooting at the first sight of this creature, Leon now dropped his gun to his side. He threw back his young head and began to laugh. He released his frightened emotions and gave warning to the oncoming figure by breaking the hanging silence.

"Claude! Claude! You don't know how close you came to being shot plum through the middle." Leon addressed his father. "What on earth are you doing up here on the mountain? I thought I was the only human being within ten miles of here."

Claude stopped shuffling his feet. He tried to bring himself erect and stood swaying over his planted feet. He squinted his red, swollen eyes in an effort to see the voice which addressed him.

"It's me, Leon, Claude. It's your fair-haired son. Don't you know me? I'm real. Here feel." Leon walked toward his daddy as he spoke.

Claude fell on his son, wrapping his arms around the boy's broad shoulders. His tears flowed from his eyes and he sobbed into Leon's overalls in uncontrolled greeting. Leon propelled him to the shelter, took the jug which had already done its job and got Claude seated on the blanket by the fire. Speechless, his father sat looking at the boy, tears brimming in his eyes, Leon commanded him.

"Now you just sit there quietly, I got some rabbits cooking on the spit for your supper. I'll just run down to the stream and get some water to make us a nice pot of coffee. We'll eat and then we'll talk. The boy hurried for the water and returned finding his father unchanged. He quickly went about making the coffee and gave the older man a hot tin cup full of the brew.

Claude wolfed down the rabbit, Mam-maws homemade bread, half of the left-over cheese and consumed two more cups of coffee in silent obedience. After he had finished, he rose more steadily from the blanket and made his way through the brush. In minutes he returned from the stream, washed, hair slicked down with water and a smile on his face. He came into the shelter and spoke to Leon as if he had just walked up the mountain for a visit.

"Why, Boy I thought I was dreaming when I saw you sitting there on that blanket. Couldn't believe my ears when you spoke. You almost scared me speechless."

"Yes, sir," Leon answered, "I bet I was a sight for sore eyes." Nervous under the scrutiny of his father's gaze the boy arose and took the coffee pot and other utensils to the stream to wash them. His efforts for composure made the encounter seem natural and when he returned, they settled down on the blanket. Talk came freely now and they answered and asked questions of each other. They appeared by the firelight to be two hunters resting casually after a day's success in the woods.

"How are the folks son?" Claude took an indirect approach to Riverby.

"Mam-maws just fine, just sitting and quilting on the front porch. Why I judge that if we laid all the quilts she's made end to end we could walk to Asheville on the bits and pieces of all our old worn out clothes," Leon pictured his grandmother.

"Speaking of blankets, Your Ma? Is she still running the Beacon mill?"

"She works pretty hard Claude. In fact, she's worked herself right up to the front office this summer. She just got promoted to secretary and now she has a desk and chair of her own. No more standing over the weavers."

"Hurrruuuump!" Claude grumbled.

"Speaking of jobs, How's yours?" Claude beamed that Leon had asked. He had been dying to tell someone his side of the story for days.

"Well, I just quit! I just up and walked out, Why, I have more sense than he has about cars. Why he doesn't know the front end of a Cadillac from the ass of a Dodge. Besides he took my car away from me. Can't sell cars without a demonstrator. Fact is you can't sell cars no how now. Folks ain't got any money to be spending on autos. Except maybe for the Vanderbilt's. Why, if I hadn't sold Mrs. Vanderbilt that new car when I was chauffeuring for her this spring, I wouldn't have had a job anyway. I made a deal with the boss right then and he knew he was getting a cracker-jack salesman when he got me."

Leon let his father ramble verbally from pillar to post, as he talked, so did he live. Hand to mouth.

"I haven't made any big money since. Least ways not on cars, I had to get myself a side line to keep eating, no demonstrator no sideline though, so I just told that Bastard, if he took my car away, I was gonna quit. And I did just that, day before yesterday. I walked right out in the middle of the morning. Boy was he surprised. Son you should have seen his face when I told him what he could do with that car!"

"I think I can see the picture, Dad." Leon smiled at the thought even though he knew his father was bragging. "What kind of sideline was it Claude?" Leon had an idea before he asked.

"Well son, you see it's like this," Claude started, stopped and then backed up. "Let's put it this way, what we don't know, don't hurt us. Everybody's doing it these days. Good money in it if you have the right contacts and son, your old dad sure knows the right folks. I got the best friends in the world. They'll help me out till I can get something else."

Leon took the opportunity to make his plea. "Claude, why don't you come home for a spell? Maybe you could get a job down at the mill. You wouldn't have to stay if you didn't like it. Just sort of come for a vacation and see all the family. Mam-maw sure misses you. I can tell cause sometimes she talks to herself and I hear her say, 'Claude please come home."

Claude cleared his throat and shifted his position to lying flat out on the blanket. Without looking directly at his son, he replied, "Well now, that would be right nice. A vacation, just what I need too. But right now, I can't. I mean, I better not. "He groped for words then the thought came to him.

"You see, I owe that old bastard some money. The one that runs the Buick place. I'm scared if I go down the mountain he'll hear and come running for it. It isn't but a few dollars but I know Mam-maw and Grandy would feel like they had to pay him off, and son, wouldn't want them to do that. I just better lay low for a while."

Claude's grandiose excuse and chivalrous gesture sort of made Leon's stomach turn uneasily. He thought of all the times his grandparents had bailed Claude out of debts and tight spots. Suddenly he felt real disgust for this flesh and blood of his flesh and blood. He thought Claude must be in real trouble this time. He never refused to let his mother and dad help him out, fact was it didn't even embarrass him to ask. The situation must be more serious than he thought at first. He hurried to retract his invitation.

"Don't know what I was thinking of anyhow, Claude. Riverby is busting at the seams with guests and family… It wouldn't be a very good time to take a vacation there any way. You better just stay up here on the mountain and rest yourself. I'll hunt you up some game tomorrow and that will hold you till I can get back up here and bring you some fresh provisions. If I can't come, I'll send Charles up. I've got to go down tomorrow. I promised Norma I would. But I'll get you some food up here day after tomorrow somehow. I'll even get some of Grandy's tobacco for you. You just settle down here and wait and see."

Claude's eyes twinkled at this proposal. He knew his son understood more than he was saying. It wouldn't be bad up here if he had food, tobacco and some, well, he knew where he could get some more of that. He'd walked over the mountain today and found it. Took him all day but it was sure worth it. He wondered how long his credit would last with the old mountaineer. He figured he could hold out a few days then he'd have to move on to new territory. Couldn't fool these 'blind tigers' long, he knew that. Besides they could find a needle in a hay stack if the haystack was on their mountain.

"That's mighty fine of you son. I'll do just that. Stay up here and you boys can come back and forth and visit me. Just mind out you don't let your mother or your Aunts on to me up here. They're worse than the Feds."

So, they agreed. The next day they caught more trout, shot more rabbit and got some squirrels. They picked dew-berries for Norma. Claude got a kick out of thinking of Norma eating dew-berries that had touched his tainted hands. They spent the day like father and son, roaming the mountain hunting and fishing and talking. Competing with their shots, telling fish tales and seeing which one could build the best spit for smoking game en masse.

Shadows fell on the mountain before Leon remembered that he had the long walk home in front of him. Claude was more fun than Glover when he was on an outing like this and Leon enjoyed his daddy's company. Claude told funny stories and laughed a lot. But Leon was late, he knew, so he pulled himself away from the companionship and prepared to return to civilization. He left the pack and gun with his father. He hung the freshly shot game on a stick and wrapped the berries in his hat, careful not to bruise them. He tied some of the string through his hat and slung it from the end of the stick which held the game.

"So long, Dad. See you tomorrow." He left the clearing, When Leon passed the Petersen's he didn't stop to tell Glover he'd been on the mountain. It was pitch black dark now and he knew his mother would be walking the floor. He shortened his stride and settled into a fast trot along the highway and into the Riverby road. Then he slowed, taking a more nonchalant gate.

On the porch knitting since four o'clock, Norma had given up her vigil only long enough to eat dinner and help wash the dishes. Dinner had been done two hours and she was almost ready to send Charles out to look for his brother when she spotted Leon coming up the drive. The porch rockers were full. The guests and family gathered there were wrapped in sweaters and were watching the kick-the-can game in progress on the lawn. Everyone breathed a sigh of relief when Leon's figure was spotted on the lower drive.

Norma left her place in the swing and walked down to meet him. Just as they came within speaking distance of each other, Norma noticed that Leon carried the fresh game. She missed the pack and his gun. He looked unnatural carrying the game on one shoulder with no gun on the other. She ran to him and hugged him tightly, standing on her tip toes to reach his neck. Neither spoke. When she disengaged her arms Norma stood back and looked behind Leon. Her eyes climbed the Mountain in much the same path as Leon had taken down. Up, up she traveled with her gaze and for a split second she thought she discerned a small wisp of smoke on the very peak. Leon saw his mother's knowing look. She didn't ask however and he didn't speak of it.

"Here Ma, I brought you some berries. They're the finest I've ever seen. Fat, ripe and juicy, just like you." Leon gave her the hat of berries. Norma made a big thing of accepting them and they walked arm in arm up to the porch.

The faceless occupants of the rockers greeted him across the dark porch as he climbed the steps. Standing in front of the door where the lamps shine through from inside, Leon displayed his fine trophies of hunting. There was a rumble of anticipative talk about tomorrows stew.

Out on the lawn, the children running to kick the can noticed that Leon had returned. They broke from the game and came to him on the porch. They hurled excited questions at him.

"Whoa there now, one at a time. I can't answer all of you at once. "Leon slowed them down.

"See any bears, this time?" La asked.

"Shot one, so big I couldn't carry him down the mountain by myself." Leon teased her.

"See any mountain lions?" Jaybo asked.

"Fought a whole tribe of them. They nearly tore me to bits. But a big elephant came along and scared them off." Leon laughed.

"Aw shucks…." Sonny scraped his shoes in the dust as he stood at the bottom step. "We had more excitement than that right here. The Feds came by this morning. They searched the whole place. They said they were looking for a bootlegger loose in these parts. Thought he might be staying here, disguised as a guest."

Leon tensed the muscles in his jaw. He sought out Norma's eyes with his and they pleaded with each other. Silently they agreed, looked back up the mountain, then back to each other. Slowly they made their way into the house. Side by side they marched in the kitchen to put up the game.

The occupants of Riverby Inn pulled up their blankets against the chill of the night. Up on the mountain, Claude tossed sleeplessly under the cover which his son had left for him. The night was clear and clusters of stars hung like chandeliers from the blue-black velvet ceiling of sky. Claude counted them, trying to forget his thoughts and put himself to sleep.

Back in the medallion room, Leon settled down in the bed with Charles and Harold. Charles questioned his brother. He probed at Leon with indirect interrogatory. Leon squirmed between the bed clothes. He repeatedly went over his trip up the mountain, step for step. He told and retold Charles trying to avoid telling of the encounter with Claude until they could discuss it alone.

Claude gave up trying to sleep. He sat up and reached for the jug. He put it down in front of himself and looked at it. "No, Claude." He spoke to himself. "You have to stay off of that stuff. You've gotta make up your mind what to do. You got your tail in a crack real good this time." He reached deep into his hip pocket and pulled out a square cut of tobacco. He bit the one remaining corner off and chewed.

Leon crawled over Harold whose turn it was to have the outside position tonight in the big bed. His feet found the floor in the darkened room. He walked over to the cot on the other side, jerked back the covers and crawled into it. The springs creaked and groaned as they gave away to his long slender body.

Charles sat up. "What do you think you're doing getting in Claude's bed? Mam-maw will take the hide off of you if she catches you in that bed. You know she likes to have it all tidy for him in case he comes home unexpectedly.

Leon laughed fiendishly and forgot himself "He's not coming tonight, expected or no. He's up there on the top of Potato Knob and he's waiting for you or me, someone to come bring him some provisions tomorrow."

Charles gasped out loud. He had suspected that something had happened that Leon wasn't telling, but he didn't dream that Leon had actually seen his father. He had thought that some more remote form of contact had been made.

Leon continued. "Scout's honor, Harold. Promise you won't tell a soul about this. It may be life or death. I really think Claude's in big trouble."

Harold nodded his head in the dark saying, "Scout's honor, I won't tell a soul. I promise, Lee."

Charles interrupted him before he could continue crossing his heart and hoping to die. "Well, I knew something was up, I saw the way Norma looked at you, she knows, doesn't she? Why did you tell her? I'm the oldest in the family. You should have told me first. I did the chores for you for the two days you were gone so you could go up on the mountain. The least you could have done was to have told me about Claude. FIRST!"

"Aw, Charles don't get hurt. I didn't tell her. She guessed. Those men that came here today put her on notice that Claude was somewhere nearby. She isn't a fool, you know."

"Yeh, and those men aren't fools either. They're Federal agents, Leon. Claude's been boot legging. He'll get us all in trouble if he doesn't watch out. They're mad as hornets this time and they swore they'd catch him."

Claude moved the quid of tobacco to his jaw and spat juice into the nearest rhododendron bush. Slowly in his mind he was letting himself consider going down to Riverby. He admitted to himself that the idea had been there all the time. The bushes moved where he had just spat, Claude stopped chewing. He listened. Nothing stirred. He moved the quid to his jaw again and spat in the same general direction. The white footed doe moved out of range. Claude picked up the gun and walked around the bush. By the light of his fire he spotted the little deer as she lept for escape. He fired once. The doe fell.

Claude had broken the law again. Once more, quickly, thoughtlessly and selfishly he stepped across the line. That fine line between moral, social, religious and legal ethics. He winced when he pulled her body into the firelight and realized she was a doe. "But I had to have something to take home, a peace offering for Mam-maw", Claude felt badly. The doe would be his dove!

———————————— ❧ ❧ ————————————

Breakfast at Riverby was grumpy. This was one of those days when every other bed emptied on the wrong side. Out-of-sorts eaters gathered to break the long nights fast.

Norma, first in the kitchen had shortened her sleepless night by putting the coffee pot on at 4 a.m. Weary and heavy of heart her hands trembled with the weight of the coffee cup. Her thoughts faltered then wandered. She greeted the break of day with impotence.

Grandy joined her enraged over the morning headline. He read to her from the Asheville Citizen, "'ICKE FIGHTS FOR FORRESTRY, GAP WIDENS BETWEEN AGRICULTURE AND INTERIOR,' Darn fools are gonna take the forest away from the farmers. Damn city slickers can't see the trees for the woods. They'll kill free enterprise in this country for sure."

LaVerne entered and quickly helped Delilah with the breakfast preparations. The children assembled on the back porch around the family board.

"Where's the cereal, mother?" Bobbie came with tray in hand.

"Bobbie, I want to talk to you right after breakfast." LaVerne had already gone over in her mind what she'd say to her daughter. Bobbie had come in at 11: 30 last night. Thirty minutes late, she had broken her curfew. "Take out the bowls then come back and I'll just give you the pot. You can dish up on the porch. We're running late this morning."

"Okay, gang! Here's a rare treat, Aunt Norma's cornmeal mash. UGH!" Bobbie made a face at the standard breakfast fare for Riverby children.

Mabel brought: out a scrap of paper which she had hidden in the top of her brushed wool beanie. She passed it up and down the table. "What is it? What is it?" They all wanted to know and tried to grab it in their sugary hands.

"Don't tear it. I found it. It's one of Mr. Bouquets checks. See his name is printed on it."

Ohs and ahs rippled up and down the table. "It looks valuable," Bill had a head for money.

"I'll show you how valuable it is," Harold took over. He brought out his fountain pen which he kept clipped to his overall pocket. He imitated Bouquets New Orleans accent. "Give me quietude everyone. I need serenity because I am a millionaire and us millionaires need peace and quiet when we write our checks. All right, mademoiselle," Harold mimicked the slight French accent, Mr. Bouquet used. "You found my personal check and I'm going to give you a reward for your honesty." The cheap pen scratched as he wrote on the pay to bearer line, "ten thousand and no/ one-hundreths dollars," Harold signed it 'Andre Bouquet.'

"Now my little upstairs maid…. go buy yourself a million new tooth brushes…. get everybody at the Inn at least five new brushes…. I, Andre Bouquet, have just cornered the tooth brush market." Harold fell over his plate laughing.

While the others joined in, jostling each other to see Harold's handy-work, Mabes, La and Hy exchanged winks with the tooth-brush bull. Sis patted it out flat, folded it neatly and put it in her overall pocket. Spooning her cereal from bowl to mouth, Sis resolved in her innocence to return it to its owner.

The boarders filed into the dining room one by one when Mose rang the first bell. Miss Mullen spoke to Mr. Bouquet.

"I couldn't sleep a wink last night, I just kept seeing those poor dead little rabbits and squirrels that boy Leon brought in here last night. You know I am a charter antivivisectionist and it's my duty to report this."

Mr. Bouquet agreed and added" Someone ought to report these little delinquents. Do you know they've been pilfering in my baggage's? I've suspected for a long time but now I am convinced of it. It's those young jezebels that clean my room, I'm sure."

Miss Adrianna charged the dining room door shrieking. "Whose been monkeying with my sunburst? I left it in the corner of the hall last night and someone's dropped some old dirty tooth brushes in it." Miss Adriana unfurled her sunburst patterned quilt. She had spent every day at Riverby piecing this latest project.

"Let's see them," Mrs. Tate refereed to the brushes. "Margaret and I seem to have misplaced ours."

Mam-maw floated into the dining room eclipsing the sunburst with her bright sunny smile. From her room just off the dining room she had overheard the disgruntled conversations.

"Good morning, Adrianna. Did I hear you say a cloud had passed over your sunburst? Mam-maw winked at Beth Taylor. Beth and the Doctor immediately held a secretly whispered conversation. "Ben, you're right, that Bouquet is a klepto. Did you see how he gagged when Miss Adrianna said toothbrushes? Boy, would Freud have fun with him," Beth confided to her husband.

"Such a lovely day, all's right with the world." Mam-maw was making a valiant: effort to cover up the ever-increasing mystery of missing tooth brushes. "Come Adrianna, sit here with me and let's have our coffee. Tell me. how is Mrs. Peake? Didn't I hear you say you were going to see her late yesterday AFTERNOON?"

Adrianna carefully folded her quilt and sat on it when she took her chair. "Oh, yes, Mrs. Blanks. I wanted to tell you; Mrs. Peake had a letter from Bonnie. You know my niece. Well, Bonnie will get out of music camp the first of July. She'll catch a bus down here right after the Fourth. Of course, Mrs. Peake really wanted us to stay up on the mountain with her, but she knew it would be better for Bonnie to be here at the Inn. With all the children, you know, its mighty lonely up at her cabin."

"How nice, I'm so glad to know that she will soon be here. She will really be an addition to the children's show nights. I hear she is so talented. I'll have to tell the Trundle-Bedders. What instrument did you say she plays?"

Margaret set up an unintelligible chatter at the little table by the window and before Miss Adriana had a chance to answer Mam-maw's question, Mam-maw excused herself and went to Margaret.

"Now, now my dear. You must mind your granny and eat your breakfast. Start the day off right, I always say." Mam-maw reached over and daintily picked off a piece of Marybelle's ham. She popped it into her mouth, chewed making noises of ecstasy for Margaret's benefit and said, "See there, It's so goodie. Now you eat the rest and I'll let you help me feed Chatter and Lucy." Mam-maw referred to her pair of pet geese.

Margaret rolled her tongue around her lips and drooled. "Gan Mudddah. . . Gan muddah Maga fee. . cha. . .tuh and ucie . . kaga . . . . . feee. . . . . . "

Mam-maw passed on to the lonely table of Miss Mullen. She slid into the ever-present vacant chair facing the old lady.

"Now Emma, what's this I hear about your leaving today? Surely you don't want to have us think you don't like our Riverby Inn?" Mam-maw saw Mr. Bouquet leave his table and head for the front hall. She quickly got up and picked up his scraps. "I'll just take these and feed my Chatter and Lucy in a minute. Here Betts, give me that cup of coffee over here." She directed Betts to her place and helped herself to a piece of toast.

"Now what was that you were saying, Emma?" Mam-maw dunked the salt rising toast in the fresh cup.

"Mrs. Blanks I must register a complaint against Leon, killing those poor animals."

A booming masculine voice stopped any further conversation. Claude had entered the deserted front hall and came toward the dining room singing. "Be it ever so humble, there's no place like home……" Draped over his shoulder was the white footed doe. Mam-maw froze as she caught his voice. A hush fell over the entire dining room and kitchen. Claude advanced up the hall.

"You hoo. Anybody home to welcome the weary traveler? Mama! your son has returned."

The swinging doors to the dining room whooshed with traffic. The family came to see if John Charles Thomas had just checked in. Claude stood erect under his burden in the doorway almost touching the top of the frame. His blue eyes rounded the large rectangular room and rested finally on the face of his mother.

"Mama, my sweetheart! Say something. I'm home. Its Claude. See here, I brought you some venison." He advanced on Miss Mullens table and let the doe slip forward over his bowed head and into his outstretched arms.

Mam-maw finally gained her feet and with arms open to encircle her son she stepped out to greet him. "Claude, Oh Claude, you mess, you scared the daylights out of me. Was that you making all that racket in the hall?"

Miss Mullen stared dumbfounded at the dead doe; its big round brown velvet eyes stared back at her. She collapsed in her chair. Her grey-green eyes stared up at the ceiling. Leon and Charles exchanged looks. Both thought gratefully of Norma's earlier departure for the mill. Banking the two brothers, the entire Blanks family had slipped in and formed a flank in front of the kitchen door.

No one knew what to say or do. Claude invariably arrived home drunk and rowdy. When he came like that the family went into action EMERGENCY. Each one had something to do to ease the embarrassment. But here he was, bright and early in the morning standing cold sober, clean and shaven in the middle of the dining room, with his arms around Mam-maw. Truly this was a breath-taking sight and the cat had everyone's tongues, except for Claude.

"Hi y'all". He waved his hand to the assemblage. "I was just passing through on a business trip. Working on a real big deal up north of here, so I said to myself, Claude you deserve a little rest and visit with your family. So! Here I am. Isn't anybody glad to see ole Claude?"

Mam-maw answered him by hugging him tightly again. The rest of the family really were glad to see him, in this condition. So glad in fact that they indulged themselves and believed his little made up explanation. A sober Claude was irresistible.

Martha Lee pushed her way up from the rear flank of Blanks while her Daddy talked. She squeezed between Grandy and her Aunt Boom on the front row and dashed toward her fathers outstretched arms. "Daddy, Oh Daddy, you're here. I knew you'd come back."

Claude swept this bundle of joy up off her feet. His stiff arms carried her up over his head like a Ferris-wheel. He threw back his sandy head and gazed up with soft blue eyes into her shining face. Transfixed, father and daughter, memorized each other, lest this split second have to last a lifetime as memory.

Martha's chubby body strained Claude's flabby muscles and at once she came back to earth. Forcing with all his might he was able to bring her down gently placing her browned bruised toes on the hard pine floor.

Grandy stood back while the whole congregation floated up and over Claude. Some buzzed his cheek while others gave him a real bear hug. Leon and Charles shook his hand. Beck regaining her strait-laced, pursed-lip composure, passed by her brother and gave him a quick peck on his mouth. She bent over Miss Mullen. "Betts, go get the gum camphor in Mam-maw's room, and Leon remove that carcass to the kitchen." Beck caught sight of LaVerne coming forward. "Stop wringing your hands in that apron sister! You've torn it from the waist band. Give me a hand, this poor thing is in a deep swoon."

The Taylors, still at their table, were enjoying this working laboratory. Claude turned, grabbed his sister LaVerne by the hand as if to hold her back lovingly from such an unpleasant duty and spoke back to Beck.

"I didn't know I had such charm left. Why this dear little lady took one look at my manly visage and keeled over. That's me, Claude the lady killer. I knock 'em dead."

Leon, carrying the soft furry head of the doe, stopped by the kitchen door. He stared down then at his father then back at the doe. He thought of the deer in his arms. Flirty little lady, so trusting and guileless.... so dead! He stroked thee long neck with true regret.

Claude continued. "Here, Beck let me help". He spoke closer to Miss Mullens ear. "Here little lady let me help you. "Miss Mullen did not answer." To what couch shall I transport the Lady of Swannanoa?"

The children snickered. Beck, in disgust of Claude's antics, gave Miss Mullen one more sniff of camphor.

"Don't poke fun Claude!"

Miss Mullen, limp as a rag in Claude's arms, fluttered; one eye lash peeped through a squinted lid at Claude and secretly enjoyed the masculine attention. Mam-maw spoke up.

"Here, Claude, bring her into my room. Put her there on Franks side." Mam-maw pointed to her husband's side of the big double bed.

Miss Mullen stiffened like a poker in Claude's arms. She opened her eyes wide and flailed her hands in the air like a desperate swimmer in the billowing surf.

"Put me down! Put me down this instant you animal killer. What time is it? I must catch the train this morning, I can't stay here one more day. I must report, I must make a report........." Her feet touched the floor running. Up the steps, down the hall, she fled for her room.

Everyone giggled. Even Beck and LaVerne could no longer contain their good senses of humor with this ridiculous performance.

"Don't worry Claude," Beck laughed, "She s been leaving Riverby every day since she arrived."

"Becks right," LaVerne added, "That's one room I wouldn't mind having vacant. Every day is a crisis with her." The two sisters joined hands with their brother and walked from the room trailing the laughing family behind.

The chilly hour of breakfast had passed. The climbing sun peeked through the amber and cranberry and Vaseline antique glass on the shelves in the dining room. Warm pools of color formed a kaleidoscope on the floor. The discontent had thawed into liquid laughter. The gayety spilled and ran over onto the front porch where the rockers lilted to and fro.

Claude took his seat in the most advantageous spot. He faced the family but he was hidden from the road by the wisteria vine. He charmed the guests and tickled the family from the same position where the Federal agents had stood on the day before. The children half covered Claude. Martha and Sis crawled on his lap.

"Daddy, you'll take us across the river for a spend-the-night, won't you? Aunt Boom, Aunt Lola, Aunt Beck and Ma said we couldn't do it without a daddy with us. You will, won't you?"

"Yeh, Uncle Claude, and you'll give me a ride over the 'pipe' won't you? So, they won't go off and leave me?" Sis added to Martha's plea.

"Whoa there. You two little Lee's aren't giving me a fair shake...." He winked at Mam-maw, the source of the "Lee". "I'll do anything your little heart's desire if you'll just let me have a visit now with my Mama."

The Trundle-Bedders scrambled off the porch and made for the tearoom to make plans. All except Sis. She was intercepted by Mr. Bouquet.

"Madam, Mrs. Hedges. May I have a word with you privately?" Mr. Bouquet intruded on the family circle and took LaVerne away. They retired to the parlor. Sis was drug along by Mr. Bouquet who had a firm grip on her hand.

"I just want you to see what your good, fine, upstanding, worthy, honorable Eagle Scout is capable of." He roared as he flashed the signed check in her face. "This little rag-a-muffin of a child who says her name is Sis.... and that's no Christian name for a child to have.... says he found this blank check of mine and filled it in. What do you think of that? Forgery! It's out and out forgery!"

"No sir, I didn't say that either. I said Mabes found it. She musta caught it in her butterfly net." Sis explained.

"Mr. Bouquet, I'm speechless. I don't know what to say. It.... it is his handwriting but I'm sure he didn't mean to do it. That is, I'm sure he didn't know what he was doing.... that is, I'm sure.... he's a fine boy.... this must have been a boyish prank. Please. Oh please! Accept my apologies. I Can assure you; he will seek you out to ask your apology."

"Madame. Those officers here yesterday, they seek out forgers and law breakers. Is your son a criminal?"

LaVerne fled the parlor room and flung herself down on Mam-maws bed just down the hall. The hot tears were overflowing and pouring down her cheeks. "Aunt Boon.... I didn't mean to...." Sis tried to comfort her.

"Madam, where did you go to! You haven't heard the last of this." Mr. Bouquet followed her up to the door of the bedroom and stopped

LaVerne buried her head in Mam-maws pillow. She had wrapped Mam-maws black shawl around and around her head. Her sobs were muffled.

Figure 15: Swannanoa River near Riverby Inn

# ⋖ *Swannanoa River* ⋗

# Grand Ole Oprey

The note read: "We're spending the night across the river. Uncle Claude is taking us over there and we're going to have a keen time. Please answer this letter and come see us." Signed Bill Fields, Riverby Inn in Swannanoa, North Carolina. While the note had been printed out with a piece of old crayon, the name was in script. Bill admired the fancy loops and swirls he had created and rolled the note into a tight spiral and inserted it into an empty pop bottle. He twisted a piece off the wad of tar he had been chewing and plugged the top of the bottle. With a professional toss, he threw the bottle into the rapids of the Swannanoa River and watched it bob out of sight.

"Bet it goes all the way to India," he remarked to the others.

"Ha! It'll just end up on the mud flats of New Orleans along with all the other messages we've sent out over the years," Tom Jr, replied with certainty.

"You all stop fooling with that stuff and get your gear loaded up. It'll get dark after a while and we want to get camp set up. I'm going to take this first load on over to the island." Charles swung a pack over his shoulders and walked rapidly across the pipe.

"I think Uncle Claude is just wonderful. Gee, he's great. Just like it says on my daddy's overall patch," Sonny patted the patch on his size eight overalls, "Anvil Brand, Hard to beat. Uncle Claude is hard to beat."

"We going to sure have a good time, that's for sure. If it wasn't for Uncle Claude, they'd never let us spend the night across the river," Jaybo agreed.

"I'm glad it's just going to be us going over for the night. Mabes and Hy and La and Harold have to go into Asheville to that old opera. Glad we don't have to suffer through culture tonight," Betty spoke up. She and Martha were packing their bed roll together on the bank of the river. They had secretly made their favorite sandwiches which they called 'hots' and hidden them in their overall pockets along with a bottle of water to assuage their burning tongues from the bread and mustard treat.

"Everybody load up and get going across the pipe. Dad will be over in a minute to inspect everything. Let's see how fast we can get the camp made up." Leon let out a Tarzan yell and preceded the children across the swirling water and disappeared into the jungle growth on the other side. The other children were frantically trying to get their things together, anxious not to be left behind, when they heard a deep-throated Tarzan yell just behind them.

"Uncle Claude! Yah--hoo, everybody! It's Uncle Claude going to go across with us!" Sis ran to meet him and threw her arms around his waist. She hung on to his belt as he walked toward the gang. Sis dangled from the sagging belt and shrieked her merriment at the game.

"What's the hold up? Everybody up and on the move, what's all this stuff for? We're not staying for a year, you know." Claude rubbed his hands together in anticipation the fun ahead. Sis had let go of the belt and was busy cramming green apples in her pockets for a midnight feast. Claude gave Martha a bear hug and swatted Sonny on his rear end to get him going across the pipe. At the last moment, Claude swung Sis to his shoulders and let out another ear-splitting yell.

"Don't be afraid of a little dew on the pipe. You won't fall. Claude's here with you. Nothing to fear! Remember what Mam-maw says, "Look straight ahead and never down." Keep the line moving up ahead. Let's get going up there in front.... It'll be dark soon."

Every one of them walked the pipe safely and once their feet hit the solid ground of the island, they ran off toward their camping grounds and prepared for the night.

---------------------- ❧ ❧ ----------------------

On the front porch of Riverby, the after-dinner rockers were watching the sun go down behind Alexander's Mountain.

"Well, how do you think we look? Do we pass inspection? Do you think we'll be mistaken for the opera stars and be hounded for our autographs?" Lola announced to the family on the porch as she slammed the screen door.

The guests smiled at the group before them and continued to rock.

Mam-maw and Beck looked up from their endeavors and eyed the aggregation before them. Mam-maw had been holding a skein of dark red yarn in her hands while Beck sat facing her and rapidly wound the yarn into a fast-growing ball.

Lola, LaVerne, Harold, Jr, Hy, Mabes and La stood in a self-conscious semi-circle just outside the front door and waited for compliments. The girls and women wore soft pastel colored voile dresses and Harold Jr. had on his Sunday suit and white shirt. All the women had on white gloves except for Lola who was busy putting on her brown pigskin driving gloves.

"Don't you think you should be wearing hats?" Beck asked critically.

"Not after six o'clock, my dear," Lola corrected, "everybody knows that. Besides Sister doesn't have anything appropriate and my hat looks lopsided. Seems Sonny sailed it off the sleeping porch to see how far it would sail and it landed against the Tearoom."

Hy said, "I could care less."

La looked her usual elegant self without a hat so she just shrugged her shoulders and said, "Let's just go on and go and get it over with."

Mabel's hair was shinny from Mam-maw's pomade which she had used with a generous hand to restrain her unruly thick curls. She couldn't have gotten a hat to stay on top of her mass of hair.

LaVerne looked anxiously about her hoping they wouldn't decide to wear hats at the last minute. She gave a little sigh as she remembered with a pang her one good hat still riding a Trailways Bus somewhere, resting on the overhead rack.

"Nonsense, girls," Mam-maw spoke up, "you all look very presentable. There will be two other operas on the series and if the other ladies are wearing hats tonight, you can wear hats for the other concerts.

The Monte Carlo Opera Company was presenting a series of three operas in Asheville. This first one was in June, then one in July and the last one would be in August. Lola had decided this form of culture, practically at the front door of Riverby, was too good a thing to pass up. Besides, it would give the older children something constructive to do. Maybe it would get the girls' minds off those silly boys.

"Let's go," Lola commanded, don't want to be late. Harold, you ride up front with your mother and myself. I'm not sure just where to turn off for the auditorium and I need your sharp eyes to point it out." They were ready to descend the steps when they heard a scream. It was a long-sustained scream that started out on a high pitch and went even higher.

"Heeeeeeelp! Merciful heav......ns, sweeeeet Lord a......boves heeeeeeeelp me!"

"That sounds like little old Miss Mullen," Harold said.

"That noise is coming from the downstairs bathroom," Lola decided.

They all ran quickly to Miss Mullen's defense. The voile dresses flowed out like silken streamers as they sped back through the front door, down the hallway, onto the little side porch and to the door of the bathroom.

Miss Mullen was standing just inside the bathroom door with her hands over her eyes. As soon as she knew help had arrived, she gave one final bleat and swayed against the door jamb.

"We're coming, we're here, what's wrong, my dear?" LaVerne comforted the frail little old maid.

Miss Mullen switched the light on and pointing to the floor she said, "Underlinens.... a man's undergarment....... There." She held on to LaVerne's arm for support. With one hand still covering her eyes, she reeled out onto the porch and used the wall to brace her back.

Grandy had vacated the bathroom only seconds before the unsuspecting Miss Mullen had entered it. As Mrs. Wilde, their mountain neighbor would say, "Hit looked like the devil had had an auction in hit".

The bath tub was one big dirty ring. All the way to the top and over the sides. Pools of water stood stagnant on the linoleum floor. The wash basin was covered with shaving soap, scum and blood. The walls around the mirror had splats of soapsuds and Grandy's whiskers studding it. A very used bar of Octagon soap, sticky with long white hair on it, lay in the bowl off the basin. The offensive man's garment sprawled where the owner had kicked it to one side. Instead of being bunched up in a ball, it lay sprawled full out on the floor at the end of the tub. For many days it had been molded to the frame of Grandy and it still assumed his shape.... from the bulging biceps in its sleeves to the bulging front of its crotch. To all intents and purposes, it was Grandy lying here nude.

"We certainly can't take time to clean up this mess," Lola said. "What on earth is Grandy doing taking a bath? It isn't Saturday! Hybernia, go get Mose before he leaves the kitchen and tell him to bring his Lysol and mop and plenty of rags. Harold, Jr. get that THING out of here," she continued, pointing to Grandy's long underwear on the floor.

"I do wish Papa would learn to raise the seat," LaVerne sighed. She looked with distaste as Harold used a long stick to snare Grandy's long johns.

"I have told Frank a thousand times not to be so messy," scolded Mam-maw "Here, son I'll take that underwear."

"Don't let it touch my red wool," cautioned Beck.

"Mose, here's a quarter.... don't stop until you have this place shining." Lola handed Mose the money from her pocket book. "Now everybody into the car. Carmen will go on without us. We mustn't miss the overture."

"Beck, the Grandfather Hopper room is in order if anybody should turn in while we are gone," said LaVerne as she settled herself in the front seat of the Franklin with Lola and Harold Jr. The three girls slammed the back doors and Lola spun her wheels as she let out the clutch too quickly. The occupants waved goodbye as their heads jerked in cadence with Lola's clutch.

After getting the children organized in their camp site, Claude had walked back across the pipe by himself and gone up the hill near the end of the front porch and over by the old Tearoom. He was gathering up sticks and twigs to make a bonfire. Watching Lola's driving sent him into peals of laughter.

"Don't forget to honk for the train," he called after the departing car. His contagious laughter cascaded onto the front porch.

"I'll ask you, Lola, what are we going to do about Grandy's baths for the remainder of the summer? We can't have him making those grand messes and taking a chance on somebody finding them like poor Miss Mullen. That was a terrible shock to her," LaVerne was so worried about this dilemma she wasn't sure she'd enjoy the opera. She wasn't quite sure what Carmen was all about. She knew it was gay and colorful.... all those South Americans are.... oh well, she'd just relax and listen to the music.

"One thing," Lola said as she blew her horn at the railroad tracks and shot over the rails, "he usually only bathes once a week and right after dinner on Saturday night. If the children won't clean it up, we'll just tip Mose every week to do the job for us. Even though he makes ten cents an hour, I feel that paying him an extra quarter is worth it. I smell smoke. Harold, Jr, check my dash board and see if anything looks hot."

"Maybe it's your emergency brake again, "he answered. Lola was known for driving with the emergency brake on.

"I smell it too," LaVerne remarked, "maybe somebody's burning trash. Do you girls smell anything?" LaVerne looked back over her shoulder in time to see Mabel blow a plume of smoke out of the open window and pass the cigarette to La.

"Lola! Lola! Stop the car! The girls are SMOKING in the back seat! Help! Murder! Stop!"

Lola gave a reflex signal to the car behind her and veered off the roadway and into the little gulley alongside the road. The Franklin bounced and swerved as it came to its resting place. Lola, in her fury, threw the car keys out onto the highway and jumped out of the car. All but wrenching the back door off its hinges, she got it open and began clawing through the smoke and grabbing at the girls.

"Give me those cigarettes this instant!" she commanded. "You can't fool me. LaVerne Hudson I thought the front of your dress looked mighty busty to me tonight. You had those cigarettes hidden in your bosom."

"Ohhhhhhhhhh Mabel...... I am so disappointed in you. And you with your God-given gift of drawing and painting." LaVerne wasn't making any sense at all, but it was hard to hear her with her head in her lap and the sounds coming out all muffled through the layers of flowered voile.

"Give me those cigarettes, young ladies, this very instant! There I've got the dastardly vile things and this is what I think of them. "Lola threw the pack out onto the highway.

Motorists were slowing down and trying to decide if they should be of assistance. Just what was going on and just what they should do to BE of assistance, they weren't sure, so they slowly drove on.

"After alllllll I've done and sacrificed! For you! And this is the thanks I get?" LaVerne was now lowering her forehead to the dashboard.

"Stop your crying, LaVerne. I've taken care of the situation, believe you me." Lola thundered as she felt the other two bosoms for contraband. Not finding any more cigarettes, she rescued her car keys from the highway and, blowing her horn, she started the car and jerked it out onto the highway.

Harold was trying very hard not to laugh. It was hard to keep his shoulders still between the two mothers. LaVerne dabbed her eyes with her handkerchief and shook her head slowly from side to side.

The three girls on the back seat were shaken and disheveled They straightened their dresses and withdrew their compacts to touch up their makeup. Mabel was very pale and her hands shook as she smoothed her hair down. It had real reason to stand on end. "I'll bet it looks just like Little Orphan Annie's," she thought as she patted it in place.

La nudged Hy and showed her one lone cigarette that had rolled under the seat when Lola had thrown the pack out onto the highway. Hy shook her head and mouthed, "Save it."

"This is the auditorium turn-off, Aunt Lola," Harold directed, glad to break the silence.

Lola gripped the wheel tightly and cut the car abruptly in front of a police car.

"Rrrrrrrrrrrr," the police siren sounded as their cruiser shot after the Franklin.

"Pull over lady."

"How dare you to address me like this," Lola said haughtily when she had stopped the car. "Just what, may I ask do you want?"

"I'm giving you a ticket for failing to signal, yield the right of way and exceeding the speed limit." the officer answered as he wrote out the ticket and tore it off his book and handed it into the window to the pigskin gloves.

"Well, of all the nerve. I spend time and money in this city every summer and THIS is the thanks I get? I will not be insulted this way. Good evening, officer." Lola tore the ticket to bits, threw the pieces in the officer startled face and drove into the parking lot of the auditorium.

---------------- ❧ ❧ ----------------

Claude had a fine fire going. Across the river, the children were sitting on the little sandy beach and were attempting to make their own small fire burn brighter. They were more interested in watching Claude cut capers in front of his bonfire. He turned a few cartwheels and did a fast-Indian dance in front of the flames for their amusement.

After a while, he grew restless and wandered into the front yard. With his hands in his pockets, he strolled over to the parked cars and inspected them.

"Beck," he called softly, "whose car is this? It has a flat tire."

"That's Dr. Taylor's car, Claude," she called back.

Turning to her mother, she continued, "That Claude is the most thoughtful person. Just imagine him taking up all that time with the children and spending the night out over there with them."

"Yes, Beck, Claude always seems to be thinking of others."

"Pardon me, doctor, but would you come out here a minute? It looks like you have a flat tire." Claude called over to where the Taylors were rocking.

"Dog-gone it, man, that was a brand-new tire," Dr. Taylor joined Claude at the rear of his car.

"It looks like you might have run over a nail. Would you like for me to take your tire off? I could do it easily and then I could take it over to Red's Service Station….. It's just around the bend. Bet they could fix it tonight and your car would be ready for you in the morning."

"That would be wonderful. Mrs. Taylor and I just might want to take a little drive tomorrow and it would be a convenience if I could get the tire fixed tonight."

"Just a minute, doctor, time for me to make another smoke signal to the kids. Come on over and see my bonfire."

Dr Taylor shaded his eyes from the bright fire and looked out across the river. He could easily make out the children sitting on their haunches around their little fire and looking toward them.

"Those children certainly do love you, Mr. Blanks. You have a real way with children," Dr. Taylor complimented.

"Call me Claude, sir. Yes, we have a high old time together. Look out, doc, I'm going to do a stunt they'll like."

Claude turned another cartwheel and then walked on his hands. The sound of applause came back from across the river.

It didn't take Claude and Dr. Taylor long to jack up the car and remove the tire. Claude adjusted his tie and called over to Beck, "I'm going back across the pipe and check on the children and then I'll walk over to Red's and leave Dr. Taylor's tire." Claude left.

The Carolina moon rose higher in the sky over Ole Hickory and the cedar trees cast their shadows across the front lawn of Riverby. Only the sound of soft voices engaged in conversation could be heard on the porch. Across the river, all was quiet.

One by one, the guests rose from their rockers and went to bed. The Taylors finally decided to call it a day and they headed for the front door, "Goodnight, Mrs. Fields and Mrs. Blanks. We have enjoyed another wonderful day in your home. Claude was so nice to attend to our tire."

"Sleep well. Don't forget to say your prayers," Mam-maw laughed, but with real sincerity.

"Well, Mama, I guess they've all gone to bed. Just the two of us are left holding down the fort. I wonder where Claude is. He should have been back by now."

"Why, you know he's going to spend the night over on the island with the children. Isn't he just wonderful, Beck? Going to all the trouble about the tire and sleeping out with the children. There's a lot of Grandfather Hopper in Claude……. doing good deeds and thinking of others."

Grandfather Hopper hung on the wall in the hallway and faced the room that bore his name. The room was furnished with an antique oak bed that had been in his home. His straight-backed chair was placed near the window. Grandfather Hopper had been dead for many years but his presence was felt in the daily lives of the family at Riverby. A large portrait of the old gentleman hung in the hallway. His frame was ornate and heavy and it needed the heavy molding to hang from.

Grandfather Hopper was Mam-maw's grandfather on her mother's side and obviously had never had a happy day in his life. The artist had painted him in somber tones of browns and blacks and tans. His heavy tan hair was parted in the middle and combed straight down on both sides. His piercing black eyes looked out from under bushy eyebrows with distaste at his future generations. The black beard was spade shaped and coarse and straight and accented the thin-lipped mouth. John Calvin could rest quietly in his grave knowing the likes of Grandfather Hopper were guarding the flocks of Presbyterians under his care.

Mam-maw treasured grandfather Hopper and proudly showed him off to the guests. As he stared with unfriendly eyes at the bewildered person hearing his history, that person would find himself diverting his eyes as if he had just been found out about some forgotten past sin.

"You see, he was Scotch-Irish and a learned man for his time, Mam-maw would begin her sermon. Through his valiant efforts he received a fine education and was destined, he thought, to teach in a college. But the Lord works in mysterious ways, and when the Lord appeared to Grandfather Hopper in a dream one night and told him to guide and direct His flocks, Grandfather turned his back on the profession of his choice and joined the ministry. We are hoping someday one of our grandchildren will become a Presbyterian minister also and take up the guiding of the flocks just like my Grandfather did.

The grandchildren, hearing this, would look from one to the other and say, "Not me".

"What about you, Lee? You have sorta beady eyes."

Then they would laugh and dart away from Leon's fast fist. Running up and down the hallway upstairs, the children would unconsciously slow down and walk with quick strides past the portrait and escape down the stairs knowing Grandfather Hopper's eyes were boring into their shoulder blades.

"Yes, Mama, Grandfather Hopper was a wonderful Christian. Claude is like him in many ways. Oh look! There's a car turning in. Do you suppose that's Red bringing back the Taylor's tire?"

"No, it must be guests."

"How could it be guests? It has Buncombe County license tags on it."

"There's a lovely looking couple in the front seat."

"Thank goodness, they don't have any children with them."

——————————— ɚ ᝡ ———————————

"Good evening, I'm Mrs. Blanks. Would you like a room for the night?"

"Never mind, Mama, I'll take care of them," said Beck as she stiff-armed her way with the guests past Mam-maw. "Sign here, please."

Grandfather Hopper looked with disdain at the middle-aged couple disappearing with Beck inside the grandfather Hopper room.

"This is the only room that is unoccupied just now." Even though the season's just starting we have rented out so many of our rooms that right now don't have a choice to show you. But the room is freshly done and there a lovely breeze through here." Beck was sure she had sold them the room.

"This will be fine for my wife and myself, the man said." My wife and I won't want breakfast in the morning. We will get up early and get a good start on continuing our trip. Let me pay you now for the room." The man handed Beck some bills and bowed her out of the bedroom and closed the door and slid the bolt.

"Rebekah, I just knew they'd take the room," Mam-maw said when Beck returned to the porch. "When I saw that black Ford turn in and stop, I said, "Jeffie, here comes some money. They gave you three dollars? That's a dollar too much. You'd better go back and give him back that dollar."

"I told him it was only two dollars but he insisted on giving me three. They must have money. They're tired from their long trip today and won't stay for breakfast in the morning. As a matter of fact, they didn't even bother to unpack their luggage. She only had a little bundle of things in her hand. Guess they just want to fall right into bed."

When Beck and Mam-maw went to bed and turned down the lights, Grandfather Hopper, by the dim light of the hallway glared straight ahead with dissatisfaction at the closed bedroom door across from him.

——————————— ɚ ᝡ ———————————

"Most unsuitable, Lola. Most unsuitable story I've heard of to take young people to." LaVerne was sitting on the back seat between Mabel and Hy. La and Harold, Jr. sat in the front seat with Lola on the way home.

"I thought we'd hear some lovely Strauss waltzes and it would be like the Student Prince, but no! Those South Americans sang those songs in a foreign tongue and that girl worked in a cigarette factory. Those Catholics will do anything! I am surprised at you, Lola! Just surprised that you would take our young people, and with that experience we had with them tonight, to an opera about Cigarette smoking." LaVerne started crying again.

"Spanish, mother. It took place in Spain. Seville, Spain. The costumes and sets were very well done, I thought," Mabel said.

"They had lovely voices," Lola remarked trying to forget about the cigarettes. Grand Opera is very trying to the vocal cords but those singers were in fine voice."

"I've never been so bored in all my life," said lovely La as she crossed her shapely legs and kicked her foot. She was thinking about the lone cigarette she had hidden under the back seat.

"Well, I loved it," Hy stated. "First time I've ever been to the opera and I didn't want to go but loved every minute of the whole thing. I'm looking forward to "Tales of Hoffman" in July. What I didn't like was Harold Jr. making those remarks about Don Jose and his skinny legs in that costume. I was frankly embarrassed when the usher asked him to stop laughing or step outside."

"I just said he looked like a balloon on tooth picks," said Harold and started laughing again.

———————— ❧ ❧ ————————

At 4:30 the next morning, Riverby was asleep. All but Grandy. He had been up for half an hour. He had dressed and gone down to check over his garden. It was pitch black dark but he could make out the rows of corn and tomatoes and watermelons by the light of the setting moon. Stirred by a hungry rumbling in his stomach, he returned to the old kitchen and stirred up the embers in the stove and shoved the pot of left-over coffee over the burner. In the tall old-fashioned kitchen cupboard, which was called a 'safe' he brought out half of a left offer dewberry pie and some cold biscuits.

The coffee was boiling hot and was strong enough to walk as he poured it in his favorite old cracked cup. Slopping some out into the saucer to blow and cool a little, he spilled a portion onto the oil cloth of the kitchen table. He ate his pie and then turned to the biscuits for dessert. He sliced them open and buttered them with thick slabs of Miss Lou's butter and up-ended the molasses pitcher over all. The sorghum poured slowly in the mountain air coolness. Grandy enjoyed his breakfast immensely. He slurped, he slopped, he burped and sucked. When his plate was cleaned, he pushed back his chair with such force it turned over with a clatter.

He made his way into the dining room and out into the hallway and headed for the upstairs.

"Got to get Verne up. Women folk'll sleep all day if tweren't for me to rouse 'em on their feet."

But LaVerne wasn't sleeping in the room Grandy was headed for. When the opera goers had returned home the night before, Beck had left a note tacked to the newel post that the Grandfather Hopper room had been taken for the night.

LaVerne ushered Mabel out onto the sleeping porch and they had slept in the green painted iron bed in the corner.

Down in her cottage, Lola bade her girls goodnight with a dressing down.

"I was mortified to think you girls would take up smoking those silly cigarettes. Don't ever let me catch you smoking again."

Under her breath, La whispered to Hy, "I plan to make sure she doesn't catch me." She tightened her fingers around the cigarette in her hand.

On the porch LaVerne whispered brokenly to Mabel on the evils of smoking and of how very disappointed she had been in her. Letting her voice crack and sniffing quite a bit, she was certain Mabel knew she was crying again. Mabel was very, very sorry she had brought down disgrace on the family and she told her mother how sad she was she had made her so miserable. Finally, they had both fallen asleep from emotion and exhaustion.

───────────── ঌ ঙ ─────────────

In the Grandfather Hopper room, the middle-aged couple were talking in low voices as the sun began to glow behind the mountain range.

The only thing pretty about the woman was her name Charmaine. She was 43 years old and an old maid. She worked in Asheville in the Buncombe County Court House as a clerk. When Vernon Ashley had come in to get a document notarized and she had been of such help to him, in a gesture of appreciation he had taken Charmaine out to lunch. Their friendship had begun.

"And now look where I am," she cried softly to Vernon.

Vernon was tired from the whole mess. As he lay next to Charmaine and patted her forehead, he couldn't for the life of him remember how he had gotten so involved with this woman. He had told her right off the bat he was married and yet she had kept after him. He had been more than a little peeved with his wife because she had taken the kids and gone for a month to nurse her sick mother in Winston-Salem and he kind of liked the attention Charmaine had shown him.

He had timidly suggested this night together and she had immediately run to her room and gathered up some things in a small bundle and beat him out to the car.

Charmaine thought the whole thing a gay and mad adventure and never mind the consequences but when they so easily had gotten the room with no questions asked, she became uneasy. Every time she thought of that Mrs. Fields with her beautiful engagement ring AND wedding ring on and the way that fat little grandmother had smiled and welcomed them, she felt a terrible twinge.

Once in the room, she had carefully removed her clothes, all but her slip, and crept between the sheets. Vernon said to himself, "What the heck?" and stripped down to the nude and jumped into bed. Charmaine was aghast. She was terrified. Every time Vernon tried to touch her, she cried all the harder and had moved over so far on the bed she was ready to fall off. After several clumsy lunges, Vernon grew tired of the game and his fifty-year-old body went to sleep.

Charmaine continued to stay awake and alert for fear Vernon would take advantage of her if she dozed off for even one split second. Now at four thirty in the morning, she was exhausted and her crying had awakened Vernon. He tried to quiet her and reassure her that nothing would happen to her.

Suddenly they heard heavy foot-steps approaching. Up the stairs they came, hesitated for a moment at the top of the steps and continued their measured tread to the door of their room. With a gasp and a hiccough Charmaine stopped her crying and Vernon grabbed for his B. V. D.'s.

"It's my wife," Vernon hissed, "I'd know her foot-steps anywhere."

At this moment, there was loud rapping at the door. A man's muffled voice said, "Verne! Verne! Git up, git up. No time sleeping. I like a GO GETTER! Git…Git."

LaVerne, out on the sleeping porch, sighed in her sleep and changed potions.

Vernon was struck dumb. That man knows my name! It must the sheriff. Lord have mercy, Catherine has sick'd the Law on me. He was having a terrible time trying to get into his pants. Somehow, he had gotten both legs into the same trouser leg and he was as hobbled as a roped calf.

When Charmaine heard the man say, "Go get her", her heart had actually stopped beating. She could already see the headlines in tomorrow's Asheville Citizen ....... LOVERS ROUTED OUT OF LOVE NEST OF RESORT HOTEL. She could just see her name and Vernon's in large letters underneath the photograph of them being driven out of the house by the police and with that sweet little grandmother shaking her head in the background. Charmaine had her skirt on up-side down and her blouse on backwards. Vernon had finally gotten his legs straightened out and in the right trouser legs but his fly was left gaping open.

While Vernon buttoned up his vest, he saw Charmaine was trying to spread up the bed. Her only thought was to make the room look normal and unlived in. If the police broke down the door, she and Vernon could just be sitting there calmly and talking. Vernon, thought to himself that Charmaine had fooled him. She knew all the tricks of covering up her immoral acts. Why that little skinny so and so, sorry I didn't just go ahead and take her right off the bat. No, I'm not sorry...... I have a clear conscience and Catherine can't divorce me if I have a clear conscience.

Grandfather Hopper's eyes seemed to soften in the dawn light at the sight of Grandy banging on the door to get the household up.

As soon as Grandy heard moving around in the room, he realized his shouting and banging had done the trick and he gave one last shout of "Time's a-wastin'" and descended the stairs.

Vernon dared to creep to the door and listen after he heard the last shout. When he heard the man's foot-steps disappearing, he hissed to Charmaine they had better make a break for it. She hastily gathered up her comb and brush and make-up and Amour Delight perfume in the little bundle and they bolted from the room and hurried down the front stairway. Afraid the sheriff might be laying for them on the first floor, they had a little trouble getting through the front door as they both ran through at the same time.

Since time had been of the essence, neither Vernon nor Charmaine had put on their shoes and they let out groans and grunts as they ran over the cinder driveway to jump into the black Ford. Leaning back and forth, back and forth on the front seat, Charmaine tried to make the car move faster with her body motion. Vernon let out the clutch and released the emergency brake at the same moment and the double action propelled the Ford forward with a giant lunge.

"We've got a head start on 'em, girl." Vernon shouted to Charmaine who was sitting right next to him with her head in her lap. She was still waiting for the newspaper photographer to snap their pictures. Vernon careened the car onto the highway and turned off onto a back road up near Oteen. He drove thirteen miles out of his way going back into Asheville, by using short cuts and back roads to elude the police he just knew were pursuing them.

On the out skirts of Asheville, Charmaine told Vernon "Goodbye forever. I never want to see you again. I plan to take the bus on home."

Vernon was terribly relieved. "Here Charmaine, you'll need some bus fare," he said thoughtfully and reached in his pocket and pulled out some money and pressed it into her hand. Charmaine felt like a very Bad Girl when she realized he had given her two dollars.

———————— ❧ ❦ ————————

LaVerne didn't get up as usual. She had a sick headache and a stiff neck. Mabel fixed a nice tray for her mother and soberly took it up to the sleeping porch.

"Thank you, dear," LaVerne said softly, "I'm just so spent out, I'll have to stay in bed, Breakfast? Dear me, let me see if I can choke something down." She stirred her coffee idly. When Mabel went sorrowfully down stairs, LaVerne plumped up her pillow, sat up in bed and ate everything on the tray.

"I must keep up my strength."

In the kitchen, Mam-Maw was helping Delilah with breakfast.

"It looks like everything's going well, Delilah, I'd better call to Mr. Claude to bring the children on back." Mam-maw went out the back door and to the edge of the flagstone steps that led down to the river. She rang the big brass bell loudly

"Yooooo----hooooooo, Claude! Bring the children. Oh, here you come." Mam-maw watched the children straggling across the pipe. "Bill your blanket is in the river. Jaybo! Hold on to Sonny. Walk the pipe carefully! Where is your Uncle Claude?"

Sis was the first to reach her grandmother waiting at the top of the steps.

"We don't know. He must have gotten scared. Leon was making scary noises and maybe he frightened him. I bet he's sleeping in a soft bed upstairs. Let's go find him, gang." Sis turned to the others who had joined her. Mam-maw looked quickly at Charles and Leon. They passed questioning looks.

"Oh, Sis, er…. not now. You children come on and get your breakfast. It's all ready. Delilah has made her good flannel pancakes and sausage, Mam-maw held open the porch door and was thankful to see that even at that moment Mose was bringing out platters of hot food. The gang took their seats and began to eat.

Charles and Leon had begun their search. Charles checked the Tearoom and Leon scoured all around the house. Both boys made a search of the parlor and the dining room, knowing full well they would not find their father.

LaVerne came down from the sleeping porch and greeted the children. She was reassured by Delilah that breakfast was going well so she strolled into the dining room and went from table to table saying "Good morning" to the guests.

"Good morning, Mrs. Hedges," greeted the Taylors.

"We want to hear about the opera, but first, I'd like to ask if the service station returned my tire?"

"Tire? I don't know anything about it but I'll ask Leon. Well good morning Beck, you're about as much a sleepy head as I've been this morning." Beck was stifling a yawn as she came into the dining room. Mam-maw was at that moment coming into the room with a pot of coffee.

"Mama, thank you for seeing to breakfast for me. I just can't keep late hours. Oh, Leon! There you are. Dr. Taylor wants to know if his tire has been returned."

"I don't think so, Aunt Boom, his car is still jacked up out front."

Mam-maw and Beck exchanged distressed looks. Leon immediately grasped the situation. He approached the Taylors table.

"Dr. Taylor, I will check on the tire at Red's Station just as soon as breakfast is over. It won't take but a minute and I'll be glad to do it."

"Why, thank you, son. No real hurry. Where is Mrs. Hedges? We want to hear about the opera."

Mam-maw, Beck and LaVerne had just gone quietly into Mam-maw's room and closed the door, Mam-maw and LaVerne sank down on the bed. Beck went to the side door and called to Bill, eating on the back porch.

"Bill, run down to the cottage and tell Aunt Lola to come up here right away. We need her this minute."

Leon entered Mam-maw's room and stood quietly staring out of the window.

Lola entered by the side door. "I was on my way up here for breakfast. What's going on? Can't I have my coffee before getting into a family wrangle?"

"It's Claude," Beck exploded. "That good for nothing has taken Dr. Taylor's tire! He told Mama and myself last night that he'd attend to getting it fixed. And now no tire!"

"He's just like a child. So irresponsible," Mam-maw pulled her black shawl around her shoulders.

Leon tells me that Claude never came back to the island last night. He left those children over there all alone. I could shake him good," LaVerne's voice was shaking.

"Claude has always been untrustworthy. I'm just mad at myself for being taken in again by him. And now this. A stolen tire from one of the guests. It's the last straw, I'll tell YOU," Lola began to put on her driving gloves as she scolded.

"Come on Leon, let's drive up to Red's and check on the tire."

"It won't be there, Aunt Lola. But I know of a man in Black Mountain who is a fence and, well, I happen to know Daddy has done business with this man before. I have a hunch that's where we'll find the tire." Leon led the way for his Aunt Lola out to her Franklin.

Girls, talk to me about something. I can't bear to think about Claude just now," Mam-maw lay back on her bed next to LaVerne and pulled the black shawl across her eyes.

"Go on, Sister, tell us about the opera last night," Beck spoke up quickly.

"I'm sorry to report it was about cigarette smoking and love affairs." LaVerne's distress was so plain that Mam-maw comforted her daughter by patting her hand.

"Those things on the stage aren't true to life. You know we don't have cigarette smoking and love affairs going on under our roof."

———————— ❧ ❧ ————————

*"It looks so dainty......so tempting*
*So fit for the taste of a queen,*
*Such epicurean colors,*
*Such garnishing's of green.*
*Such art! But I turn from it bravely.*
*I dare not do more than look;*
*For I know, were I but to taste it,*
*I would fall in love with the cook.*

Dr Taylor finished his poem and sat grinning at
LaVerne who stood by his plate with her big bowl of salad.

"Why Dr. Taylor, I'll declare you're going to make me blush and right in front of your wife, too!"

"Mrs. Hedges, I insist you sit down here at our table and tell me what all you put in your salad bowl. This is a whole lunch by itself," Beth Taylor pulled out a chair and motioned for LaVerne to sit down.

"I like to go to the garden early and get one of Grandy's green pebbly cabbages and then I gather the other vegetables for the salad. I scoop out the center of the cabbage and set it to one side to chill. Then I chop up the middle part of the cabbage along with tender yellow neck squash, cucumbers, tomatoes, radishes, green onions oh, I don't know, just anything that is tender and bright. This is added to the cabbage 'bowl' and tossed with an oil and vinegar dressing."

"Excuse me. I'm going to go to my room and write this all down before I forget it," Beth Taylor excused herself.

Left alone with Dr. Taylor, LaVerne blurted out an apology, "I'm so sorry about your tire, Dr. Taylor. Claude was very wicked to mislead you the way he did. I'm sure his heart was in the right place at first but he is most irresponsible we're all terribly sorry."

"No harm done, Mrs. Hedges. Leon brought the tire back from Black Mountain and put it back on himself. He's a fine young lad, and Charles, too. Certainly, don't hold you ladies responsible for what your brother did."

"Thank you for your kind understanding. Claude has always been a trial to the family. He has hurt my mother so deeply. As a matter of fact, Mama has made me promise that I'll always see to Claude. It is her deepest desire and I'll never betray her faith but he makes it so difficult for me and for us all."

"My dear woman, you have your work cut out for you. May the good Lord be with you."

———————— ❧ ❧ ————————

Hy and La and Mabel marched right up to their mothers begging them for one more chance.

"We've told you we were sorry to disgrace the whole family by smoking," they pleaded. "We think we've been punished enough. After all, we're practically GROWN. You've been treating us like babies."

"When we caught you puffing on those silly cigarettes, we TOLD you that you couldn't leave the hill for a week. It's your own fault for even trying such a fool thing." Lola was adamant.

"Mabel, you know how disappointed I was in you," her mother sadly shook her head. LaVerne didn't think she'd ever get over the terrible shock.

"We're not asking for the moon," Hy said. "Just let us walk to the village and get the afternoon mail."

"Sorry! We can't trust you by yourselves. So don't keep nagging." Lola wasn't giving an inch.

"we'll just rot. Dry up and blow away and nobody will ever know what happened to us," La entreated.

"You should have thought of that in the first place," Lola replied. "You'll certainly dry up and blow away if you keep on smoking those cigarettes," She twisted out the last word.

"If we have a chaperone, can we go?" La had an inspiration. "Aunt Beck said she was thinking about taking a walk. Surely, if your own sister goes with us, you'd let us go."

"I'll take them under my wing. I want to walk some before suppertime, anyway, to see if I can walk off all the calories in Delilah's strawberry shortcake," Beck patted her heavy thighs.

"I'll trust Mabel with Beck," LaVerne decided.

With that, Lola decided she might just as well give in, too, so with a whoop and a squeal, the girls ran upstairs to comb their hair and apply fresh Tangee lipstick.

"Oh, I can just feel those pounds melting away on my legs," Beck declared as they walked down Lover's Lane to the village.

"I know something better than walking to take-off weight," Hy laughed.

"I do diet all I can," Beck complained, "but my metabolism is off and even if I eat a soda cracker it ends up on my hips."

"I've got something right here that will make you lose pounds and pounds," said La as she pulled out a pack of cigarettes from her bra.

"Why............! I'm speechless! Hy, La, Mabes! I'm horrified and surprised at you for thinking you could smoke in front of me. How dare you? I will not betray my sisters' trust like this. Give me those cigarettes this instant. There, now, I'm going to throw them in the river. Oh, I'm surprised at you. Mabel, stop your crying. I'm not going to tell on any of you. It would break my sisters' hearts if they knew what ingrates you all are. Don't you EVER try such a thing again.

"I'd rather weigh five hundred pounds than lose weight by smoking."

"I can see that," whispered La to Hy as Beck waddled on ahead of them muttering to herself.

# Chapter 11

# A Full House

As usual, there was a chill to the morning air as the children gathered on the back porch for breakfast. They wore heavy sweaters over their Anvil Brand overalls and the hot bowls of Riverby Inn cereal tasted good and warm to their hungry stomachs as they fortified themselves for the work of the day. They were going to dam up the stream that fed into the Swannanoa River and make a swimming hole.

Lola appeared on the porch and yodeled for attention. "Work before play. You know there are many chores to do before you can run off and get in that river.

"I want Hy, Mabes and La to get started on the rooms immediately. There will be NO further pie beds made for the summer! Is that clear, girls? You are much too old for that kind of foolishness and since I am the complaint department, I don't want to have to make any more apologies. It's a wonder someone didn't get a broken leg last night trying to get into bed. And worst of all, most of our sheets are old and someone could tear them."

The older girls giggled and stole glances at each other as they remembered the oaths and mutterings of last night's bedtime.

"Now, you older boys are to clean up the yard. Pick up the papers, mow the grass and clean out the fish pond. There will not be any more paper boat regattas on the fish pond

"Martha Lee and Betty, I want you to go back up on the mountain and get more wild flowers.

"Sonny and Bill sweep the porch. Sis, you stay here and help snap beans for Delilah. Bobbie, your department is the front part of the house. Clean the parlor rooms and the hallway.

"Everybody better stay out of my way. I do a good and thorough job when I dust and polish and I don't want anybody messing it up." Bobbie warned as she went to get her broom and furniture polish.

———— *❧ ❧* ————

Deep in the heart of Ole Hickory, cold streams formed. At one particular place in the midst of towering laurel bushes, they gushed to the surface and spilled down the side of the mountain. The water was pure and crystalline clear as it gurgled along its course down the bed of dull gray sand, speckled with pebbles and bits of mica, 'fool's gold', and joined the mother water of the Swannanoa River.

Between the little bridge of Lover's Lane and the river lay the area to be dammed.

The construction of the dam took real manual labor. It had to be built on a foundation of large rocks, held together with gummy clay from the river bank and lathed with sticks and branches of leaves against all possible seepage of water. The older boys carried large stones from the river and the girls hauled clay and moss and small branches and twigs and the construction began.

Sweaters had long been shed and overall trousers had been rolled up above the knees and the children were covered with mud and clay. Before Ernest rang the big brass dinner bell for the noon meal, he came grinning down the hill to report that the children would be served lunch right at the dam site.

The older children formed a procession and carried trays of food down to the branch and left word that under no circumstances were the Trundle Bed Trash to come up to the house tracking mud.

Sitting around the big flat boulder that served for a table, they ate their cornbread and squash and black-eyed peas while the water behind the dam rose higher and higher.

Early in the afternoon, the water was deep enough to swim in. The first private swimming pool of the summer had been completed.

Out of sight of the stream, the swimmers and the divers and behind a small white Pine tree, Aubrey was well hidden. He pressed his thin body flat against the crinkly bark trunk and his hands clutched a low hanging limb. He had been hiding there for almost an hour and from time to time when he would see an especially daring feat performed from the rude diving board, his hands became clinched even more tightly around the limb.

Aubrey had arrived at Riverby two days before with his widowed mother. He was eleven years old and small for his age. Really quite a handsome lad in a quaint poetic way.

He had dark brown hair and alabaster skin. Large brown eyes peered through long lashes. When he had first arrived, shortly before supper, he was taken back by all the children he saw. His mother placed her arm around his shoulder and discretely drew him away from the boisterous gang that had just come trudging across the lawn from an afternoon on Little Hickory and The Ridge. Sonny and Bill were bombarding each other with small green crab apples. Old Queen sedately strolled alongside the children and one of the boarder girls was bringing up the rear and luring a stray cat along by dropping the remnants of her meat loaf sandwich. Some of the girls had bouquets of mountain flowers that were long overdue for a drink of water.

Aubrey was excited beyond words to see this menagerie struggling across the lower yard. If only his mother would let him go barefooted and get his Best and Co. shorts and shirts dirty and worn and torn! But he did a strange thing. As the parade of children went past the porch and he felt the pressure of his mother's arm on his shoulder, he said in a loud, high voice, "Well, look at the dirty peasants!" He then quickly turned on his heel and retreated into the front parlor.

By these words, Aubrey had ostracized himself from the comradery of the Riverby children. Aubrey longed to swim with the children but he stayed hidden.

"I'll get even with them."

"Mrs. Hedges, are you going to permit your daughter to talk to me like this?" Mr. Bouquet was looking at LaVerne but pointing at Bobbie.

"Mother, I have just finished cleaning up all these rooms. I have slaved and slaved and mopped and waxed and just as I was backing out of the room mopping behind me, in cones Mr. Bouquet through the other door with his hiking boots on and those old fossils and he plopped them all down on MY clean floor."

"These are not fossils, young lady. They are artifacts. Science may very well be interested in what I have discovered. I intend to take these 'fossils' as you call them and sort them out and catalogue them and take them back to a friend of mine who is a geologist. I may even present them to a museum someday."

"I'm sorry if Bobbie has offended you, sir, but she has worked hard to have the parlor neat and tidy. Why don't you take these, er, things out to the Tearoom? It's empty and you could use that place to clean them up. Let me help you gather them together. "

"Clean them up? Madam, you don't understand. These must be kept in their original condition but I'll move them, I'll move them, this Bobbie might sweep them into her trash."

Muttering under his breath, Andre Bouquet collected his treasures and left the room.

"All my efforts have gone to waste," walled Bobbie.

"Now dear, don't take on so. See I'm smoothing out the sofa pillows. There, isn't that better? Just like it was before. You've worked so hard and everything is lovely, just lovely. Why don't you go take a sun bath? Grandy is down in the garden and he won't see you. Put some shorts on and slip down to the river by the pipe and relax on the big rocks. The sun will do you good," LaVerne placated.

Back again on the back porch, LaVerne rejoined Lola and Rebekah in snapping the beans Sis had started that morning.

Lola looked up at her sister's long drawn out sigh as she continued with her snapping.

"Isn't it funny that we haven't heard a word from the Thompson's. I know that Tommy wouldn't miss a summer at Riverby unless something dreadful had happened. I wonder what's wrong?"

"Don't go putting the poor mouth on that sweet family," LaVerne sighed. "Mary Ann has just probably had one of her spells, crying and all that. Tommy is probably waiting for her to sweeten up before making the long drive."

"I know if I was Tommy Thompson, I'd march her straight up to Mayos and have her checked over from head to toe. It's not right for those two children to have her moaning around all the time, Melancholia indeed! She's just plain lazy." Beck put in her two cents worth.

"Better send Martha and Betts after more flowers. I'm running low on daisies," Lola observed.

"Never mind worrying about flowers now, Lola, let's just get these beans snapped. I have one of my feelings about the Hailes. Something tells me they'll be pulling in today. Their rooms are all ready and I've put their names in the pot for supper."

A loud, wailing scream penetrated the semi-quietness of the hillside. The three mothers jumped to their feet wondering which of their children had been drowned in the river. LaVerne, allergic to sudden unpredictable noises, lurched off the bench toward the door. The snapped beans popped and cracked as they spilled to the floor. Beck and Lola slipped and squished through them in wild pursuit of the continuing wail.

Bobbie appeared at the top of the flagstone steps from the river clad in halter and shorts and bare feet. She collapsed in her mother arms and sobbed out her story.

"My good shoes, my good shoes…. washed away in the current. Oh mother, I'm soooo sorry I wore my good shoes to the river. I just wanted to protect my toe polish from the cinders. Oh, they cost you so much money and now they are gone! I don't know how it happened. I must have rolled over on the part of the rock where had carefully placed them and knocked them in the river. Kill me! Please go ahead and kill me. I deserve it. They're gone." The last word was a choked sob.

LaVerne and Bobbie clutched each other and swayed down in a heap on the steps moaning in anguish over the loss.

Lola broke the death knell, "Lordy, Lordy. Sarah Bernhardt and Zazu Pitts couldn't have put on a better show."

Grandy appeared with the Asheville Citizen rolled up under his arm.

"Verne! Verne! Get up you lazy girl and git in that kitchen. I'm goin' to be a-wantin' my dinner. What you gals mean lolly-gagging around the kitchen door when you got work to do? Bobbie! What you got on? You are indecent in them underclothes. Git in that house and cover your body." The rolled-up newspaper hit its mark on the backside of the shorts, Bobbie took up her screaming and ran up the back steps.

Mam-maw stood huffing and puffing studying the situation for clues as to the commotion and the whole gang arrived from the river, dripping puddles into the soft dust and all asking questions in one breath.

Tooooooooooooot....... toooooooooooot! A car horn down on the highway interrupted the drama by the kitchen porch. Suddenly everyone stopped talking and there was for a split-second complete silence.

"Hail! Hail! The gangs all here!" came a chorus of female voices up the front drive. The chorus repeated itself.

"The Hailes are here! The Hailes just came up the driveway," chorused the children standing like wet puppies on the steps. A whoop went up from the family group by the kitchen. They all joined hands and walked toward the front of the house singing in answer, "Hail! Hail! The Blanks gang is here! "

Mr. Haile behind the wheel, Mrs. Haile at his side and their five black haired girl moppets screamed out the back windows, "Haile! Haile!"

"Last one in the river's a rotten egg."

Shoes off, their bathing suits on under their dresses they made a dash for the river as they tumbled over each other out of the car.

"Hey Jean, you lost your front teeth," Sis said with envy to the youngest Haile.

"Leon do I look ugly in these braces?" The willowy Janet asked her counterpart in age.

The girls eagerly renewed their friendships with the Blanks children.

Mrs. Haile turned to Beck. "I can't wait to show you the new crochet pattern, the nuns at the convent showed me. Remember when you were down in New Orleans in the fall and we visited the convent to buy some lace? Well, I went back several times to learn to tat, but I just couldn't do it…. puts your eyes out…. but I got a new crochet pattern anyway."

Lola interrupted the reunion by saying," we've given you the big double rooms at the end of the hall. You know, the calico rooms that look out over the highway toward Alexander's mountain?"

Aubrey had the swimming hole to himself. He paddled around and around playing like he was swimming. He jumped-off the diving board and then he methodically kicked at the dam until a large chunk of mud and moss collapsed and the flow of backed-up water went hurtling through the opening carrying bits of the dam into the river. He watched quietly as more and more of the dam gave way. It took less than fifteen minutes for the stream to become once again shallow and clear.

Aubrey skipped and sang as he made his way up the cinder path to his mother.

After supper, Aubrey rocked on the porch with the grown-ups. In the yard, the children held a pow-wow.

"I vote we declare war on him," Bill argued.

"Yeah, I'll take him on. That coward. We KNOW he broke down the dam. All that hard work for nothing." Sonny rolled back his sleeves from his thin white arms.

"I never plan to speak to him, he's mean and spoiled," Martha said and Betty agreed to go along with the silent treatment.

"You're all wrong," Leon said as he lounged against the sycamore tree taking in the situation. "I think we should invite him on out here in the yard and play some games with him." The gang was about ready to jump on Leon and thump his head when they saw 'that look' in his twinkling blue eyes.

"Yeahhhhhhhhh, you're right!" They quickly jumped to the bait.

When they called to Aubrey to come play Crack the Whip with them, he mistrusted them and declined the invitation.

"Go on Aubrey," Mam-maw encouraged, "you'll have a lot of fun." Mam-maw knew the child longed to be part of the gang and that it would be good for this protected boy to engage in rough housing and get momentarily away from his mother.

Mrs. White made small cooing noises about how delicate he was and it had been a long day and, in a stage whisper behind her hand, that he was constipated. But Mam-maw heartily assured her that an evening on the lawn would cure her son of being delicate, tired and constipated.

By the time the whip chain had lined up, there were twenty youngsters in a row. Hands were tightly clasped and a thrill of expectation rippled down the chain. Bill stepped forward with a crooked smile, said, "Audrey we're going to let you be on the whip end. It's in honor of your first night in our games."

Martha Lee and Betty sent out a bleat of giggles that quickly ran up and down the line.

"My name is Aubrey, not Audrey," he shrieked," and you'd better give me the best place in line because your Mam-maw said so."

With a shout, Leon started the gang running. Faster, faster, faster, their bare feet raced over the grass and through the stray black-eyed Susan's that bloomed over the yard.

Suddenly Leon, the cracker, stopped short, dug his heels in the turf and began the pulling motion that would repeat itself along the children.......... gathering momentum until the end man flew off his feet and sailed through the air with arms and legs flailing.

It was no accident that Aubrey landed in one of Sally Kate's cow cakes. It had been almost dried out until a night shower had revitalized it.

Immediately laughter, whistling, screaming and cat calls echoed through the chill of the evening.

"Oh little Audrey, how's your constipation?"

"Gang, look at the dirty peasant."

Aubrey looked at his Best and Company shorts and ran to his mother.

Dr. Taylor turned to his wife and said softly, "I wouldn't have missed this 'cure' for anything in the world. Let's see if Aubrey rejoins them. Something very important is happening to that little boy and his mother doesn't even know it."

Charles began to count off the fists before him. "One potato, two potato, three potato, four; five potato, Oh hi Aubrey! Come on back and join the gang. We're getting ready to play Kick the Can."

Aubrey hung back for a moment and pressed his hands against the sides of his clean shorts. His mother was in the rear of the yard hanging out the hastily laundered soiled ones. His indecision was growing until Mam-maw called out, "Of course, he wants to play. Put out your potatoes, son, and go get counted off."

"………. seven potato more. O-U-T spells YOU." This continued until Jaybo was 'it'. He covered his eyes and counted to one hundred by fives.

The children scrambled for their favorite hiding places. By the time Jaybo was droning twen-ty five, thir-ty, thirty-five, for-ty, Aubrey was still standing by the tree unsure of which way to go.

Flat on his stomach under the big box bush by the end of the porch, Bill hissed loudly to attract Aubrey's attention and pointed to the tearoom.

"Sixty, sixty five, seventy….."

Aubrey was desperate and ran to the door of the Tearoom. He was a little anxious about this little house since he had heard a man say he was going to put his artifacts in it. Aubrey wasn't sure what artifacts were and he wondered if they would hurt him. What if those artifacts were still inside? At the sound of "Coming ready or not," Aubrey took a deep breath and eased himself inside the door.

Gosh it was dark! The moonlight shone through a window and Aubrey saw some furniture with sheets spread over them. Panic was rising in his throat until he heard a child shout, "Home free". He was determined to stick it out.

When Aubrey heard Jaybo's feet approaching the Tearoom he knelt behind the nearest sheet-draped chair and the chair moved! Another chair moved and the small table moved!

They not only moved but were surrounding him. He had never been so terrified in his life. He was ready to scream for his mother when he saw an inner tube sandal protruding from beneath a sheet. He mustered all his courage and yanked off first one sheet and then another until the chairs turned out to be members of the gang in sitting position with arms akimbo.

Aubrey was so relieved and weak from fright that at the sound of laughter from the furniture he guffawed and rolled on the floor. Kick the Can disbanded immediately and all the gang gathered in the Tearoom to hear the story.

"I thought you all were artifacts," Aubrey loved being the center of attention. He sat on the floor and took off his shoes and socks.

"If you really want to be one of us," Bill said, "Tomorrow I'll show you how to make some inner tube sandals."

"Yeah, and the next dam we build, you have to carry the big rocks," Sonny warned.

Aubrey grinned and ducked his head. He hoped they would stay there all summer.

# Chapter 12

# The Cornbread Express

On the broad front porch, the rocking chairs were moving in two-four time. They were heavily occupied at this hour of the day. It was in the hour before lunch. The family had done their morning chores. The guests had taken their daily constitutionals up the side of Old Hickory.

The mornings repose was interspersed with casual conversation of the day's events and of lazy chatter about what the day was yet to bring. Grandy, a full day's work already done in his garden, was stretched out on the long porch swing. The Asheville Citizen was spread over his face while he slept, nosily. Down in the broad Swannanoa River, the younger contingent took many last bumps down the slippery rapids, whetting already full-blown appetites.

Mam-maw occupied her usual chair, front door left. Her sun visor with its yellow green shade was pulled forward to cover her eyes from the noon-day sun. The rug she was braiding lay quietly on her lap. Her soft hands rested as she shared conversation with the rocker nearby.

Little Aubrey's mother, down the porch from Mam-maw, sat silently fidgeting. Her hands were nervous reminders of her constant anxiety. "Where was Aubrey?" they said. "Down the river with that rowdy bunch of children," her hands answered. "Maybe he'll slip on a rock and hurt himself," they argued. "He's too sensitive and fragile to play with those ruffians," they pleaded, pulling at a stray thread on her skirt. She began to chirp like a caged canary, not aware that her whining broke the silence.

"There now, Mrs. White, Aubrey is having a grand day in the river with the children." Mam-maw assured her. "I can hear him, listen! Can't you tell he's having such fun? He's really becoming one of the crowd with the children, isn't that nice?"

Mrs. White gulped down a large knot in her throat, making a hideous hiccup, and turned pink in Mam-maws all-knowing analogy.

Mr. Bouquet, the fat, repulsive old fuss-pot, approached the porch from the lawn and collapsed on the front steps. Wiping his wet brow, he mumbled, "My, it's a hot one today, must be gonna have another cloud burst after lunch." The rocking chairs came to a sudden stop as the occupants arched their backs at the incursion. Mr. Bouquet, the tolerated, sat misconstruing the charged atmosphere for attention. He greeted the clouds of chilly silence. "You'll never guess what I discovered on Old Hickory this morning." The bored shuffle of feet answered this daily revelation. "There's a dried-up lake, prehistoric no doubt, right on top of that mountain. I just know the bed is deep in fossils. Tomorrow, I'm going back up there and dig some up and I'll show you all."

The rocking chairs returned to their two-four beat. "There, that's over for the day." they whispered as they resumed the back and forward, back and forward shhhhhhhh.

The front door slammed. The rockers didn't miss a beat. The occupants knew that poor little Miss Mullen was in their midst. Surrounded by paper bags and one tired old suit case, she stood, her worn paper fan fluttering in the stillness. Miss Mullen had been leaving Riverby daily for three weeks. Her mode of departure was always the same. Her check-out hour was 11:30 sharp. Each day she transferred herself from her room to the porch, bag and baggage, then back again, never quite making the train, never quite intending to make it, never finalizing the status of her bed and board. The very air Miss Mullen breathed was indefinite.

Dr. Taylor stopped buzzing with his wife and looked on with a wry smile. Academic interest was written all over his face.

"Can I flag the train for you, Miss Mullen? Mam-maw tempted the fluttering bird, knowing it would never leave the nest.

"Yes, would you please, Mrs. Blanks." Miss Mullen pleaded. Mam-maw hummed, "Tit willow," softly and rocked, her head bobbing a yes.

"Do come and sit a spell, Miss Mullen, haven't seen any smoke yet." Mam-maw assured as she scanned the horizon for the train to Old Fort and points north.

The train which ran in front of Riverby nuzzled the tracks and hugged the edge of Ole Hickory. It usually passed in the distance around 11:30. It had been dubbed the 'cornbread express' because it signaled Mam-maw kitchen ward. "Time to put the cornbread in the oven for lunch", she said by way of excusing herself. This had become a daily routine reminder that lunch would be ready, or that at least the cornbread would be ready, in twenty-five minutes. The sharp piercing whistle… toot…toot… and everyone waited patiently to butter the cornbread.

"There, there, Miss Mullen, I see some smoke now," Mam-maw coddled the poor little old maid.

"Toot!….Toot!……TOOT! The Whistle sounded.

"Shall I flag her down?" Mam-maw addressed Miss Mullen.

"Cornbread express is a coming." The children chorused as they rounded the side of the house, in from play in the river to wash up for lunch.

"Get my flag, Betts," Mam-maw commanded. Betts ran inside the front door to get the old piece of quilt, Mam-maw used to flag the train whenever guests were departing by steam locomotion.

The rockers hissed forward and stopped on tippy-toe as occupants strained their necks to see the oncoming arrival. Mam-maw had the tired old signal in her broad fat hands. The quiet repose was broken by the chug… chug… chug. The mongrel train, all freight except for one passenger car, climbed the rise. Like one big long caterpillar, it rounded the bend of Ole Hickory and came onto the Riverby horizon.

All of a sudden, the peaceful patchwork picture of mountain, train, cornfields and midday sun split at the seams. The lazy cornbread train had gone awry. It set the Riverby world topsy turvey as it left its prescribed path and jack-knifed into the adjoining cornfield. Like the game "pop the whip" which the children played, there was suddenly a break in the line and several box cars broke regimentation and careened off the tracks, finding a resting place sideways, upside down, coming to rest without the circumscribed perimeter of traindom.

Mam-maw stood frozen over the top step of the porch with the tattered and torn dismal piece unfurled in her hands. The rockers were as quiet as straight legged chairs. Miss Mullen stood resigned, another twenty-four hours at Riverby had been decided for her. The children stared in disbelief, quiet and shocked. Like a star out of orbit, the train represented for them, the impossible, the crazy, the unexplored abnormal of everyday events. "Siiii," The old engine hissed, spun and belched its last gulp of steam, it wafted out over Hickory becoming a soft white cloud on the clear blue sky.

"The train had a wreck," Mam-maw stated calmly and quietly to the onrushing kitchen crew who curiously sought the front porch. The children went into action as quickly as they had come to rest. Down the lawn, across the road, through the cornfield, they hurtled headlong to the rescue.

The front porch rocking chair group came alive. "Train wreck, right before our eyes, can you believe it…." A hodgepodge of reaction stirred the peaceful scene. Grandy shot up like a bolt, the Asheville Citizen old news now, wafted in the breeze. The swing took an angry jerk backwards.

"Time to put the cornbread in the oven. Mam-maw tried hard to regain universal composure as she turned toward the kitchen. She desperately willed an amen over the scene of havoc and went about her daily routine. "Hot cornbread for lunch, that would bring the dizzy picture into focus." She said to herself.

Through the fields and up the hill the children reached the accident scene before the engineer let go the whistle of distress. "Toot! Tooooooooooooooot! Toot! Toot! wailed the disaster tune.

Jaybo pulled up short of the overturned car as he caught sight of Leon descending to the scene from off the side of hickory. He too, had heard the crash while hunting rabbits on the mountain and arrived simultaneously on the scene, gun on one shoulder and two rabbits hung from the other.[7]

Jaybo inched his bare feet along unsure of his footing in all the debris. Tobacco, big green-brown

Figure 16: Train Wreck

leaves spilled all over the ground making a path from the sprung door of the car. He reached down and took a leaf from between his toes.

"Hey Lee! Leeeeeeon look here, come see what!" Jaybo screamed. Suddenly the gang was all there, surrounding him mouths open, eyes searching.

"Gooooood Granny alive!" Leon gasped "Look at all that 'baccie', there must be two tons of it laying here at our feet." His blue eyes twinkled, telegraphing message to all the older 'Trundle-Bedders' standing around. Mabes, Charles, Harold and La got the message immediately and went into action. Gathering arm loads they transferred it to the nearest cousin, Bobbie, Tom, Bill, Sonny or Martha.

"Into the cave, quick about it," Lee ordered his regiments. There was complete understanding throughout the forces. The cave was a secret hide-away. Its hidden entrance lay only a few feet away across the track. No one knew of this place except the little black turtles with orange spots who made it their home on hot days. Like the turtles the kids abandoned it in the cool damp days of August.

Within minutes the children had stacked many piles of cured tobacco in a dark dry corner. Their filching of the cargo was brought up short by the arrival of half the valley, come to satisfy their curiosity and lend assistance. No longer unobserved, they dared not return to the cave and give away its existence. Ringing out loud over the commotion on the hillside, the Riverby dinner bell summoned the gang home.

"Cornbread must be done," Betts allowed. "Last one home is a smelly rotten egg." A cloud of dust pursued the bare feet of the 'Trundle-Bed-Trash' as they dug into the layer of topsoil wildly charging down the road, up the lawn and round the house side to the back screened porch.

"Martha Lee is a rotten egg! Moffin Nee is a rotten egg," they teased.

"Cornbread's ready, hurry and wash up," Aunt Boom greeted the mob. Lunch on the back porch the day of the train wreck was very subdued. The gang deftly and expertly did away with mounds of rice and gravy, four or five fried chickens, a peck of green beans and two pans of hot cornbread. Mabes remarked, "Thank goodness the cornbread express got round the bend before it wrecked. Mam-maw might have jumped the track herself and forgotten this yummy hot bread."

Just about everyone was silent, as visions of the cache in the cave stirred each little mind. For weeks, since Hy, La and Mabes had experimented with the habit, the rest of the gang had determined to have a try at smoking. They had tried smoking corn silks, grape vines and rabbit tobacco, all to no avail. It burned up before one good drag and several eyebrows had been taken in the trial. Some of the middle age set of children had rummaged into Grandy's trunk to find his pipe tobacco only to be found out before having a good try at it. Betts had squealed inadvertently by vomiting all over the hall after a couple of puffs. The whole group got stinging fannies for this effort.

Now! Fate had delivered a train load of tobacco right in front of Riverby. A goodly part of it was now in the cave. Surely this day, before the sun set over Ole Hickory, every member of the 'Trundle Bed Trash' would have experienced the weed. Each little mind contemplated the effects. Would it make them dope friends? Would it make them sick, like it did Betts? Was it sinful, as their mothers had sworn? Would it make them grown-up and sophisticated ladies and gentlemen? Would puffing become a habit? Would it stunt the growth of their tanned sturdy legs?

Every single one was impatient to get on with it and see. They couldn't wait to get through with lunch and have a go at their doubts. The boys beat the girls to the cave. Sis was made to take a nap. Hy, La and Mabes decided to walk a mile to town for a Camel rather than roll their own. Martha and Betts got nabbed for duty in their mother's room, giving facials, setting hair and caring for split nails. The Aunts even extracted a half promise from Leon that he would give them a foot rub while their faces were being massaged.

Leon got them all settled, stretched out on their beds in the downstairs room, feet propped up. Then he made the pretext of needing the Dr. Tichenor's antiseptic from the upstairs medicine cabinet. He was gone, leaving the nerve ends in their fat feet jangling with thirst for the refrigerant. He went up the front steps, down the long hall upstairs, down the back-porch steps and out. Mam-maw just barely caught sight of him as he prepared to leave for the cave. She smiled, nodded and joined him in his little game of escape. She promptly forgot that she saw him. She had no idea, of course about the tobacco.

When Leon arrived in the secret hide-away, it looked like Venusburg. Bobbie, who somehow had escaped her after lunch chores was lying back on a couch of stone. She tried to light her self-rolled cigarette. Jaybo had swiped some toilet paper and they had spent the first few minutes in the cave rolling up a supply of more or less cylindrical shapes. Tom and Sonny decided to join with the gang in this bit of mischief and they were striking matches under Bobbies cigarette egging her on to a big deep breath. Jaybo served as temporary look-out and had just passed Leon through the entrance.

Bobbie nibbled on the end of the cigarette and took a dramatic Hollywood type drag on it. Her jaw fell open and smoke bellowed forth, her nose itched as smoke dribbled out there too. She tried desperately to conceal a convulsive cough. The wet end of her cigarette came unraveled, spilling the crumbled tobacco out. This gave her the opportunity to avoid another drag and she took the weed from her lip putting it back together in her fingers.

Betts and Martha arrived late and immediately struck up a light for their cigarettes. Leon and Jaybo were close behind and in moments the small cave was a smoke-filled den. The little family of black turtles evacuated, slowly wending their way to the entrance

Feeling giddy in the head, the smokers were relieved to stop a bit to roll up some more Then the process began again no one was really sure how long this had gone on, or how many cigarettes had actually been consumed but by the time the older girls got back from town and got to the cave entrance, Ole Hickory looked as if it was on fire. Smoke was pouring from the bushes in front of the entrance and there were ominous groans coming close behind the smoke. Hy and La braved the inferno only to be greeted by five green faced cousins seeking the outward reaches of fresh air. Clutching their stomachs and lol-a-gaging their heads about on their shoulders, they crawled out in much the same manner as did the turtles.

The wrecked train still lay a few yards off, down the hill Charles was more fascinated with the train then the smoking and had spent his after-luncheon hour investigating the wreck. Hearing the new arrivals approach the cave, he had come up to see what was going on. He rapidly went into action nursing the nicotinic drunks with gentle hands. He laid them all down on the soft grass of the incline. Carefully he placed their heads, elevating them above their feet. He took off the boy's shirts and dispensed the older girls to the nearby stream with them. They hurried and dipped the shirts in cold water, returning like Indian messengers, swift of foot lest the cloth lose the chill of the steam.

In minutes the scene truly looked like a tragic train wreck, with victims laid out for proper identification. Hardly recognizable, these victims, overcome by smoke had screwed up faces, walled eyes and a pea green pallor.

Bill Fields stood back, his gaze falling first on the wreck, next on the Florence Nightingales hovering over the tobacco addicts. He could not resist an observation and said, "Well the cornbread express didn't quite make it through today. I wonder if them puffers will?" He motioned in the direction of his ailing relatives, "Me, I'm gonna try Grandy's chewing t'baccie, like a man."

———————————— ❧ ❧ ————————————

Grandy stopped by the children's table on the back porch after his breakfast. "I've got an idea." He startled the cereal eaters. "Why don't you younguns hunt up some frogs this morning and tomorrow we'll have a frog jumping contest. Why, when I was a boy out in Arkansas, it wasn't the Fourth of July without a frog jump!"

"Hooray for Grandy." Leon was really taken by his idea.

"That's a good plan." Sonny agreed.

"Now Papa, don't put wild ideas in their heads." LaVerne warned. "You know we have enough going on now for a three-ring circus." Behind her the kitchen forces were in high gear with food preparations for the morrow. "On top of everything else Lola got the bright idea of inviting all our neighbors for breakfast. Then Beck came along and decided she wanted this opportunity to show off her nature trail on the back hill to Mrs. Hunnicutt and then, so as of now we are having brunch by the river in the morning and a picnic on the side lawn in evening. We're just blessed that Delilah and Mose will give up their holiday to stay on and help us. I told them they could leave early tonight. Central just sent word out from the village that Tizzie Newcomb called. She's coming for the weekend and she'll help us gals clean up after dinner tonight."

"The mad hatter's, coming for the weekend?" The children asked excitedly. Their mother's cousin was very special to them.

She had been orphaned by Grandy's sister at an early age and Mam-maw had adopted her. She was like a fourth sister to the Blanks gals.

She had a job as a traveling milliner and thus the kids had named her the mad hatter. Periodically when she was traveling in the vicinity of Riverby she would drop in for a weekend to be in the bosom of the family.

"Good Granny alive, LaVerne!" Grandy gasped at his daughter. "After all, its Independence Day and we oughta celebrate proper. I'll just stop by the preachers and ask the Reverend Coffin and his missus to join us. He can bless all us'ins vittles."

"Have Mercy Papa!" Lola came out on the porch with a bowl of cold boiled potatoes to be cut-up for the salad. "Don't let's have another baptizing, that's all we need." Lola referred to the year the colored minister had persuaded Grandy to let them have a baptizing in the river behind the house. Half the Blanks Presbyterian children had become members of the Mt. Sinai Baptist church on that Independence Day.

Beck came through the door with a dozen stalks of celery and a basket of bell peppers. The children slipped quickly out. They wanted to disappear before someone realized that they had not been given their chores for the day. They would be slicers and dicers gathered in the tearoom.

— ❧ ❧ —

"Gee Whiz," Harold quieted the babbling. "Grandy's idea really is peachy. Let's take some of these old tea boxes and go find some frogs."

"Yea, I know a place up on Ole Hickory by the branch where there are a jillion frogs." Charles lead the way.

They spent the morning collecting frogs in bottles, jars and cans. Martha Lee discovered in a calm pool above the frog territory, that there were millions of tadpoles. She and Betts devoted their morning to collecting jars full of these little babies while their cousins captured bulls.

Summoned home by the Riverby wash-up, clean-up bell, they were confronted with an immediate problem. What on earth were they going to do with their precious pets over night?

Mam-maw came to their rescue by offering the tub in the empty guest room as a compound for the leaping captives. Martha and Betts smuggled their taddies up to the sleeping porch. They went unchallenged in a house hold which was a stir with preparations for the Fourth. In fact, the only complaint raised was "You children are covered in mud and downright smelly from all those frogs, get up those steps and get cleaned up for supper."

"Gee Martha, look at all those cakes on the sideboard," Bets noted as they peeked in the dining room window from the stairs. Mam-maw had lined up five cakes on the big family piece of furniture.

The boys took over one bath room and the girls another. The upstairs baths were back to back. Martha Lee concerned that she had spilled some water from her jar of taddies, smuggled them into the bathroom to slake their thirst. The tub was running over three little bare bodies. The sink was in use by two more fem-fatales taking a short cut to cleanliness so Martha resorted to the toilet. She dumped her tads into the bowl of the potty and stood in line at the sink to refill her empty jar. One of the bare skinned babes from the tub had to make use of the facilities and somehow before Martha realized what had transpired, her foundlings had been flushed.

Utter panic ensued. Martha burst into tears while the other girls giggled. The tragic news got out in the male quarters. There was a mad dash on their part to regain clothing. Leon announced that he would retrieve his sweet sister's pets. Off he went like the Pied Piper, down the back steps and down the hill to the river, with a partially clothed, half bathed gang close on his heels. Lee lead then to the sewer opening at the riverside. Immediate vigil began for the great passing of tadpoles. After a few minutes of no results, a runner was sent back up the hill and up the stairs. It had been decided that Betts tadpoles should be flushed as an experiment to ascertain how quickly the tad poles would arrive at the river.

It didn't take long and a whoop went up at the riverside when the second batch arrived and were retrieved. Martha was told the terrible truth that her pets had made the river before they could be caught. But she was assured that they were now swimming happily in the Swannanoa, no harm done. Greatly relieved with this news she joined the others in the new found sport of flushing and retrieving. The girls in the upstairs bath were the flushers and the boys on the river bank were the retrievers.

The boys sent Bett's tads back up to the bathroom. Flush went the taddies and in a minute they were fished out of the river, carried back upstairs to the bathroom and so on. Over and over again, hundreds of little tadpoles traveled back and forth through the pipes of Riverby. A few from each batch made an escape and swam freely into the river.

--- &infin; ---

Lola took her stance in the middle of the group of family children with LaVerne standing just behind her. She gave a high-pitched yodel for quiet and attention and made her speech.

"Your Aunt Rebekah has taken a big group of guests over to Mt Pisgah and the Rat to show then the blooming Laurel."

Fourteen frogs jumped.... Each child had selected their frog and was testing his or her frog, tickling the hind leg to see how far his frog could jump.

"Aunt Boom and I are going in to Black Mountain to the beauty parlor, Estell and Sarah are going to do us at the same time so we shouldn't be gone more than an hour and a half."

Satisfied that their frog could jump farther than anyone else's, the children set about tagging them, preparatory to returning them to the tub.

"You are under Mam-maw's care while we are gone. She will be in her room taking a nap so don't disturb her unless an emergency comes up."

"Will you please put those frogs back in the tub in the downstairs bathroom this moment!" Aunt Boom had stood all the racket she could cope with in one day and the children ran to return their charges to the. tub.

"You are not to leave the hill under any circumstances! You are not to go swimming in the river or climb trees or play croquet and don't adopt anymore pets! Hibernia, La and Mabes are to watch out for anyone turning in. The rest of you just sit quietly and practice your songs for the Fourth of July song fest. We will be back just as soon as we can. Come on LaVerne, Let's go."

The children stood in a circle and watched the pool of dust hurrying along behind the Franklin as it moved down the driveway and turned onto the highway towards Black Mountain.

"Does anybody know any stories?" Giggled Jaybo.

"Once there was this traveling salesman who stopped at a farm house…." Began Charles who laughed wildly and slapped his thighs.

"Cut it out, that's not nice. Maybe we could sing. Like Aunt Lola says, we better get ready for the Fourth." Martha suggested.

"Sure," Bobby said "Listen to the song I heard Charlie Parker sing one time…. "Bobbie glanced up at the window of the pink room where Hy, Mabes and La were creating new hair-dos. When she saw a wisp of smoke come through the screen, she raised her voice and sang….

"I just dropped in to tell you, I'm ragged but right,
 A thief and a gambler's gal, I get drunk every night;

Her song was interrupted. Betty said "Oooooooooooh, I'm going to tell YOU."

"Tattletale, a lotta good it'll do you."

"Come on Martha, let's go get that box of apples we picked yesterday and make some cider and sell it. Maybe we could go to the village and get the afternoons mail and sell the cider by the post office. I know they said not to leave the place but somebody's got to get the mail and Mam-maw will let us go when she wakes up." Martha and Betty and Sis went onto the back porch and wrestled the box of apples out from under the old washing machine.

"If somebody will go down the hill aways, by Grandy's root cellar, and chunk into the river these old tin cans, I'll let somebody have two free shots." Leon had just appeared smiling with his .22 rifle.

"Lee you're going to get into trouble. They'll kill you if you shoot that gun in the yard." Bobbie warned Leon.

"They didn't SAY not to shoot the gun. I'll let everybody have a shot then nobody can tell on me." Jaybo ran down the back hill and threw the cans into the river's strong current.

"Crack, crack, ping, ping." Leon hit every one of them with a bullet a piece. The kids lined up behind him and each had a chance to shoot the .22 but no one else hit a can.

"Don't get your fingers caught in the wringer, Sis." the girls warned. As Martha turned the wringer, Betty and Sis fed apple slices into it and caught the juice in a molasses bucket.

"Man, these are juicy, won't take long to fill the whole bucket. Bet we get at least a quarter for it." They figured.

"This kind of shootin' is too easy for me." Leon said letting Jaybo have a chance at the target practice. "Bill, run get me a deck of cards and I'll show you a trick.

When Bill returned Leon riffled through them until he found the ace of diamonds. "Sonny you run down the river and stand by the pipe and hold this card out like so…. and I'll shoot right through the diamond in the middle."

"Well, I don't know. I'd hate to have my hand shot off."

"Mamma's boy! Old buddy." Egged on by Bill.

Sonny grabbed the card and scurried down the flagstone steps to the pipe. He held the card by the very tip and closed his eyes. "Ready." He called.

In one motion, Leon raised the rifle to his shoulder, aimed and squeezed the trigger. All the kids held their breath. The bullet went dead center through the diamond and pinged on the pipe.

Sonny was the man of the hour. He showed the card with the bullet hole in it and repeated his performance in pantomime for the gang. He felt very brave.

"What can we do now?" The kids turned from one to the other for suggestions. "All the laws THEY laid down, doesn't leave room for anything fun to do."

"Mam-maw says we can walk to the village for the mail." Reported Martha and Betty. They began to walk down the back driveway towards lover's lane with the bucket of apple juice sloshing in between them. Sis skipped alongside with two jelly glasses in her hands.

"Look what I found in the root cellar," Jaybo whispered as he produced a pint bottle. It was an old gin bottle and had the remnants of some gin still in the bottom of it.

"Must be Grandy's conversation water," said Charles as he claimed it.

"You're not going to drink it, are you? Tom asked.

"No but I know somebody who will," grinned Leon. He ran into the kitchen and picked up a handful of cold biscuits and a bowl and came back out into the yard. He saturated the broken biscuit pieces with the half cup of gin. Then he stood back and called loudly …." Coo…. Coo…. Coooooooooeeeeee!

In answer to his clear call, Leon's pet pigeons coooeeeed in reply and winged in for a hand out. On and on they came landing with grateful flutter of wings at his feet.

"Here, pige, pige, piggey…. good corn for you…… liquid corn this time."

The pigeons didn't hesitate. They strutted and cooed and pecked at the gin biscuits. One or two became a little bold and began pecking at the bare toes around them. The gang jumped back out of the way. Some pigeons were beginning to blink their beady little pink eyes and some were walking with the roll of a sailor's gait. "Can they fly?" Bill asked Leon.

Leon picked one of the pigeons up and threw her in the air. Her wings flapped and the bird went straight up like a helicopter. The others tried out their wings and they too went straight up and down. The back yard was beginning to look like a pigeon yo-yo game.

The gang was laughing until someone cautioned them to shut up or else Mam-maw would come out and boy! If she found a lot of drunk pigeons everybody would be in serious trouble. "Well they didn't tell us not to get the pigeons drunk!" Tom declared. "How are you going to sober 'em up? With black coffee and tomato juice?" The laughter could not be controlled this time.

———————— ❧ ❦ ————————

*Figure 17: Children at the post office*

*The children often walked to the town of Swannanoa to get the mail.*
*From left to right: friend, Harold, Hy, La, Mabes, Charles, Leon*

When the girls got to the post office to pick up the mail, the postmaster, Mr. Jones said. "We've been waiting for some of you folks to come down here today! A package came in on Number 514 out of Charlotte. Samson has it over on the loading platform."

"Where is it? Hey Samson where's our package? "

Samson pushed back his baseball cap and scratched his head. "I don't think you little girls can manage it. I might have to ride you back home in my truck." He pointed to the large crate in the station house.

A deep rumbling whine came from the crate. The girls dropped their buckets of apple juice and rushed forward. On the tag it read…." To my loved ones," it was signed Claude.

"Uncle Claude sent us a dog," yelled Sis to the town.[8]

"It's mine," Martha said. "He's my daddy and he sent this dog to me."

Betty stepped back from the crate as a large tail began wagging-and slapping at the boards.

"Poor fella,", mourned Martha," all cooped up in here. Samson help us get him out. He's such a nice old thing. Just a minute boy, you'll be free."

Samson pulled off the top boards and jumped back. An adolescent St. Bernard dog jumped out of the crate and greeted his owners. He ran around and around the station house, upsetting the spittoon and a small bench. Then eyeing the bucket bounded over and lapped up all the apple juice.

"We'll have to get a rope and tie it around his neck and get him up in your truck somehow!" Martha said hugging the big dog around the neck.

Samson backed up his truck and the dog joined in the fun and frolic of being hauled in the back of the big red truck. The girls tried to settle the dog on the bed of the truck as Samson drove slowly off. "I'm going to name him Pee-Wee." Martha announced to all the sidewalk gallery as they passed through the village. "I'll bet he'll be ten feet tall when he gets his growth." Betts wise cracked.

When LaVerne and Lola returned from Black Mountain with their new finger waves and red necks, they thought the heat of the dryer had caused brain damage. "Lola, that looks like and enormous dog out there in the middle of the children." LaVerne stared at the mirage.

"Dog, nothing. It's a full-grown elephant! And what on earth is wrong with those pigeons? They can't stand up on their feet." As the Franklin nudged into its favorite parking place by the kitchen door, and an intoxicated pigeon jumped upon the radiator and began to nuzzle the flying naked lady on the radiator ornament. "Well, I do declare, Lola, that's the strangest acting bird I've ever seen. Something must have gotten into their mash."

"Aunt Boom, Aunt Lola, Mam-maw! Everybody come and see Pee-Wee." Martha said just as the St. Bernard left his calling card against the tearoom door.

"Let's hear the worst! What happened?" Aunt LaVerne demanded. "And don't tell me one of those bull frogs grew shaggy hair and answers to the name of Pee-wee!"

"Oh, nothing unusual happened. No one turned in for a room. We didn't have much excitement at all." The gang chorused.

Tizzie Newcomb's model-A came up the driveway just in time for supper. There was mass rejoicing among the family and as soon as the meal was done and the dishes washed, the children were rushed off to bed. They were hurried through their "now I lay me down to sleep" and directed to go right to sleep.

Tizzie was assigned the downstairs guest room all to herself. This was a rare experience for any member of the family for it was seldom a vacant room was available for relatives. Lola, Beck and Boom besieged her with the latest gossip. Tizzie, in turn brought them up to date on recent happenings in her life as a traveling sales lady.

Mabes, Hy and La, fascinated as teenagers by the exciting life cousin Tizzie must live out in the world on her own, slipped down the back steps. They sneaked around the house and crawled up the side porch floor and flattened themselves under Tizzie's window to eaves drop. They were not disappointed, for Tizzie launched into a dialogue of her travels.

"................ And last week I stopped off in New Market to visit cousin Kate. I was simply mortified. I had been given a marvelous recipe by my feather and ribbon merchant for Angel food cake.... well you know what a wonderful cook Kate is...Well I thought I'd just show her how to make this cake. I followed the recipe just perfectly. It said to beat the fourteen eggs separately and I followed it to the letter. Beat each egg.... separately......And...."

Jeffie's cousins broke into giggles. She didn't have to go any further with her most embarrassing story.

"Well, I don't know what you think is so funny. I nearly died. I used up every egg Kate had in the house. Darn cake never rose an inch."

"Not even backwards?" Laverne teased her.

".........Well, after that, I went on into West Virginia. I had to work around Charleston and so I decided to go spend the weekend in White Sulphur Springs. I just decided to treat myself to a real plush treat. I checked into the Greenbriar late Saturday afternoon. I got a lovely room overlooking the springs and park. I just had time to take a mineral bath and a short nap before dinner.

"......I forgot to put on a slip. You know that pretty flowered voile dress I wore last time I was here? Well I was going to wear that to dinner. I had put a hand towel under the top of my corset at my waist in the back.... You know.... I had been breaking in a new corset and it had cut me around the waist .... I simply have to lose some weight!

"Well anyway.... I just stuck the towel in between my bra and corset.... I had to have relief.... I didn't know I had forgotten to put on my slip till I had had dinner. Imagine.... I was listening to the orchestra in the grand salon.... had punch and some cake and then I got back to my room and looked in the mirror.... I died.... I just died...

"You could see straight through that dress…. see everything, my corset, my bra…. And in the back, there was that towel in plain view…. It had The Greenbriar written in red right down the middle…. Well! I'll just tell you I got up before day and checked right out of that swanky hotel. L couldn't have stood to have stayed for breakfast. Imagine eating in the dining room again…. with all those dowagers looking at me and remembering what a sight I had been the night before…."

The gals talked on and on till it was very late. Mabes, Hy and La had long since been overcome by sleep and lay snoozing under the window. Finally, Lola, Beck and Boom retired upstairs and left Tizzie to prepare for bed.

Tizzie decided on the spur of the moment to take a quick bath. She slipped into the bathroom, and afraid of disturbing someone, she left the light turned off. Determined to soak her weary bones she drew a tub of water. She slipped out of her corset, bra and slip in the dark and sunk her backsides into the brimming hot tub.

"E-e-e-e-e-e-e-e-e-e-e-e!" Tizzie's voice penetrated the still night. "M-m-m-m-m-m-m-m-! Mam-m-m-m-m-mw! She screamed.

Mabes, Hy, and La were bolted from their sleep and got to their feet. They stood in frozen panic. Lights went on in windows all over the house…. Footsteps hurried down stairs. Mam-maw fumbled for her glasses and shook Grandy saying.

"Frank! Frank wake up! Sounds as if Tizzie is being raped under our very roof." The three eavesdroppers were closest to Tizzie in the bathroom and realized what had happened.

They heard her say in horror.

"Frogs, Oh No! My God! A million frogs!" There was a thud as Tizzie got herself out of the tub full of frogs only to slip on the wet linoleum floor. Mabes started to giggle. Hy and La joined her and they rolled on the floor in hysterics. Everyone at Riverby crashed into Jeffie's room calling to her.

Tizzie regaining her wits, jumped to her feet. She realized that she was stark naked. She forgot about the frogs in her fear of being caught in her nudity by the herd of onrushing feet and pounding fists on the bathroom door. She called out to the mob, "Mam-maw this bathroom is full of frogs!"

She pushed open the screen on the window and jumped through the opening to the side porch. The bright moonlight fell on her nude figure, outlining every bulge and casting a shadow the side wall of the house which resembled the silhouette of the Fat Lady at the circus. The bright beam also picked out three little toe-headed teenagers staring speechless at this moonlit lady Godiva. The four, caught in each-others embarrassment, remained dumb.

The bathroom door crashed open. Mam-maw screamed. "Frank go get the gun. Tizzie's been raped and kidnapped. He took her out the window. Quick! Frank! Poor thing is stark naked, she left her clothes on the floor."

"Might do her some good." Grandy grumbled to himself as he ran for his gun.

By this time, the poor scared frogs came leaping out of the open bathroom window and flopped and flipped, helpless with fear. They lay siege to the porch. This prompted Tizzie to start shrieking anew. The side porch door from the guest room opened. The three teenage girls quickly moved in front of Tizzie's pitiful modest body.

When Mam-maw, leading her posse, caught sight of the four on the porch, no one could tell that Tizzie was attired in her birthday dress. Mabes gaining composure far beyond her years calmly greeted the staring mass of faces.

"Poor cousin Tizzie has had an awful time, Mam-maw. Our frogs were in her bath tub. No one told her. She's been frightened out of her wits." Tizzie whimpered in the background. Mabes continued. "She jumped out of the window with all her clothes off. You all go out into the hall and we'll get her into bed."

They all retreated save Mam-maw. She grabbed up the Beacon blanket off the end of the bed and embraced, Tizzie's shaking body. Cooing and comforting her, Mam-maw guided her to the big old double bed and got her tucked in.

The girls stole out and up the stairs lest some mother get curious as to their part in all this commotion. Gaining the upstairs hall, they were surrounded by inquisitive cousins who had been hanging over the banisters. They kept mum as they sashayed down the hall to the back-sleeping porch.

Leon was the first to speak. "What happened. You all?"

"It's females' business and we aren't telling." La replied.

"mum's the word", Hy said.

"Poor, poor dear mad hatter." Mabes all but wept.

"Aw, you all. Come on now. Tell us. PLEASE!" Chorused the mob of moppets. Mabes, Hy and La, no longer able to keep straight faces, collapsed across the cots. Tears of laughter streamed down their faces as they slowly unfolded the evenings drama.

# Chapter 13

## Breakfast With Feet

"Here it is the Fourth of July and no help. We might just as well face facts. Delilah has gone off on a ginned-up toot and Mose is going to celebrate somewhere else. That means it will be up to us to cook breakfast, lug all the food down those flags stone steps to the riverbank…. not counting getting the trestle tables set up down there and hauling the silverware and china down to set them." LaVerne stood in the middle of cold kitchen and addressed her sisters.

"No use crying over spilt milk or swigged down gin," answered Lola with her hands on her ample hips, "I'll go right now and organize the child labor forces. Get the range fired up and get started on breakfast. We don't have a minute to spare."

"Sister, this is terrible! If there were some way to get in touch with the neighbors, we could cancel the breakfast. I wish papa would install a phone here." Beck dreaded to think of the work ahead.

"I can't cancel the whole day. Most of the itinerant guests we have will be leaving after today and we want to have their last day with us something to remember." LaVerne jammed some more coal into the range and filled the Riverby coffee pot to the brim and set it on the middle eye. "Brunch will be served at the river at ten o'clock as scheduled."

Lola stood at the top of the flagstone steps that led down to the river and cupped her hand around her mouth to shout her instructions for the work forces on the riverbank or to the back porch.

The older boys were down below setting up the long trestle tables and benches. The three tables were lined up in a row and as soon as they could get one set up on the sawhorses some of the girls began to decorate them. One table had a bolt of blue overall denim on it for a cloth. The middle table had a white sheet on it (Martha and Betty grumbled about sheets being used for a table cloth and table cloths being used for sheets on their bed). The other table had a red cloth of theatrical gauze which had been left over from making the dining room curtains. Fern fronds were laid down the centers of the tables and daisy chains were hastily woven and placed on the ferns. Baskets of peaches and berries were placed on the tables.

The other children formed a human chain and passed down from the kitchen to the riverbank the silverware and china.

In the kitchen LaVerne, Beck and Mam-maw cooked the breakfast of Delilah's flannel pancakes, fried sausage, scrambled eggs and homemade applesauce. By the time the neighbors and guests took their seats, the sun was sparkling on the river. The picturesque setting was a solo of color played on the symphonic sounds of the river.

Reverend Coffin returned the blessing, "Bless oh Lord this day in the life of our great country. Bless this gracious family, this bountiful table, this joyous occasion. With hearts full of thanksgiving, let us not forget the miserable sinners…... the poor, pitiful victims of night gin sessions and dear Lord we thank you for this beautiful spot by the river where we are gathered together to break the long night's fast in this restful setting…."

"Restful for the guests," LaVerne whispered to her sisters.

"Amen".

The neighbors sat together at one of the tables. It wasn't often that there was an opportunity for them to gather together and they shared conversation as well as the food.

Violet Wilde pushed back the sleeves of her dark green cable knit sweater and laid her beaded evening bag on the bench beside her as she helped herself to more pancakes. As she passed the platter to Bynum Harwood, he delicately took one pancake off the plate and said, "I thertainly do admire your thweater. What thize needles did you uth?"

"Oh shucks, who bothers about needle sizes? Seems to me I used two different needles for this sweater. Never can keep up with my sewing gear. I just use what's handy. Flossie, I noticed you run up your flag right on the dot this morning." She turned to Flossie Hunnicutt who never failed to run up her flag a minute after sunrise.

"You can count on me, Violet. I'm patriotic 365 days a year. It doesn't take the Fourth of July to make me remember I'm an American."

Miss Bishop turned to her neighbor who lived in a lodge on the side of Little Hickory.

"Miss Peake, when is Bonnie coming?"

"…….. so there I was up to my elbows making chow-chow and hears all this screaming going on in the yard and I go tearing out to see what's up and do you know one of my peacocks had, well, I won't mention no names, but he had this woman backed up to the chicken shed. Don't know who was screaming the loudest. Well sir, I calls him off and this certain woman says, 'You oughta put a muzzle on that varmint.' Well, that made me mad, her calling anything as pretty as my peacocks a varmint so says I to her, well honey if you'll get me a peacock muzzle, I'll put it, on him. She better watch out! That fellow lost three big feathers out of his tail from the excitement and all. I brought them feathers to Mrs. Blanks today. She can put 'em in a jar." Violet speared another sausage onto her plate.

"I'd thertainly admire to have thome of thoth featherth,", Bynum remarked.

"Beth, I don't, see how we can leave this place." Dr, Taylor looked out over the scene before him. "The lovely river, the hillside there with the ferns and mountain ivy and violets growing on it, the beautiful mountains and these dear, dear people we have come to know and to love."

His wife looked with affection on her husband. He looked like a new man.

Up and down the tables the other guests were thinking with a pang how they, too, would miss Riverby. Many of their suitcases were already packed. Andre Bouquet, was already wondering how he would pack his artifacts in with all his other, things.

The pleasant mood and conversations were interrupted by an automobile horn.

"Ahhhhhh----------oooooo--------gah"

Claude sounded the horn again and turned the steering sharply as a front wheel of the Auburn balanced on the edge of the flagstone steps.

"Hold her steady, Claude, hold her steady," said his companion, Dr. McFee, not too steady himself.

"Mac would you look at the scene below! My sisters' idea of Venice. Breakfast at a sidewalk cafe on Swannanoa's own grand Canal." Claude began to back up the car. He ground the gears and lurched off down the driveway.

"Where ya, where ya going? where you going, old buddy?"

"We better run for our lives. I'm gettin' outta here."

Claude's laughter floated down to the river.

The happy conversation of the breakfasters stopped as they watched the scene above them. Hardly a sound was made.

Lola took charge. "Girls! Get your trays and start, stacking the dishes. We have work to do. We have a long and busy day ahead of us."

While the forces carried all the equipment back up to the kitchen and the boys carried the tables and benches up to the side yard near the fish pond for the late afternoon buffet they discussed excitedly the events of the day.

"I'm warming up my pitching arm," said Jaybo. "We are going to choose up sides for softball. The Reds will play against the Blues."

"Not until after the croquet tournament," corrected Bobbie.

"I'm taking on anybody in the place in horseshoe pitching," called Harold, Jr.

"Don't forget we're going to do some tumbling out on the front yard," Leon called back. "Remember, we have that trick to practice for tonight."

"Did you find your jumping frog, Sonny?" Bill patted his own frog buried deep in his overall pockets.

"Don't worry about MY frog. He'll beat yours by a country mile."

———————— ❧ ❧ ————————

"It does seem to me that either Delilah could have sent someone in her place if she wanted to get tanked up," LaVerne addressed her sisters above the top of a platter piled high with fried chicken.

"We've done all the work for today. No use thinking about the help. Well, here's the potato salad. This is ready to go out to the tables. Norma, have you finished your deviled eggs and pickle platter?" Lola turned to her sister in-law.

"Yes, and everything looks very pretty if I do say so myself. Now I'm arranging some of those pickled cherries I invented. Let's taste them and see how they turned out it."

"Awg. Pfew….alllooggg."

"Oh Norm, these have turned my mouth wrong side out!"

"Give me some water quick!"

"How could anything look so pretty and taste that terrible?"

"I canned two dozen jars of these hideous things and was going to send the recipe into Woman's Home Companion and see if I could get a prize. I guess I'll have to donate all these jars to charity."

"Norma, the most charitable thing you can do is throw these things in the river," Mam-maw laughed.

Supper was served buffet style and once again the tables groaned and sagged under the weight of the food. Plates were piled high and the guests and family sat on the grass around the yard. The watermelons had been cooling since early morning in the branch and they would be cut later. But now Mam-maw had a patriotic dessert. The younger grandchildren formed a line and each child carried a cake she had made.

"From the Southland, I present an Old South caramel cake made with plenty of butter and fresh eggs. From the East, a Lord Baltimore cake. I highly recommend this cake to anyone who has a sweet tooth. Next, we have one of my favorites, Rocky Mountain Rocky Cake with thick fudge icing and pecans and cherries in it. To the western shores of this wonderful country I take pride in my California coconut cake. I have to be honest, Rebekah insisted on having a finger in the making of this one. And bringing up the rear is a cake I've made for the first time in my life and can't really vouch for it because the recipe was new to me…. A Yankee cake! Line them up here, children, and I'll cut them. Step up everyone and take your pick. We also have a big pitcher of Apollinaris lemonade if you want it."

Andre Bouquet rinsed his mouth out with the lemonade and dumped his cake into the shrubbery. He turned to his companion and coughed, "I can't recommend the Yankee cake. It's a crazy cake…. Mrs. Blanks must have used salt for sugar!"

Dr. Taylor was having the time of his life. He complimented Mam-maw on her baking skills.

Lola said "I wish you could stay on here for a while longer. The apples from the orchard will be ripe soon and Mama will be making her good apple scruple."

"Leon" LaVerne called. "Set a match to the bonfire, the sun is going down and there's a chill in the air."

When the bonfire was thrusting its flames upward, the Riverby children stopped chasing the lightning bugs and June bugs and ran in front of the blazing fire. They formed a human pyramid. Sis struggled to reach her position on top and slowly stood up and waved an American flag while all of Riverby sang 'My Country Tis of Thee'.

Then everyone grouped around the fire and sang songs of America. They saluted every section of the country with Dixie, Home on the Range and even Yankee Doodle Dandy.

LaVerne, sitting between Lola and Beck sighed, "Beautiful, just beautiful."

"Yes, we worked hard but it was worth it," answered Lola.

"Just look at the happy faces of the children and the contentment of the guests. Yes, it was worth every back-breaking minute."

# Summer Madness

Mam-maw, Lola, LaVerne and Rebekah were doing an unusual thing. They were all sitting idly on the front porch rocking, resting and talking. The itinerant guests had left and the summer regulars had been checking into the Inn in a steady stream. There had been a tender good-bye scene with the Taylors who were most reluctant to leave and then Cousin Tizzie Newcomb decided she had better get back to work.

"Girls, I am just, worn out," LaVerne admitted as she stopped rocking for a moment. "I ache all over and especially my feet."

"I must say, the Fourth of July took a lot out of us all," agreed Lola.

"But daughters, you gave the guests a wonderful time and the children have been marvelous. They are having such a good time this summer. Proverbs says "Women looketh well to the ways of their household and eateth not the bread of idleness. Their children shall rise up and call them blessed!'"

"Mama, what do you mean?" Snorted Beck. "The children have been a mess! Frogs in the bath tub, Tom Jr. cracked Bobbie over the head with a croquet mallet and the blood flowed like the Swannanoa River, and during show night, that wild kitty bit Tom's sore toe.... all the way through the bandage."

"Bobbie has been a problem," LaVerne stated. "She and Mr. Bouquet got into several wrangles and she let her new shoes.... float down the river.... never to be heard from again and that incident with the chloroform was too much. I don't know what on earth possessed Bobbie to smell that chloroform and pass out like that. I had it out with Mabes good and proper. She can use ammonia to kill those butterflies in her collection."

"Don forget, Mama," Lola sniffed," that siege with the mumps early in the summer: And Claude bringing that drunk doctor on the premises during our breakfast at the river. I was mortified. And pie beds! I have warned those girls for the last time about pie beds. I think that was what really sent Miss Mullen packing."

"Surely, we have gone through the worst. Nothing more can possibly happen," LaVerne hoped.

The rockers stopped abruptly as screaming, crying and loud oaths broke their conversation.

"He's killed Me! He's killed me! Call the police...... call an ambulance."

The mothers wasted no time in propelling themselves into action. They ran down the front steps in time to see Bill and Sonny engaged in a monstrous fight. Blood poured from every pore. They kept plowing into each other with all the ire their bodies could produce. Sonny kept swinging all the time he was screaming.

"Well, country hick, hope you're satisfied. You've just killed your city cousin." With that last Will and Testament, he slumped over on the driveway.

The women were genuinely alarmed and rushed to pull them apart. It turned out to be cherry juice. Sonny and Bill had been picking cherries and gotten into an argument over whether it was better to live in the city or country and ended up pelting each other with cherries. All the Riverby children gathered around to watch the excitement.

Sonny and Bill were punished and the rest of the children were sent back up into the cherry trees to pick. Grandy said the birds were going to get all the cherries and he wanted all those trees stripped today!

"Oh boy, we should have a good time with all of us kids in the trees. Come on gang, let's go," Martha shouted.

"Not you and Betty," Lola stopped the girls. "You two are to go up on the mountain and get blackberries and flowers." She didn't notice how their faces fell.

Martha and Betty were distinctly disgruntled as they set off down the curling country road in their overalls with empty lard buckets swinging from their arms. They passed the Bishops house without stopping. They passed the wild crab apple tree, their bare feet leaving splayed footprints in the dust.

The country road became a mountain trail at the rail road tracks and the girls turned left at the fork of the trail and trudged up the mountain past Mrs. Peake's log cabin.

For the next two hours they followed the trail leaving it only once to snitch some summer apples from Mr. McLain's orchard. It was a point of honor to steal at least one apple since Mr. McLain had once blasted away with a shotgun at the gang. They always enjoyed getting even and having the thrill of wondering if they would be shot at again.

As they left the orchard munching the green fruit and started over toward the Ridge, they entered a small glade filled with May apples and fern and jack in the Pulpits. The source of their favorite branch by the edge of the Riverby property was here. An eternal fountain of pure cold mountain water bubbled up like icy champagne from the heart springs of the mountain onto a bed of pebbles studded with mica.

They considered this clear pool and secluded glade as their very own private property. The girls lay flat on their stomachs and buried their faces in the cold water and drank deeply. Their thirst quenched, they washed their faces and hands and lay down on the ground to rest.

The wonderful odor of the wooded mountains permeated the air. Coolness, dampness, leaf mold and the aroma of wild flowers filled the air.

"Well, I'm just not going to do any more work," said Martha, "let's just stage a sit-down strike."

"Yeah and Grandy would sit down on us, too, after he thumped our heads good and hard," answered Betty.

"The other kids get to have all the fun and we're stuck with the hard work." Then Martha imitated Lola's voice, "Girls, shake the hall rugs. Girls, bring your dust mops in here. Where have you girls been? These tables aren't dusted."

"And the orders we get at meal time. Girls, pass the biscuits. Girls, get your trays Blah, blah, blah. I'm tired of all that. And I tired of wearing cast-off clothes and having my aunts buying me clothes. I feel just like Ella Cinders in the funnies. Only she ran away and met a millionaire last week."

"That's it! Let's run away! We can hop the afternoon freight train and ride in the cute caboose. They have a stove and bunks and everything. We'll just ride until we come to a strange big town…. maybe Chicago, even."

"Wonderful! We sure wouldn't have trouble getting jobs…... cleaning, cooking and being waitresses. I'd bet we'd make enough between us to rent an apartment. Man, that would really be living. The kids would sure be jealous."

"Yeah, and best of all, they'd have to do the work at Riverby and everybody would be so sorry they'd mistreated us. I bet we could pass for sixteen with lipstick on and dresses. We already know how to smoke and that will make us look older."

"Let's pick the blackberries and sell them to Mr. Bart's store and that'll give us some money to eat on and we'll take some of the money and buy a pack of real cigarettes. Funny, seems I can smell smoke now."

The girls stood up and sniffed the air. They walked around the big boulders to the back of the spring and gasped. They had stumbled onto a blind tiger! A rough looking man had been left guarding the still and he jumped up from his nap at the first gasp and already had his hands on his gun.

"What are you girls staring at?"

"N-nothing, mister, we're looking for blackberries."

"Thar ain't no berries 'round hyar. But they is bears. You girls git on."

"Yes, sir, we're going. We don't want to meet any bears…. or anything else," replied Betty. "Come on Martha, let's start home."

The lard cans clanked against their legs as they walked rapidly away not looking back.

Once out of sight of the still, the girls ran down the mountainside until they had put several hundred yards behind them. The end of their downhill run brought them to a stop in a thicket of blackberry bushes.

"Let's pick our berries and get out of here."

It didn't take the girls long to fill the lard cans and to eat their fill. Afterwards, they strolled along and then lay down for a while on a sunny slope waiting for the whistle of the freight train that would take them to Chicago.

"I'm sure tired," Betty remarked.

"And hungry," answered Martha. "You know, we'll miss supper and we missed dinner…. that was hours ago. I wonder who served lunch and shelled that bushel basket of lima beans on the porch?"

"Yep, and Aunt Lola waiting for the iron weed to go in the big crocks. They are really sorry now they treated us the way they did. And think about in the morning. They'll be up all night with the cops looking for us and worrying about us and what with all the crying and carrying on, they'll be too worn out to do all our chores in the morning."

"Too bad about the movie, though."

"Movie? What do you mean?"

"Mr. Parkerson is going to stand treat tonight for the movie in the village. Tom Mix is in it."

"Dad blast it! We get all the dirty breaks. They even go to the picture show when we're running away from home. No heart, that's what I call it."

The train didn't stop. It hardly even slowed down. The engineer just gave a blast on his whistle and waved to the station master as he sped through the village.

The girls waved and called and ran to the water tower but by the time they got there, the 23 cars had dashed past, and the tail end of the red caboose wig-wagged a good-bye as it swayed down the tracks.

The girls held on to the supports of the water tower with one hand and still clutched the pails of blackberries with the other and panted.

Betty sat down and put her head on her knees. Too much exertion caused her heart to beat wildly. Martha dropped her lard can and pointed.

"Look! There's Aunt Beck and all the kids. She's driving up and down the street and the kids are going in and out of all the stores. They've been looking for us since before noon, I'll bet. Boy, do they look worried. We're going to really catch it."

"Let's just go on over and give ourselves up. We've let them worry enough and I'm too tired to walk home," panted Betty.

The girls sidled up to the LaSalle and "Hey, you all, here we are."

"You girls will just have to walk home. I don't have room for another child They're already riding the running boards. We're trying to sell Grandy's surplus cherries. The back seat is loaded with buckets of them. Delilah needs those blackberries for cobbler…. hurry along on home…. It's almost five o clock now. Where's the iron weed? Lola's waiting for that, too."

"Where have you all been?" asked Tom Jr. as he ran up to the car. "Mr. Parkerson took us to North Fork to swim and we yodeled for you. When you didn't come, we just went on. Boy, that water felt good. See you later at the house."

They hadn't even been missed. The girls bawled all the way back to Riverby… every step of the two miles.

Mam-maw was seated at her quilt frame when the girls came straggling up the cinder road of the back driveway. After a few leading questions to the worn-out girls, she called a meeting of her daughters.

Martha and Betty were given a brief vacation from house work and they gladly gave up the idea of a flat in Chicago.

Early the next morning the girls set up a roadside stand. They rolled four large rocks from the rock wall to the edge of the highway and placed a large empty box on top. On the surface of their 'table' they had eight quarts of cherries arranged. Four of them were bright red pie cherries and four boxes held the dark and plump sweet Bing cherries. The cherries had been picked while the dew was still on them and arranged with care, stems down in the boxes. Bright green cherry leaves stuck out here and there offering a pleasant contrast to the red cherries. On the corners of the table were lard cans filled with flowers. The bouquets were mostly made up of wild flowers but a few choice blossoms from Lola's cultivated garden were added. Framing the edge of the table were ears of popcorn with the husks off. The kernels were full and colorful.

In a small box on the ground next to the table were two gray and black and white striped kittens. They were quite angry about being cooped up in the box and tried frantically to escape over the side. Their claw marks were evident on all four sides of their box.

The sturdy rock pillars that stood sentinel at the driveway entrance each supported a twelve-year-old girl. They had on clean overalls and khaki shirts. Their brown bare feet hung down from the posts and lazily kicked at the rocks. Betty had a clover necklace around her neck and Martha wore a crown of field daisies on her blond hair.

They smiled and waved to the strings of cars that zipped past them.

"That one was from South Carolina," called out Martha

"Who cares about old South Carolina? I want to see one from Iowa or California. Hey, look! Here comes one from Florida and he's going to turn in."

"That's the Thompsons in a new car. Hey Mr. and Mrs. Thompson! Hey Helen and Chris. We've been waiting for you."

Mr. Thompson stopped the car momentarily to greet the girls but remembering how tired Mary Ann must be, he changed gears and drove up the driveway to the front door.

"I noticed Mrs. Thompson had already started crying. Last time we saw her she was crying. She's nice once you get used to her crying all the time. Betts, do you think we should lower our prices again? Nobody's going to stop.

Martha, jumped down off the pillar and picked up the sign in front of their table. It read:

*Fresh eating cherries and pie cherries….25¢ a quart.* (A line had been drawn through the 25' to read 15)
*Beautiful flowers for home or graveyard….10¢ a bunch*
*Two wild tigers….5¢ a piece*
*Popcorn……. pop it yourself*

"If we keep lowering the prices, we'll never get enough money to go to the Recreation Park. Those rides are expensive over there."

"I think I'll lower the flowers to 5 a bunch. They look pretty droopy. Do you think I should get some fresh water for them from the river? 'Member, too, we've got to get rid of these kitties. Nine different times this summer cats have been dumped on the yard at Riverby. Grandy said he'd better see these tigers gone by dinner time or else…."

"Guess it's just as well. Can't tame 'em. I think they must be half puma. They don't even purr…. just snarl and scratch and claw."

"Here little kitties, want a nice cherry?" Martha dropped a couple of cherries into their box. "Spit out the seeds little Stripes. Oh, Zebra, don't eat so bossy, nobody will want to buy you."

"Look at this, Martha," Betty called as she inserted a cherry into the leather pad of her sling shot. She drew back the inner tube catapult and let fly on the bumper of an Oldsmobile. Zing! Serves him right for not stopping. Go on back to West Virginia... you're missing some good old North Carolina cherries," she called after the speeding car.

"Ah……. oooo…gah! "Lola honked the Franklin's horn as she slowed down and stopped. The girls hadn't seen her approaching from behind them. From practice, they jumped back into the day lily beds to escape her off-course driving. Lola kept one hand on the horn and with the other she twisted and turned the steering wheel aiming first for one post and then the other. Putting on the emergency brake with her 'horn hand! she jerked to a stop. LaVerne, in the seat beside her, clutched the doorknob and let out a little squeal.

"Just what do you young ladies think you are doing? We saw you throwing cherries at cars. This mess looks terrible…. and right here at the main gate." Lola began to adjust the snap on her driving gloves.

"Mam-maw said we could earn some money to go to the Rec Park. We'll pick everything up, honest we will," they pleaded.

"Oh girls, you are standing in Mam-maw's day lilies. She brought the roots wrapped in wet cotton from her girlhood home in Tennessee and planted them with loving care," LaVerne scolded. "Now disband this stand right away and take those cherries up to Delilah. I'll tell you what," she suddenly decided upon seeing their crestfallen faces, "hull that popcorn and we can pop it tonight over the open fire. You give us that box of kitties and we'll take them out to Miss Lou's. She can use some good mousers in her barn.

While Martha loaded the snarling tigers into the car, Betty tried to fluff up the trodden day lilies.

Lola honked the horn and burst out onto the highway. The girls stood staring after the car and caught a fleeting glimpse of Zebra stealthily climbing along the back of the front seat. As the Franklin disappeared from sight, Zebra raised one paw and struck out at one of Lola free-swinging curls.

The Trail ways bus had stopped right by their stand before they knew it.

Martha and Betty grabbed up their boxes of cherries and boarded the bus, squeezing quickly past a passenger.

"Get your cherries here!"

"Red, ripe deee--licious home grown cherries. Yes mam, that'll be 15 cents. Two boxes, sir? Glad to see you have the change.

Up and down the aisles the girls ran peddling their fruit and not paying heed to the driver's outraged orders to get off the bus. As the last box was being sold and the girls were getting off the bus, Martha quickly placed on the floor of the bus, next to the driver's feet, two of the lard cans with the wilted wild flowers.

"Thanks a lot for stopping, mister. Give the flowers to your wife."

The driver let out an oath and closed the doors and rolled off.

"Wheee, Marth, look at the loot I got. Here, put your money on the table and let's count it. Start with the pennies and then count the dimes and nickels. One, two, three, four....

"ONE, TWO, THREE, FOUR.......ONE TWO THREE FOUR GARB OF OLD GAUL! Sssssssqqqqquuuuiiiirrrrllll, lllllleeeeooooummmm, wwasaaaa sssssssskkkkkkeeeelllll...."

"Martha Lee: What is it? What happened?" Betty dropped her pennies and clutched for Martha.

"It's a boy in a skirt! No, it's a girl. I see her pigtails. It musta gotten off the bus. Look! Yonder!"

"It's got on a plaid outfit and long socks to match. There's a knife in the top of one sock and look at that funny looking pocket book swinging back and forth in front!"

— ❧ ❧ —

Bonnie MacLeod never missed a beat. On and on up the long driveway she continued to march and play her to bagpipe. After the long bus ride, it was wonderful to feel solid ground under her feet and to exercise her lungs. She knew aunt Adrianna would be proud.

Grandy ran out of his garden with his hoe held over his head.

Up at the house, men, women and children burst out of the house to see what was loose on the hill. Bonnie had a captive audience. As she neared the front steps, she kept right on playing and smartened up her marching steps.

"Surprise! Surprise!" Screamed Miss Adrianna as she ran down the steps past the startled assemblage. With a ceremonial sword in each hand she all but ran the family through as she joined Bonnie in the driveway. Bonnie continued to pipe as she turned about and began a march around the front yard with Miss Adrianna behind her. When the marching stopped, Miss Adrianna crisscrossed the swords on the grass and Bonnie deftly changed tunes while Miss Adrianna performed the sword dance

For once in their lives, the family was speechless. The guests wished someone would explain it all. Mam-maw felt her salts beginning to work so she headed for the privacy of her room. The Highland Fling was too much for her system.

When the mountain air began to regain its silence, all the children ran forward

"Let me have a crack at that bag of wind," Bill demanded.

"Look out, everybody, Jaybo and I are going to have a duel," Tom Jr. and Jaybo were flashing the swords in the air and making tentative lunges at each other.

"How do you pump this thing up, girl? Which part do I blow?" Sis was punching the bag.

"Children, children. Stand back. Boys! Put those weapons down before somebody gets stabbed in the heart." Mam-maw had reappeared and taken charge.

"Now, Miss Adrianna, here are your knives. You'd better put them back in your room. Hello, Bonnie, dear... welcome to Riverby Inn. My you play, you play, nice and loud. I know you are proud of your bag pipes and I can imagine how expensive they must be. So, you take them to your room, child, and put them away carefully. We wouldn't want them to get broken." Mam-maw carefully withdrew the instrument from Sonny's sticky hands and handed it back to Bonnie.

———————————— ❧ ❧ ————————————

The bridge game wasn't going at all well. Gloria Parkerson, Birdie Rogers and Jewel Barnett had begged Mam-maw to leave her quilt frame for an hour or two and make up a foursome.

"The house and hill are quiet as can be and we can really concentrate on our game," they had begged. So, Mam-maw joined them in the parlor room.

"Looks like Mam-maw and I won that rubber, girls. Four spades doubled did the trick. Mam-maw you should play for money with the luck you have at cards."

"Your long suit of clubs helped me out, Gloria. You know me well enough to know that I'd never play for money. That's gambling, pure and simple, and I won't permit it in my house. Once a person takes to gambling, no telling what else he might do," Mam-maw shook her head sternly.

"Oh, she didn't mean to imply that we should gamble," corrected Birdie in her soft Alabama accent.

"Hurumph," said Mam-maw, "Well I should hope NOT."

"Shuffle those cards well this time, Birdie," said Jewel. "We've gotten the worst hands. I'll never know why you doubled last hand. Your heart singleton didn't warrant it."

Jewel's dissatisfaction was interrupted savagely.

"Sssssssqqqquuuuiiiirrrrllll, aaaaaooooolllll, wasaaaa ssskkkkkeeeelllll."

Mam-maw placed her hand over her heart and adjusted her glasses with the other one. Jewel, stubbing out her cigarette burned her index finger. Gloria clutched the table with both hands and held on tight while Birdie, shuffling the cards, sat quietly as she watched the cards spew out into the air and flutter all over the room.

"What is it?"

"My God! There it goes again. Did Queen get her tail caught in the door?"

"Don't take the Lord's name in vain!" commanded Mam-maw.

"It must be Bonnie again with that bagpipe. Twice in the same day is too much. I'll never get used to that sound."

Bonnie came piping her way down the big stairway and into the hall.

Little Beetle Parkerson, playing dolls on the end of the porch ran crying to her mother, "Something's coming to eat me!"

Lola and LaVerne hadn't been on the hill when Bonnie had first arrived and at the first sounds of the skirling, LaVerne, in the kitchen, dropped her paring knife and ran for the front of the house. Lola was right on her heels with her garden scissors in one hand and a stalk of iron weed in the other.

"Surprise!" cried out Miss Adrianna as she stood next to her little niece. "Bet you didn't know she could play 'Gaily Through the World.' This is an authentic outfit. Black Watch is her tartan. Hello Mrs. Hedges and Mrs. Hudson…. how do you like it?"

"Do you mean to tell me that, ----that----that horrible screeching came out of that THING? Are we going to have to listen to that for the rest of the summer?!" Lola blamed LaVerne.

"Well, Miss Adrianna did say Bonnie would bring an instrument. I didn't think it mattered. After all, we've had flutes, accordions, violins, jews harps, snare drums, trombones and bugles. I play ragtime, myself. But a bagpipe. I never thought of that." LaVerne recalled rapidly to her mind the arrival of Miss Adrianna the week before. "I should have been prepared for anything," she said to herself.

---------------------- ❧ ❧ ----------------------

Miss Adrianna was 85 pounds of active dynamite. Single handed she had driven her big Buick touring car 850 miles without stopping off somewhere to sleep. The old car had turned the corner on two wheels as she swung it between the rock posts at the end of the driveway and put it in high to make the grade to the front steps. She had spurned all offers to help her unload the car and had frisked and frolicked up and down the steps unloading the automobile.

At dinner, Miss Adrianna had had three helpings of everything that had been passed to her and then took her seat on the front porch in the center rocker. Out of her large knitting bag she had first produced some tatting which she attacked with a vengeance. The shuttle flew in and out of the designs so fast it was impossible to watch it. Growing tired of the pattern, she tossed the tatting back into the bag and brought out some argyle socks already half finished. The faster she rocked, the faster she knitted. Even Norma who held the Riverby record for fast knitting was bug-eyed as she watched Miss Adrianna finish the five-color socks and turn the heel and within minutes bind off the toe.

Next, Miss Adrianna brought out a piece of cheese from her knitting bag and ate it in three quick bites. "I burn up a lot of energy," she needlessly explained.

As she munched on a smokehouse apple, she explained to the assembled ladies the brilliant mind of her little niece who would soon be coming.

"The child can do anything! Anything at all. Only 11 years old and knows astronomy. She has skipped three grades in school and will be going into high school in the fall."

"Can you imagine that, Beck?" Mam-maw winked.

"I have a son who…." Beck didn't get a chance to go on.

"Brilliant mind, just brilliant. Plays four musical instruments and three of those she can play at the same time. One girl band."

"My Martha has a lovely voice," Norma put in.

"All star athlete, too. Basketball, tennis, hopscotch, polo. Not to mention running, racing and jumping."

"Our children play games here, too," Lola was getting her dander up.

"Pole vault. She's got to practice her pole vaulting some. Got beat by 1/100th of an inch by the state champion. Anybody want a bite of my almond Hershey bar? Good for you. Puts iron in your system."

"I'd like to put some iron in her system," murmured LaVerne behind her hand.

"Wonderful cook, my little Bonnie. You should taste her Scotch scones. Melt in your mouth. Won six blue ribbons at the State Fair in the spring for her desserts and preserves."

"No, Mama, I can't imagine it," Beck finally answered her mother.

"She's an eater like me. Burns up lots of energy. Gets it from her Scottish great-great-grandfather. He was a caution. Hated the British and gave old Queen Victoria a terrible time. Always trying to urge the Scots into another uprising. Rugged man. Wore his kilts all winter long…. rain, sleet, or snow. You know there's only one thing more sacred to a Scot than his Presbyterianism… and that's his tartan."

"I asked you, Mrs. Hedges, do you like her tartan?

"Er, look, Miss Adrianna, we're just as Presbyterian as you are but…."

"No buts about Bonnie, give us next 'Scotland the Brave' and let's see how you sound on that." Miss. Adrianna sat down on a footstool in the middle of the hall-way and opened up her sewing basket. "While Bonnie blows up the air in the bag, I'll tell you about my sunburst quilt I'm piecing. Take your time, Bonnie, and don't get too winded before you start."

"Maybe we could get a better idea of how her piece sounds if she went down by the Bing cherry trees," LaVerne suggested after looking at the unbelieving faces of Jevel, Birdie, Gloria and Lola.

"Now this sunburst quilt is a secret recipe, you might say. Ha, ha. All the way from Scotland. Very dark winters up there and long ones, too…. lots of fog. I'm doing a sunburst to end all sunbursts. See, this big round orange fellow is the sun. That goes square in the middle. Then those colored pieces go bursting out from the sun in all directions…. like rays. I'll start out with this purple, then add rays of this yellow and blue and mulberry and pink and take a look this shade of green. Unusual isn't it? That's enough air in the bag, Bonnie, now grab that chanter and let's hear you give it all you've got. I want to KNOW that Rob Roy and Robby Burns are right in this very room."

"I have something cooking on the stove," LaVerne said and left the room. Lola was fast on her heels. "Sister, you better take a firm stand about that thing."

"Oh, Lola, how can I take a firm stand? They might leave and, oh dear, I don't know what to do. We can't offend Mrs. Peake's relatives. Mrs. Peake is our good friend and neighbor."

"So good a friend and neighbor she highly recommended Riverby for those Highland refugees." She slammed the dining room door as the first screams of the bagpipe began their dying agony.

The bridge foursome closed all the doors of the parlor room. As Birdie picked up the cards from the floor, Jevel shut the windows. "We'll never be able to concentrate on our game with that wounded water buffalo out there in the hall."

"Sorry, girls, I can't play bridge with that noise. I'm going to take my nap with my shawl over my eyes and ears. The sound of that bagpipe hurts my eardrums and the sight of that sunburst quilt hurts my eyes."

"Mam-maw," asked Gloria, "what did you think of those colors? That green. Ugh. What did you think of it?"

"It's all right if you like goose shit green in the middle of an Aurora Borealis." Mam-maw slammed the door of her bedroom.

"Come on girls," Gloria motioned, "let's head for the john and settle up. Jewel you owe me fourteen cents and Birdie you owe me a dime. Don't take on so, you'll get lucky one of these days, too, and cut Mammaw for a partner."

# Chapter 15

# The Blue Bonnet Plague

"And the Lord told a great whale to swallow up Jonah; and Jonah was in the belly of the fish for three days and three nights." Mam-maw quoted from the Bible.

Sis and Beetle Parkerson were gazing into the depths of Mam-maws gold fish pond. One of their favorite quiet places, the pool was a swimming mass of gold fish with Old Testament names. Mam-maw had slipped quietly into their daydreaming and was taking the opportunity to give them a Sunday School lesson. As Mam-maw told of Jonah inside the deep dark cavernous stomach of the whale, the tow-heads nestled up to her breast and suckled from her main spring of knowledge of the scriptures.

"And then, the Lord spoke to the fish and it vomited out Jonah upon the dry land" Mam-maw told of God's miracle. Both little girls put their faces down close to the water, sure that they would see Jonah emerge from a big, fat gold fish.

Gloria Parkerson, Beetle's mother, came out on the side porch and finding Mam-maw, she came with tears in her eyes to seek her comfort and knowledge.

"Mam-maw, she's got it. She's got it again and we haven't been here a week. What on earth am I to do?"

"Now, now, Gloria. What is it? Back up now and tell me again. What's the trouble?"

"It's Evangeline. She's all broken out with poison ivy. I watched her carefully all last week and forbade her to go across 'the pipe' to the island with the other children because of all that undergrowth over there. And here she is this morning a mass of little white blisters. What am I going to do with her?"

"There, there, Gloria. Don't get upset. There's just nothing you can do to stop her from getting it. She's just one of those children prone to this thing." Mam-maw tried to stop the tears which kept welling up in Gloria's eyes. "If it's any comfort to you, Beck said this morning that she thought Jaybo had it too."

Most of the children at Riverby could wade through forests of poison ivy and poison oak and never have a poisonous blister to show for it. Some few would have it in various stages on their legs, feet, arms or hands but nothing serious, it just kept them scratching. But Jaybo and Evangeline were so allergic to it that their heads ballooned out of all proportion to the rest of their bodies. Last summer, Evangeline's face was so swollen with it that her eyes became slits and her little nose disappeared in her contorted face.

LaVerne overheard Gloria's and Mam-maw's conversation from the pantry where she was making birds nest pudding for lunch. She left the egg whites she was whipping and joined the two women by the fish pond

"Mother, I am suspicious of the older girls. Bobbie has a terrible rash on her elbow and Mabes complained this morning that she and the Hudson girls have been itching too."

Beck came down the side porch and joined the clinical discussion. "Well, Jaybo has poison ivy. No doubt about it. His face is covered in it. We'll have to keep them shut up inside Gloria. We can't have it spread all over them like it did last summer. That was awful."

Lola had come up from her cottage below just in time to hear the diagnosis. "Yes, you better shut them up somewhere. It's bad for business having those two pitiful looking children around. it scares people away. After all who wants to stay at an Inn where the children look as if they had some plague."

"Come on, Gloria. Let's go into town and see if Dr. Mac has something to stop it from spreading. Maybe something new has been discovered," Beck spoke to Gloria. They left immediately for the La Salle in the parking area.

LaVerne continued her story. "But mother, the girls don't look like they have poison ivy. It's more like a rash. Maybe its poison oak. I don't know, but I wish you'd take a look at them and see what you think."

"Alright, LaVerne, go find them and line 'em up. I'll give them a going over." Mam-maw sent her daughter off to bring in the itchers.

"SEVEN YEARS?!" Bobbie shrieked. "I'm ruined for life. ALL those Palmolive facials, wasted. No one will want to date me, not even Sam."

"Lordy! Wait till mother hears about this," Hy said dryly.

"Mother? What about Miss Finney? Can't you just see her face when she hears that two of her debutante coteries have the ITCH!" La broke into laughter.

"I'm going to get my Sulphur and lard mixture and go to work on then right this minute. Mam-maw declared. "Come on LaVerne, we have to rub it into their hair and scalps. If it gets in their hair, we'll never. cure it."

LaVerne stood dumb struck, looking at her two daughters in disbelief.

"Put that in my hair?" Bobbie came near to striking her grandmother when she saw the mixture Mam-maw had in her hands. "I'd rather die. Please Mam-maw, isn't there something else that we can use? I just gave myself a shampoo and set last night."

LaVerne looked at her lovely blond curls, so natural and wavy. Then she looked at Mabes' curls, almost kinky with bounce and abundance. "Mama maybe we should take them into the public health hospital at Oteen. I just can't do it." She winced at the thought of her beautiful daughters being swathed in pig fat.

"Come on, daughter. Just make up your mind, it's the right thing to do, and do it. I know it looks awful and smells worse, but It's the best and quickest cure known for this stubborn ailment."

When Beck and Gloria returned from town, they could hear squeals all the way out on the front lawn. Mam-maw finally had to sit on Bobbie to get her to succumb to the treatment. Lola had been called in to suave her daughters and all three of the older women were crying as loudly as the younger girls.

"This looks like the immolation of the heathens! What one earth are you all doing?" Beck stood in the doorway wondering who was giving who the treatment.

"Don't laugh, Beck, this isn't funny. Our girls have the seven-year itch." LaVerne wailed to Beck as she put the last blob of lard on Mabes' eyebrows.

"Well, what on earth are you putting on them? Wait I have the latest cure for poison ivy, maybe it will help the itch too. Want me to go back and ask Dr. Mac?" Beck tried to stop them from lathing their girls with one more ounce of fat.

"Heavens, no! Do you want the whole village to know that the Blanks have the itch? Shhhhhh don't tell a soul. Just come on in here and help us."

"Well the whole town's going to have it too!" Bobbie regained her tongue. "I'm sure of that. I just know I got this in the movie the other night. You remember you all let us girls go into the village to see that Tom Mix Movie? Well, there was a little boy sitting next to me all night and he itched throughout all the gun battles. I bet you a nickel, that's where we got this from."

LaVerne, done with the disfigurement of her daughters, sat pitifully on the edge of Mam-maws bed." I just don't think I can stand it. First, we have a grade B kitchen. Now we have the seven-year itch. We might as well close up the Inn and put up a big Health card out on the gate that says we have the blue bonnet plague." In her depression, LaVerne failed to get her words straight

"Now, now, daughters. Just take it easy. It isn't the end of the world. Just remember it could be worse. If these poor things are still itching this afternoon, I'm going to give them a hot oatmeal bath."

Bobbie fainted dead away on the daybed.

Gloria had rounded up Jaybo and Evangeline. Beck joined her on the back porch and they read all the promises on the label disregarding the deep indigo mixture inside. They swabbed Jaybo and Evangeline thoroughly.

"Um, that feels good." Jaybo told his mother.

"Uh huh, it sure stops the itching." Evangeline agreed.

Greatly encouraged by his reaction, Beck yodeled down the hill to the rest of the children in the river and commanded their presence.

"All right, stop shoving and pushing. I'm going to cure this epidemic once and for all." Beck used her usual lavish hand in wielding the blue dipped swab.

"But, Mama. I never had poison ivy in my life, why do have to get that messy stuff all over me?" Bill protested.

Beck looked up to admire her handiwork. She was aghast at the site before her. The children looked like they had just come up out of a purple lagoon. They were purple from stem to stern.

Lola came from the kitchen to warn them. "It must be clearly understood now, that if a car load of tourists turns in you are to hide yourselves at the first shout of warning."

"Yes, and remember no swimming! Absolutely not a toe the river. I don't want you to wash off this medicine till everyone stops itching." Beck added the final edict.

Later in the morning a light blue car headed up the driveway.

"They're turning in! They're turning in. Everybody!" Lola sounded the general alarm.

LaVerne had just dumped a pound of oatmeal into hot, salted boiling water. She ran to the pantry window and told the crowd playing croquet on the side lawn to hide.

"Quick you all! Psssst! You purple creatures from Mars, the Moon is attacking. Run for your lives!" She tried to make a game of the emergency.

Betts, Martha, Sis and the two younger Parkerson girls were already safe within the Music parlor room. They had been singing and playing through the music book Martha had gotten in Asheville. They stopped their music and peered through the double windows, a safe distance from the prospective guests.

Sonny and Bill remained on their tummies under the front porch, chewing a stolen quid of Grandy's tobacco. They rolled over, spat through the boxwood bush and remained on vigil.

Bobbie a white fluffy terry cloth towel wrapped around her Sulphur-lard hairdo, sat calmly on the end of the porch filling in the latest Palmolive-Peet contest.

The sedan came slowly and cautiously up the driveway. It stopped in front of the steps, trapping Evangeline and Jaybo. They were playing mumble-peg just across the drive from the steps.

There was a neat and tidy mother and father in the front seat with a neat and tidy only child in the back. This girl child was lily white. and had on a smocked dress and a crisp-bow-ribbon around her sausage curls.

Just as the car settled by the front door, the Riverby alarm bell rang loud and clear… Mam-maw caught the last of Lola's warning as she sat reading the bible in her room. Having no idea where any one of her grandchildren were, she ran to the dining room and grabbed the bell.

Jaybo and Evangeline answered her summons, running right across the path of the little sedan. The driver stopped, turned off the ignition and then caught sight of the two monstrous looking children in the path of this auto. He restarted the engine, roared the horn and prepared to make a fast exit. Sonny and Bill popped from under the big boxwood, they too thought the bell was for them. Betts and the other girls came out on the porch while the croquet teams rounded the corner. The prospective lodgers were surrounded by gentian violet.

Lola and LaVerne had removed their aprons and were coming across the welcome mat at the front door, hands extended just in time to see the Father put the car in gear and move off in a whirl of dust The children looked from one to the other and sensing the poor man's panic at the sight of them, they began to giggle. Lola and LaVerne, their Blanks senses of humor overcoming their disappointment joined the children in a hearty laugh.

La and Hy remained in their room at the cottage all morning. Greased from head to toe they were unfit for household chores.

"La, I'm going to write Charley and the boys and tell them that we'll be home the first of the week." Hy spoke to her sister.

"We can't go home like this. I know it's funny but the Highpoint police will quarantine us in a jail cell!"

"Aw La, you know Mam-maw said she caught it in time and that we'll be cured in a couple of days. And if Mam-maw says so, you know she's right. Come on help me think up something to tell the fellas."

"Well, you could tell them about the square dance on Saturday night. Just to show them we are doing SOMETHING up here beside sitting on the hill."

"Yeah, that's good. Boy will I be glad to get home even if we do have to fit those ole dresses and all. A few days by ourselves with Daddy ought to be fun."

"So will the bus ride. I nearly fainted when Mother said we could ride the bus home by ourselves. Hey tell the gang about that too! That's exciting."

The last dish was washed. LaVerne was returning them to their proper shelves, rearranging and straightening the cupboards as she went. It had been hot and sticky in the kitchen. It was a relief to LaVerne to have the noon-meal over and done. Now she would join her sisters in the downstairs bedroom for a quiet rest. Betts and Martha had promised to roll up her hair and give her a facial while she stretched her weary bones out on the big bed. "My hair is a mess". She thought, "I really do need some working on." LaVerne caught sight of her reflection in the glass door of the cupboard.

"LaVerne, where is my yeast cake? Mam-maw had come into the kitchen, gone to the back porch and was looking through the ice-box.

"It's right there on the second shelf Mother, I put it there yesterday after I came from the market." LaVerne answered with impatience. Mam-maw could never find anything. She couldn't even find her glasses and she couldn't see a thing without them. Yet, her store-bought eyes were always pushed back over her forehead and rested half hidden in her topknot of snow-white hair.

"Well Delilah will just have to come here and find it for me, I can't see it anywhere."

"Mother, Delilah went down to her house twenty minutes ago, poor thing was just dead from the heat after standing over that old wood stove all morning."

"LaVerne you'll have to come then. You asked me to make rolls for supper tonight and I have to set my yeast right now if going to get them to rise by night. I really should have done it this morning but you know I had to help Gloria Parkerson with that hooked rug pattern. Then Martha Lee wanted me to hear her piano practice and now it's my nap time and I should be resting in my room this very minute." Mam-maw was out of patience herself.

"Alright, mother, I'm coming." LaVerne put down the stack of plates and went to the old wooden ice-box on the back porch.

"Why that's funny, I know I put the yeast right here yesterday." LaVerne placed her hand on an empty space on the second shelf where she knew the yeast cake should be. "It was in a new kind of wrapping, Mama, all done up like a piece of store-bought candy, I know cause I noticed it was different when I bought it at the store. Now what do you suppose could have happened to it? I put it right here in front so you would see it. Now it's gone. It's not anywhere." LaVerne felt completely exasperated with the mystery.

"It looked like candy, did it?" Mam-maw began to smile. "Well I just bet I know where that yeast is right now."

"You do?"

"I sure do!" Mam-maw began a low secretive laugh. "Leon Blanks, that little devil." She shook her finger at the empty space at the head of the table where Leon had eaten at noon. "LaVerne, that little rascal came to me this morning and said he felt bloated. He asked me for a dose of salts. I gave it to him right away. His tummy was swollen and he did look downright peaked." LaVerne wondered what on earth had gotten her mother off on to this tangent. She often dosed her grandchildren with salts or gave them an NR tablet, with less provocation than a swollen tummy.

"Good for you mother, he'll feel better by night, I'm sure. Now what are we going to do about your yeast?"

"Why, I'm just going to make him go to the village right now and get me another cake. He ate it! So, it serves him right."

"He WHAT?" LaVerne gasped.

"He ate it. Of course he did. He must have thought it was nougat and just gobbled it up. Well it serves him right to be rising in the stomach. I hope he rises double. If he doesn't get to town right now and get me some more, I'm going to kneed him just like a loaf of bread. That'll take the wind out of him."

LaVerne was beginning to understand what her mother was trying to tell her. Leon and the big boys, frequently slipped down the back steps to raid the ice-box in the night. It had been the bane of her existence all summer to come in to the kitchen in the morning only to find half the breakfast fixings gone, vanished. They grinned like cats at her early morning tantrums and paid no heed to her warnings.

"Well, this was the last straw." LaVerne said. "It's past one-o-clock and I was counting on those rolls for supper. She sat down on the long bench at the children's table, wiped the perspiration from her forehead and began to cry. Tears poured. She couldn't stop them. She was worn out, hot and ready to scream with indignation.

"Aw, LaVerne, don't get upset. They didn't mean to do it. You know boys have to be boys. You take it too personally. Now you just go on and get yourself a little rest. I'll round up that young offender and head him to the store this minute." LaVerne checked her flooding emotions, mopped at her eyes and rose to her mother's side. She gave her a little hug around the neck. Mam-maw squeezed her back and left the kitchen in search of Leon, satisfied LaVerne had passed her crisis.

LaVerne returned to the cupboard to finish putting the plates away. Tears welled up in her eyes again. "I just can't help it." She thought. "If only I could talk to somebody. But I dare not tell anyone. Oh, Dear Lord". She Whispered. "What am I to do? Another summer of hard work and I haven't been able to save but fifty dollars. How am I to manage? I don't think I can take another long cold, hungry winter in Fort Smith. I don't mind, Lord, it's the children. Bless their little souls, we just don't have enough to eat. They live in hand me down clothes from Lola's girls and Becks nephews on Toms side. And Harold, my Harold, I don't know what he does with his money. He must make more. Forgive me dear God forgive me, but I love him I can't help it, he's my husband and I love him." Her tears poured. She was sobbing out loud and couldn't control herself.

"I'm lucky everyone's in the front of the house," she thought, "I can't let them see me like this." The tears stopped and she seemed to feel better all over. She didn't feel hot and tired anymore. She went out on the back porch and put her face close to the pump and gave a plunging pull on the handle. The cool spring water came splashing out and she stuck her swollen eyes into the palms of her hands as she caught the fresh water in her cupped hands.

"Now, you silly girl, get back to that cupboard and finish up so you can get your hair screwed up. She fussed at herself. "A facial and set will make me feel better. I really do need to go to the beauty parlor. Tomorrow I'll make an appointment. Darn it, I don't care if Papa does throw a scene about it. It's my money and I deserve it more than anyone, hard as I work around here." She talked on to herself as she placed the cups and saucers on the second shelf.

"What's this I thought I'd thrown that cup without a handle out in the trash, and this saucer with the crack in it. I know I threw it away day before yesterday. Ah! Ha! Mr. Blanks, think you're pretty smart, do you?" She spoke to an invisible image of her father. "You sly old miser, can't stand to see anything thrown out, can you, well I'll show you a thing or two." Out the back door she carried the broken cups and saucers. She walked to the edge of the hill and looked down on the river. I'll show you what Verne does with broken dishes Papa." She said out loud as she drew back her pitching arm and threw the abused china over the edge and down into the river.

The river accepted this contribution just as it did the dyes of the blanket mill, the garbage of the valley and the litter of passing motorists. "The river is filthy, we really ought not to let the children swim there so much." She mused.

"LaVerne, LaVerne," Her mother called from the kitchen.

"Where on earth are you?" She discovered her daughter as she stood still looking into the river. "What on earth are you doing out there? I thought you were going to take a rest."

"Nothing Mother, just getting a little fresh air." She lied.

"Well come in here! There's someone out front. You'd better go see what they want. We have one room available, maybe they'll take it. Thank goodness all the children are taking a rest. Beck and Lola are undressed and lying down, Norma's gone back to the mill and I was half asleep. You'll just have to be the one on duty. Get that apron off and get up front. Hurry now!"

"Oh NO!" LaVerne thought. "There goes my rest." She remembered the little room upstairs with the double wedding ring quilt at the foot of the bed. It was vacant and she lost four dollars every day it stayed that way. She ran to the kitchen porch. She took off her apron and glanced in the mirror by the wash bowl. She patted down her stray hairs and walked calmly to the front door. All the activity of the morning, the extreme heat and her recent emotional outburst had left her feeling light headed.

Two figures stood on the porch. As LaVerne neared, she saw that they were an elderly couple, most respectable looking. They were just the right sort for the double wedding ring quilt room she was sure. They'd love it at Riverby. "Oops hope they don't object to children," she thought, as she made a mental recount. "20 . . . 21 . . . 22. .23. .24. Heavens to Betsy, were there that many? No wonder we dirtied up every pot and pan in the house for lunch. The kitchen sink looked as much like and orphanage as the back porch did."

She opened the screen and found a pleasant looking woman. The man at her side, her husband, was the hulking remains of a Clemson fullback. His suit bagged. He had obviously lost weight recently. His hair was permanently gray and he had deep lines in his face.

His wife did the talking and like a soft magnolia opening, she gained breadth with each breath. "I'm so sorry to bother you at this hour of the day but I wonder if by any chance your dining room is still open?"

LaVerne opened her mouth but nothing came out. She was afraid to let herself answer this fragile, underworked, over privileged appearance.

"My name is Amelia Sharp and this is my husband John." LaVerne nodded, half-heartedly at this introduction.

"We are from Atlanta. My husband isn't well. He had a little spell at the bank last week and our physician told us to get away and come right up to the mountains. We've been just driving along with no reservations anywhere. When we came over that hill yonder, John said, 'look at that house, Amelia. It looks just like my mothers and I bet they have some real fine southern cooking there'."

"Well, our lunch hour is over." LaVerne found her tongue. "But I guess I could find something left in the kitchen. I'll have to warm it up, so there'll be a little wait."

"Oh, thank you. We don't mind." Mrs. Sharp assured her.

"Just have a seat in one of the rockers and rest yourselves. I'll call you when its ready. LaVerne slipped through the door and started down the hall toward the kitchen. Becks head popped around the door to the downstairs bedroom.

"Come on, LaVerne. Lola and I have been waiting for you. Lola's almost asleep and I'm dying to tell you all about that antique blanket chest I heard about in the village today."

*The Blue Bonnet Plague*　　171

LaVerne gave her a brief resume of what had transpired and gestured toward the front porch where the two Georgians rocked. Beck peeked through the front screen and looked them over, while LaVerne went on to the kitchen.

She sliced some Tennessee ham and placed it in the skillet, warmed up the biscuits and the mustard greens on the back eye and then went to the icebox to get out the left-over cold slaw. While she waited for the ham to fry and the other things to warm, she sliced up a big red tomato and put it on two salad plates with the slaw. She went into the dining room and set two places at one of the small tables. Everything was neat and clean, set for the evening meal. She went back to the porch to call the couple in to their luncheon.

LaVerne consoled herself on the way to the porch by thinking of the seventy-five cents per person, she would receive for her efforts. As she neared the front door, she heard Becks voice.

"Of all things" LaVerne thought. "She was undressed and resting, now what's she doing on the porch?"

"Yes, this is a quaint old country Inn. My parents retired and bought this place for all us family to come home to each summer. We had so many people stop and ask, just as you did, if we wouldn't please let them eat or spend the night. We just couldn't turn them down. So here we are doing our Christian duty to poor tired, hungry travelers. Why, we never dreamed of running an Inn but it got so we had to start taking reservations. We're booked solid for the whole summer." Beck was laying back in her rocker, playing the Queen Bee.

"Oh! so sorry to hear that, I was just going to ask if we couldn't take a room for a week or two." Mrs. Sharp was truly disappointed.

LaVerne caught herself on the hall banister and felt her way along to the big newel post where she got a tight grip and had a real battle with herself. "Just wait till get my hands on you, Miss Rebekah." She talked to herself. "You'll starve for the rest of the summer before I give you another mouthful from my kitchen. If you'd just stayed in your room and kept your mouth shut, I would have rented that room upstairs."

LaVerne came upon an idea. She ran upstairs and got Beck's son Jaybo and Evangeline Parkerson. They were both swollen beyond recognition already and with the gentian violet spread all over them, they looked like lost souls from a leper colony. She gave them rapid instructions and, in a minute, the two children were back down at the front door.

LaVerne opened the screen for them, Jay half crawled, half walked to his mother and collapsed over her new pink voile dress.

Evangeline sidled up alongside of Beck and said. "Mother, dear mother, where have you been? We've been locked up in the tower room all morning, hiding like you told us. Did you rent the room? Can't we have something to eat?"

Beck struck dumb for once in her life viewed the scene at her feet in chocked horror.

Mr. and Mrs. Sharp stunned, turned their heads and saw LaVerne laughing in the doorway. The over played drama staged for Becks benefit was such a farce that even they had to laugh.
"Oh heavens! The Ham. I left it on the fire." LaVerne regained her composure. "Come on into the dining room, you two, your lunch is ready to be served."

---------------------- & *Chapter 16* & ----------------------

# Festus Lead Off!

Riverby Inn broke out with another contagion, Quilting fever! While the children were scratching and itching from poison ivy and the itch, the front porch was having a patch-work epidemic!

Gloria Parkerson was sitting on one end of the porch cutting out pieces of pink material. She hoped to assemble them into a tulip pattern quilt. Next to her sat Jewel Barnett working with her needle. She sewed fig leaves all over squares of white material.

Mam-maw was in her usual chair with her quilting frame. She was quilting the patch work design she had already sewed together. Mary Ann Thompson sat next to her.

"That's right Mary Ann, just rip up those old ties of Tommy's. Take out all the lining aid when you're done, I'll show you the next step." Mam-maw patiently tried to help Mary Ann.

"Poor Tommy," Beck chimed in, "He won't have a tie left for church." Beck was copying her mother's wedding ring pattern.

Lola on her left was creating the flower garden design.

Mary Haile and Birdie Rogers, not caring for quilting continued to crochet luncheon sets. LaVerne sat near the door, her fine needle whipping and rolling the lace insertion on a shirt waist for Mabes graduation. Although it was nearly a year off, LaVerne's time for handwork was limited. Her work was exquisite but painstaking, she wanted the dress to be very special though homemade.

"Tomorrow I'm going to ask Bynum Harwood to come show us how to petit point. He does beautiful work and you know petit point is a lost art." Mam-maw promised the girls a treat.

Beck picked up a grape panel Vaseline goblet off the floor and sipped her cool water. Looking into the bottom she admired the antique with the sun shining through it. "Speaking of lost arts, you know we gals haven't been antiquing this year. Mrs. Hunnicutt was telling me just the other day about an old cherry blanket chest she knew about over near Bat Cove. She says there's an old mountaineer woman says she wants to sell it. Seems it belonged to her first husband and her second husband won't let her keep the blankets in it."

"Sounds interesting Beck. Will you ever forget the time we heard about the Jenny Lind beds?" Lola reminded Beck of the wild experience they had, had the summer before.

"Well Beck may want to forget it, but I never will," LaVerne chuckled. "I can see Beck now caught up under the rafters of the root cellar with that prize pair of beds in plain sight. But she and the beds were wedged tight. She couldn't get to the beds and no human on earth could have gotten them out without tearing down the house. Fact was, I thought for a while there, that we were going to have to dismantle Beck to get her out."

The quilters laughed at the comic-scene LaVerne pictured.

"You think that's funny, do you?" Beck came right back.

"Well what about the time you and Lola found the nest of hornets in the top dresser drawer of that Maple dresser. I laughed till I cried at the expression on the old man's face when you two jumped through his kitchen window and stampeded his flock of goats."

"Well you girls cured me last summer." Gloria Parkerson hastened to add. "I'll do my antiquing in shops from now on. Claude scared me out of ten years growth driving around Craggy mountain in… in… in… well you remember." Gloria realized she was about to make reference to Claude's drunken condition in front of Mam-maw. She bit her tongue and hedged.

"Come on gals, let's go! Right now. We keep saying we're gonna antique but there never seems to be a good time. Well there's no time like right now. The children are all confined to the hill to recuperate and can't get into too much trouble."

Beck had the bug.

"That's a good idea Beck. Somebody has to go over to Bat Cove to tell the Weaver brothers to come play for the square dance Saturday. You all could kill two birds with one stone. I'll keep an eye on my grandchildren and that means yours too if you girls want to go." Mam-maw offered to baby-sit for the entire female group.

"Are you sure you can manage Mama? We could always just leave a message for the Weavers at the General delivery window in the village?" Lola didn't want to burden her mother.

"P'shaw, Lola, don't be such a worry wart. Course I can manage. I raised you, didn't I?" Mam-maw insisted.

"Well, alright but I do think we'd better take Bill and Sonny with us. Don't you Beck? The gentian violet hasn't helped the fist fights one iota." Lola and Beck agreed. They each took their own cars. Everyone loaded up leaving their quilting pieces with Mary Ann, who hung back shyly from the excursion.

"Go on while the spirit is moving you. I'll be glad to pick up for you. I'll just stay here and keep Mam-maw company." Mary Ann excused herself rather gracefully, Mam-maw thought.

"Mary Ann you were sweet to stay here with me. You're always so thoughtful and considerate. My but Tommy is a lucky man to have such a dear wife." Mary Ann knew Mam-maw was exaggerating her offer to stay behind and pick up the sewing. She understood and still Mam-maw's white-lie bolstered her ego.

"I'm just sick that Tommy won't be here for the Square dance. He loves to dance and you're both so good doing the Texas Star." Mam-maw continued.

"Well, I'm glad he isn't going to drive straight through all alone. Jewel and Birdie's husbands are taking turns in Jewels car so they'll make it alright. Tommy will be in on Sunday sometime."

"We tried to wait till everyone got here to have the dance but the children couldn't wait. You know Hybernia and La have to leave Sunday to go back to Highpoint and fit their debutante dresses. So, it was this Saturday or never. Gloria's Joe will miss it too. We'll do something special over Labor Day weekend though. You just wait and see!"

———————— ❧ ❦ ————————

Dan Wilde showered, shaved, shampooed, polished his brown and white shoes and put on his Palm Beach suit. It was light blue and the thought crossed his mind that if Bobbie wore a blue dress tonight, they would look like a couple that belonged together. He patted some Italian Balm on his white handkerchief before he put it into his breast pocket and adjusted his tie in front of the bathroom mirror.

Dan could hardly contain himself he was so excited. Bobbie had asked HIM to the Riverby Square Dance, not one of her other beaus in the village, but HIM. Dan Wilde couldn't get over it! And Mrs. Hedges had said that she would put his name in the pot for the buffet supper before the dance.

George his brother-in law had even offered Dan his car to drive over in. "Course it isn't but a mile up to Riverby, but maybe Bobbie and I can take a little moonlight ride after the dance." Dan thought with relish. He made a left-hand turn into the driveway, he honked and waved to the children playing in their Sunday school clothes on the lower lawn. He eased the car carefully up the drive. "In case Mrs. Hedges is on the porch, I want her to see what a good driver I am". He thought as he squeezed into the last vacant spot on the parking area.

Bobbie came down the steps before Dan got the keys out of the ignition. The skirt of her blue eyelet cotton dress made a full circle and showed off her shapely legs as she purposefully swished it with each step. Dan was in a trance. Bobbie dressed and waiting for HIM? Dan looked quickly into the rear-view mirror to see if it was really HIM sitting there.

"Well Hello Danny boy. I thought you'd never get here. What a lovely car, whose is it?" Bobbie floated up to the left front window and leaned in through it with her elbows on the frame. Dan was trapped.

"Oh, Bobbie. You… you... you… sure look purty in that dress. I sure louuuuuuuuuu uh like you in blue." Bobbie made a quick curtsey to Dan's compliment, and he opened the door and got out.

"It's Georges! The car is, I mean well he let me borrow it for tonight. Hey Bobbie, I'm gonna ask your mother if you can't ride in it with me later. After the dance, maybe just take a spin up to the village and back."

"I don't want to ride JUST to the village and back." She teased and Dan's hopes wilted. His face showed his immediate let down. "I'll tell you where I want to ride." Bobbie twisted the toe of Hy's white pumps in the grass. coyly." I want to ride to the recreation park."

"Bu…uh… uh…uh't Bobbie. There won't be enough time after the dance. You know you have to be home by eleven. Sides George would have a duck fit if I took his car to Asheville without asking, I mean."

"Well do you suppose you could ask him? For another night I mean, we could go skating! ALL alone!" Dan was unaware that he was twisting slowly around her little finger.

"Sure, sure he would. I mean I could ask. When? I mean when could we go?"

"Well, I don't have any place to go for Labor Day weekend, yet. All the other girls have made their plans. You know it's a big holiday weekend and most couples plan special, way ahead. It'll be our last weekend together and you know…. and that's pretty special, and and… well just everybody's going skating at the park".

Dan gulped his Adam's apple and rubbed his sweaty palms together. He couldn't believe his eyes or his ears. Here before him stood the prettiest girl in the valley, just waiting for him to ask her.

"Bobbie, will you go skating with me on Labor Day Weekend? Our special occasion, a goodbye for the summer. I'll get the car, I promise." Dan vowed to heaven he'd be George's slave for life if he could just have the car.

"It's a date!" Bobbie laughed, grabbed Dan's hand and pulled him toward the porch.

"Hey Dan, did ja see our powder horn? Genuine antique of the Revolutionary war?" Bill and Sonny came down the steps both wearing a powder horn. Like Siamese twins, they had made a rope loop big enough to surround the two of them and they had it over their shoulders.

"I tell you; I get the hysterics every time I see those two and that powder horn." Gloria was telling the story for the fiftieth time to the guests on the porch. "There we were out antiquing. We found the house where the blanket chest was reputed to be, but the old codger wouldn't let us past the parlor room. While we were trying to talk him into letting us into the bedroom, those two boys slipped off. We didn't even miss them. All the while we were arguing, those two were scouring the house. They got all the way up to the attic before we knew it. Here they came shouting down the steps, 'we found an antique... we found a real antique' And they had. Somewhere in their rummaging they had found that old powder horn. It really is a prize. It's got the date whittled into the cow horn." Her audience laughed every time she told the tale.

The dinner bell sounded. The rocking chairs were vacated as the guests and family rose to form a line into the dining room. Platters of fried chicken, LaVerne's German potato salad, sliced tomatoes and hot biscuits were waiting. Home canned pickled peaches and watermelon pickles and green onions were placed here and there. Mam-maw presided over the desserts laid out on her monstrous carved sideboard. There was a four-layer jam cake with caramel icing, a cherry pie, a blackberry cobbler and Sally Lunn. Norma filled the coffee cups and poured milk for the children.

The crowd moved around taking their places outside on the porch, around the fish pond in the side yard and the children moved out onto the front lawn. All but Grandy. His regular place was set at the head of the family table. He dined alone in the middle of the big room presiding over his plate with grand gestures of the silverware.

"Papa, please don't ask for seconds, we're running awful low on food. Take all the desserts you want and enjoy THAT piece of chicken." LaVerne whispered to her father as she passed through to the kitchen for hot biscuits.

"Auuuuuuuuuuuuuga! Auuuuuuuuuuuuuga! The peaceful meeting and eating on the lawn were interrupted by an antique horn mounted on a pre-historic car. The 'fellas' from Highpoint drove up the driveway in the fossilized remains from a graveyard for cars. They had received Hy's letter just in time to make the long expedition from Highpoint to Swannanoa and had survived fifteen breakdowns, no sleep and less food in order to arrive in time for the dance.

"Hey Hy! How you like it? We named it Shake, Run and Rattle. Isn't she keen?" The boys had spotted Hybernia on the front lawn with her buffet plate in her lap.

"Gee, fellas, you came? Hey! La, Mabes, the fellas are here, one for all of us."

"Yea, they chorused. Hey buddy look at that plate." One of the boys had seen Hy's loaded dinner plate. "Boy we are starved, haven't eaten a thing since we left home."

"Come on, park that contraption. There's lots of food." Hy extended an invitation to all.

"More mouths to feed? Good heavens Lola, there isn't a chicken bone left in the place. If only Hy had told me we would have prepared enough to take care of these boys, like I did for Dan. You know I asked him myself. But these boys really have a nerve just arriving here starved like this." LaVerne was really outdone.

"Isn't there any squirrel stew on the back of the stove sister?" Beck had gotten her head into the conference. Tell 'em its stewed pheasant, they're so hungry, they'll never know the difference."

"Where are they going to stay Lola?" LaVerne was really as concerned over bed space as she was over food rations.

"Well if you could double-up the girls up here, I could sleep them all down on the loft at my cottage. I just can't turn these boys out LaVerne, unfortunately they are among the finest families in Highpoint." Lola pleaded.

After the dishes were taken to the kitchen and the floor was sprinkled with cornmeal, the Weaver brothers wiped their chicken sticky fingers with their red bandanas and stepped forward to begin tuning up their instruments.

Grandpappy Weaver stood up, "Folks, we're proud to be hyar tonight. We've had good vittles and the Lord willin' my boys'll give ya good fiddlin'. Ah aim to do the callin'. Now they's plenty of seats over to your wall, so if ye don't keer to jine the dancin', just have a cheer and help with the clappin'. All right boys Let's go…. Festus, lead off…. Now all jine hands and circle right……"

Leon had claimed Mam-maw as his partner and they led off the circle. Grandy stepped up and tapped Lola who was a part of the circle before she realized what had happened. Charles had asked his mother early that morning if he could have her first dance. Harold Jr, grabbed his Aunt Beck and in turn Jaybo had gotten his mother's signal to choose his Aunt Boom. The teenage group gathered into a separate circle in a corner by the kitchen and were clowning around with the little ones sitting on the sidelines.

"Go on, Tom Jr. get Martha Lee. It doesn't matter if she's your cousin. Come on Sonny, get Betts, Bill you get Sis, come on, we'll let you in our circle." Hy tried to get them into the swing of things.

"Aw shucks, I always get stuck with Sis. Here Sonny you dance with her," Bill complained.

Bobbie and Dan were sitting in the corner. They stuck out like sore thumbs. Bobbie was very peaked that she had been left out of the teenage circle. She had been more shocked than anyone on the hill when the car load of attractive ivy leaguers had arrived from Highpoint. The extra boy they brought along for her was dancing with Evangeline Parkerson.

"Here, Dan, you and Bobbie take my place. I'm all tuckered out." Mam-maw sensing the situation had broken the circle in favor of letting the two wall-flowers in.

"As a final number, my boys'll play 'I Dreamt I Waltzed my Darlin Back Home' and I want all you men out thar to claim your darlin' and waltz nice and easy like."

"Night, Miz Blanks. We Weavers shore enjoyed your party, I warn't a feelin' to pert last week, but when I got your message about the callin' tonight, I jus perked right up." Grandpappy Weaver paid his final respects to Mam-maw and took his leave.

---

Tommy Thomson pulled into the Riverby Inn gates before noon. He didn't mind missing the Saturday Night Square Dance but he was sure not to miss Sunday Dinner.

Grandy had just come up the driveway minutes before, trailing his flock of Trundle Bed Trash behind him. The Reverend Coffin had delivered a short sermon on tithing and Grandy didn't wait around as usual to shake his hand.

After Tommy had greeted everyone, he sought out Mary Ann in their downstairs bedroom.
"Honey, I could have sworn I saw Hybernia and LaVerne Hudson getting off a Trailways bus in Black Mountain. They got into a dilapidated looking car with a bunch of boys and started off over Old Fort mountain. I guess it couldn't have been them, but it sure did look like them. Cute looking bunch of kids though. They had written on the rumble seat, 'Shake Run and Rattle.'"

# Chapter 17

# Wheelamania

All of Riverby was on wheels. The upper part of the lawn was used for a parking lot for the guests and their cars were going and coming all day long as they took side trips to Chimney Rock, Mt. Mitchell and into the Smokies. Beck's LaSalle was hardly still a minute. Even Norma was trying out an old Model T Ford and dickering with the owner to come down on his price, Charles and Leon had surreptitiously acquired a motorcycle and practiced riding it down on Lovers' Lane.

A teenage car craze had swept the Swannanoa Valley until wheelamania had become an epidemic for which there seemed to be no cure.

Glover Petersen, Dan Wilde and many of the other neighbor boys drove their homemade cars up to the front steps of Riverby and with much backfiring and honking of horns, proudly showed off their half-breed automobiles. Sons of Buicks and daughters of Dodge were blended together in what appeared to be a shotgun marriage. The foundation was any old chassis the junk yard offered and odd fenders and running boards and engines of dubious character were installed. A steering wheel, blasting horn and crooked headlights completed the ensemble.

Some were so low slung the driver was inches off the road and some were so high off the ground, the girls had to be boosted on board. Harold Jr. had created the car supreme by welding the front end of an old Stutz Bear Cat onto the rear of a Plymouth. Conversation centered around spark plugs and carburetors and exhaust pipes and, most important of all, a proper name for the car. The name was gaily painted on the side of the car and the front porch rockers watched with amusement as Flying Jenny, Pegasus, and Petunia lurched past.

"Glover, why did you name your car The Mayflower?" Harold Jr. asked Leon's best friend.

"Because so many Puritans have come across in it," he laughed and adjusted one cockeyed headlight.

"You'd better not let Grandy hear you say that. Are you sure this thing is safe?" Harold ignored the fact his car didn't have a single door on it.

"Oh sure, it runs fine. Have a little trouble with the floor boards, though. Took Bobbie for a little spin the other day out Bee Tree Road and when I changed gears to make that curve near the church, I'll be darned the floor boards didn't give away on Bobbie's side and when I looked back, there she was sitting in the middle of the road. Laugh? Thought I'd die"

Leon had the motorcycle hidden in Mr. McClain's cornfield while he tried to adjust the brakes. He finished what he hoped was a thorough job and stood up to wipe his hands on some corn silks. Coming down the lane toward the Village was Grandy. He walked with his usual stance. His back was straight as an Indian's and his hands were clasped together behind his back.

"Hope I beat Verne and Lola to the post office," Leon heard him mutter.

Leon decided to take the bull by the horns and show Grandy the motorcycle. If he could get, his approval, then he knew he and Charles could bring the machine on the hill. He jumped on the seat and roared the engine for a moment and sped up to Grandy who was trying to jump out of the way.

"Hey Grandy! Want a ride to the Village?"

"Leon! What is that thing? Where did you get that Devil's Horse? Get off that contraption quick before it turns on you."

"This is my motorcycle. Charles and I went in halves on it. If you like it, I can even ride you into Asheville and think of all that bus fare you'll save... twenty cents each way. Come on and get on behind me. I can get you to the Post Office in two minutes flat."

That decided Grandy. He gingerly climbed astride the cycle and with one hand holding on to his hat and the other holding on to Leon, he clinched his pipe in his teeth and yelled, "Fire away."

Leon gave her the gun and roared off. He dipped and swerved and laughed his fiendish laugh. "How do you like it, Grandy? See, I have her under control.... she steers easy as pie. Look! No hands!"

"Let me off this thing! Grab them handle bars, boy."

"Nothing to it, Grandy, look! I can drive with my eyes closed." Leon turned around to show Grandy that indeed he did have his eyes closed.

"A cow! Look out for that cow, dad blame you."

Grandy started beating Leon on the head with his brown felt hat and tried to grab the handle bars.

It was too late. A nice plump dumb Jersey had wandered into their path and stood there watching the Devil's Horse and its two riders plow right into her. Leon had opened his eyes and applied the skittish brakes too late. Grandy and Leon landed in a poison ivy bed and watched the still active motorcycle lunge and cavort after the unhurt but startled cow.

"Somebody's going to have buttermilk for dinner tonight," Leon laughed as he watched the cow lurch into the cornfield.

Grandy continued to thrash Leon with the fedora. "If I'm going to be killed on wheels, it, it'll be a Cadillac and not a Devil's Horse."

"Pride goeth before a mighty fall, Grandy," Leon lay back full length in the poison ivy and rolled over and over laughing all the while as he quoted Grandy's favorite quotation from the Bible.

"What did you call that thing again, Sonny?" asked Bill

"It's not a thing, it's a soapbox racer and it is called a B-Nanny.

"Looks about as crazy as its name, to me. But if it will go as fast as you say it will, I'm game to try to make one." Tom Jr. said encouragingly.

The gang looked at the drawing in the dirt and tried to visualize the finished product. They were dying to get on wheels, too.

They had gone Indian fashion over the pipe that morning to the island to swing on the big grapevine swing. Taking turns at the swing and giving the usual Tarzan yells, they soon graduated to the more dangerous sport of shimmying up a young sapling until the weight of their bodies near the top of the tree made it bend down and snap the rider back up into a wide arche.

Two of the boys had made the long climb up the big pine tree to the crow's nest and were bombarding the children below with buckeyes.

Several had climbed into the old crooked tree that a winter storm had bent over and down into a big U shape. It was almost like a hammock. Lolling back against the rough bark and sucking on the juice from the mountain honey suckle blossoms, they were plotting their adventures for the day. Sonny had come up with the idea of making the B Nanny's.

"I saw a boy make one of these last winter and it was something. You just need four wheels, a seat and two ropes to guide it by. Course if you want to fancy it up, you can tie the ropes to a wheel and use it for a steering wheel and put a box on the front for a hood and use old license plates on the back. Some kids nail Cherry Smash bottle caps on the front like headlights," Sonny explained. He was squatted down under the tree and drawing a sketch of the car in the hard-packed dirt with a stick.

"We'll have to get partners. With all of us looking for wheels and things, we'll need one to be making the B-Nanny and the other to be collecting the stuff we'll need. Then, too, we can have teams and race against each other," Jaybo advised.

The idea caught like wild fire and the gang left the trees and grapevine and ran back across the pipe to scour the yard, dump and neighbors for B-Nanny parts.

"No darn it, I don't have any wheels or two by fours or rope or anything else," Mabes said to the children. "You all go somewhere else and don't disturb us because we're working on a new contest. Mam-maw have you thought, of a seven-letter word meaning round, slender and blunt?"

"Sounds like 'cigarette' to me, except it has too many letters," Mam-maw laughed as she continued her cross-word puzzle.

"Aw, I don't know why everybody keeps on with those contests. All summer long somebody has been sending in entries or jingles to a soap company hoping to win a hundred dollars. Prissy Bobbie thought she was going to be Miss Palmolive Soap Complexion Girl and all she got was a pink celluloid hair brush. Who cares about soap anyway? We need wheels". Tom Jr. and Jaybo stomped off.

"Come on Mam-maw, tell me in ten words why you like P and G soap," Mabes ignored the boys and turned again to Mam-maw in the next rocker.

Martha and Betty stepped back to appraise their B-Nanny. They had found a nice wide plank from the old barn. Actually, the plank was very loose on the back side and with their help it had come off the siding very easily. They hoped Grandy wouldn't notice the hole it had left. Two small doll baby buggy wheels were attached to the front end of the planks on the original axil from the buggy and two stout jumping ropes with red knobs, on the ends were already attached to the wheels. It worked fine.

"Come on, Betts, let's go into the Village and canvass some of the stores and yards up there. We have to have two more wheels for the back. We just, can't let those boys get ahead of us.

"I'll tell you what! Let's go over to the Harwood's and maybe if we hint around enough, Mr. Harwood will give us some of those wheels he has. It's worth a try. Anyway, we can play with little Billie Mae. She's a darling baby."

Sis joined Mabes and Mam-maw on the porch and pulled up a rocker next to them. "My mama says that in this picture if I find thirty things that begin with the letter "S" I'll get a year's supply of Juicy Fruit gum. Will somebody help me? I'll give you a stick if I win," she said generously.

Martha Lee and Betty found the Harwood at home in their brown painted cottage. "Hey you all," they called as they entered the yard.

Patricia and Bynum were sitting on the porch swing. Patricia went right on shelling black-eyed peas and looked up from under her bright red mop of shaggy hair to smile at the girls. Bynum laid aside the baby nightgown he was feather stitching and stretched his long-freckled arms.

"Well, hey right back at you. We're glad to have thome company. I've been buthy with my rolling and whipping, my eyeth are ready to burth right out of my head. When you get ready to leave, I want you to return the crothet hook I borrowed from Mam-maw."

"Did you finish crocheting Billie Mae's christening dress?" Martha giggled shyly.

"thertainly did and the lookth adorable in it. How about thome homemade root beer? A glath would hit the thpot right now. Patritha, darling, how about it?"

"It did set up right good, girls. Bynum made it last week and while most of it is in a big crock, he put some of it in Orange Crush bottles. Wait here and I'll bring some out."

"Mr. Bynum," Martha began, "do you have any old wheels and an axle to go with them that you don't want? We're making soapbox racers at Riverby and Betts and I are trying to beat the boys getting theirs made. In payment for your kindness, maybe we could be nursemaid to little Bynum and Billie Mae for you someday while you and Miss Patricia go into Asheville."

Bynum was thoughtful as he once again picked up the baby nightgown and began the feather stitching. He held the garment up close to his nearsighted eyes as he pushed and pulled the needle expertly in and out of the material.

"Ith a deal," he decided. "We won't leave our babieth with juth anybody but I truth you girlthe. It tho happenth that I do have two wheel barrow wheelth. I'll let you borrow them and when you're through you can give them back to me. They'll make thwell wheelth and I'll throw in thome athll greath too. Bet thoth boyth will be jealouth when you all with path them. Hee, hee, hee. Oh, here, Patrith, let me help you. Thith thure lookth refrething. Why didn't you youth thoth new glatheth with the flowerth painted on them? Girlth, tell Mabeth I've taken up drawing and painting…. I've done thome pathtelth that are lovely."

Patricia blushed for being called down in front of the girls. She could never do anything right in Bynum's eyes. They all drank deeply of the root beer. It was so highly carbonated it stung all the way down.

"Pretty good, eh?" Bynum bragged. "I muth thay it hath a powerful kick."

The girls held their hands over their mouths politely as they burped. Tears were in their eyes from the chemical reaction.

Lugging home the wheel barrow wheels…. each girl balanced one on her head…. they took turns carrying the christening dress which Bynum had insisted they take back to show Mam-maw. He had tied it up in a box with tissue paper around it and returned the crochet hook in the box also. The small can of axle grease was in Betty's overall watch pocket.

"Boy oh boy, was this our lucky day! Free wheels, axel grease and free root beer. Man, that stuff nearly took off the top of my head. Do you think that it had REAL beer in it? I was sorta fraid to drink mine. Do I act drunk?" Martha was worried.

"Nah, it's perfectly all right to drink root beer. It's not THAT kind of beer at all. They just cook up some kind of root, like snakeroot or sassafras roots and add it to ginger ale or yeast cakes."

—————————— ❧ ❧ ——————————

"Do you know what's gotten into Lola and LaVerne? Are they actually serious about walking all the way to Black Mountain?" Mam-maw stopped rocking and turned to Beck who had just turned off her motor and joined her mother on the porch

"It's only four miles up there and the exercise will do them good. Maybe it'll take some of the starch out of the major general. I Just passed them coming out of the entrance and nearly wrecked the car I was laughing so hard. The two 'hikers' were walking like they were taught how young ladies should walk at their dear Alma Mater, the Memphis Conference Female Seminary…. bosoms out, stomachs in, behinds poked out, and feet pointed right and then left. Lola tried to get me to go with them and set an example to everyone on the hill. They are disgusted with everybody being on wheels and they, of all people, want all of Riverby to profit by their example and start walking."

"They must be serious, there they go across the bridge and around the bend in the highway," Mam-maw lowered her eye shade." I'm waiting right here until they get back safely."

"Safely? What on earth could possibly happen to those two? I don't care if that LaSalle steering wheel becomes glued to my hands, you won't catch me walking." Beck went into the kitchen to make a sandwich and get a Coca-Cola. It might be a long time until dinner with LaVerne out of the kitchen.

*Figure 18: Distant bridge over the Swannanoa*

———————— ❧ ❧ ————————

Beck put down her crocheting and peered through the vines on the porch. "Well, well, Mama, here come the hikers. I thought, I heard some moaning and groaning."

Lola refused to look at Beck as she came up the front steps stiff-legged and took her seat in the first rocker. She leaned down and began to untie her Enna Jettick shoes. LaVerne's blond-gray hair was disheveled and escaping the hair pins she tried without success to use to get it under control. She couldn't make it up the steps so just collapsed on the top step and leaned against the post.

"Daughters, speak to me. I know something happened to you. What's the matter?" Mam-maw didn't know whether to get some hot salts water to soak their feet in or give them a dose of salts.

"We started out fine. We were enjoying our walk and looking at the joys of nature. We had gone about a mile; you know where that roadside spring is? We decided to stop and get a drink of water."

"Lola, that's not a mile from here. It's just around the bend," Beck corrected.

"Well, have it your way. Anyway, we decided to get a cool drink of mountain spring water to quench our thirst. While we were standing there with the dippers in our hands, a car stopped on the side of the highway and a young man jumped from his car and joined us," Lola said.

"He was most polite," LaVerne remembered. "A gentleman through and through. I'm a good judge of character."

"We fell into conversation and when he found out we were walking to Black Mountain he asked us if we didn't want to ride up there with him. He opened the car door for us and we stepped into the back seat," Lola continued without looking at the faces of Beck and Mam-maw. "He banged the door and started with a jerk. As we took our seats, we both noticed this long wicked looking sawed-off shot gun on the front seat by his side.... in very convenient reaching distance. We nudged each other but dared not speak."

"YOU dared not speak?" laughed Beck.

"Daughter, what was the gun for?" Mam-maw was most concerned.

"I'm coming to that part, if I may continue to have the floor and not have any more side remarks. Well, across the valley to our right and running parallel with the highway was a long endless freight train. It was headed toward Black Mountain, too. The young man kept turning his head in the direction of the train. He seemed to me to be trying to race it." Lola stopped to catch her breath.

"Mam-maw we were too frightened to ask any questions or even attempt to make polite conversation," LaVerne put in. "But suddenly he began to smile at us and said he guessed we were wondering about his gun and why he was racing the train. Lola spoke up and said we certainly were entitled to an explanation. I was open and honest with him and admitted I was scared stiff."

"To make a long story short. It turned out he was a deputy sheriff out of Asheville and was racing the train to Black Mountain for there was every reason to believe there was a hobo hiding somewhere on the train. He was wanted for murdering a man in Asheville last night."

"Murder?" Gasped Beck and Mam-maw.

"Yes, and they believed he was trying to escape by way of the train. He could have been underneath one of the cars or hanging between two freight cars. Well, you can imagine how relieved we were to know we weren't victims of a kidnapping! By this time, we were rounding the curve on two wheels as we came into town and sighted the station. The young man drove right up to the side of the tracks and LaVerne and I nearly fell in front of the train trying to get out of that car. There were officers lined up and ready for action. The young man in his haste seemed to have for gotten he had two passengers in the back seat of his car."

"What would Emily Post say?" Giggled Beck.

"He grabbed his gun and ran to join the other officers," Lola went on not looking at Beck.

"Little did he know he had the major general on board," Beck couldn't resist saying.

"Do you want to hear the rest of the story, Miss Smarty? Anyway, we ran in the opposite direction toward the main street before the shooting began. And that's all we know about it. No shots were fired because we surely would have heard them. We were so un-nerved by the whole experience that we decided not to walk back home. Fortunately, we ran into Flossie Hunnicutt on the main street and she brought us back as far as the bridge." Lola massaged her feet.

LaVerne said, "Weren't we silly to have climbed into a car with a man we did not know? That's the biggest fool thing I ever heard of two old married women with children being guilty of doing. Why in this wild mountain area, anything could have happened to us."

"Like what?" Beck was having a wonderful time at their expense.

"Beck, this is serious. I'm going to have a good long talk with my girls about not accepting rides with strangers. Who knows what might happen in this day and age and everybody on wheels?" LaVerne made a mental note to talk privately with Mabes and, especially, Bobbie.

"If that young man was in such a hurry to catch a racing freight train and a murderer, I wonder why he stopped to get a cool drink of water by the side of the road?" Mam-maw wondered out loud.

# Chapter 18

# Anvil Brand

Not a rocker on the porch moved. Empty, they stood erect and quiet, pushed slightly back against the wall by the early morning cleaning crew, Martha and Betts. Grandy the sole occupant of the porch, sat as erect as the rockers in his favorite cradle. He slept. His firm chin resting on his chest. Occasionally a snore would arose him but then he'd return to the arms of Morpheus.

The house was a beehive of activity. Cleaning, preparing lunch, arranging flowers, baking the bread; all took place somewhere within the large frame house. The porch remained desolate. The children vanished earlier in the morning for a hike up the mountain. All except for Leon who was now rounding the corner of the house to join the others. He spotted Grandy, peacefully oblivious to the world, asleep in his rocker.

Leon took the steps two at a time. Unable to resist the blissful picture Grandy made and still smarting from the thumps Grandy had given him this morning, Leon took advantage of the situation. He took his prized good luck token, a rabbit's foot from his pocket and stealthily began to tickle Grandy under the nose. The old man stirred slightly and swatted at what he mistook to be a fly. Leon backed around the corner out of sight and waited. Grandy settled back into a deep sleep. Leon advanced once again. This time he tickled behind the old man's ear. Grandy stirred and scratched. His one good eye blinked open then shut. He pulled his hat down over his ears, letting it rest on his nose.

Leon feeling more audacious, stooped over the front of the rocker and worked the rabbit's foot vigorously back and forth under his grandfather's chin. Grandy squirmed and wiggled. He came up out of the chair fighting mad at the varmints which he thought were interfering with his nap time.

Leon couldn't resist a fiendish laugh. Grandy awake now recognized his grandson.

"Why, you little rascal, get yourself out of here right now." Leon put the porch behind him as he dashed to the front yard and began to tease.

"I'll be glad when you're dead, you rascal you! I'll be glad when......." Leon sang down the driveway.

Grandy stood there and shook his fist at the imp who was fast disappearing toward Old Hickory.

"What on earth ales you Papa?" Lola said as she came out of the house.

"That Leon, Lola, I tell you something has to be done about this Trundle Bed Trash. They're gettin too uppity for their own good."

Any further discussion on their part was forestalled by a procession of adults onto the porch. LaVerne and Mam-maw came out, aprons on, with buckets of green apples to be peeled for a lunch time cobbler. Mam-maw's advent to the porch each morning always brought out half the guests as well. Becks La Salle came up the road and parked near the tearoom. She and Gloria Parkerson and Mary Haile climbed out laden with pounds of butter and pints of cream plus several gallons of milk.

"They're my grandchildren and that's my river and if they want to swim and play down there, you're not going to stop them LaVerne." Mam-maw announced her text for the day. She and LaVerne continued a conversation which they had apparently gotten underway in the kitchen.

"It's so filthy. Everybody in the valley throws any and everything into it and......" LaVerne was cut short by her mother.

"Hush now! Don't go telling such tales. You'll scare these poor guests to death. The idea. Such nonsense. Here, take this pan on back to Delilah and get her started. I'll finish these others in a few minutes." Mam-maw. got rid of LaVerne.

"Just a minute there Miss Verne," Grandy stopped LaVerne at the door. "Talk about dirtying up the river, do you. Well just tell me young lady, how these got in there?" Grandy pulled several bits of broken china from his coat pocket.

"I don't want to discuss it any further," LaVerne skirted around him and made through the door. Grandy followed close on her heels shouting.

"Don't know how you all can be so careless with the china? I just picked some out of the trash can the other day, now I finds these in the river.... Lord sakes, gal, y'all think we're china millionaires?????" His voice faded and LaVerne's answer, if she gave one, went unheard.

"Mam-maw, we are going to have to be more careful, sure enough. Norma came home last night and said there was talk at the factory about Infantile Paralysis in the valley." Lola introduced this new thought. Beck and Mary Haile came out onto the porch from the house.

"Beck that's the prettiest butter I ever saw." Mary described Miss Lou Patton's butter.

"It's delicious too!" Beck spoke through a mouthful of salt rising bread. She held a slice in one hand. It was at least and inch deep in the golden yellow butter.

"Hear anything up at the post office, Beck?" Lola asked. "You know, about the Infantile Paralysis?"

"Yes, they say it's pretty bad back around Bat Cove. Not a single case here in Swannanoa yet though." Beck gave her report.

"See! that settles it. Y'all are always getting worked up over nothing. They're always having some queer thing in Bat Cove. Those folks are all inter-married with Indians. What do you expect?" Mam-maw tried to close the issue.

"What do you think?". LaVerne returned to the porch and continued to pursue the subject.

"Oh, I think Mama's right, just queer folks having some queer disease. They don't really know whether it's Infantile Paralysis or just Indian. They won't let a doctor near the place, those folks practice their own kind of medicine, don't believe in doctors. You know, like Papa, wouldn't see a doctor if he cut his head off." Beck stuffed a stick of gum in her mouth.

"Rebekah; don't talk about your Papa. He's just a healthy man and he doesn't need doctors." Mam-maw explained.

"Healthy nothing, he's just too tight to pay the bill." Lola chimed in.

"I'm going to ignore that remark young lady. You'd better keep any others to yourself." Mam-maw gasped.

"Wonder what that trains doing stopped over there on the track?" Lola observed.

"It's been there all morning. It's near time for the cornbread express to come around the bend. That engineer had better hurry and move on or we'll be having another train wreck out there." Mam-maw raised her heavy frame from the rocker and went toward the kitchen.

"Well I know what I'm going to do about the river. Hudson's coming to bring the girls back this week and I'm just going to have him go into Asheville and buy them a canoe. It won't keep them away from the river but at least it will keep them out of the water for the most part." Lola had had the canoe on her mind all summer but just never seemed to get around to buying it.

"Look over there at that train sister," Beck broke in, "Don't you see some little children playing on top of one of those cars?"

"I see something moving around up there." Mary Haile added.

"Yes, you're right. There are some children up there. Probably some of that mountaineer clan that runs the still up on Hickory." LaVerne surmised.

"Poor untended little fellows, they're pitiful. Don't have any toys or playthings except the trains and mountains, I guess." Lola joined in.

"They's women's children," LaVerne smiled. "You know last week they came through the yard and were hanging around the back door. I was in the kitchen and I took them out some cookies. But do you know they wouldn't touch them? I asked them who their Pa was and you know what they said? They said, 'we ain't got no Pa mam', we'uns women's chillun'."

"That trains moving!" Mary Haile raised her voice. "It's moving, those children are gonna be killed."

"Verne! Verne!" Grandy yelled. He was running up the driveway from his garden.

"Here I am Papa, good heavens, what's wrong? Stop that running. You'll have a heat stroke!"

"I may have a heat stroke but you're gonna have a hissin' duck fit." He gasped for more breath. "The chillun', our chillun' is over yonder climbing all over that train. If that train starts to move…." Grandy was unaware that the train had moved since he first spotted the children and started to the house in his pell-mell flight to warn his daughters.

Mam-maw came bolting through the front door, her piece of quilt she used to flag the train was in her hands.

"Yoo Hoo!! Yoo Hooooooooooooooo! She screamed at the train.

The train had gathered steam and moved around the curve to town. The cornbread express was close behind.

"Well, I'll be a damn yankee!" Grandy spotted the children coming across the corn patch. "There they are, them rascals. I'll wail the tar out of 'em with a black cherry bough. Just let me get my hands on 'em, dad burned little idiots."

The wind had shifted and the Trundle Bed Trash, downwind of the commotion on the hill, took a sudden detour. They spread out over the field in all directions, looking for cover. Leon took his torn soiled white handkerchief out of his pocket and began to wave it, in surrender.

"None of that foolishness, Leon Blanks. You've got your come-uppance coming, Now get yourself up this hill this minute." Lola called from the bottom step of the porch.

A car sped up the road to the house and stopped, screeching its brakes. When the dust cleared, Lola noted her Homer, pale and shaking in the back seat. Under the wheel, his teenage daughter, LaVerne raced the engine, reversed the gears, grating the machinery under the hood and shot backwards to the steps. She had over-run her first attempt to land squarely in front. Hybernia was dragging on a long cigarette holder.

*Anvil Brand*   189

Her hair hung limp unpinned over one eye. She turned around and unlocked the back door to let her pent-up father out. Lola stared speechless at her family.

"Well General, don't just stand there." LaVerne opened the car door and reached for the ground, her lovely long legs showing from the thigh down. "We your loyal staff, reporting for duty. Attention!" She pulled her two tanned feet together and gave a halfhearted salute. Homer had made his way to the steps. He stopped short of embracing his wife and opened fire.

"Lola, your girls almost killed me in that car. They brought me over Old Fort mountain at forty miles an hour. FOR---TY miles an hour! I'm a dead man. Look at me… you know my nerves can't stand much. My ulcers are eating each other up. Just feel my heart. It's about to jump out of my chest. Do something. Don't just stand there…. do SOMETHING!" Homer collapsed on the bottom step. Then rose on second thought and put his linen pocket handkerchief under his seat. He spread it on the step and sat again moaning and groaning, his head between his hands.

"Do you want me to call an ambulance for you or the juvenile authorities for them?" Lola was embarrassed in front of the porch full of family and guests.

Hy rounded the car from the right-side suitcase in hand. The mahogany cowhide matched her tanned skin and nearly outweighed her frail figure. Its contents were twelve pair of shoes.

"Well Moll, aren't you glad to see your hubby and us Highpoint Debs? Dad just insisted that we come on today. Funny he was so anxious to get here. I think Richard Sanders must have really scared him. He put the ladder right up to my window. Why we were as good as eloped. Guess I'll have to marry that boy yet. He just insists on it!"

Sixteen-year-old LaVerne, addressed her sister one year her senior. "Child bride! Isn't she a floozie? About to disgrace us all at the tender age of seventeen." La threw back her long blond hair and chuckled.

The porch silently witnessed the Hudson's arrival in embarrassed amusement, Lola regained her tongue.

"Son, where is Sonny Hudson? Did anyone see him out there?" She motioned toward the corn patch in front where the children were beginning to reassemble. Since the train crisis seemed diverted, they were ready to make their re-entry to the family group.

"There he is Lola. Next to Jay. See him?" Mam-maw had spotted him." Now you and Homer come on up out of the noonday sun and sit yourselves here by me."

"You gals unload the car. Open the trunk and the big boys will help you carry things in." Beck advised the two teenage rebels.

The Trundle Bed Trash with hang-dog expressions greeting to Hy and La. They nodded to their mothers and relatives on the front porch. Betts was the first one to spot him. Sitting next to Mam-maw, hunched forward, head in hands, Homer Hudson had gone unnoticed to the other children.

"Uncle Hudson. Uncle Huddy! Did'ja bring us some new overalls? Hey gang, Look! Uncle Huddy is here," Betts incited the gang. They leapt to the porch and surrounded their uncle. The nervous overall tycoon rocked back in his chair, pulled his knees up to his chest to defend himself and mumbled to his wife, "Get 'em away Lola! I'm having a nervous breakdown. Get them out of here. Mrs. Blanks make them go away. I brought a car load of overalls to them. They're in the car… in the trunk. Tell them. They're there… get 'em away from me."

Lola sprang into action. "Now children, you know your Uncle Hudson is a very nervous man. You're going to make him sick. Get off the porch and let him rest. He brought you all overalls, they're in the car. See those big boxes Leon is unloading? Take them into Mamas room, Leon, we'll try them on after lunch."

"Lunch!" Mam-maw came to life. "Land sakes my cornbread. Wash up everybody. Lunch will be ready in a minute." She addressed the whole porch. "Come on Son, you can use my bathroom to gee tidied up for lunch." She invited Homer into her room.

The gang skirted the house and made their way to the back porch, where they washed up under the cold-water pump. Lola insisted that Hy and La take their meal in the main dining room with her. She wanted a more coherent explanation of their untimely arrival. The main eatery of Riverby held a subdued group of adults. The elders of the Blanks family held their tongues and waited the entrance of Hudson. He entered silently, looked around at the guests and took his seat daring anyone to disturb his peace at the table.

He quickly threw down the glass of warm soda water, Lola had provided as a starter course in his dinner plate. At Grandy's request he belched out a blessing.

"Bleeeeeeeeeeess            thiiiiiiiiiis   fooooooo, and uhhhhhs  to thiiiiiiiiiii……Hurummmmmmmmp , Amen." No one ever understood a word of Uncle Huddy's blessings.

At the same time on the back porch the gang was quiet as mice, lest some mother in the kitchen overhear. They whispered a discussion of the mornings near catastrophe.

"Boy that was too close for comfort." Bill rubbed his backsides.

"We should have hidden in the cave. I told you all we had better get down off that train before someone saw us." Jaybo interjected his cautious outlook.

"Hid in the cave and missed all the fireworks?" Sonny chimed in. Why you're chicken, Jaybo, always being so smart with your I told you so's, after we're in trouble."

"Who you calling a coward? Sonny Hudson." Bill swung to his older brother's defense.

"Sides I wouldn't have missed seeing Daddy and those crazy girls for all the lickings in Buncombe county." Sonny continued.

"Boy, was he mad at Hy and La. I thought he was gonna kill 'em when got out of that car. Crazy old gals. They're always pootin' around with Daddy. Why if I did that, he'd skin me alive."

"Hush, they'll hear you." Betts cautioned. "Mother will wash your mouth out with octagon soap if you don't mind your manners Sonny Hudson, that's not a nice word to use around us girls."

"Nothin' wrong with pootin'," Son pursued the usage of his latest nasty word. "Mam-maw poots every morning on that chamber pot in her room. Lordy, you can hear her all over the downstairs. If it's good enough for Mam-maw, then its good enough for you, Miss Priss."

"Aw, shut up Son." Tom Jr, blushed.

"Well anyhow, we were sure lucky that Uncle Huddy and the girls arrived when they did. Boy that sure got us off the hook. Aunt Lola was ready to lay into me." Leon sighed.

"Don't think you're off the hook, young man. Any of you!" Aunt LaVerne stuck her head around the kitchen door hearing the last of their conversation. "I heard what you said and I'm going to have a talk with all of you. Just you wait." She turned and came out to Betts. "Here, take this in to your Uncle Hudson." LaVerne gave her daughter a dish of boiled, unseasoned green beans. "You all got your poor uncle so upset he can't eat his dinner. He has to have a soft diet."

"Soft diet, nothing. He's just plain finicky. He's always got to have something different from the rest of us." Betts balked at this special chore. "Like to see what I'd get if I refused to eat what was put in front of me."

"You'll see what you'll get if you don't hush up and get this into that dining room, young lady." Aunt Boom patted Betts on her backsides.

"I sure do hope Uncle Huddy brung some small overalls for me." Little Sis wondered out loud. "I hate wearing these ole lace panties. I wanna look like you all do. Wonder why that ole silly factory of his don't make lil' gulls overalls?"

"Cause lil' gulls don't s'posed to wear overalls." Sonny mocked Sis's southern drawl." Sides you don't gotta wear no lace pants either. Just don't wear nothing. Like Hy, she doesn't wear any underpants. She goes plum buck under her pleated skirts. Fact is she doesn't wear anything under her middy either."

"Why Sonny Hudson, shame on you." Martha's fair skin turned a deep red. "Boys aren't supposed to know such things, much less discuss them."

"I can hardly wait till we get to opening up the boxes. I sure hope he didn't forget my bathing suit. I want to go up to Lake Eden with Glover and the boys on Saturday and I sure can't go in my old overalls." Leon thought out loud.

"Hey, guess what?" Betts dashed back onto the porch. "They're gonna buy us a canoe. A canoe. Did you hear me?"

"A what? What are you talking about?" Jaybo asked.

"I heard Aunt Lola tell Uncle Hudson to go into Asheville tomorrow and get us a canoe."

"Your dreaming Betts, they'd never let us have a boat. Besides Uncle Hudson would be the last one to by US one," Leon argued.

"She's right," Son confirmed. "Mother told me last night she was gonna get us one. Better treat me nice or I won't let you ride in it. You hear, Bill Fields?"

"Alright children, now that you've finished, go on out and play. Martha you and Betts help clear the tables." Aunt Boom broke into the revelry.

<hr />

Hudson was at the end of his rope. LaVerne yawned openly but remained silent.

"Well go on. What did the neighbors think of all this commotion?" Lola wanted to hear the whole story.

"I didn't give a damn what they thought. I just wanted to get some sleep. I came within an inch of telling Hy to just go on out and marry him and let me have some peace. Anyhow, I told him if he'd go away and leave us alone, he could come up here this weekend and see Hy. You can talk to him. I'm leaving Friday, I've got to get back to that CCC contract at the factory."

"Alright, don't get yourself all worked up. I'll take care of Mr. Sandy Sanders…." Lola assured her husband.

"Better not show his face in these parts. That young whipper snapper. I'll send him straight home to help his Pappy. And you two young women listen to me. I'll tan your hides good if you even look like acting so grown up. You think your Ma and Pa is old as God, do you? Well you've got another thing coming. I'm the boss around here and I'll have none of your sashaying around acting like young Jezebels. That goes for your t'baccie too! Don't be huffin' and puffin' round here. Any baccie here is mine, mind I don't find any of it missing either." Grandy was Lord and Master of the table. He had spoken! He left no room for further conversation so the family broke up and left the dining room. Betts and Martha hovering over the guest tables in the background rattled dishes and made like they were busy while the Hudson saga unfolded.

With their trays loaded they dashed to the kitchen and dumped the unscraped plates right into Delilah's dishwater.

"What are you all doing in here in Mam-maw's room?" Betts and Martha had sought the gang out.

"We're waiting." Leon was stretched out on Mam-maws bed. He had his eyes covered with her black shawl. Sis was rifling through Mam-maws dresser drawers, a piece of Mam-maw's home dried orange peel was dangling from her mouth. Harold had Grandy's straight razor and was about to cut his throat experimenting with it on his peach fuzz. Charles had Grandy's shotgun and was sighting down the barrel straight at the two girls in the doorway.

"Put that thing down, Charles Blanks. You know better than to point a gun at anyone." Martha chastised her older brother.

Jaybo and Tom Jr. were poking, squishing and picking at the two big boxes in the center of the room." ANVIL BRAND, Hard to Beat, Highpoint, North Carolina; H. T. Hudson, manufacturer They read the big stickers.

"Where's Mabes?" Betts asked.

"Waitin' by the dining room door for Hy and La to get free of Aunt Lola. Where else?" answered Harold Jr.

"Quit it Bubs, you're gonna hurt yourself with that Ole rusty razor." Betts warned her brother.

"Pffffffffft............. pfffffffft............... Kabooooooooom !"

The sound coming from the thin, tight pressed lips of Bill Fields focused everyone's attention to Mam-maws closet.

Sonny Hudson sat on Mam-maws rambling rose' chamber pot in the half open door. Bill supplied the sound effects.

"Pfffffffffft....... pffffffffffffffft........Kabooooooooooom!" Bill accompanied the last boom by dropping the covered brick bat door stop, Mam-maw kept by her door.

"Stop that! You naughty boys. Stop this minute. It's not funny to make fun of Mam-maw like that." Martha was in tears.

"You need a dose of salts Bill, your sound effects ain't bombastic enough." Sonny ignored Martha. Leon rolled on the bed with laughter and the whole room erupted into giggles.

"Shhhhhhhh, you want to bring the whole household down on our heads? You know we aren't supposed to be in Mam-maw and Grandy's room. It's absolutely off limits, "Betts warned.

"Off limits, Huh?" Sonny challenged. Then how come you and Martha and Sis are always slipping in here to look at Grandy's eye when he's asleep?"

"Cuz we wants to see whut it looks like up close, silly." Sis matter of factly answered. "It's awful looking. Gives me the creeps. Looks just like that ole red wrinkled skin of rooster's comb. Leon is it really a birthmark, like you said?"

"Sure is, lil' Sis. His Ma got scared by a big ole red rooster before he was born." Leon teased.

"Now Leon don't tell her that, she'll go straight and ask Grandy about it and then we will be in for some thumps." Harold was worried.

"I heard how he got it." Son took up the explanation.

"You know how all the mountain children wear asfidity balls? Well his Ma forgot to wear hers and borned him like that. That's what Miz Wright tole me."

"Granny Blanks was not scared by a rooster and she didn't wear asfidity balls." Martha's soft heart bled. "Sometimes people are just born wrong. Babies inside their mothers don't grow right, that's what happened. It wasn't Granny's fault one bit. Look at Margaret Fry, she wasn't born right. Something went wrong and Mother says she'll always be a little girl. Her brain isn't ever going to grow up either."

"Shhhhhhh! I hear them coming."

Hudson lead the way into the room with his wife and her sisters backing him up. He spotted Sonny for the first time since his arrival.

"Well, Hi, there son, wondered where you were. Glad to see you looking so fit." He gave a halfhearted wave with one hand to his son. Sonny waved back. The father-son cordialities had been taken care of.

Hudson took his sterling silver penknife from the watch pocket of his plus-fours and went to work on the boxes. One contained khaki shorts and shirts, the other contained navy-blue denim overalls. In a few seconds Mam-maws room looked like third-avenue dry goods store. Uncle Hudson ripped out his brand of goods, heedless up size and sex, he tossed several sets in each child's direction.

The girls adjourned across the hall to the music parlor room, while the boys maintained their places in Mam-maws room.

"Anvil Brand is hard to beat, that's my slogan, but quit snatching. Here Jaybo try these on." Hudson tossed a man-sized pair at Jay. They would have fit fine, if Jay had been six foot three. "Okay, kids. That's it. I'm going to get myself a nap. Now keep quiet, I want some rest."

"Thank you, Uncle Huddy." The mob sang out as he went down the hall.

"Mama look." Betts vied for her mother's attention. Aunt Boom turned to find her daughter swallowed up in a size 46.

"Look Betts, I found me a pair. How do I Look?" Sis asked. "Good heavens Baby, those are big enough for me, here let's trade." She swapped with Sis who looked like one pocket would have fit her.

The boys brought over a batch from their room that didn't fit them and in turn the girls swapped some back. The mass fitting continued. The coveralls had bib-tops, country style, with large metal loops which fit over a button to fasten on the shoulders. Their main feature was pockets. There were big ones, small ones, deep ones and short ones. Pencil shaped ones, watch shaped ones and even loops on the sides for hammers.

The overalls were highly favored over the khakis. They had no fit. One button on each side, they hung from the shoulders rather than the waist and they hid a multitude of skinny, fat and lopsided adolescent shapes. The children would take their old ones now and cut them off at the thigh level. They made the best bathing suits for the river. They survived the slippery rocks time and again where a regular tank suit, lost its bottom after a couple of slides.

At last everyone found the closest fit. The closest was never closer than three sizes to the natural shape. The scissors came out. The girls lined up in front of Aunt LaVerne and one by one got trimmed. If the shoulder straps were too long, and if too much of their chests were exposed, the hooks were cut off, the straps shortened, then the hooks were pinned back on with a large safety pin.

The legs were cut somewhere between the knee and the ankle. The older girls cut them up in a series of three-inch slits around the bottom edge. This they called shagging and it was the sole distinction between a male and female overall. The same effect was achieved with the khakis. The shirt tail was cut off and shagged and left to hang over the shorts like a middy.

Inside forty-five minutes the Blanks grandchildren had acquired a new summer wardrobe. They were hard to beat. They presented a solid front to the whole valley. It was easy to lose oneself in the group in case of trouble, one was indistinguishable from the other.

"Aunt Lola where's my bathing suit?" Leon had patiently waited for his promised bathing attire. Aunt Lola was caught short for once in her life. She realized that Hudson had forgotten to bring the muchly needed suit and she saw Leon's disappointment. She did some quick thinking.

"Oh, Leon, Uncle Hudson must have forgotten. Don't worry though, just wait right here. I think we can fix you up."

She raced upstairs to search through Hy's suitcase. There was little distinction between a girl's and a boy's tank suit. Lola thought that maybe Leon could make do with Hy's tank suit. She hurried back to Mam-maws room, praying it would fit. Leon welcomed it with open arms and disappeared into Mam-maws closet to slip it on.

He opened the closet door in a grand gesture and sauntered out into the room where all were waiting to see him in a real bathing suit. His manly body swathed in Hy's suit was poking out in all the wrong places. The top, darted and shaped, hung loose on his broad flat chest and showed his first crop of masculine filament, rather than the soft feminine curves for which it was designed. The armholes, stretched and pulled to allow his biceps passage, cut into his shoulder blades. His thin, taut buttocks didn't fill out the generous weave of the seat and the material dropped in rivulets to his thighs. A pity the excess in back wouldn't give to the front, because in the crotch he had real problems. He moved awkwardly in front of Mam-maw's floor length mirror. The audience feared that his first movement would burst the seam. They tried to cover their giggles as his joyous expression changed to humiliation.

"Aw shucks. Guess I'll just wear my old sawed-off overalls up to Lake Eden with the boys. I don't think these new-fangled suits become me." Leon broke into everyone's embarrassment.

"You'll do no such thing, Leon." Aunt Lola was so ashamed. "You'll just get a suit that fits you, your very own size from the Boys shop at Ivy's in Asheville. We're going into town tomorrow to buy you all a canoe and you'll just march yourself in there and pick out a suit that does become you and charge it to me."

"A canoe?" Every little voice in the room said it. They were ecstatic with thoughts of a real boat all their very own. Leon could only see himself, as Johnny Weismuller.

Early the next morning, Leon sneaked into Grandy's room and persuaded the old man to take the straight razor to his neck hairs, which badly needed barbering. Grandy and Norma put their heads together and decided to give him a first class hair-cut. They took a soup bowl from the kitchen, put it on top of Leon's head, they draped a table cloth around his shoulders and sat him on top of a kitchen stool, on the back porch by the wash stand, where Grandy shaved daily.

Norma got the quilting scissors and between her snippin' and Grandy's shaving they turned out a reasonably cherubic haircut. Leon had bangs front and aft but was shaved from the ear lobe down. His Octagon soap scrubbed face shone like a mirror above his out-grown buster brown shirt. His Sunday knickers didn't quite make it below his knees, but Grandy gave him some of his own long socks and the area of skin seemed in proper proportion. He had on the one pair of good shoes which he and Charles shared back and forth between them.

Charles loaned him his old beat up wallet and Grandy of all things put two nickels inside of it. He swatted him on the backsides with his Asheville Citizen and Norma cautioned him to BEHAVE. They sent him to wait in Hudson's car.

"And keep your mouth shut!" Norma gave a final word to her heart and soul.

Hudson, breakfast finished, paced back and forth on the front porch while Lola got herself dressed for the journey to town. One by one their cereal still clinging to their lips, the Blanks grandchildren rounded the house and gathered on the porch to watch the departure.

"Is it gonna be a real injun canoe, Uncle Huddy?" Bill one leg hooked over the railing dangled a question.

"Can we have an out-board motor too?" Tom Jr. pestered.

"How about a small Chriscraft to sleep four?" Jaybo giggled.

"No, No, No! ! ! !" Homer Hudson was ready to go.

"Now Homer, not so hard on them. Here you are a snarling mess and it isn't even 9 0'clock. I hate to think what you'll be like by the time we get lunch at the S & W cafeteria." Lola had come out on the porch to settle her husbands jangled nerves.

"S & W! Now Lola, I told you I'd never set foot in that mad house again. You take the children there if you want to. I'm going to check by Merril, Lynch, Pierce, Fenner and Bean. Then I'm going up to the Grove Park Inn and eat my lunch.

Lola, defeated again in her efforts to bring the family together began to call, "Son? Son? come on Mama and Daddy are ready to go."

Homer T. Hudson Jr. appeared in the doorway, hesitatingly. He was clothed in all white. Buster Brown shirt and shore white pants with long white knee length stockings. His white skin, never tanned like the others. He constantly turned red, blistered, peeled and was white again. His straight wiry hair was so blond, only his fierce blue eyes, squinting out from white eyelashes under his white brows, broke his albino like coloring. Only his fierce temper and fierce determination to be one of the crowd saved him from appearing delicate looking.

"Homer T." The Trundle-Bed Trash started a teasing chant.

"Oh, Homer T., Mommie, and Daddykins are waiting to go go bye bye car…."

Sonny never showed his face any further than the screen door. He turned on his heels and ran to his room. A moment later he passed through the screen door, wearing his dirty old overalls. He had carefully mussed up his hair and a toad frog beeped in his side pocket.

"Now, then Miz Hudson, don't you open your mouth. I'm going to Asheville like this or I stay on this front porch." Lola gasped. "Why Homer Hudson, how dare you talk to your mother like that. Now go put a shirt on under those overalls. Take that frog out of your pocket and get yourself into that car." A compromise had been reached. Hudson sank into the back seat next to Leon, rolled up the windows and lit a cigarette.

"And now for you," Lola turned on the teasers. Jay, Tom and Bill tumbled off the porch railing. "Get yourselves down to that river and build a dock. Make a place to tie this canoe too before we get back, or there'll be no boat on these premises. Charles, I put you in charge and see that it's done properly."

Lola bounced down the steps and got into the front seat, tugging and pulling herself all under the steering wheel. Sonny came dashing out the front door and around the car. He joined her on the front seat.

Lola turned on the ignition, gave the klaxons a trial blast and put her whole right foot on the accelerator. The car lurched forward and came to an immediate stall. She inadvertently flooded the engine.

"Too much bunion action." Charles commented drolly.

She finally regained the engine, stripped the gears into reverse and backed wide into a deadly arc across the lawn.

"Thank goodness, you children are up on the porch," Mam-maw commented as she came through the door and witnessed Lola at the wheel.

"Schreeeeeeeeeeech" She released the clutch and the Franklin bucked and lurched straight for the front steps. By some stroke of luck Lola got the car righted in the road, pointed in the general direction of the highway, sounded the klaxon again and gave more bunion action to the accelerator.

"Bye Y all!" Everyone on the porch cried out with relief. Lola hit the first juniper bush, taking half the greenery off on the bumper and finally found the two ruts which would take her safely to the highway. Uncle Hudson's head sank below the horizon of the back window while Leon waved and laughed all the way to the highway.

Figure 19: Leon in front of juniper bushes

———————— ❧ ❧ ————————

When the train whistle blew on the Cornbread express, Aunt LaVerne went down to supervise the crew working on the dock. Seeing that they were half through, she suggested that all the children go with her back up the hill for the "talking to" she had promised yesterday. They begged forgiveness all the way up the hill, but Aunt Boom insisted that they hear her out.

She led the gang into the Music-parlor room. She pulled the big sliding doors shut and sat on the backless piano stool facing each one by swinging back and forth on the corkscrew base.

"Now you children must realize that trains are dangerous." She took her text. "You older boys shouldn't lead these little ones into such a silly prank where you might get hurt. We have a big responsibility running this Inn and we need all your cooperation. I was soo disappointed in you. Never dreamed you'd do such a thing… Now, I know you won't let me down…etc. etc. etc. etc." The children became mesmerized by her soft, voiced lecture tone. After a few preliminary, "yes Mam'" they became soporific.

"BANG!!! "Aunt Booms hand struck a bass chord and the nodding heads jerked awake.

"Come ona here. Come ona here…. Alexanders Ragtime Band." Aunt Boom burst into song at her own accompaniment. Her right hand heavy on the bass, boom boomed away, seemingly unconscious of what her right hand was doing with the melody. They raised their squeaky little voices in song, uniting with this "once Upon a Time" Auntie Boom in her Wizard of Oz mood.

———————— ❧ ❧ ————————

Beck closed the door tightly so that she and LaVerne could talk privately while they rested. They looked at each other and got the giggles. Beck unbuttoned her dress and began to struggle with her corset. LaVerne followed suite.

"Well, did you ever see such a sight as those two little hussy's ripping up the driveway in Hudson's Franklin?" Beck had waited twenty-four hours to get on this subject.

Outside the window, three lithe young bodies slithered along the dusty porch floor and lay prone on the porch beneath the windows of the downstairs bedroom.

"Geesum," La whispered. "You two sure goofed when you swept this porch this morning. Its filthy! I got chicken whackey on the palm of my hand! UGH!"

In the bedroom, Beck and Boom were prone. Each in the middle of a big double bed, they ohhhhhed and ahhhhhhed in delight to have ungirded their flesh. LaVerne started the discussion.

"Beck I simply cannot understand what sister has done to deserve this! You know it embarrassed her to death."

"Just like Hudson. Just like him!" Beck agreed.

"Now Beck, Lola adores him and he's wonderful. A good provider, so successful, why he's considered one of THE LEADING BUSINESS MEN OF HIGHPOINT.I just think he's busy, hasn't time to give to his family.

"Well that's true. Lola is president of her book club, chairlady of her music club and a blue-ribbon winner for her garden club. I must give the devil his due They're certainly among the prominent families of Highpoint and Hudson does have a good background. He comes from good southern stock. I guess he's just plain spoiled."

"An only child That's it. I never saw one yet that wasn't spoiled, self-centered and miserable. I'm convinced that if it wasn't for only children, the world wouldn't be in the mess it's in. There ought to be a law against people having one child. My Harold is one, I ought to know. Spoiled rotten, selfish, nervous, sensitive......."

The mother of four, laughed, bypassing the reference to Harold and picked up the thread of conversation.

"I wouldn't know, anything about that only child business. The stork didn't give me but fifteen months with my only child". LaVerne laughed with Beck and continued.

"Well, I'll tell you what I think. It's a shame to say it but I really do believe that all that success is what's caused all this to do with the girls. They've had too much and I think Lola is making a big mistake letting them make their debut. It has given them airs. And did you know that she lets them run up to the University of Virginia and to Washington and Lee for weekends. College campuses are the breeding grounds for this wild living. Young ladies today are far too lax. Why when Lola and I were at the Memphis Female Seminary, gentleman callers were made to sit across the room, on the other side of the proctor..."

"Well you certainly have a point there. You know Tom never even kissed me until after we were engaged. I wouldn't have thought of doing such a thing with anyone except the man I was to marry. And Tom respected me for it too. Why you know he told me so."

"You know, Beck, Lola spoke to me about this Sandy when she first came down. The Sanders are a very prominent family in Highpoint. Lovely mother, great big house, prominent father, son a problem! Sometimes I wonder what the world is coming to? Just take my Harold Jr. He's got that job in the college cafeteria that will help. But I still don't know if I can afford the tuition to college. There's nothing spoiled or wild about him. He's an excellent student. He makes me so proud. He deserves a college education. Sometimes I just don't think it's fair!

"Well sister, you know I'll help out. Just tell me how much."

"No! No! I don't mean for you to help. Beck you and Lola are so good to me but I don't want you to help. It's just the depression and all, things are hard. Harold just doesn't make enough. Someday it will be different. I'll manage somehow. Thanks anyway." LaVerne leaned over and squeezed her sister's generous hand.

"Sister? Have you heard from Harold? Lately I mean."

"He's awful busy you know. He's been working night and day. I'll get a letter tomorrow." LaVerne refused to give a direct answer.

"Of course, it's preposterous to think that Hy would marry anyone. After all she's only eighteen."

"How old were you when you married Harold?" The direct comparison made LaVerne want to cry out, in protest.

"Well that was different. I'd finished college and was teaching school before I ever considered marriage. I was a grown woman. Beck, do you think I made a mistake?"

Beck caught her breath. She could not answer.

"What do you suppose Lola will do when this boy Sandy shows up?" Beck had to ignore the conversation and go on. Her heart was broken. She had given up her husband but now, she learned that LaVerne had had to give hers up too. Oh, my God, Beck prayed for guidance.

"Well, you know Lola. No telling. But I bet you one thing. She'll just ignore the whole situation. That's her usual approach to this kind of thing. Ignore it and it'll go away, that's Lola." LaVerne sighed deeply.

Beck was on the verge of tears. The conversation was getting too pointed for her. "Oh, Sister. Is that what you're doing? Ignoring it? Aren't you going back? Tell me. Aren't you going back?

"I don't know, Beck. I don't know. I just don't know." LaVerne had said it. Somehow the weight of the world lifted from her shoulders. It was out. The horrible truth, was out. She was glad, Beck sobbed. "Now Beck, don't. Don't. We have to walk the pipe in life too. Who's to say whether we should fall in together or walk on alone? No one can always look straight ahead. The current, the rapids, the birds, the beautiful wild flowers, they are distracting. For one short moment, we all look down or up. The pipe is ugly, why must we never see the beauty around us without falling off?" Beck could not answer. She had buried her head in her pillow.

"Beck, Beck. Don't. I didn't want to upset you. Just think, we have our children. Our beautiful children, our bright, talented children. We must live for them. We will, nothing else really matters."

LaVerne sighed, from deep within, her the trembling died away, one final wave of faith engulfed her being, the weary gale had blown itself out. She was very tired. Beck had calmed. The bed next to her no longer tossed. The afternoon sun sought out the design of the double wedding ring quilt and blazed across it in youthful innocence. It was the last thing LaVerne remembered before she sank into the long even breaths of sleep. Behind her lay Hell! Fort Smith, Arkansas was scalded with the midwestern heat. Harold her husband still waved farewell.

———————————— ❧ ❧ ————————————

A car door slammed in the yard. There was commotion outside.

"What's that?" LaVerne sat bolt upright in bed. Sounds like someone on the porch.

Beck roused herself from sleep and went to the window. She pulled on the shade, it zipped up spinning wildly around the cylinder at the top. Face to face she encountered the laughing countenance of Hy, La and Mabes. Behind them hanging onto the post of the porch with bare feet crossed over in monkey like fashion was a boy. He had several days growth of beard and a guitar hung from the back of his dirty white knit sweater UVA was emblazoned down the front in Orange and Purple. He was squeaking his baritone vocal cords. "Girl of My Dreams, I Love you" Beck was sure she must be still dreaming.

LaVerne roused herself and looked at Beck." What is it? No! No! Stop Beck. You're undressed."

LaVerne stopped Beck who forgetting lack of attire was bolting for the door to the side porch.

"Oh, Sandy, you just won't do." Hybernia caressed the admonition.

"Sandy???!!!!!!!" Beck and LaVerne went into action. Beck struggled with her girdle, felt for her shoes with her feet and shook her finger all at the same time.

"Mama, Mama. That's it lets get Mama. She'll know what to do." LaVerne was trying to get her dress on.

"No, Mamas napping. Anyway, leave her out of this. If Papa gets wind that the boy's here, he's apt to get out his shotgun. Beck gave up the fight with her girdle and just pulled on her dress, wrong side out. Once covered she opened the door.

"Hybernia Hudson, you come in this house at once." Beck commanded.

"You too! Mabel and LaVerne" Boom added from Becks rear. "How de do, Mam." The boy disentangled himself from the post and swooped down on Beck and LaVerne with a grand Rudolph Valentino hand gesture.

"My name is Richard Fennel Sanders III, Esquire. At your command, gentle ladies." He addressed the two dumbfounded aunts. He flipped the guitar over his shoulder and began to enlighten them further.

"A wandering minstrel I, a thing of threads and patches……" By the time he reached the bit about, "I will charm your ears with songs of lovers fears," He had indeed won his suit with Beck and LaVerne.

"Now see here, young man. Mr. Richard whatever your name is Sanders we know all about you. I'm Mrs. Harold Hedges and this is my sister, Mrs. Tom Fields. We are Hybernia's mother's sisters and at this moment Hybernia is in our charge. We mean to keep her that way till her mother and daddy get beck from Asheville."

"By your Leave, Madam," Sandy made another of those Valentino sweeps." I came to call on this fair flower of womanhood. I came to sing ballads at her feet. I would not dare touch a strand of her long golden tresses.

Mabel looked at Hybernia's hair. "Why this poor simpering idiot, Hy's hair is as brown as mine and shingled up the back."

"Cast not stones at this fragile love sick figure, mademoiselle, I may be sick, but not like that. I'm sick with love. A love sick madman." Sandy spoke this ridiculous line strictly for Hy's benefit and she broke up. Even LaVerne and Beck snickered.

"Aw, Sandy, come on, don't tease us." Hy said. She turned to her aunts. "Can't we sit here on the porch and visit till mother and daddy come? Sandy's a lot of fun and he'll play some more on his guitar."

"I can't see any harm in that. Can you Sister?" Beck sought her older sister's approval.

"Well I guess it will be alright. You all sit yourselves there in the side swing and don't disturb the household with your giggling. I'll make you a pitcher of lemonade." LaVerne turned the riot into a pink tea party.

Sandys guitar playing soon brought the whole gang up from the river. One by one the boarders strolled out onto the porch to join in the singing which sprang spontaneously from Sandys G string.

It turned into one of the loveliest afternoons of the summer. LaVerne returned to the kitchen many times to replenish the lemonade, while some forty odd voices young and old became wandering minstrels for a little while. Beck sought out LaVerne on one of her trips to the rear of the house.

"Sister, he's a real nice boy. Isn't it fun having all the young people singing on the front porch? And did you see, even Mary Ann Thompson joined in on 'Shine on Harvest Moon.' I even saw Grandy singing the chorus of 'Carolina Moon' and he hasn't said a word about sending the young man packing."

"It's certainly not what we thought. He's a fine young man. It makes me feel guilty that I accused him of wild living and all those things." LaVerne felt badly.

"It's alright, Sister, we both said a lot of things this afternoon that we shouldn't have, I guess." They passed knowing looks which sealed their secret.

———————————— ๑ ๑ ————————————

The Franklin came quietly up the road to the big house. No klaxons gave warning, no gear stripping, no juniper eating movements disturbed the happy singing group on the front porch. Homer was driving! Slowly, precisely he maneuvered the car up the long road from the highway. Strapped across the car top was a bright shiny green canoe.

The Trundle Bed Trash dashed from the porch at all angles and were hanging onto the car before it even fully stopped. Charles jumped onto the hood of the car and started to undo the knot in the rope which secured the front end of the canoe. Tom Jr. and Jay were on the back bumper jumping up and down with anticipation.

Hudson alighted from his position behind the wheel and tried to disengage his nephews and nieces.

"Get down from there you little rascals. You'll have my car torn up before I can get that fool thing off. Leave me something to get back to Highpoint in tomorrow. Scat now! Leon, you and Charles get the canoe down."

Leon stole out of the other door of the front seat and ran for the porch. He fondled his new bathing suit, his first bathing suit, in his raw-boned hands.

"Look Mama." He went to his mother, "Isn't it pretty? It's got an Ivy's label in it." He held the navy-blue tank suit over his front to model it. "And Look, Aunt Lola bought these. He lifted his right foot to display a brand-new pair of saddle oxfords.

Lola advanced toward the porch laden with boxes and bags. She was greeted by silence.

"Hybernia Hudson, what is the meaning of this? No sooner is my back turned than this young man shows up in Swannanoa. Have you no thought or feelings at all for me? How could you?" Lola had spotted Sandy right off.

"Aw, mother, take it easy. Sandy just came up to say hello. I didn't even know he was coming."

Sandy spoke up. "That's right Mrs. Hudson, Hy didn't know I was coming. It isn't her fault. I just decided myself this morning. I stuck up my thumb and got a ride here. I had a swell time here, your sisters are sure nice, Mrs. Hudson."

Lola gained a rocker and sat her shopping worn body down. The surrounding rockers buzzed with tales of the delightful afternoon.

While the cool late evening shadows fell across the porch and the kitchen came a live with its warmth from the Royal Oak stove, several left their chairs and went into the hall. They took down woolen stoles and sweaters from the communal rack by Mam-maws bedroom door and wrapped themselves against the early chill of night. Mam-maw spoke.

"Hudson, don't you think someone had better go down and herd those young sailors up for baths and dry clothes. It's a might chill these late August evenings. Lola's back in the kitchen putting the finishing touches on her spaghetti and I know the children don't want to miss their favorite meal."

"I better go man the lifeboats and give a little artificial respiration." Hudson answered her and left the porch.

During dinner some changing and rearranging took place. It was decided by the mothers that it would be more seemly if Hybernia, La and Mabes spent the night up at the big house. In exchange, Lola would bunk Charley down with the remaining children at her cottage. Leon, Charles and Harold would occupy the medallion room at the end of the hall while the girls slept close by on the sleeping porch.

"Pssssssst!" Mabes warned as she sneaked into the boy's room. Y'all want to hear what Beck and Mother were saying this afternoon when we were listening under their window?" She asked Charles, Leon and her brother.

"Can't wait," Harold said as she crawled over the other two boys in the big double bed and came to Mabes. Leon and Charles scurried behind them to the sleeping porch. Mabes perched herself atop a pile of pillows at one end of a cot and took the floor. She summed up the entire conversation in regard to Hy and her family. LaVerne added her impressions by saying,

"Gee, I didn't know we were rich! She said daddy was one of the leading business men. She said he was so successful, well that means we must have a lot of money, Huh?"

Leon teased. "At the rate you and Hy spend it I doubt that he's got anything. De-but-ing all over Highpoint in fancy clothes. Galivanting around the countryside to parties. You two will bankrupt poor ole Huddy."

"I sure got a laugh out of the way they described daddy." Hy took her turn. "Well Hudson does have a good background, comes from good stock." Hy mimicked Becks voice. "These Blanks women kill me with their 'holier than thou' attitude toward all in-laws. You'd think that being a Blanks made you real special. They lay all the faults of us children to our father's feet. Boy! They just ought to hear what daddy says about the Blanks. That would kill 'em for sure."

"Yes, the strait-laced females from the Seminary. Young ladies are far too lax with the boys." La mimicked her Aunt Boom. "Why Beck said, Tom Fields never kissed her till they were engaged. How in pity's name did she know whether she wanted to marry him or not? Suppose she hadn't liked the way he kissed? She'd have been in a fine pickle."

"You reckon she never kissed anybody else?" Charles asked.

"Shucks, I kissed Evangeline Parkerson last summer, and nothing happened. Nothing at all, I didn't feel nothing. Evangeline said she pretended like I was Leon so I don't think anything happened to her either."

"What do you mean nothing happened?" Leon quizzed. "Didn't you get stuck by those steel braces she wears? Shoot, I told her I wasn't going to kiss her anymore. Those things stuck me in the lip."

The girls went into gales of giggles at the boys' description of kissing.

"Hey Scout!" Mabes addressed her brother. "Don't fine upstanding young men like you have any secret romances to tell us about?"

"I'm waiting for Fanny Farmer to woe me with her cooking." Harold made a plump joke.

"Mother sure threw bouquets at you in that talk. About how proud she was of you. How she was going to send you to college no matter if she had to work her fingers to the bone." Mabes complimented her brother with this little ego booster.

"Hush! Mabes, you know I can't go to college. You think I'm going off to Arkansas U. when there isn't even enough to buy food for the rest of the family? I'm going to get a job and go to work. It might kill mother, but at least we all won't starve!" Harold had without thinking brought up the sore subject.

Mabes cowered on her pile of pillows, embarrassed that Harold had let the cold hard facts slip out. She and her brother had shared their private thoughts with each other on previous occasions but the public they had kept a carefully falsified front.

"Aw, don't worry Harold, Beck said she would send you to college. You know she will. I'm sure mother and daddy would help you too, so don't worry you'll get your edification one way or another."

Now both Harold and Mabes felt like they'd like to crawl through a hole in the floor. Charity. Always charity, they were galled by the thought.

"Well that's all we heard. Sandy came up about that time and we didn't hear anymore." Mabes wanted to close the conversation.

"What was that?" La had heard a noise. "Sounds like someone scratching on the screen downstairs."

"Hy? HY? is that you up there?" It was Sandy's voice coming from below. "Come on, let's go for a ride in the canoe. I got the key off your daddy's dresser," Sandy entreated.

"How'd you get out?" Leon called down to him.

"Slipped." Sandy answered. "Come on Hy we haven't been alone all day. I have to talk to you."

"Okay! Sounds peachy. Let me get some cloches." Hy called back.

"Shhhhhhhhhhhhh, you want to wake the whole house. Here take these overalls," Leon handed Hy his. Hy pulled them on over her gown and scurried down the back steps and out into the moonlit backyard

"Now, you two behave yourselves, remember you don't have any chaperones." Harold teased.

The two young romantics joined hands and hurried down to the riverbank giggling softly over this midnight rendezvous. On the porch, the conversation lagged with Hy's departure. The five remaining heads peered through the screen for a glimpse of the canoe going down the river. The moon was bright enough for them to see the river right where the pipe crossed over to the island. Several minutes passed before Leon spotted them.

"Hey, there they are, see, lifting the canoe over the pipe. That crazy boy is really going to put that canoe in the rapids."

All of a sudden, the quiet stillness of the hillside erupted.

"Help! Help! They're eloping!" It was Lola's voice ringing clear and true up the hill from her cottage. "Help somebody stop them. Help! Hybernia Hudson come back here. I'll annul it, you hear? I'll annul you!" Lola went racing along the river bank draped in a sheet and thrashing her arms about trying to keep her balance on the rocks.

Hy and Sandy jumped into the canoe and began to paddle frantically away from the shore and out into the deep shadows of mid-stream, hoping to be covered by the darkness. Hudson came out of the cottage, calling, "Lola! Lola, come back here. You'll dash yourself to death on those rocks." He too had donned a sheet and was trailing in Lola's wake up the shore. Delilah, disturbed in her little room in Lola's cottage, opened her door and began to wail. "Lord have mercy, Miz Hudson. You'll catch your death of cold going swimming at night!" She grabbed a checkered table cloth off the laundry pile on her porch, threw it around her shoulders and braved the night to try and overtake Miz Hudson.

"Jesus, look at 'em go." Leon observed out loud. "Hy's in for it now. They'll never believe it was just an innocent little canoe ride on the river."

The back hall came alive with running feet. Beck and LaVerne led the pack coming onto the porch.

"Are you all alright?" Beck asked. "What in heavens name is going on down by the river?"

Before anyone could answer, they all peeked through the screen and saw the whole scene unfold in front of them. At that point, Lola again took up her wail.

"Richard Sanders, I'll call the police! I'll call the coast guard! I'll call the FBI! This is kidnap! Bring my daughter back here this minute. I'LL annul her! So help me, I'll annul her!"

"Bubba, what does annul mean?" Mabes asked, "Decapitation?"

They stood speechless and watched the frantic pair in the canoe, take a giddy roll. They had lost a paddle and were trying to regain it. The canoe pitched and rolled, over it went. Making a semi-circular motion, the canoe pitched its occupants into the cold dark waters of the Swannanoa. The three draped figures stopped their running and observed the ship wreck.

Hudson regained his voice.

"Lola! They'll drown, do something. Quick. They'll drown."

"I've saved her, Mrs. Hudson I've saved her." Sandy's head bobbed into the moonlight patch of the River near the pipe where they had lifted the boat over. He was struggling against the rapids to hold himself and Hy up above the water. Leon dashed wildly down the back stairs and down the steps to the river. Charles was close on his heels and ran downstream to catch the canoe. Leon went for the two canoers, he got Sandy by the hand and pulled him ashore.

Hudson, Lola and Delilah shed their sheets and table cloth and began to wrap up the young couple. Somewhere in midstream Hy had lost Leon's oversized overalls and was now shivering in her flimsy nightgown.

She gasped for breath and turned to see about Sandy. "He saved my life. Mother Sandy saved my life. The boat caught me on the head and knocked me out and I would have drowned for sure. Oh, Sandy you saved me." Lola herded the sopping twosome toward her cottage, ignoring Hy's dramatics.

The whole hillside got quiet. The Hudson family along with Delilah disappeared into the cottage down the hill. The group on the upstairs sleeping porch dispersed, disgusted that no one would hear Lola's final words that night. All were instructed to go directly to sleep and try and forget the whole affair. LaVerne gave a final benediction. "Now that ends the whole affair. I don't want to hear another word about it from anyone. Poor Lola has had enough today to drive any woman to the State Sanitorium. I'll just make a pot of hot tea and slip down to her cottage and see if I can help warm her cold soul."

# Chapter 19

# TB or Not TB in a Model T

The mid-afternoon sun was warm on the front porch. As the family and some of the guests joined forces there, they looked forward to cutting the big snake-striped watermelons which had been placed in the branch that morning. The cold mountain stream chilled them till crispy flakes of ice formed in the red liquid fruit. By mid-afternoon they were ready to fill the between-meal need of vacationing stomachs.

Mam-maw had finished her nap, removed the black shawl from her eyes and taken her rocker on the porch. She was busy now over a braided rug she was making for the living room of Lola's cottage.

Her girls had joined her after a session on the beds on the sleeping porch. There they swathed their faces in cream, let go the laces of their corsets and had what they laughingly referred to as, their pillow talk.

Gloria Parkerson came forth looking for a foursome. They waited for some of the others to appear before bringing the big melon up the hill.

"Let's cut for partners," Beck spoke to Gloria.

Lola lectured: "While you all waste away the afternoon around the bridge table, LaVerne and I are going to Miss Lou's for butter and cream."

"Now, don't you all slip off and go antiquing on the side...."

Beck didn't finish her sentence. A Model T Ford coupe had turned in the driveway and was making its way up the hill.

"Where are the children?" LaVerne. was eager to send out the alarm.

"No need to worry," Beck calmed her. "This car is loaded with little people. One.... two.... three.... heavens, they look like they've got more in that coupe than we have hidden in the hills."

The six women on the porch chuckled at Beck's observation. The little Model T chugged and gasped up the steep climb. As it came closer to the house, the women were able to ascertain it had a rumble seat. The rumble seat contained, three more towheads.

Finally, the little Ford gave up the ghost and stopped at the far end of the porch from the steps. Out rolled five little boys, a travel-worn looking woman and her husband. The little boys scattered hither and yon not waiting to be introduced. The father alighted with the dignity of a Cadillac owner and turned immediately to gaze up at the mountain scenery across the valley, leaving his back turned to the women on the porch.

The small woman advanced toward the porch and said, "Do you mind if we look around a little?" She took a step nearer the porch and continued.

"My husband and I met here in this house fifteen years ago and we've never been back…. since we married and left. We are just passing through and couldn't resist showing the children this place."

Mam-maw, in her hospitable way answered, "You just spend as much time as you care to spend looking around."

"Would you like to come inside the house?"

"Oh, thank you, no. We'd love to go to the river and sit one more time on the big rocks."

By that time the man had shifted his view from the mountains to the porch and he seemed quite relieved that his wife had obtained permission for both of them. Hand in hand, they trailed off toward the river. The five little boys had disappeared somewhere over the six acres of yard.

"Mama," Lola addressed her parent, "you ought to be careful whom you let roam around the house and grounds. After all, you don't know a thing about those people. They may be public enemy's number one, for all we know. "

"Now, listen here, Mrs. Hudson, this is still my house and anyone passing is welcome to it. You don't think for one minute that I would turn away a sweet little family like that."

Gloria, silent through the whole encounter spoke up. "Isn't that romantic? Just think of it! They met right here in this house and they married and now they have their own little family."

LaVerne sat quietly rocking. She seemed to be adding something mentally on her fingers. She started to speak but thought better of it and remained silent.

"Come on, Miss Truelove, let's go get that watermelon and cut it. Then we can get to our bridge game." Beck was impatient to get her hands on the cards. "It really looked like a beautiful, juicy melon when I plugged it this morning and I've got my mouth all set for a piece."

Lola couldn't resist a barb. "Just what you need, Beck. A big fat slice of watermelon. just what your diet calls for."

"Not a calorie in it," Beck was quick to retort. "Not a single calorie. You're so hepped on not eating between meals, you'd starve the poor Armenians before you'd let them eat between a meal."

"Hold on there a minute, daughters, I want to offer those poor weary travelers and those little boys some melon. Wait till they come back before you eat it all up."

LaVerne decided it was time to speak of her figuring. She had calculated back some fifteen years into the history of the big old house and now she was sure her first thoughts were verified.

"Maybe we'd better not do that." She held out a hand to stop her mother from protesting before she was through with her story.

"That couple said they had met here fifteen years ago. Now just wait a minute and think back. We bought this place in 1921 from Dr. Wilson who was running a small clinic for the mountain people in the tearoom there in the side yard."

"Now LaVerne," Mam-maw interrupted, "that's all past history. What on earth does that have to do with eating a watermelon on an August day in 1934?"

"It might have a lot to do with having them sit down to the table and eat with us and all our children……. spreading TB with every mouthful."

"TB?" Lola gasped. "What on earth are you talking about, sister?"

"If you all will just be quiet a minute and let me tell you, I will explain it to you very clearly." LaVerne continued, looking at the group around her who now sat in shocked silence.

"Before Dr. Wilson had his clinic here, his father, who was also a doctor ran this house as a TB Sanitarium. Good heavens, you don't think anyone ever built this twenty-bedroom house just to live in as a family, do you?"

LaVerne let that bit of information which she recalled to them soak in a minute and continued.

"So, if that couple met here fifteen years ago, they must have been TB patients here. You know full well that no one is ever cured of TB. And I'm not convinced they don't still have the germ. You know, like those yellow fever carriers."

Mam-maw exploded, "Stop this nonsense this minute! Dr. Wilson only used the place for a few months as a sanitarium. He told Grandy he accepted only the cured patients. This house was used to get their systems built up and put some meat on their bones before they rejoined their families. You know Frank wouldn't have bought this place if there had been the least question about it."

"Well, I don't know. You know how papa is about germs…" Lola didn't get to finish her sentence.

"Stop! Wait a minute! Listen!" Gloria tried to get the attention of the women. "Before you make fools of yourselves, hear me out. Remember, I was threatened with TB and that's how I came here. I know all about it and believe me this couple is perfectly safe. Fifteen years of marital bliss and five strapping young sons is hardly the work of two active TB patients. They're cured. Clean as a whistle. They couldn't infect a soul. I bet they're in better health than any one of us."

The three sisters listened to Gloria as she talked sense. They walked to the flagstone steps and looked down below. Perched on the largest rock by the river sat the couple. Their five sons had joined them there. They huddled their heads together, while their father pointed in one direction and then the other…no doubt re-living and re-telling the days of court ship spent there.

The sky began to grow dark and at the first streak of lightning, the little family rose and quickly made their way back up the hill.

They thanked Mam-maw for letting them view her domain, climbed back into their Model T, while the man cranked vigorously on the engine. With great effort the car was persuaded to continue the journey.

———————— ❧ ❦ ————————

The storm was going to be a true mountain thunder-storm… quickly conceived, suffering violent birth pangs but soon dying out with a sigh.

The sun had been high in the sky over Ole Hickory all day. There it had hung, going about its job of adding a blush of a burn to the already deeply tanned faces and arms of the children. Soft, clouds flirted across its face from time to time but within a few moments, the upper air currents had swished in large dark thunderheads and Thor was in his chaotic glory. Jagged lightning vied for attention with the great rolls of thunder that echoed across the valley and shook the air.

The children were scared to death of these storms and at the first indication of darkness, they fled from the river, jumped from the trees and quickly abandoned the croquet court.

Grown-ups dashed for the parking area to roll up the car windows and returned drenched to the skin.

Nature didn't fool around with a soft drizzle or a sleepy pitter patter of rain drops. The rain slanted down from The Ridge in saucer-sized drops and rapidly continued with a full-blown cloud burst.

The river turned muddy and turbulent and the branches of the cherry trees dipped low and then were flung backwards in their own version of a modern dance.

Even Grandy dropped his hoe at the first crack of thunder and headed for the kitchen to steam his wet back against the glowing coal range.

The population of Riverby crowded through the front doors and stood momentarily in the great hallway to chatter excitedly about the suddenness and power of the storm.

Martha Lee secretly pushed open the screen doors to let the dogs and cats inside.

Mam-maw was the first to go into the front parlor room and light the fire and turn on the lamps. The children fanned out in all directions. Some in the upstairs back hall to play hide and seek and some gathered on the sleeping porch to watch debris tossing down the river.

"Man, this is really a good storm. The water is already over the pipe. Oh no! There go the watermelons... floating down the river."

Some of the more adventuresome children preferred to stay out on the front porch to shout back at the thunder and stomp their feet at the capricious lightning. It was easy to be brave and daring when solid security was just through the door behind them.

But the most popular spot in the house was the music parlor room.

To the piano accompaniment and loud singing of "mama, mama, have you heard? Papa's goin' to buy me a mocking bird. If that mockin' bird don't sing, Papa's goin' to buy me a diamond ring," the sliding doors banged shut after the children raced inside the room.

Card tables were pushed together and chairs were drawn up. Three decks of cards were shuffled together and dealt out. Just about every card was marked from the back so the players could tell what kind of hand they had even before turning them over and sorting them.

Bill and Sonny engaged in a vicious slap-jack game on the floor and the air was pierced by cries of, "you cheater!"

"If that diamond ring turns brass, Papa' goin' to buy me a lookin' glass...."

The picture of Cousin Tizzie on the piano top was in serious danger of falling off. A bad omen, for it meant she would die immediately... no matter where she was or what she was doing. Her fixed smile continued to gaze out at the crowd with sweet serenity. She was completely unaware that her demise was so imminent. Her frizzled Marcel seemed to bounce with the beat of each bass note.

"Take a card, any card. You all come on now and take a card," urged Sis. "I know a card trick."

"Yeah, yeah, yeah. We all know that stupid trick." The older kids wouldn't cooperate at all. She wondered how anyone else could possibly know that wonderful trick Uncle Claude had taught her. She didn't know it was the same old trick that was old hat to the older children. It was a wonder of cleverness and brilliance to her.

"Go find Little Beetle, Sis. She'll think it's great," one of the older girls said to her.

"Cheaters never win, you cheater! I'm going to tell Mam-maw on you, you cheatn' devil. I saw you hide that card in your pocket. Look! It's even got dewberry jam on it. Where did you get bread and jam this time of day, you cheater?" Bill and Sonny began to wrestle on the floor and rolled under the rickety leg of the end card table and collapsed the Rook Game in progress.

"Free for all, free for all. Everybody fight." Urged Tom Jr.

Cards, tables, children and dewberry jam and bread blended into a rolling, surging free for all.

"If that looking glass gets broke, Papa's goin' to buy me a billy goat. If that billy goat runs a-way, Papa's goin' to buy me a bale of hay." The sound of music stood out from the wrestling match on the floor.

———————————— ❧ ❧ ————————————

At long last Bobbie had nabbed a bathroom all to herself!

In the midst of the storm, she claimed the back bath-room for her very own. She propped up a straight-backed chair under the doorknob to ensure privacy and carefully arranged her clean undergarments on the seat. She gave a thorough cleaning to the tub and the wash basin and began to run straight hot water from the tap. By gum, I'll just drain the darned tank dry, she decided selfishly. Into the fast filling tub, she tossed an embroidered hand towel to serve as a wash cloth and just as promptly she tossed in a fairly new bar of Woodbury's soap.

She had borrowed the soap from Gloria Parkerson. Gloria wasn't aware it had been borrowed, though. The embossed profile of Mr. Woodbury was still apparent on the bar and Bobbie agreed with herself to still have his profile apparent when she returned the soap to Gloria's room after her bath.

Skinning off her clothes and chucking them into a wad on the floor, she quickly admired her fully developed sixteen-year old figure before stepping into the tub. Oh heck, the water is beginning to cool off. I'd better turn off the tap so I'll have some warm water to rinse my hair.

She didn't waste motion. She quickly lathered up her hair, rinsed it in the clean tub water and re-lathered it. Swishing it, up on top of her head in a Martha Washington style, she set about to soap the rest of herself.

She just loved the aroma of Woodbury soap. It was great good luck that, Big Gloria had the same taste in toiletries as she did. Mmmmmmm, her razor could stand a new blade, but it'll do for now. Wish I could find a gold Gillette somewhere.

She luxuriated in the water. This is life for me. Boy, one of these days, I'll have a sunken tub with perfume coming out of a tap…. just like Jean Harlow.

She rinsed her hair until it was squeaky clean and rinsed the lather off her body. Reluctantly letting the sudsy water go down the drain, she got out and dried off on the last clean towel she had found in the linen closet. Too bad for new guests arriving tonight. They'll have to dry off on their imaginations.

Bobbie slipped into her step-ins and adjusted the brassiere. La will have to gain some weight and get bigger bras or I'll have a case of risen breasts, she thought as she tried to poke her 34's into a 32. She gave her head a thorough towel rubbing and combed out the tangles. Since her blond hair was naturally curly, it wasn't necessary to put it in curlers.

Pressing the waves into place and combing back her widow's peak did the trick.

I just hate Pepsodent tooth paste! On my next bed making rounds, I'm going to locate some Listerine… gives you such a good clean taste. Making a face into the mirror, she brushed thoroughly with the Pepsodent and tapped her brush on the side of the basin.

Carefully drying off the soap and the razor, she cautiously opened the bathroom door and peaked out. Good! No one in sight! She ran on tip toes down the hallway and slipped into the blue checked bedroom and replaced the soap and razor. On the way out she carefully closed the door. People should keep their doors closed, she thought, to herself, no telling who might just walk right in.

Back in the bathroom, she wiped out the tub and basin, picked up her toothbrush, comb and soiled garments and went to the sleeping porch to dress for her date.

———————— ✌ ✌ ————————

Mary Ann was as usual undecided what to do. She had slept badly last night and when she retired to her room with her son, Chris, for a rest after lunch, she had only succeeded in tossing and turning and listening to the sounds of the big house and the frightening storm.

She eased herself off the big double bed of dark cherry and cracked open the door to the hallway and listened to the sounds coming from the hallway and parlor rooms.

"Mrs. Hudson, you create the loveliest flower arrangements I think I've ever seen." Birdie Rogers' lilting voice ended on a high note. "That's a real potpourri of flowers in that old ironstone pitcher. I don't know how you can get such a lovely affect with wild flowers in their garish nature colors and blend them so perfectly with tea roses and that French Iris. And that one perfect full-blown deep pink rose in the center is…. well, words just fail me. I'm going to describe this to my garden club in Jacksonville when I get back. On second thought, I'm going to commission Mabel to paint me a picture of this very arrangement to show the Green Thumb Garden Club."

While Lola made soft noises of 'thank you' and gave the flowers an extra tug, Mary Ann softly closed the door.

Her thoughts were running away with her. That sounds like Birdie, giving praise where it is needed and thinking of sharing the arrangement with our garden club. Why can't I think of such things?

She looked at her reflection in the mirror of the antique dressing table. She was so tall she had to bend down a bit to study the complete portrait of herself standing there. Her tallness was accentuated by her thinness. The Ivory satin slip she had been resting in hung straight down with scarcely a ripple to outline the curves of a woman's figure. The lace insert at the bosom was meant to soften and sexually reveal a woman's breast. On Mary Ann the lace was just a mockery. Her face looked back at her with frankness… plain, no make-up to point up the soft brown eyes, her jaw bones too pronounced and her hair set in a Marcel that was unbecoming. The reflection was too much for her to stand. She turned away from the mirror and looked at her son lying sprawled on the other double cherry bed. I wish he wouldn't sleep with his eyes open! It's un-natural and gives me a spooky feeling. An eight-year-old boy should sleep with his eyes closed. I'll have to speak to Mam-maw about that. When Tommy comes back to the room, I'll ask him first.

Tommy.

When his name popped in her mind her heart did a little double skip. It always did. I'll never know how I could be so lucky to catch him. A whirlwind courtship, just like in novels. What a stroke of luck to meet him in my senior year at Agnes Scott. He just took me in tow, swept me right off my feet and insisted on marrying me the week after graduation.

He's such a good provider. He has gone right to the top with his insurance company and one of these days he'll be president. I just know it. That is, if I can be more of a help to him…. entertaining and all. But I can't help it if I am so shy. And these tears! For no reason at all, these tears fill my eyes and no matter how hard I try to blink them back they are plain as day to everybody. Why am I so sad all the time? Melancholia the doctor calls it. Grande Melancholia with a broad "A".

I have everything to make me happy. A handsome loving husband and so tall. The only boy I ever dated I could wear high heels with. There I go again kidding myself... he was the only boy I ever dated... unless you count the Matthews boy. I think I could have married him. He liked me and we had such fun reading poetry together, let me see, how did that Elizabeth Barrett Browning poem go that we liked so much? "How do I love thee, let me count the ways. I love thee to the depth and breadth and height my soul can reach when feeling out of space…." Her thoughts trailed off as her memory failed her. That certainly describes the way I feel about Tommy. But if I feel that way, why can't I show him? I looked so forward to his return from Jacksonville the other day and yet when he pulled up in our gunmetal gray Packard, I hid in my room and played like I didn't even know he had arrived.

The women fawned over him.

"Tommy," they called to him, "Tommy Thompson how GOOD it is to see you! We thought you were coming yesterday and watched for you to turn in all day long."

Mary Ann remembered how he had laughed. So genuine and deep and rolling. "Where's the most wonderful wife in the world?" He had shouted.

"Well lookie here …. Here's my beautiful daughter. Helen darling you've grown a mile. I LIKE those white shorts and that pretty blue shirt on you." He had burled his head in her brown curls and hugged her close.

"Chris, son, get, down out of that tree and shake hands with your daddy. I've brought you a bow and arrow set." Reaching his tall frame on tip toes he helped his son down from the large dogwood tree and tousled his hair.

"Retriever! Look at old Retriever! Hy ya old fella. Glad to see me?" He patted and stroked the black Cocker Spaniel that danced around his long legs. "Been taking care of my family, boy? That's a good dog."

After greeting his children and asking repeatedly for Mary Ann, he went to the porch and kissed Mam-maw and shook hands with the men. The Riverby children gathered excitedly about him and tried immediately to get him in a game.

Mary Ann, hearing all this, cowered in the yellow bed-room with her heart beating wildly as his measured steps approached the downstairs bedroom. When he flung open the door her heart actually stopped beating with terror.

"Darling!" He boomed. "You look wonderful! Let me get a good look at you. I couldn't wait to cover the miles to see you. I know I was due yesterday but I stopped off near Brevard to investigate camps for the children. One of these summers they'll want to go to camp and then you and I can take a real trip together. Maybe even Europe. You'd like that wouldn't you?"

Lying back down on her bed, Mary Ann stretched out carefully and quietly so as not to wake up Chris. Just thinking about Tommy had made her perspire heavily. Her hands shook as she pulled up the Wedding Ring quilt over her body so she wouldn't get a chill.

"Now why should I be so frightened of my own husband? She had been over this a million times in her own mind and never could come up with an answer. It's just that he over powers me. He is handsome, out-going, has charm and personality. I am unattractive, gawky, shy and withdrawn. Just like the Roosevelts. The President so handsome and attractive and his wife so, so, so like me. Buck teeth and all.

"Tommy can't fool me, though. He could have picked any place in this country to send the children and me for the summers but he chose this place above all others. This fabulous family with their out-going personalities. They DO things. Each one is so talented in some way or other.

"Mam-maw is so kind and helpful. She loves me… really loves me and wants to help me. What was that Bible verse she wrote down for me, from Timothy, I think. 'For God did not give us the spirit of fear, but of power and of love and of a sound mind'. She said it had helped her so many times and she wanted me to commit it to memory and say to myself whenever I feel upset. I don't know whether it does or not.

Haven't really given it a good test. All I know is that she comforts me… just by being next to her, I know no harm will come to me.

"Tommy insists every year that we have this bright sunny bedroom with the dotted swiss curtain. The only bedroom with a private bath and the only guest room on the first floor. Mam-maw and Grandy are right across the hall, in case I should need them in the night. The food is so good for me, too.

"I'm going right now to force myself to gain five pounds. And I swear to myself that I'll start taking an interest in cosmetics and do something becoming with my hair. Tonight, I'll wear that aqua voile dress Tommy likes so much and I'll wear that jade ring he gave me. Now, I've sworn to it and I'll do it even if it kills me. While I'm at it I might just as well go 'whole hog' as Grandy says. I'll get Mam-maw and Beck to teach me to knit. Oh, nothing complicated, but maybe I could knit Tommy a muffler. No, not a muffler, too hot to wear in Florida, but I'll learn something. Maybe I could crochet. I can start Helen a bed-spread for her trousseau. Crocheting looks busier than knitting anyway. The way the hook darts in and out, in and out.

"I must remember to laugh some. With a little practice I could even learn to whoop like Rebekah. I could hear her whooping and laughing the day I arrived and was unpacking here in my room. She sounded so gay that I stopped what I was doing and watched her from the window.

"Step back, everybody, I'm going to give it the acid test," whooped Beck.

Between two pine trees Leon had hammered in the hooks securely and strung up the last of the eight hammocks Beck had bought in Asheville weeks before. She was cautiously settling her 200 pounds in it while Harold Jr, steadied the striped canvas. Beck lay back and put her head on the little orange pillow attached to the hammock.

"This one will be mine. It's away from the river and has a gorgeous view of the mountains. Sis, run get me a glass of iced tea. I want three spoons of sugar and at least a quarter of a lemon…and a nice bouquet of mint on top. I'm going to hold court here for the rest of the summer. Anybody who wants to see me can find me here. Heavenly, just heavenly."

"That was a lie, remembered Mary Ann. She spent just time enough in that hammock to drink the tea and was off like a shot.

"Beck made her very conscious of her shortcomings. Tommy should have married a woman like Rebekah. She knits, she sews, she crochets, she drives a car, she laughs a lot, she is a good cook and plays bridge like a professional. Her energy makes me feel like a snail. On top of all she does, she set up an outdoor canning kitchen. Incredible! When she found out Grandy had vegetables enough to feed Riverby and then some left over to sell, she started canning. Mrs. Hedges couldn't let her take over the kitchen to do it so Beck just went down under that big mimosa tree on the back hill and went to work. Chris and Helen told me all about it. She got the children busy building fires and peeling vegetables and she canned food all day long. There's nothing that woman can't do.

"And Mrs. Hudson. There another one. Plays the piano like a concert artist and arranges flowers and is always on the go. It's common knowledge she has plenty of money… her husband being that overall tycoon and all. Dorothy Jackson told me herself she visited her in High Point and her house and yard are a show place. Gorgeous home with columns and plenty of servants. And yet, she spends her summers here in the mountains. Works from sun up to sun down and sleeps two in a bed and just loves it.

"Mrs. Hedges is so dear to me. So feminine…even with the hard work she does all day long she is still all woman. She has to wear those cheap house dresses and homemade aprons but she wears them with a real air. She takes up so much time with my children. When Chris had that bad case of poison ivy, Mrs. Hedges told him such charming fairy tales he didn't scratch once. And Helen! Always quoting Mrs. Hedges.

"Mrs. Hedges says it's all right, for us to go to the Village movie." "Mrs. Hedges says she'll save some hamburger for Retriever." "Mrs. Hedges says……"

"These sisters are too much for me." She went into her private bathroom and poured herself a drink of water from the tap. Instead of being caught up in their enthusiasm," I'm just overwhelmed by it. I can't measure up to any of them and no use trying. Now the other lady guests aren't like that. They enter in to the flow of things and do whatever appeals to them. If they like to sew, they piece quilts; if they like to knit, they make a pair of socks; if they like to play bridge, they organize a tournament. They enjoy the food and games and go on hikes with the children and some-times they even take part in Show Night. Now that I'd never do! Making a spectacle of myself in front of all those people. Never!

"But I'm turning over a new leaf today and I'm going to get dressed and go right out there in the parlor and ask that cute Gloria to sit on the porch as soon as the storm is over and rock, and explain Contract Bridge to me. I might catch on to it quickly and wouldn't that surprise Tommy!

"Tommy, let's take on the Parkerson's in a game of bridge." He would just faint.

"I'll be brave and follow my new regime, I'll make my husband proud of me yet. And I'll take more of an interest with the children, too.

"Wonder what makes me feel so brave all of a sudden, she thought. She'd been in her room all day long and every-thing was the same as it had always been. Or was it? It was Mam-maw this morning…. that's what it was!

At six thirty that morning Mary Ann was lying wide awake with her eyes open staring into the gloom of the room. The night, had been so long and so dark but now the first rays of the sun were running across the mountains and right up the front steps of Riverby Inn. Mary Ann sensed the sun rather than seeing it.

The bedroom door across the hall opened quietly and Mary Arm heard the slippered feet of Mam-maw going toward the front door. Her heavy frame jarred the cut glass ash trays on the hall tables.

Then Mary Ann heard talking. Just one voice. It was Mam-maw's.

"I will lift up mine eyes unto the hills, from whence cometh my strength. My strength cometh from the Lord."

"Mother," Chris called out waking up from his nap. Where is Dad? I Just had the best dream. I dreamed Dad was going to take us all hiking with a picnic lunch…. all of Riverby Inn going up Mt. Mitchell."

Mary Ann held onto the cherry bed post with her right hand and tried to hold herself together.

———————— ❧ ❧ ————————

"Sun's out! Sun's out!" One of the captains of the storm on the porch pushed back the double sliding doors of the music parlor room and continued to yell above the din.

Everything stopped at once. The rugs were straightened, tables folded up and stacked, cards were placed in their three-deck high stack. Another chorus on the piano and Cousin Tizzie would have been dead. Her smiling face was an inch from the edge of the top of the upright. The storm was over.

# Chapter 20

# Stewed Rooster

"LaVerne there's a Major and Mrs. Collins from Montgomery, Alabama who have heard about Riverby from our old friends the Jacksons. He has written and wants to know if I would rent him the entire cottage for the last week in August. I am to send him a wire this morning so he can make his plans. There would be the Major, his wife Kitty, her mother Pearl and their three children. It would mean we would have to have the family double up on the sleeping porch to a fare-thee-well but it would mean $25 in your pocket and it would be just for a week. They would take their meals up here at the big house. I'll make it clear that we close on Labor Day and they'd have to be out by then. What do you think?" Lola showed the letter to LaVerne.

"I think it is a stroke of luck. We are running over with vegetables and I say this is a direct answer to my prayers. Last night I had a talk with the Lord about my finances and He has sent us this family. Lola, you're so good to give up your cottage. Please send the wire right off. I'll make all the arrangements. The family will have to double up and hold back like they've never done before."

The children were pressed into service at once. Extra cots and pallets were set up on the already crowded sleeping porch and in the second-floor back bedroom of the big house. The cottage was scoured and cleaned and polished to a high shine. Lola made some flower arrangements in amber and antique Vaseline/glass bowls and Beck contributed an artistic fruit arrangement in the wooden knitting holder that sat by the maple rocker. The small welcome mat was shaken free of dust and lovingly replaced at the front door.

———— ❧ ❧ ————

Mam-maw was working over her quilt frame on the far side of the porch. From where she sat, she could listen out for the children playing in the river. On the pumpkin pin cushion Hy had given her, stood a dozen needles with long streamers of white thread hanging down. Mam-maw, having difficulty threading her needles, had pressed the children into being her needle threaders. One or two would leave their duties around the house and run to her quilting frame, thread up all the empty needles and run back for the next chore. Now they were swimming in the river and she was pleased to hear their happy laughter. When the front door screen banged shut, Mam-maw looked up from her quilt.

"You come here to me, Tommy Thompson, and stick out your tongue. Just as I thought. It's coated. You sit down here and I'm going to get you an N. R. tablet. You've been eating out at those restaurants while your family is up here and I can tell you haven't been eating properly. I know you men; you've been living on fried foods. You need some good turnip greens and cornbread. I'll tell Delilah to fix up some especially for you." She rose to get the N.R. tablet.

Tommy caught her hand and pulled her gently back down on the straight-backed chair with the woven rush seat.

"I do have a bitter taste in my mouth, Mam-maw," he confessed, "but it's not my digestion. I am very worried about Mary Ann. She looks so thin and tired. I don't have to tell you how much she means to me. She is my life. The only woman I have ever loved. She clings to me and needs me to make her decisions. She'll be all right. She's had a busy summer looking after the children. That's hard work, you know. Helen and Chris are growing children with lots of energy and I think it has been too much for Mary Ann. Next summer I plan to put them in camp and let her have a real vacation."

"Tommy, Mary Ann is a complicated person and has a nervous temperament. She needs to get out of herself…. Give out a little more. No, dear boy, don't wince like that. It's so true. She's a very fine woman and there are many of us here who love her dearly. Helen and Chris have had a wonderful summer. They play right along with the family children and I listen out for them just like I do the family youngsters. Why don't you and Mary Ann plan a little trip together for a few days? It would do you both world of good to get off together. I'll look after your children for you."

Tommy threw back his head and laughed his deep-down rolling laugh. "Mam-maw you are quite a woman. Were you born with a caul over your face? You're the girl of my dreams and I love you so much that I'm going to kiss you right now in front of God and everybody. You've just solved my problem. My Insurance sales have been ahead of all the other salesmen in the southeast and my boss wants Mary Ann and me to be the guests of the Company at the Waldorf Astoria Hotel in New York City. Would you look after our children and let us go, really? It would be for only a few days and Mary Ann could even get to see her Aunt Gay she loves so much."

"Of course, you'll go! Get in there and start packing. Your children can eat on the porch with the family and I'll get one of the older girls to sleep in your bed to keep Chris and Helen company at night." Mam-maw watched Tommy bound through the doors to tell Mary Ann.

"I'd better go tell LaVerne," she said out laud. She hoisted herself off the chair and like a beautiful clipper ship in full sail she swept through the dining room into the kitchen.

"Mama, just please don't bring me any bad news," LaVerne begged. This has been one of those mornings when everything has gone wrong. We strongly suspect that the Major drinks beer down at the cottage. At least there is some kind of a whiskey odor on his breath and he acts very peculiar. This morning at breakfast he was very unpleasant about the coffee. Said it wasn't hot enough. So, I personally boiled it, and you know what that does to coffee, and poured it in his cup so he could see with his own eyes how hot it was. Next thing I know, Mose comes in and says the Major he wants an ice cube to go 'long side his-coffee'. Where does he think he is? At the Biltmore in Asheville? So, I chopped off a hunk of ice and sent it in by Mose. The major just proceeded to put the ice in his cup: It's so hard to satisfy drinkers."

"Daughter, just do the best you can. No one can ask for more. I came to tell you the Thompson's are going to New York for a few days and I have promised to look after their children for them."

"Mama, why on earth would you do that? I don't want any added responsibility." LaVerne was furious.

"Don't take on so. The change will do Mary Ann good and it will give her a lift, to know she can be a real help to Tommy in appearing with him in New York for his big meeting. I have a feeling all the big bosses will want to look them over. In any case, it will free their bed for some of the family girls to use it."

"That's something I hadn't thought of. I'm sorry I was cross with you but I have had more than I can say grace over today. Even the children have been a trial today. Sis and Little Beetle came screaming in here a while ago to report that Miss Prissy Bobbie told them they had balls in their eyes, drums in their ears, nostrils in their noses and soles on their feet. I could switch her legs good for stirring up an unnecessary fuss." LaVerne collapsed on the bench on the back porch and sat down on half a dozen of Grandy's rotten tomatoes. Up she jumped like a shot and looked at Mam-maw without saying a word.

Mam-maw had to talk to herself very sternly. Now don't laugh. That's the funniest sight I've ever seen. LaVerne's, seat covered with Frank's rotten tomatoes. Jeffie, don't you dare laugh. LaVerne is worn out and all to pieces with her worries and responsibilities. Jeffie, I think you are smiling don't you dare laugh; you'll never stop.

"Delilah! Bring me a wet towel. Mam-maw was glad for the opportunity to turn her back on LaVerne. "Daughter, go change your dress. I'll tomato that Frank if he doesn't stop bringing those squashed vegetables up here. Thank you, Delilah. Here, LaVerne, stop shaking and wipe your face and your dress in back."

LaVerne started to laugh. She stopped shaking her shoulders but peals of laughter burst from her throat. Her mother joined her. They shrieked. They laughed. They wiped their tears and laughed some more. LaVerne ran up the back-porch steps to the sleeping porch and fell across a cot and held her sides. The outburst of laughing had upset Mam-Maw's system so she retired to her room.

"Miz Delilah, wha's de matteh with Miz Mam-Maw and Miz LouVun? Is de having a white lady fit?" Mose edged close to Delilah for protection in case the fit throwers returned

"Boy, you jus don' unnerstan womenfolk," replied Delilah a little uncertain. She wasn't sure what it was all about herself

"No'm ah sure don'."

——————— ❧ ❦ ———————

Major Collins wanted to get rid of Kitty and her mother. He was fed up to the teeth with them. Pearl was the most ridiculous excuse for a mother-in-law he had ever seen. Kitty catered to her constantly.

"Mother darling, let me get you a cup of hot tea. I can very easily fire up that little coal range in the kitchen."

"No Kitty, angel, you sit here and talk to your husband like a good wife should. Don't worry about me, precious, I'll take the Woman's Home Companion in my back bedroom and read a story. Of course, my bedroom is the one near the highway and the noise of the cars whizzing by makes it hard to concentrate but you and the Major deserve some time alone away from the old folks like me."

Kitty was aghast. She had made her own darling mother feel unwanted. I knew she should have taken the other bedroom but hers has a better breeze, she agonized quietly.

"Mother darling, how can you say such a thing? This very minute I'm moving your things in our bedroom. Yes, you shall have it…. the highway noise won't bother the Major and myself and you deserve to get some peace and quiet. And Mother darling, you have never looked younger than you do now. That henna rinse," she whispered, "is so becoming. Of course, you didn't need it... that one little tiny gray strand was cute on you. And I never did think it was gray…. just a lovely ash blonde "

"Oh, for corn's sake," the Major bellowed. "Am I going to have to listen to all this fol-de-rol again? 'Mother darling-Kitty- angel— let- me- wait- on- you- hand- and- foot- mother- darling- you- look- young- just- like- my- sister routine??" The Major was surprised at his own outburst but he was fed up to his bushy eyebrows with this play acting.

He adored his beautiful Kitty with her turned up nose and sexy figure and black ringlets. He had put up with Mother Darling as long as he could for today, anyway. Whining, complaining, working on Kitty's good nature. He muttered an Army oath under his breath. He decided to get drunk... all by himself. He had a fifth of bourbon hidden in his shirt drawer and he decided to drink the whole bottle.

"Major, precious, how can you say such a thing to me and to Mother Darling. You are no true gentleman of the South to talk like that. Mother Darling he IS sorry, I can tell. Let's you and me go up to the Big House and sit on the porch with those nice ladies and talk. Maybe we could get up a bridge game. Major, you're worn out. We'll leave you here in peace and quiet and you can take a rest. The children went on a hike with some of the other children and it'll be nice and quiet for you down here."

Pearl was trying hard not to cry. She knew she looked like a hag next to her beautiful daughter but it was important to keep up your appearance especially after forty. No one, not even Kitty, knew just exactly how many years beyond forty Mother Darling was.

"Major, get out the car, and drive us up to the Big House. Mother Darling has such delicate ankles I'm afraid she might turn them on the path and get a sprain."

"You mean you want me to drive you up the driveway to the front porch?" It was beyond him but he badly needed that drink so he took his car keys and helped Mother Darling out to the flagstone walk and into the car. He resisted a real urge to push her down. He roared the engine and backed the car all the way up the driveway until it reached the porch steps. The knitters and crocheting groups looked up in amazement to see a car backing up to a halt. The sides of the black car were so highly polished the rockers could see their faces in them.

The Major opened the front door and helped Mother Darling and her race horse ankles out. He slammed the door and helped her settle into a rocker next to Mam-maw. Kitty jumped out of the back seat and was pleased to see her mother seated next to Mam-maw. The contrast will make Mother Darling look just like my sister, she thought.

At this moment, Grandy's big red rooster who had been strutting on the driveway eating cigarette butts and gravel caught sight of his reflection in the side of the polished Dodge. With a hoarse cry of cockle-doodle-do he jumped on the running board and attacked the finish with foul zeal. Again and again he fought his image until his beak was blunted and the finish scratched and marred.

Scat! Shoo!" Mam-maw jumped from her rocker and parried her knitting needles at the rooster until he ran off around the house with a great flopping of wings.

The Major never said a word. He gave Mother Darling's chair a shove which started her rocking treacherously fast and jumped into the Dodge and went all the way back to the cottage in first gear. He turned off the ignition, ran into the house, slammed the door of his bedroom and uncorked the bourbon bottle.

—————————— ঌ ঌ ——————————

Grandy was around by the back porch at the Big House cleaning out the well. The big wooden cover was propped up to one side and Grandy had two bamboo fishing poles tied together with a butterfly net attached to the end.

"Trundle Bed Trash got nothing better to do, I'll give 'em something to do. Wished I knew who threw this rag doll and red balloon down here. Taint fittin' and it stales up the drinking water."

He had just dragged up the drowned baby doll and the red balloon that said "Eat at the S & W, Asheville, North Carolina" and was preparing to put the cover back over the well when his red rooster came flopping around the corner. Seeing his old friend, Grandy, rooster jumped on his shoulders in his flight from the mean rooster on the side of the car out front. While Grandy was trying to de-rooster himself, the bird looked down into the well and saw his reflection in the water. Of course, he thought that mad rival out front had followed him and he jumped into the well to fight to the finish.

By the time Grandy got out the rooster with his poles and net, the rooster had drowned. Grandy brought his old friend with droopy feathers to the kitchen and said, "Verne, cook him up."

"Why Papa, he'll be tough but if we stew him long enough, he might just do. I'll use three or four plump hens along with him and that way maybe no one will notice.

But they did notice. As fate would have it, every picky eater in the household got a portion of that old red rooster while the people who would eat anything got a portion of the nice tender hens.

Tommy's picture post card from New York was passed around for everyone to read. On one side was a picture of the Waldorf Astoria rising straight up with its head towering over the other buildings. An X marked a window where their room was. On the reverse side was the message: "Having a wonderful time. Mary Ann is in her glory. The chef here is terrible. Put on that pot of greens, we'll be home soon. Love, The Thompsons."

Major Collins weaved slightly in his chair and said in a loud voice to his wife, "Food at the Waldorf, my eye! The food at the Village drugstore would beat the food here today. This chicken is tough as an Army saddle."

Pearl was quick to agree. "Tastes like a tough old rooster to me. Everything else is delicious, though. Kitty, remind me to get Delilah's recipe for these dumplings. They are wonderful. Not at all like the doughy things we are used to at home. These are like a flat noodle."

"Everything tastes delicious to me. I'm going to have to go on a diet when I get home," she motioned at the food.

There was the main course of chicken and dumplings, green beans cooked with a ham bone and tender okra. Baked squash stuffed with white corn and blackberry cobbler.
Overhearing Major Collins complaint, LaVerne said to Beck, "I bet he's been drinking again. Alcohol kills the taste buds. Well, one stewed rooster deserves another, in my opinion."

# Free For All

LaVerne had to rearrange the sleeping quarters. Cousin Tizzie had stopped by unexpectedly and since she and Mam-maw wanted to gossip together all night, Grandy was moved temporarily to the back bedroom upstairs. LaVerne moved the bed rolls and pallets out of the room and piled them into a corner of the sleeping porch. She finished making up Grandy's bed and sat tiredly down on the edge.

"Bobbie, I want to know just exactly what your plans are for the evening." Her feet hurt her terribly. No wonder, she had been on them since early, early morning and had only sat down to eat her meals.

Bobbie was preening herself in the mirror over the wash stand. She had a hair brush in one hand and a comb in the other. Brush, comb, brush, comb, brush, comb... her hands were in a violent windmill motion as she trained a curl here and there and slicked back her widow's peak. She was hoping her mother wouldn't notice how much make-up she had applied to her pretty face and she was careful to keep her back to LaVerne.

"You look very pretty, my dear. That blue blouse and drindle skirt are most becoming on you. Are you going out with Dan Wilde tonight? Are you going square dancing or to a movie? Look at me and answer my questions. I want to know where you are going."

Bobbie took a deep breath and turned around. The sudden motion whirled the full skirt out in a circle and revealed a white petticoat with eyelet braid on it.

"Dan will take me any place I want to go and I haven't made up my mind yet. All I have to do is snap my fingers and take my pick.... Myrna Loy at the Ashville movie, the Recreation Park for roller skating, Black Mountain for square dancing. It entirely depends on me."

"Young lady, don't take that attitude with me! I'm tired, but not too tired to turn you over my knee and wear you out. Before you leave the house, you are to wipe off twenty layers of that lipstick. I don't like your attitude about spending boy's money. Dan works hard at the mill and is saving up for his expenses at Duke and I don't want you spending all his hard-earned money. Just because he is one of the village boys, you think you can treat him like dirt. If you continue with this attitude all through your life you will end up with ashes in your mouth."

"When you come in tonight, you are to sleep with me on the porch in that iron bed in the corner. Be very quiet and considerate because there will be more people sleeping on the porch than I care to count."

LaVerne considered the conversation closed and she rose to her feet, giving the bedspread one last smoothing and went out.

Bobbie, who had been making a big display of blotting her carmine lips with toilet paper in front of her mother, quickly opened her tube of lipstick and re-applied a layer to her mouth. Just for good measure, she traced over and over again her cupid's bow and heavy lower lip. Boy, does she love to boss me around. I'll be SO glad when I leave home. She blames me for everything that happens around here and criticizes me all of the darned time. One of these days, boy...! Her thoughts stopped. She was trying to picture just how she would go about getting even with her mother. I don't have to worry about that now, she consoled herself. My eyes change color when I get mad and I want to look beautiful tonight. I'm in the mood for dancing under the stars and I want to knock those boy's eyes out of their heads. That silly Dan acts like a puppy dog around me... does everything but lick my hand.

When Bobbie left Grandy's room she moved quickly down the hall toward the stairway. As she passed Mrs. Todd's room, she noticed through the open door of the empty room a large glass atomizer on the dresser. She ducked inside the room and pumped the atomizer several times into the air. She counted to three very slowly and walked with precision through the falling mist of French perfume. Just like in the movies, she thought.

Sweeping down the stairway, she paused at the newel post and flashed a dazzling smile at Dan. He was rooted to the spot. Never in all his life had he seen anything as beautiful as Bobbie, he thought.

———————— ❧ ❧ ————————

By nine o'clock the sleeping porch was a beehive of activity. Children of all ages and sizes were squirming into their cots and pallets. There was scarcely space to walk between the beds.

"Doggone it, Bill," yelled Jaybo, "I'm going to beat your brains in. You've got bubble gum all over me. Ugh, it's in my hair." He began a systematic pounding on the lump in bed with him.

"Ouch, I'm not Bill, you big bully. You'd better stop punching me," Sonny. screeched.

"The next lump that moves is bound to be Bill and I'll get him good." Jaybo was on his knees pulling at the ropes of bubble gum that threatened to bind him up for life.

Bill finally had to come up for air and the minute his head showed out of the covers, Jaybo began pounding him and smearing the gum on his face.

"Everybody quiet down," Charles ordered, "pretty soon Grandy will come barreling out of his room next door and thump everybody."

The boys settled down at once and as soon as their restless bodies became quiet, they dropped off into deep sleep.

Martha and Betty had spread their pallet quilts so close to the back steps it would be nip and tuck all night long to keep from falling down onto the back porch below.

They were a little late in staking out their floor space. The afternoon mail had brought them a small package. For five cents apiece and a three-cent stamp, they had been sent a small jar of Pond's Cold Cream. Hiding their package in the watch pocket of Martha overalls, they had giggled all the way home from the Village. All through dinner they had continued to giggle and make secret motions to each other.

Grandy, washing up at the pump, ordered them to stop giggling immediately.

"Good granny alive, I'm tired and I don't aim to listen to that nanny goat giggling while I wash my face. Verne! Come tend to these girls. They's found a tee-hee nest in a ha-ha bush again." He strode toward the dining room. As he passed by them, he flicked out his big rough hand and gave them each a resounding thump on the head.

"Guess that'll settle your hash," LaVerne said as she appeared on the porch with a fresh plate of hot biscuits. "Don't say you haven't been warned, girls. We're all worn out with those incessant giggles."

They quieted down at once and quickly finished their meal. At bedtime they went to the back bathroom and carefully soaped their faces with Octagon soap.

"Next time we send off for something, let's get some complexion soap," said Martha. "I think I have a pimple."

"I was thinking more on the lines of a razor kit. Look at all the black hair on my legs. Ugh. I hate it. You're so blond the hair on your legs doesn't even show up."

"Oh, doesn't that Ponds smell delicious?"

"Good enough to eat. Feel how smooth and creamy it is."

"Now you take just a dab and stroke up, stroke up, stroke up. That way you don't get wrinkles."

By the time they made up their pallets and crawled into it with their faces shiny and fragrant from the cold cream and their dirty necks, all the other children were sleeping like logs.

"Don't forget to say your prayers," prompted Martha sleepily.

Betty was trying to get to the end of the Lord Prayer without falling asleep. She was ready to say Amen when she heard a movement on the steps. The noise was slow, steady, and alarming. Instantly her senses came wide awake and she lay there stiff with her eyes tightly closed. The noise made a sound. Then another. "Gggururm, huuuh, rrrurughem, manerrrmen."

She couldn't stand it another minute! Betty opened her eyes and let out one blood curdling scream after another. On the steps she saw a horrible animal. It was coming to get her! Oh, that awful smell! A WILD animal. Its mangey coat was even loose over its bones…. it was hungry and had come to eat her up. That hideous face with its big rabies teeth showing. That dread disease, Black Tongue, even.

She couldn't stop her screaming. The whole sleeping porch was on its feet. Quilts, bedrolls, pillows, children whirled into one big jumble as they tried to get away from the horrible monster…. their nightmares had come true. The Beast was ON the porch.

Suddenly it stopped its horrible animal noises and stood up on its hind legs and began to dance. The spotted hide fell off and out jumped that devil Leon. His fiendish laugh sounding worse than the animal's. Laughing and laughing and holding his sides he curled up in a ball and rolled over and over on all the beds.

The children started laughing and crying. 'Free for all' and joined in the fracas. Betty stopped her shaking and gave her face several extra upward strokes to ward off any wrinkles that might have appeared since the Great Beast came.

"Stop it! Stop it! This instant!" Beck, Lola and LaVerne were wading through the surging mass on the porch. Slapping at the children, stopping pillow fights and grabbing at flying shirt-tails they soon had the porch under control. Leon was banished with the old goat hide, beds were remade and children were forced down into them. LaVerne was so exhausted she decided to come on to bed and THAT would certainly put an end to any further uprisings. Lola said that since she had to go to Black Mountain early the next morning that she, too, would come on to bed.

LaVerne was sound asleep as soon as she hit the pillow. Lola on the opposite side of the porch was wrestling with her corset in the dark. She got it unhooked, shimmied out of it, and put it, under her pillow along with her slip, brassiere and teddy bears, the silk all-in-one she wore next to her skin. She was rolling down her stockings and slipping her nightie over her head when Sonny started throwing up.

Whoops, whoops, whoops. All over the quilt.

"Maaaaaammmrnmmmaaaaaa! I'm sick at my stomach."

The understatement of the year thought Lola as she made her way by the light of the moon to his side and held his head. In the moonlight, she could see it was green apples.

"I have told you and told you and told you, you can't eat green apples. You disobey me and I have to pay for it. Stop throwing up and listen to me."

Since Sonny was totally unable to control his stomach, Lola snatched him up with the soggy quilt and headed for the bathroom.

"l was real good, mama, I kept it all on MY quilt," he said proudly as he heaved once more into the toilet bowl.

By eleven thirty everyone was sound asleep on the porch. Leon's goat hide was hanging on a nail on the big sycamore tree out by the Tearoom and the throw-up had been cleaned up. Snores, purrs, bubbling's and sleep talking's formed an orchestra with the croaking frogs and locusts outside the sleeping porch screens. A mother hoot owl sang her hideous song to her babies and the river bubbled along just down the hill.

---

Dan quietly stopped his mother's dark blue Chevy at the front door of Riverby Inn. He no sooner turned off the ignition than he jumped out and ran around to open the door for Bobbie. He slid a little on the gravel as he rounded the back of the car but, regained his balance and swept open the car door.

"Gee, Bobbie, I sure had a swell time. I hope you had a good time, too. How about next week? I think I could get my brother-in-law's maroon Oldsmobile and we could go skating at the Rec Park or over to Bee Tree Dam and maybe dance...... round dancing, not square," he coaxed and promised.

"I can't say, right now, Dan. You'd better let me hear from you before then. Let's check and see where the crowd is going." She continued to look straight ahead of her, knowing full well the effect her profile had on boys. Her turned up nose was just like the profile of a movie star. Finally, she turned and looked Dan full in the face and smiled.

"You're sweet, Dan, really you are. You check about the Olds and let me know." She slid out of the car and languidly made her way up the front steps.

Dan couldn't take his eyes off here. "Can I kiss you goodnight, Bobbie?"

Bobbie leaned toward him. "Just be sure you get that snazzy car on Saturday night. Goodnight."

Dan watched her enter the house and he reluctantly returned to the car and got behind the steering wheel. The fragrance of French perfume lingered in the car as he let the clutch out and drove off. Rounding the corner by the Tearoom, he misjudged the curve and got a face full of Mam-maw's cedar bush.

Joe and Gloria Parkerson were sitting in the shadows of the porch on the glider. They were holding hands and talking quietly together. When Dan and Bobbie drove up, they stilled their voices and played like there was no one there as they had the porch to themselves and didn't want company.

"I've had my eye on that young miss," said Gloria after Bobbie had gone into the house, "she is a little devil with these boys."

"She's a beautiful girl but I'm afraid she is headed for trouble one of these days," Joe agreed.

By midnight the household was very dark and everyone was sound asleep. Bobbie left the small light burning in the bathroom as was the custom and made her way down the back hallway. She had carefully removed her shoes, skirt and blouse. I'll just sleep in my undergarments she said to herself, then I'll be ready to slip my skirt on in the morning. She felt along the passage way and entered the back bedroom. Putting her clothes carefully on the floor to the right of the door, she eased in under the covers and snuggled up next to her mother for warmth.

"Hold on thar. Hold on thar, I say! What is it? Who is it? Jeffie, that ain't you!" Grandy jumped out of bed and danced first on one foot and then the other as he hung onto his hat and grabbed for his glasses.

"Grandy...... Grandy......... oh no! I've gotten in bed with Gran--------dYYYYYYY. Mother---------moth-------er where are you?" Bobbie held the bedspread over her front and pounded out on the porch, remembering for the first time her mother's instructions about the sleeping arrangements. She jumped into her mother's bed.

"Get the Lysol and Octagon soap. I've Just been in bed with Grandy."

"Verne! Verne!" Grandy appeared at the sleeping porch door and rapped on the frame for attention. Can't a man get his sleep around here? This Trundle Bed Trash is surrounding me. It takes the cake, that's what it does. They're even getting' right into my bed with me, that's what they're doin'. This is the last time I sleep without Jeffie. Dang nab it. A man can't even get his rest without them rascals getting' right into his bed." He stalked back into his room and slammed the door.

Lola, Beck, LaVerne and Norma took turns-sitting up in bed repeating the incident, then laughing and flopping back down on their cots. The quartet hit every note of the musical scale and still they continued to shriek and shake with paroxysms of glee.

"Laugh all you want to but I don't think it's funny. I'm taking a bath right now. I don't care if it is midnight. Imagine me in bed with Grandy, ugh."
Even with the bathroom door closed and both taps on full blast, Bobbie could still hear the laughter from the sleeping porch.

---- ❧ *Chapter 22* ❧ ----

# Signal of Distress

Mam-maw was in a reflective mood. Her knitting lay idle in her lap and she was looking at her favorite view…. the mountains that stood serene and tall across the way from the porch.

"If there's anything I love, it's a tenor voice," she confided to Gloria. "My Grandfather Hopper had a beautiful clear tenor voice. I have always felt that in our family background somewhere there must have been a Welshman. The Welsh have beautiful untrained singing voices… especially the men. We've had so much going on this summer that I haven't heard my favorite radio program for weeks. Every day, out of Chicago, there is a fifteen-minute program. A young man sings all the old-time songs. He's Irish I think and his voice is clear and high and it just sort of catches at my heartstrings."

"Let me go tune in the radio for you, Mam-maw," Gloria offered. "What time is the program and what station do I turn to?"

"We can't get Chicago on this old machine we have. I'll have to walk over to the Bishops. We sit and talk for a while and when the radio warms up and the static clears, we listen to this young man sing. What time is it? He comes on at ten o'clock."

"It's just now nine thirty. You'll have plenty of time to stroll over to the Bishops. I'll get your cane for you. I know how you like to take your cane when you walk on country roads." Gloria went to the back hallway and selected a cane from the umbrella stand. When she returned to the porch, Lola was talking to her mother.

"Mama, when you get to the Bishops, ask them if they could let a couple of the girls sleep in their spare room for the night. The sleeping porch is entirely too crowded. We haven't had a decent sleep for nights. The Thompsons are due back sometime today and the older girls will have to have some place to sleep. Beck and I are going over to Mrs. Wilde's and Flossie Hunnicutt's to see if they could take some of the gang. It was a mistake to rent out the cottage. We've doubled up and doubled up until we are ready to burst at the seams

"You could let our three girls sleep over there if you want to. We'd be glad to let the family take over their room," said Gloria as she reappeared with Mam-maw's cane.

"Thank you, Gloria. I'm sure it will be alright with the Bishops. I'm so glad I thought about my program, I hope he will sing Wagon Wheels and In the Garden. At Easter he sang The Palms and I wrote him a thank you letter." Mam-maw waved goodbye to Gloria and Lola and walked slowly across the long front yard to the curving country lane toward her neighbor's house.

"Beck! Beee— ck! Re----bekah! Where are you? Come   along, we have to run our errands before it gets any later in the day." Lola called loudly into the hallway and scanned the premises for Beck.

They had agreed to leave right after breakfast and go to the homes of two neighbors over near the Presbyterian Church and ask if they would take in a few of the family for the night. Major and Mrs. Colling planned to leave the next day and the family could once again spread out in the cottage and relieve the crowded conditions on the sleeping porch.

What a week it had been. The old house and cottage were groaning with people. Mealtimes were a nightmare. LaVerne not only had the regular guests to prepare for but tourists turned in off the highway at all hours looking for lunch or dinner before continuing their journey. Frequently a car would turn in as the dinner bell rang and the family food would be swept right off the table in front of the children's eager eyes and quivering nostrils and passed to the migratory flocks in the dining room.

Leon was sent repeatedly up into the mountains with his .22 rifle to bring back squirrels. Delilah kept a large kettle of squirrel stew simmering on the back of the big stove. The family would start to whimper and cry out when LaVerne would swoop out on the back porch and grab the pieces of fried chicken off their plates, load them on a platter and whisk them into the dining room. At this moment, Delilah would appear at the back door with the squirrel stew and dip it up.

"Let's us poor masses do like they did in Russia and start a revolution," Charles urged. "We studied about that in school last year. Those peasants were down-trodden and hungry and they just rebelled and overthrew the Czar."

"I wouldn't try to overthrow Czar Grandy the Great but there are three Czarinas that I'd like to take a crack at."

"Just remember to take a big bite out of your meat as soon as you sit down. They can't serve it to the guests if you do that. The Health Department won't allow it," Harold informed the group.

Beck and Lola took their own cars and each went her own way to the neighbors.

Beck skillfully backed her car out of the driveway and eased it out onto the highway. She crossed the bridge over the Swannanoa River and turned left on the gravel road that split the middle of two cornfields. Her destination was a mile and a half down this road to the little white cottage nestled in a grove of poplar trees on the right.

Lola, who had been in such a hurry to get off, waited for Rebekah to get onto the highway before she climbed into the Franklin. She put on her driving gloves, rattled the keys a little before inserting the key to the trunk into the ignition. When it wouldn't lock 'home', she pulled it out and tried the other one on her key ring. When it fitted properly, she gave it a sharp twist to the right and was gratified when the engine sprang to life. Spurning the rearview mirror and looking casually to the right and left, she backed out of her parking place and stopped inches from the door of the Tearoom. Tugging at the awkward steering wheel, she let out the clutch and lurched off down to the driveway.

When, she too, took the gravel road, Rebekah's dust was beginning to settle. Lola was headed for the red brick two story house on the left-hand side of the road… right across from Flossie Hunnicutt's.

Lola turned into the driveway of Mrs. Wilde's house and blew the horn. Violet Wilde was just coming out of the barn and she waved a greeting. Her heavy frame was encased in a soiled house dress with a large apron over it. Men's rubber hip boots were on her feet with the tops doubled back at the kneecap. She had on her dark green cable-knit sweater and a tam o'shanter hat was socked down over her head. Her peacocks squawked at her heels.

"Miiiiiizzzzz Hutson, I've been busier than two frogs fighten' over a lily pad. My spotted cow just birthed a calf at four o clock this morning. Never saw an animal with such little hips. She had a terrible birthin' but she's alright now…only thing, she's just as thin as a racer. I've put her on double rations," Her loud shrieking voice diminished as she reached the car.

"Get out and come on my porch for a spell. I ain't seen you since the Fourth of July. Dan tells me you folks got more guests than my old dog has fleas. Looks like you all have took Dan on to raise. He spends near 'bout every night at Riverby with that pretty Bobbie. You tell Miz Hedges when she can't hardly stand the sight of him any more to send him on back home. Lordy, these boys in love can sure be a nuisance."

"Mrs. Wilde, these geraniums in the porch boxes are absolutely gorgeous," complimented Lola as she and Violet settled themselves in the wicker chairs on the porch. "What on earth do you do to them? Those blooms look as big as Grandy's cabbages."

"Blood! Honey, I puts fresh chicken blood on 'em. Every time I wring a chicken's neck, I let the blood drain right out on those geraniums. They are purty, I must say. Just pleasures my eyes to look at 'em."

"Mrs. Wilde," Lola was glad to change the subject, "do you have room to take in two or three of our boys for tonight? We have doubled up all week and we are bursting at the seams. It would be for just one night. Tomorrow we will have the cottage free. We'll send over sheets and pillows for the boys to use."

"Why, I'd be glad to help out. Never mind the bed clothes. I got more than enough. They can sleep in Dan's room. I think he and Bobbie have a date tonight. That Dan is such a good boy. He's my baby, you know, and he's a real comfort to me. Good sense, too. Last night I caught a low-down tramp in my hen house. Rascal has been riding the rods from Asheville to Black Mountain. When he gets to this junction, he jumps off, rung over here, takes a couple of my hens, runs back and catches the next freight to Black Mountain. How do you like that for a sneak? Well, I fixed him up. Rigged up an alarm system from my room to the hen house and last night the bell went off just before midnight.

I jumped out of bed and grabs my shot gun and strikes out for the hen house and caught that devil with a Rhode Island Red under each arm. 'Stand where you are. I've got a bead on you.' Well, I would have shot him right then and there but Dan was just then coming in from his date and saw all the commotion and he says, 'Ma, you can't shoot that man at such close range, that buckshot will just tear him up.' And he was right. So, I kept a bead on him and Dan went to the house and called the Law. That was smart thinking."

"Dan has nice manners, Mrs. Wilde, you've done a good job raising him."

"One of these days he'll be gettin' married and leaving me. Did I ever tell you that Mr. Wilde, bless his memory, took me to Mexico City on our honeymoon? Well, he did. We took in a bull fight and hit just tore me up. I'll declare, Miz Hutson, those horses were soooo pretty. They had on fancy trappin's and their hooves were shining like mother's pearls. Those bulls are mean devils, though. Glad to get home to civilization. Oh, you have to leave? I can't spend all day jawing neither. Got to go check on my spotted cow. Hope she'll have enough milk for her calf. You send those boys on over I'll be ready for them."

The two women waved goodbye and Lola made her erratic course around the circular driveway and headed out on the gravel road back to Riverby.

In the distance, approaching her was a tornado of dust swirling angrily behind a salmon colored Oldsmobile. Like a real Kansas twister, it couldn't decide which way it wanted to go. It darted from one side of the road to the other and back again. At times it careened the car almost into the cornfield and then jerked back again into the center of the road.

———————— ❧ ❧ ————————

"Here comes Flossie," said Lola to herself, as she blew her horn and signaled for the Oldsmobile to stop.

It was touch and go for a while as the two cars approached each other... each driver trying to bring her horse power under control and stay away from other.

Skidding to a stop, Lola called out, "Beck's waiting for you at your house. See you later." Flossie called out something in reply which was muffled by the dust, and each driver ground her gears and leapt off in opposite directions.

Flossie was in a dither. She had left the house early and had gone to the Village, to attend to some banking. As she passed Red's Shell Station she decided to get tanked up. She pulled sharply on the steering wheel cutting across the highway and bumped to a stop with the front end of the car kissing the gas pump.

"Can you reach me from here, Red?"

Red hurried to her side. "Don't back up Mrs. Hunnicutt," he warned. "I'll stretch the hose. You're just fine. Fill er up?"

It was the third time in a week Flossie Hunnicutt had been into the station. She could never remember if her tank was full or dry. The Indicator on the dashboard had been a mystery to her from the beginning and she never paid attention to them. Consequently, her tank was either full to the brim in town or bone dry on a country road somewhere.

Red was washing off her windshield, Flossie looked about her and when she saw a red, white and blue poster in his window with an American Eagle on it and the initials NRA, she gasped and clutched her heart.

"My flag, Red, my flag! I forgot to put out my flag this morning. Never mind the windshield. Put the gas on my account and I'll sign later." She turned the key, pumped on the accelerator and turned the car around in the middle of the highway.

Red was left standing there with a stretched hose in his hand which was belching gasoline out on the ground. "That woman isn't safe on the road. Darned fool women drivers."

Flossie was appalled at herself! The first time in her life she had forgotten to put up her flag. And with Labor Day coming up. What if I forget to run it up on a national holiday?

Beck was getting tired of waiting. She had been sitting on the glassed-in sun porch for close to thirty minutes and she was getting restless. When Flossie hadn't answered her calls, Beck had gone into the house and waited for her on the sun porch.

Such a lovely home. Flossie takes real pleasure in decorating and is go good at it. She is cultured and educated. I don't know why she doesn't want to live in the city. The little cottage was orderly and spic and span. Well, no wonder, they don't have any children. Mr. Hunnicutt leaves early every morning for his job in Asheville and gets home after six. Flossie can devote her time to making a lovely home. Now, how on earth can she be so scatterbrained when her home is so well appointed and tidy? She has collected some real treasures of mountain craft and blended them quite skillfully with her traditional furniture. I love that soft Oriental rug in her living room. The colors are muted and toned down. Not like so many Orientals with those wild purples, reds, roses and blues all jumping out at you. Only the sound of a dozen clocks ticking kept Beck company.

The sound of a car skidding on the blue-chip driveway brought Beck to her feet. The car door slammed and Flossie ran into the house, said, "Hi Beck, I'll be with you in a minute," grabbed up the American flag from its stand on the sun porch and ran out to the flag pole. She ran it up to the top with quick jerks on the rope.

"Rebekah, you'll just have to excuse my rudeness," Flossie apologized when she came back into the house. "I'm on a new diet and it has done something to my memory. Can you imagine? I forgot to put up my flag this morning. First time in fifteen years...if you don't count the time of the heavy snow when I had to leave it out overnight. Too frozen to work the ropes. Well, it is good to see you. Tell me all the Riverby news." Flossie moved into the kitchen and put on the percolator and slipped some cinnamon buns into the oven. "I'm through with diets, "she announced.

"I try to diet, too," said Beck. "But it's hard with low blood pressure and thyroid trouble. I think I also tend to be anemic. The doctors don't say as much, but I think I know myself better than they do. Well, I'm here, Flossie, to ask you if some of the older girls could use your little guest house for the night. We have guests coming out of our ears. Sister is exhausted and I had put my foot down, and said she is going to have a good night's sleep That puts her into shape better than anything else."

"Rebekah, I can take three on that big bed out there in my Riverby Overflow house. You send them over."

Flossie pointed to the little house standing at the edge of her garden. Once upon a time it had been a hen house but she had had it scoured and painted and a new roof put on and had turned it into a charming one room guest house. A large antique bed dominated the room but there was room for a chair or two and a washstand.

Flossie poured the coffee and passed the heavy cream and cinnamon buns warm from the oven. She and Beck were having a good time gossiping when Glover, Red's boy, rapped at the door.

"Mrs. Hunnicutt, Dad says to please sign your ticket for three gallons of gas."

"Oh dear yes. I was in a hurry to get home. I don't have my glasses. Where do I sign? Oh well, it doesn't make any difference." She signed her name several times on the receipt in rolling script.

"By the way, Mrs. Hunnicutt, is everything all right here? I noticed your flag was upside down and in an army manual my father has it says a flag flown upside down is a signal of distress."

"Upside down! What will I do next? Goodbye Rebekah, I'm going to fix my flag and take a pill and lie down for a while. Send the girls on over." Flossie upset her coffee cup as she dashed past Beck and Glover and headed for the fish pond. "Hang on, Old Glory, Flossie's coming."

━━━━━━━━━━━━ ❧ *Chapter 23* ❦ ━━━━━━━━━━━━

# Double Up and Hold Back

The big old-fashioned kitchen had been alive with activity since the middle of the afternoon. Inside the oven of the Royal Oak stove, several legs o' lamb were being roasted. Every half hour, Delilah would open the big door of the oven and baste the lamb with the drippings. Mose was attempting to keep all pots and pans washed and scoured as they were re-used promptly.

"Miss Lou-Vun", Delilah said quietly at her elbow, "youss all wore out. Yo' nerves are just all a frazzled No need for you to stand here in this hot kitchen at that counter fixin' that mint sauce. Ah's cleared a space in the pantry and set you up a stool to sit on. The window is open and they's a cool breeze sweeping in right off that Alice-zander' mountain across the way. You go on in and settle down. Mose! Take Miss Lou-Vun's fixin's in yonder and don' drag you's feet so!"

LaVerne moved into the pantry as though in a trance. It seemed the summer would never end. It seemed to her that her whole life was made up of 'walking the pipe' in some way or other. Her days revolved around the meals. She could hardly enjoy her breakfast for thinking out the luncheon menu. At lunch, her mind was already on suppertime. If I can make it through this Labor Day weekend, I'll be alright she comforted herself.

When she settled herself on the stool, she turned her attention to the sprigs of fresh mint leaves standing in water in the big yellow crockery bowl. She pressed her face close to the fragrant leaves and breathed deeply. How refreshing it was!

With the kitchen scissors, she cut the leaves into small pieces in an ironstone pitcher and added some boiling water. As they steeped, she added sugar, salt, pepper and homemade apple vinegar.

With that out of the way, she started on her salad bowl. She used the large wooden chopping block and tackled the garden vegetables lying washed and cleaned in the big canning kettle. She assembled watercress from the branch, leaf lettuce, rosy radishes, tender yellow raw squash, spring onions... tops and all, small cauliflower bouquets, cucumbers and red, red ripe tomatoes. She added sliced green pepper rings for a final garnish and submerged the whole salad into a large bowl of ice water. She went over the menu again in her mind.

Leg O' Lamb with mint sauce, riced potatoes and gravy. Baby beets, creamed corn cut fresh off the cob. Let's see now, we're a little low on green vegetables so I'll invent a new dish... I'll mix peas and lima beans together.... maybe mince in some pimiento for color. Hot rolls, salad, and cherry cobbler. If anyone turns in at the last minute, I'll have Delilah fry some bacon for the family. They've been well fed all summer and they'll have to hold back tonight in case we get some paying customers off the road.

"Oh Lord," she prayed with bowed head, "I ask for strength of body to get through this next meal and this day. Thank you. Amen."

LaVerne never would have made it without the Lord's help. When the guests filed into the dining room after the dinner bell rang and the family pushed and shoved into their places on the back porch, the wave of people was like the rush of water going over Niagara Falls. Three extra car loads turned off the highway and were seated for dinner.

"More hot rolls! They're calling for more hot rolls, Delilah." Hy refilled the big platter with rolls right out of the oven and covered them with a large linen napkin.

"More meat!" Ordered Bobbie. "Some of the men want some more of that lamb with the mint sauce."

LaVerne said, "I was afraid of that. That lamb is absolutely delicious…. so juicy and tender on the inside but crisp on the outer edges. Delilah, you're too good a cook," she laughed and attacked the left-over meat with the sharp knife and cut off thin slivers to arrange on the tray. "I hope this will be enough to satisfy them, we're down to the bare bone."

"Peppa sauce!" Shouted out Mose. "De Majah want peppa sauce."

"Mose, are you sure you understood him? We don't have any pepper sauce. What on earth would he want pepper sauce on? That's to be served with greens and turnips and we're all out of it. Pass him that mint sauce again.

"No'm I passed him de mince sauce and he say damn it boy I said peppa sauce."

"I will not tolerate that kind of talk in my dining room. The very idea of such talk. Mose, I'm very sorry he talked to you that way. I know Mrs. Collins and her mother were highly embarrassed. I'll fix some kind of pepper sauce and serve it to him myself. Go tell him that Mrs. Hedges is attending to it personally."

Mose grinned his widest and swung back into the dining room.

LaVerne grabbed a small glass antique bowl of dark green. Smiling to herself she quickly minced and chopped up some green Bell peppers and some very hot red peppers. To this she added a cup of vinegar that had begun to ferment and plenty of salt. Her soft blue eyes were smiling as she decided to really spice it up. Working even more quickly, she added plenty of black pepper and everything else hot she could think of from her spice shelf. Stirring up the brew which was looking a little bubbly and frothy on top, she said to herself as she took off her apron, "This should be peppery enough. Maybe it will burn out that bad talk in his mouth and cut through that whiskey breath."

She patted her hair into place and smiled her most charming smile and sailed into the dining room.

"Major, I'm so sorry you were inconvenienced. Here is your pepper sauce…a specialty of the house I'm rather proud of. On your meat? Fine, let me ladle it on for you." She was generous in serving him.

"Thank you so much, Mrs. Hedges," Kitty said with real appreciation. "The Major likes hot sauces on his meat. Mother Darling and I prefer this delicious mint sauce. It's such a complement to the lamb."

"Mrs. Green," LaVerne addressed Kitty's mother, "I hope your ankles are alright. I see you have them taped up." As she acknowledged Pearl's ankles, she stole a look sideways at the Major. He was carefully cutting his meat into neat little regulation squares and helping himself to more of his special sauce.

"Oh, dear yes," Pearl replied. "I have such delicate ankles. The doctor told me that my legs are really much younger than my body and I have to remember that and try not to let them run away with me. You see, I'm really older than I look," she smiled demurely.

"Major, Major precious, what is the matter?" Kitty interrupted her mother's favorite conversation. "Your face and neck are lobster red. Speak to me. Somebody DO something!"

"I expect he needs something to drink," LaVerne could hardly keep from laughing. "Good, Mose, pour the Major some of that hot coffee. See, Major, boiling right out of the pot just like you like it."

Never in all his life had the Major been so taken by surprise. What on earth did that woman put in this sauce? It looks so innocent sitting there in that dark green bowl but she must have piped it in straight from hell. He was choking and coughing and clutching his throat. Not even Indian curry had set him on fire like this. If that woman didn't look so sweet and smiling at me so nicely, I would swear she did this to me on purpose. And that red-hot coffee going down my throat, on top of that witch's brew.

People were beginning to stare at all the commotion and Joe Parkerson began pounding him on the back.

The memory of it and the agony of his burnt tongue and throat made him rush from the table, out through the kitchen and onto the back porch. The family diners looked in amazement while the Major pumped up the pump handle and hung his head beneath it. The cold well water flushed and drained and purified his mouth and throat. He slowly made his way to the front porch and took a rocker for the first time at Riverby. He leaned back and wiped his eyes and kept his mouth open. The cool evening mountain air felt good, Kitty found him there with his necktie untied and his shirt collar open.

"Precious, are you all right? Here's a dish of cracked ice that thoughtful Mrs. Hedges sent out for you. Just suck on a piece. She said for you to rest quietly and try not to talk. She said sometimes she gets things she can't swallow either."

When the other diners had finished their meal, they too, gravitated to the porch and politely inquired after the Major's health. Kitty thanked them and did the talking for him. Pearl sat on his other side and patted his hand. She had her taped-up ankles resting on a low footstool Kitty had thoughtfully provided for her.

———————————— ❧ ❧ ————————————

The migrant diners paid for their dinners and said they would certainly call again next time they were up that way. "You give folks a good meal for .75," they said, climbed back into their cars and drove off... after a wistful look at the permanent residents rocking on the cool porch.

Beck called to the children on the lawn as they began counting off for Kick the Can.

"Just one short game then I want you to get your things lined up so we can take you to the neighbors for the night."

"Gloria," Mam-maw called as Gloria strolled past her on the porch, "I wanted you to know I heard my program. Radio is a marvel. There we were in the Bishop's living room and way out in Chicago that tenor was singing. He sang "The Last Round-Up", an Appalachian folk song and "The Lord's Prayer" It was so inspirational."

Gloria smiled at Mam-maw with affection. "Joe wants me to play the piano for him. Do you have any special request?"

"Do you know 'Day is Dying in the West'? I love those old hymns, but anything you play will be fine with me. I like the way you play 'Painting the clouds with Sunshine'......anything will be nice."

Mam-maw turned her attention to the lovely mountains in front of her and the children at happy play in the yard. The late afternoon sun was almost gone. Alexander's Mountain was fast swallowing it up. The brilliant glow in the West was a forecast of tomorrow's glow in the East. Lightning bugs were turning their little flashing beacon lights on and the locusts and crickets were starting their serenades to the tune of the slowly moving rocking chairs.

Mam-maw closed her eyes and her quiet thoughts went as usual to Claude. She was wondering if he was remembering the hymn she had taught him so many years ago. She went over the words in her secret mind and listened carefully to them:

Lead kindly light, amid the encircling gloom, Lead thou me on;

The night is dark, and I am far from home; Lead thou me on;

Keep Thou my feet; I do not ask to see, The distant scene, one step enough for me.

"Hey gang, there's Samson's truck. Look! He's turning in," Bill's shout broke up the game.

Samson maneuvered the big red truck carefully through the rock posts at the entrance of Riverby and changed gears as he started up the incline to the front porch.

The children emerged from their hiding places and gathered around home base waiting for Samson to stop.

"Hey Samson, how about a ride?"

"Whatcha got in your truck?"

"Are you coming to do any hauling?"

"You'd better pull on around to the back door. Aunt Beck gets awful mad when you stop in front."

By the time Samson had stopped and put on the emergency brake, the rockers were stilled with expectancy. In the momentary quietness, loud and slurred hymn singing was coming from the back of the truck.

*"I would be true.... for there are those who trush me....*

*I would be pure.... for.... there are those whoooo carrrree...*

*I would be stroooooong. for I know my weak....ness*

*I would .....Whassa matter, whassa matter? why we stop----ing?"*

A tousled blond head arose from the bed of the truck. The face was swollen and flushed with a purple bruise just under the left eye. As the figure attempted to stand up, it swayed and caught itself from falling by clutching out for the top of the cab and using it for leverage. Claude was very drunk and very dirty.

The silence was unbearable. The children stood back, stock still and tried to recognize the uncle they adored. This wasn't he.... this man looked different and mean. Norma half rose from her chair and gathered her stole tightly about her as if for protection.

Mam-maw's girls were furious and terribly embarrassed. they tried to leave their chairs and go toward the steps but like underwater swimmers, their motions were absurdly inept.

Mam-maw's arms were held out in front of her as though she were about to take an infant in them and cuddle it.

Grandy was on his feet at once but stood quietly not daring to believe the prodigal son was home once again.

"Mr. Blanks," Samson stood humbly at the foot of the porch steps with his head bowed, "I seen Mr. Claude lying in Park's Square in Asheville and I brung him home long with the order of grain for Mr. Bart's sto'" Samson stood uneasily shifting from one foot to the other and scratching at his large overalled backside. He was trying to think out if he had done the right thing.

A banging sound erupted from the truck. Claude was pounding on the top of the cab with both fists for attention.

"Now tha ah've gath'ed you all together," he intoned with an expansive sweep of his arm at the family and guests on the porch and the children in the yard, "th' meetin' will now COME TO ORDER." When his eyes met Mam-maw's, he slowly slumped back into unconsciousness on the bed of the truck.

Samson was fast on his feet for someone who weighed 300 pounds. He jumped up in the back of the truck, hoisted Claude over his shoulders and climbed down again. Charles and Leon rushed forward, and relieving Samson of his burden, they attempted to stand Claude on his feet with their arms supporting him. They looked from face to face for a word or signal as to what should be done with him.

"The Tearoom," LaVerne ordered as she stepped forward. "I'll be right there."

She rushed off the porch and swung open the Tearoom door. Unused for several weeks, it smelled musty. She quickly cleared some stored chairs out of the way and glanced at the cot in the far corner. It needed sheets and a pillow she thought as she opened the windows to the cool night air.

"I can STAND ALONE. I am NOT drunk. Boys.... Chars.... Le-on outta my way," His boys continued to hold him up as they dodged the swinging and flapping arms.

Norma was rigid with humiliation as she left the porch and went to Mam-maw's room. Safely inside, she buried her head in her lap and convulsive sobs racked her body.

Lola was already in the linen closet gathering up sheets and a torn towel. No need for a pillow she reasoned, he'll just mess it up.

Grandy put his calloused hand on Samson's shoulder. For a moment their eyes met.

"Ah hopes ah done the right thing, Mr. Blanks."

"It is always right to bring my son home, Samson. Here's something for your trouble. Grandy opened his coin purse with the snap fastener and withdrew a bill.

"Ah don' wants no money, Sir."

"Take it, Samson. He probably would have taken a taxi cab like he usually does and they charge more than that."

Mam-maw was making her way through the startled and embarrassed guests toward the Tearoom. Her head was held high and her eyes were straight ahead so she wouldn't have to look at the eyes full of pity for her.

"Don't come in, Mama," LaVerne beseeched. We have him sitting quietly in a chair until we get the cot made up. He in a belligerent mood and he'll just upset you. Wait until tomorrow when he's more himself."

Mam-maw glared at her daughter and pushed her way into the darkened Tearoom. The vile odor of whiskey almost took her breath away.

"Oh Claude."

"Now don't go 'Oh Clauding' me again. I'm not eve....... n goin' to look at you. I know THAT look and I don' have to take it off you or ennnnybody else." He closed his eyes tightly so he wouldn't have to look at his mother's face.

In the face and eyes of Jeffie Gill Blanks was the look of all women of all time looking at the destruction of a Golden One. She turned her head and groped with unseeing eyes out of the Tearoom. Her great age and weight and spirit were bowed and seemed to be crumbling. LaVerne went to her mother's side. She put her arm around her mother and walked with her slowly to her bedroom.

Lola shot a contemptuous look at Claude as she jerked the sheet into slipshod place. Charles and Leon strained at their young muscles until Claude was on his feet and slumping over on the bed.

Grandy appeared in the doorway of the Tearoom with a cup of coffee in his hand, his hand shook as he entered the little room and the cup rattled in the saucer. Placatingly, he said, "Boy, I've brung you some coffee."

Claude didn't hear him. He had passed out again.

Charles and Leon took off Claude shoes and slipped outside.

Grandy pulled up a small stool and set the coffee down next to the cot. He pulled up the worn coverlet over the unconscious body and with his rough hand gently smoothed back the blond hair from Claude's brow.

"It's good to have you home, son."

Grandy went, outside and carefully and quietly closed the Tearoom door.

Beck was acting as though nothing had happened. Her voice was a little too loud and rather high pitched as she began organizing the children for bedtime.

"Bobbie, check with your mother about where you are to sleep before you go on your date. I want my boys to get in the back seat of my car. I'm taking you to the Wilde's. All you girl's going to Mrs. Hunnicutt's…. Hy, Mabes, La…… get in the front seat. I'll help sort out the rest of you when I get back. Do you have your pajamas and tooth brushes? Let me get the car keys and I'll be right out." She bustled back into the house

"Psst, Gloria," she whispered, "start playing the piano again. I don't care, anything."

Gloria was standing uncertainly at the door of the music parlor room where she had watched the whole episode. She felt such compassion for the family she loved. How humiliating for them. But knowing they would want things to proceed normally, she sat back down on the round stool and began playing and singing in a loud voice.

"I'm painting the clouds with sunshine…"

"When Beck drove off with the carload of children, Lola appeared on the porch and announced in no uncertain terms that is was bedtime for all children. For once they didn't argue with her. Even the boarder children took the hint and kissed their parent's goodnight and went quietly up to bed.

"Don't cry, Marth. Please don't cry." Betty was trying hard to fight back her own tears. "I can't stand to see you cry. It wasn't so bad this time. At least he was standing up. Maybe not everybody noticed. Here, if you'll stop crying, I'll let you wear my diamond ring." She tugged at the dime store ring that had formed a green circle around her finger. The large stone was loose in the mounting. "And you can have my dessert tomorrow. He'll be all right tomorrow and we'll have a good time. He'll play with us across the river and I bet we have a songfest after supper. Marth, please don't cry."

With their arms locked around each other out of fear and, trying hard to derive comfort from each other, they lay on their bed on the sleeping porch and slowly went to sleep.

Norma was lying next to Mam-maw and talking quietly." I'm going to leave him, Mam-maw. I can't put up with this. It's hard enough on me but worse on the children. I support us anyway and know I can get a divorce……. I'll charge desertion and non-support. "

Norma had repeated this story for so many years, Mam-maw knew it by heart.

Mam-maw didn't answer her. Long ago she had said everything to her that could be said. She pulled her black shawl higher up over her eyes and, with Norma beside her talking on, she withdrew into herself and began to pray her prayer of thanksgiving for Claude's safe journey home. The usual hymn came into her mind and she gave herself over to going over the words in her heart.

*The Lord my Shep-herd, I'll not want;*
*He makes me down to lie*
*In pastures green; He leadeth me*
*The quiet wa-ters by.*

As soon as Claude was safely put away in the Tearoom and the children had gone to bed, the guests left the front porch. Some of them decided to take a walk and when Gloria couldn't get anyone to join her in song, she stopped her playing and closed the lid to the piano. She took a book and sat with Joe in the parlor room in case they could be of help to the family. Maybe Joe would have to go for the doctor.

Mary Ann Thompson lay on her bed and arranged a cool cloth over her eyes.

Major Collins, carrying his bowl of cracked ice, motioned to kitty and Pearl and they made their way back to the cottage.

Pearl slipped on her glasses in the darkness so she could see the path better and not hurt her ankles.

By ten thirty most of the lights were out in the Big House and the cottage

"LaVerne! LaVerne! Is that you?" Lola's anxious voice called down Lover's Lane to the solitary figure seated on a large gray boulder. "Sister, I've been looking everywhere for you. You have no business worrying me like this," she scolded.

LaVerne didn't answer Lola's remarks. The long summer, the long day and now the long night ahead had left her depleted. Now that the summer was almost over, she thought back on all those meals and hard days. She had accumulated less than a hundred dollars for all the backbreaking work. It would soon be time to close up the Big House and go back to Arkansas. There was nothing else she could do. Tonight, everything was just too much for her. Claude coming home 'that way'. Her sympathetic nature cried out for her mother and father and for Norma and her children. If only I could have had time to talk to Claude quietly this summer: But I didn't have a quiet moment and I couldn't take on an extra burden of responsibility. And Bobbie! She couldn't shake off that terrible feeling!

Finally, she answered her sister's call, "I'm here, Lola. I'm so worried about Bobbie. I have one of my terrible premonitions about her."

"Sister, you're just exhausted. You've worked so hard today and with that fool Claude coming in like that. I could crown him with a croquet mallet. I'll tell you, he's uncanny. He seems to know instinctively when he shouldn't appear."

"I well remember last summer, at the height of the season, when he came home drunk and threatened suicide and locked himself in the Parkerson's room and shot the gun out of the window. He has no consideration at all."

"Did you know that Papa is dozing in a chair outside the Tearoom? Guess he's waiting for Claude to wake up and call for something. Did you know that Papa even took him a cup of coffee? I've never known Papa to wait on anybody before. He's spoiled Claude to death. Well, I'm going to see that Papa goes on to bed. Claude won't come to until noon tomorrow."

"Watch and see...... he'll get up and bathe and shave and put on clean clothes and march right into the dining room as big as life and with his charm he'll put all the guests at ease. They'll forget all about tonight. But not me! Wait until I get my hands on him. What's the matter, LaVerne?"

"I know something has happened to Bobbie."

"Go on to bed. You'll feel better tomorrow. Bobbie's all right. You worry too much."

# Chapter 24

# Labor Day

On the sleeping porch, a child stirred and talked out in his sleep, "I got last tag, Kig's X........."Norma sat up in bed. She had been sleeping lightly. Waking at any noise but drifting off again into an uneasy slumber.

"I'll get up and take and aspirin, it's just a headache or that time of life." Norma knew she was just looking for an excuse to get out of bed and look out at the Tearoom again to see if there was any sign of light or movement.

She made her way carefully through the cots on the porch, and went down the hallway to the bathroom. She noted to herself, 'the front porch lights on! That Bobbie is so careless and wasteful. Now I'll have to go down and turn it off and here I am in my nightgown and with cold cream all over my face.'

Not only was the front porch light still lit but Norma found the front door was standing wide open and a strong cool breeze was coming in. Norma checked the old-fashioned clock on the mantel in the hallway. Twelve o'clock! I wonder if Bobbie is in this house! LaVerne will tan her hide.

Norma picked up some papers that had blown off a table and lay scattered on the floor. She closed the double front door and snapped off the front porch light. She turned on a small lamp in the hallway and tipped toed to Mam-maw and Grandy's room and peered in. The two large lumps on the double bed were sleeping soundly. The cot at the foot of the bed was empty

She went back up the long stairway. On the second floor she began a systematic check of the family rooms, took a quick peek into the Medallion room, the wall paper still made her cringe, and went out onto the sleeping porch. She went from cot to pallet checking each occupant to see if Bobbie was snuggled up with Sis, or Bill or Sonny. She checked each sleeping form. She tried to remember if Bobbie had had instructions to go to the Bishop's or Mrs. Hunnicutt's or if she was going to double up in the room with their girls, or did they go over to the Bishops? She couldn't remember. Since Claude's arrival that afternoon, everything had emptied from her mind except him. She hesitated only for a moment before touching LaVerne on the shoulder. Instantly LaVerne was awake.

"Is that you Bobbie? Oh Norma. What's the matter? What time is it?"

"Where was Bobbie supposed to sleep tonight? I found the front porch light on and the doors open and I can't find her anywhere in the house. I thought I'd better wake you up."

"What time is it? Norma, I told Leon to set up a cot for her in Mam-maws room. Now let's see, yes, I told her to sleep down there so she wouldn't disturb everyone up here when she came in. Yes, I'm sure I told her that. Isn't she there? Did you look?" Norma shook her head in answer.

The two women went back down the stairs and checked the time again. It was almost 12: 30 a.m.

———————————— ✈ ✈ ————————————

12:30, Bobbie checked the clock on the dashboard. Dan's brother in-law's car was speeding. The white side wall tires were overheated and they cried on the corkscrew curves of Old Fort mountain. Dan jerked the wheel left then right, left, right, swaying his body weight as if to help the auto maintain balance. Bobbie watched with suspended interest as tree tops danced in weird shapes across the windshield and ran into walls of sheer granite and dropped into black valleys.

"Rrrrrrrrrrrrrrrrrrrrrrrrrrrrrrrrrrrrrr." The siren penetrated Bobbie's pre-occupation of the car's flirtation with the mountain sides.

"Ok kid, slow down. There's a side road around the next curve. I want you to take a quick left on to it. Easy, brakes, EASY! Hold her steady, Now, NOW!" The car took a dangerous roll to the right and faltered precariously before swinging back to the left.

"There, good going kid. Now take a good look ahead. Throw the Lights!" Dan obeyed and drove up the straight clay road.

"Stop, now cut the engine! No monkey business!"

Bobbie felt the cold steel barrel on her temple.

"If you so much as bat an eye to attract those lousy cops, I'll blow your girlfriends head off "

"Rrrrrrrrrrrrrrrrrrrrrrrrrrrrrrrrrrrrrrrrrr." The incessant siren echoed from peak to peak down the blue ridge. Bobbie watched the head beam of the police car flash bright then dark, bright, dark, as they wove in and out of the curves and moved up and down the grade of the road

"Rrrrrrrrrrrrrrrrrrrrrrrrrrrrrrrr". The gun point bored into her skull. She was paralyzed, she felt faint. The evening flashed before her.

The large Ferris wheel turned its slow and incessant circuit and the white light bulbs strung on its superstructure could be seen for miles around. The wire cages upon reaching the apex of the circle, swayed back and forth as they caught the air currents from the mountains. In the center of the Park, the large swimming pool had its under-water lights on and the swimmers swam with quick strokes to keep warm.

The merry go 'round went in its endless circles with the wide-eyed stallions straining at their leashes. The loud music was a natural come-on and the rotating spotlight on top blinked like a lighthouse beacon.

The smell of hot dogs and popcorn and cotton candy and roasted peanuts was irresistible. The park concessionaires smiled as their cash boxes rapidly filled up. The crowd surged from one amusement to another; The Lopp, the Loop, the Whip and the putt putt course. The roller-skating rink was alive with young people and grown-ups from Asheville, Black Mountain and all the hidden coves in between. Over the public address system, records of leading dance bands were playing alternately with a Hammond organ in the corner.

At 10: 30 Bobbie looked up and saw Dan leaning against the guard railing of the skating rink. He was scanning the crowd for her. All evening long as soon as he claimed her for a skating session, and they would circle the rink once or twice, she would be tapped on the shoulder by a boy and they'd skate off together. Finally, Dan had given up. His two-tone shoes were scuffed up from his skates which didn't fit properly. The blue and yellow tie which Bobbie had made fun of, was hidden in his jacket pocket and his shirt collar was open. He had taken off his jacket and was holding it by the collar with one finger while it hung limp against his damp back.

It was time for them to leave get back to Riverby by eleven o clock. Dan skated fast to catch up with her and since he couldn't make himself heard to her over the noise of the rink, he pointed with obvious gestures to his watch. Bobbie, finished the session with her momentary partner and whirled up to Dan skating fast. At the last possible moment, she turned her skates skillfully and spun to a graceful stop in front of him. His face lit up in admiration. He knelt down and unfastened her skates and steered her in a manner to the exit.

"Oh Dan, I had a wonderful time tonight. Wasn't this more fun than dancing? You show a girl a good time." Bobbie said generously as they made their way across the dark parking lot toward the Oldsmobile. Dan smiled self-consciously in the darkness and helped her into the car. He made his way around to the front of the car and stooped to tie his shoe laces.

Bobbie switched on the dashboard lights, sank back against the luxurious cushions and felt in her purse for her compact. Still smiling a bit at her social success of the night, she opened the compact and looked into the mirror, her face did not smile back at her. Instead there appeared the face of a MAN. Gaunt, bearded and red-eyed, the rotating spot light on top of the merry go 'round momentarily lit up the left side of the man's face to reveal a nasty red scar that extended from the corner of his eye to the hollow of his sunken cheek.

"Rrrrrrrrrrrrrrrrrrrrrrrrrrrrrrrr" The police spot light peeked up the red clay side road. It passed and all hope seemed to die with the wailing siren. Bobbie fought to remain alert. She was terrified. Then she slowly and deliberately made herself remember. She had withdrawn the small pink powder puff and keeping her eye on the Man in the mirror, she patted her face with the puff. As Dan got behind the wheel, she saw reflected in the mirror the glint of blue steel as the spot light made its flashing circuit again.

The Man spoke. "If you don't shout or attract attention in any way, I promise you I won't shoot. Do exactly as I say, Buddy. Move over girlie, get in the middle. I'm coming up front with you and I'll sit next to the door. O.K. Buddy, start the car. Drive quickly, but not too fast, out of the Park to the highway. Remember, I have a gun on the girl and I'll use it if I have to."

The smile on Dan's face froze. He had a terrible time getting the key out of his pocket. It was tangled up in the blue and yellow stripped tie and when he finally got it loose and tried to put it into the ignition his had shook so hard he couldn't get it in. Bobbie remembered how she had leaned over and placed her hand on Dan's and said. "Just take it easy, Dan, do what the Man says."

"Just act natural, you two. When you get to the highway, Buddy, turn right and head toward Black Mountain. Keep within the speed limit till we get out of here. No tricks, either one of you or the girl will get it."

The maroon Oldsmobile had gone right past the rock pillars of the driveway of Riverby. The house was dark except for the front porch light and a light in one of the bathrooms.

---------------------- ❧ ❦ ----------------------

Norma and LaVerne came out onto the front porch of Riverby Inn.

"I'm taking my seat and when that young lady comes home, I'm going to take a hairbrush and wear her out. I don't blame Dan; I know he's dependable and would bring her home at the regular hour but Bobbie has gotten completely out of hand this summer. Well, this is the last straw and when I get through talking to her she'll change ways, believe me!"

"Here, LaVerne, here is a wool shawl. It's chilly out here on the porch." Norma had taken two large shawls off the hook in the back hallway and the women wrapped up in them and took their seats in the rockers on the porch.

"She is thoughtless, Norma......I'm worried. I had a powerful intuition about Bobbie earlier this evening and I still feel very odd, somehow. "

"You're just tired. I'll sit here with you for a while. You know how young people are; they get to having a good time and forget the hour." Norma didn't believe a word of what she said as she adjusted her shawl around her small frame and stole a glance at the tearoom.

LaVerne put her head back against the rocker and closed her eyes to think. "I must get my thoughts quieted down. Even out here in the night air, my face feels flushed. Must be my blood pressure rising. I wonder if I'm sick. I'm sick all right. Sick of worrying; sick of working like a slave. My feet hurt and I have a low backache. All this hard work and I'm hardly better off financially than when I came up here this summer. I can't keep a proper eye on the children when I have to devote every minute to the kitchen and the meals. Bobbie has slipped away from me this summer. She is so determined and strong-willed and selfish. I had so counted on clearing enough money this summer to try making a move to Washington, D.C. Cousin Nonnie Lee has made a mint up there. I could get a rooming house, too, like she has and put Mabel in art school. I could take Betty to a heart specialist for a thorough going over. Harold could take a nice government job and go to college at night. I might even be able to place Bobbie in a strict girls' school. No use making those plans now!

"These problems, my responsibilities, they're entirely too much for one parent to handle. I can't cope with any of it alone. The children love their father. If I can just get through these next few days; the trial of running the Inn; closing it for the winter... If Bobbie gets home all right. I'll go on back to Fort Smith and try it another year. Yes, that's what I'll do. I promise. LaVerne sighed involuntarily. Bobbie, where are you? It's comforting to have Norma sitting out here with me. She certainly has her worries, too."

Norma rearranged her shawl thinking that if that Bobbie was her daughter. "I'd blister her behind so hard she wouldn't: be able to sit down for a week. LaVerne is too easy going with her. But I must admit, it isn't like Bobbie to be this late. And Dan, he's so dependable. I hope they aren't up to something. But What? Maybe we should call the police. POLICE! Oh Lord no, Claude's still out there in the tearoom and the police want him for questioning. Oh, Claude! How can I go on like this? How much more of this can I take? What have you done to me? Our children? Why?" Humiliation spread through Norma like a critical disease.

"Norma I can't sit here another minute. My nerves are ready to snap. Would you go wake Mama and tell her what's happened? I'll wake up Lola and Beck and they can drive us to Asheville. Those children have had a flat tire or run out of gas or something. And at this hour there's no one to stop and help them." LaVerne tried hard to derive comfort from her words.

Mam-maw slipped her wrapper on, pushed her feet into her warm carpet slippers and came onto the porch. Lola, Beck and LaVerne were quietly getting dressed. They laid their plans. Lola and LaVerne would drive slowly toward Asheville checking the highway for the stalled car. Each of them secretly determined she would check the ditches for a wreck.

Beck you and Norma go to the Bishops and check quietly, then maybe you'd better cheek by the Hunnicutt's guest house and just see if by mistake Bobbie went to sleep there with Hy, La and Mabes." LaVerne requested them to do this for her.

"Then we'll all check back here with Mama. If there's still no word, we'll drive over to the Wilde's and see if they know anything." Lola advised,

Lola and LaVerne drove slowly to Asheville checking the highway and scanning the road for sight of a car.

"Check the ditches, Sister. They may have slipped off the road," Lola was becoming desperate

Beck turned off her head lights as she drove into the Bishops

"Norma, you don't think Bobbie has done something foolish do you? Girls act mighty silly over summer romances." Beck stopped the car. Norma nodded agreement with Becks theory and slipped from the car. She eased herself into the familiar neighbor's house and up to the guest room.

"Evangeline! Evangeline! Don't make a sound, child. It is Miss Norma. Do you know where Bobbie and Dan were going tonight? She hasn't come home."

"What's happened? Oooooooooh, it's late. Gosh darn it why couldn't I have gone too? Here she's turned up missing and I never get to have any fun. They went to the Recreation Park at Asheville. They were going to skate."

"Where you going Miss Norma? Can't I go too and get in on the excitement? Why, who knows? They might have gotten married. Bobbie had on a blue dress and that's a bride's color…. after…white Miss Norma, I could be dressed in a jiffy. Oh, all right. I'll stay here, I NEVER get to have any fun. Do you think Dan gave her a solitaire?"

Lola and LaVerne had passed Oteen and hadn't seen anything unusual. They were silent.

Norma and Beck backed out of the Bishops yard and headed for the Hunnicutt's to double check.

Mam-maw sat on the porch and wished she'd thought to bring out her can of snuff. She was afraid to go back and get it for fear she'd wake up Frank or her girls might come back with some news. As she rocked, she talked to herself and from time to time as the conversation progressed, she shook her head at the mountains for emphasis.

"I feel very responsible for Bobbies action. I said to myself at the beginning of the summer, Jeffie, I want you to spend a lot of time with Bobbie. Adolescence is a trying time for a girl under the best of circumstances and with a girl as lovely looking as Bobbie and with her high-strung personality, it's an explosive mixture. I understand that young woman very well. The looks, the personality, the love of life. I was just such a young miss once. But the quiet influence of Grandfather Hopper made such an impression on me. I was able to channel all my love and joy and strength into marriage, husband and children. When did Claude begin to elude my grasp? It happened so fast that it was suddenly too late.

I had Beck so late in life and with an infant to care for and then, I went through the Change and with one thing and another, Claude was gone. The damage is done. I saw the whole thing happening again this summer. LaVerne is so torn up inside and working so hard during the day. I saw this situation coming and I should have helped her with Bobbie. But somehow, I've felt so tired this summer. We've never had so many here before and instead of being stimulating, it has left me feeling exhausted and spent.

Strength, Jeffie, take strength from the mountains over there. Hang on, the summer will soon be over. The children will be gone, I'll miss them. The winters are long and cold. I'm getting old, oh, nonsense Jeffie, you're just tired and sleepy. I must stay awake. Get up and walk a little. Go out to the tearoom and wake up Claude. He'll know what to do. NO! He'll still be under the influence and he spoke so roughly to me this evening." For the first time in all these years, Claude was ugly add rough with her.

"While I'm up, I'll just slip in and get my snuff. That'll keep me awake until I get some news."

As Jeffie returned from her room, she heard a sound on the stairway. She was startled to see Betty padding down the stairs half asleep and in her bare feet.

"Mam-maw, Where's my mother? Is something wrong? I heard a noise and then some cars and I can't find mama anywhere. Is she sick? I think I heard her crying a little when she came to bed." She looked ready to cry herself as she paused uncertainly at the foot of the steps. The light from the lamp shown through the skimpy nightgown she wore and revealed her thin brown body. Her ribs stood out in bas relief but the growing buds of her twelve-year-old breasts were already beginning to swell.

"Shhhhh, child, don't wake up the household. Your mother is alright. Come out on the porch with me. You can sit on my lap if you think you can find room for those long legs of yours. Here, wrap this shawl around your shoulders while I take a dip of snuff."

Betty leaned back against the soft bosom and laid her head quite close to her Mam-maw's neck. The blend of sweet and acrid tobacco was comforting and familiar to the young girl. Mam-maw told her briefly that Dan and Bobbie were late getting home. "They just got to having a good time somewhere and didn't realize how late it was, and your mother and aunts have gone to find them. Now you run up to bed and don't worry. Everything is going to be all right. Kiss me goodnight."

Betty returned to the sleeping porch. She started to get back in the bed she had shared with her mother. Then she saw Martha in bed alone so she climbed in beside her and whispered in her ear urgently.

"Marth, Marth! wake up. Somethings happened to Bobbie and I'm scared."

"Lemme 'lone. Somethings always happening to Bobbie. I'm sleepy."

"Martha, please wake up, I think Bobbie is dead or married or something."

"Dead? Married?" Martha popped her eyes open.

"Well she hasn't come home yet. Mother, Aunt Lola and Aunt Beck and your mother have gone to look for her and Mam-maw's on the front porch. I'm scared, Mam-maws worried too, I can tell."

"Don't worry about Bobbie. She leads a charmed life. I heard some of the grown-ups say so the other day. You're sure sweet to be so worried about her. She hasn't been very nice to you this summer or to anybody else for that matter."

"Well, she is my sister.… just the same as Mabes is. And she told me she might give me her green culots. If she' s dead do you think I'd still get em? She wouldn't have to make out a will or anything, d'ya think? Anyway, I think she talked Dan into eloping. Just to get even with Mother. Dan for a brother-in law. How do you like that?"

———————— ❧ ❧ ————————

"I don't care if it is after two o'clock, Lola, if you don't take me over to the Wilde's I'll walk." LaVerne was on the verge of hysteria. The two cars of sisters had returned to Riverby. Lola and LaVerne had driven all the way into Asheville and circled back by the Recreation Park which was now completely dark. After Beck and Norma had checked their two neighbors' houses, they had driven up the road toward Black Mountain for several miles.

Mam-maw took the initiative. "Yes, I think you girls should go over to Mrs. Wilde's. She might have some news of them.… If not, she has a phone there, in case you need it. Her daughter and son-in-law live there with her and they might have some suggestions to make. I'll stay right here at my post until I hear from you." Mam-maw went over and put her arms around LaVerne and whispered in her ear. "Now, LaVerne, don't cry I've just had a talk with the Lord and I feel much better. Now you girls go on over there. For all you know, they may have heard something from Dan and Bobbie."

When the two cars arrived at Mrs. Wilde's house, the lights were on in every room except one. Dan's bedroom on the corner of the second floor overlooking the cornfield was dark.

At the sound of the car doors slamming, Mrs. Wilde ran out of the front door letting the screen slam.

"Dan? Dan! That you? WHO is out there?" She screamed excitedly. She recognized the women approaching her, she said in a loud voice.

"Well, well, Miz Hutson, Miz Norma, Miz Fields… yore boys is fast asleep up there in Dan's room. That's where my Dan should be, but he ain't. Miz Hedges, should I call you mother-in-law?" The last was a sneer.

"Mother in-law? Why? What do you mean Mrs. Wild? Have you heard from the children?"

"Not airy a word. But mind you, now, I know that Bobbie of yourn. She's been teasing and tormentin' Dan all summer long. Bet she twisted him around her little finger and made him drive dun to South Carolina to the Jedge of the Peach. I just know'd they was up to somethin' cause Sam spent all afternoon shining up George's car and got it all tanked up with gaze."

Beck placed her arm around LaVerne's shoulder. Lola stepped forward. "Mrs. Wilde control yourself. I know Bobbie and Dan did not run off and get married. Why, I promised Bobbie I'd give her Expression Lessons this fall and she was looking forward to it. This kind of talk is ridiculous. Norma, get Central on the phone and get connected with the Asheville hospital. They might have been in an accident."

"You're right Miz Hutson," Mrs. Wilde felt genuinely sorry, "I been actin' turrible. I'm awful sorry I said all them mean things about Bobbie. I'm near out of my scalp worrin' over Dan. George, if I hear you say one more word about that dang blasted car of yourn, I'll break your neck. If Miz Norma don't get no satisfaction from them people at the hospital…. about accidents and all, George, I want you to call the sheriff."

Norma was alarmed and stepped to LaVerne's side. LaVerne held up her hand slightly and said, "No, not the sheriff. That's not at all necessary."

"Come in the house and take a cheer, we'll stick together and we'll see it through…. one way or tother." Mrs. Wilde sank down on a large footstool and pulled her rose-red chenille robe together in front and gave a twist to the rope belt. She stretched her feet in front of her and stared intently at her white legs and the tops of her feet encased in men's oxfords.

"Carrie," she addressed her daughter, "Go fix up that big campin' pot of coffee. We could all use something to warm us up."

George was pacing up and down in front of the house and anxiously scanning the darkness toward the highway when an apparition appeared before him.

"What's the matter? What's happened? I got here as fast as I could. This is Mrs. Hunnicutt, s'that you George?"

"Yassum, Mrs. Hunnicutt. Go on in the house." Flossie Hunnicutt drew her Japanese kimono together over her bosom. The gold dragon on the back of the robe twisted and turned with her sudden movements.

"Violet! Violet Wilde, I'm coming in." Flossie announced as she opened the screen door and let herself inside.

"Rebekah! Lola! LaVerne! Norma! Do tell whatever is the matter?"

LaVerne stood up and came toward Agnes. "Agnes, would you let me call long distance on your phone? Bobbie and Dan are missing and I want to call my husband and talk to him." She ignored the stares of her sisters. "I don't have my purse with me but I'll ask the Operator the exact amount of the call and reimburse you tomorrow. LaVerne felt the railroad passes in her brassiere. She put her hand over her bosom as if to protect them and continued. "I'll tell you what has happened on the way over to your house." LaVerne paused to address her sisters.

"I'm alright. Beck, suppose you take Norma home. She has to be on the early shift at the Mill tomorrow and maybe you could get Mam-maw to go to bed too."

Violet's eyes were misty as she watched the women go. "I wish I could talk to Harry," She said to Lola. "Harry, who?"

"Harry Wilde, my husband, God rest his soul."

When LaVerne hung up the telephone on the drum table she said to Flossie.

"Harold is terribly upset."

"LaVerne this is a real crisis. If you want me to, I could run up my flag, upside down. They tell me that's an international distress signal and somebody might see it and………"

"Thank you, Flossie, I don't think that will be necessary, I'll go on back to the Wilde's. Maybe someone has called by now. Thank you for letting me use your phone. Friends mean so much at a time like this." Flossie leaned over and kissed LaVerne's cheek.

"I'll say a little prayer for you LaVerne."

──────────── ❧ ❧ ────────────

"Riiiiiiiiiiinng. Riiiiiiiiiiiinnnng. Ring!"

It was five o'clock in the morning and the telephone rang in Violet Wilde's living room. Two Longs and a short; two longs and a short. The occupants in the room had been dosing but the loud ring propelled them to their feet and sped them to the instrument.

"Hello-hello-hello HELLO? Is that you Dan, darlin' Speak to me Dan!"

"This is the long dis----tance Op—er—a—tor. Will you accept a col-lect call from a Mr. Dan-ie-l Wil-de in High Point, North Caro lina?"

"Get off'n the phone you dang fool idiot. That's my Dan. Put him on. Put him on! Of course, I'll take the call. Hurry up you fool, put Dan on. Hello Dan? Dan?"

"Dan, where have you been?! You've had me out of my mind with worry! Are you all right? What are doing in High Point? Are you Married? Answer me right now!"

"Mrs. Wilde, please ask him about Bobbie. Is Bobbie alright?" LaVerne could not stand it another minute.

"Hello. Hello. Here Mrs. Hedges, you talk, I'm too nervous."

"Hello, Dan? Bobbie? Oh, Bobbie is that really you, Are you alright? What happened?"

"Just a minute Mother. The reporters are trying to take my picture and Dan is fussing with them. I can't hear a thing. There now, the police are helping."

"Police? POLICE?" Gasped LaVerne.

"Yessum, we're at the police station in High Point. You see, this man poked a gun in my ribs at the Recreation Park just as we were leaving, Mother, please don't be mad with me, I didn't do anything wrong, and we would have been home right on the dot of eleven if this man hadn't kidnapped us."

"Kidnapped, KIDNAPPED!" LaVerne gasped.[9]

"Oh, mother, I was so scared." Bobbie began to cry. "We're at the police station in High Point now. The police called Uncle Hudson and, Oh, here he is now! Uncle Hudson." Bobbie sobbed.

"Is my car in one piece?" George leaned over LaVerne's shoulder and shouted into the mouthpiece of the phone.

"Mrs. Hedges, Mrs. Hedges? Is that you?" Dans voice came over the phone. "This is Dan, and we're all right. Bobbie doesn't have a scratch on her, I promise. She's just a little upset now that it's all over. She was so brave the whole time. Even when he put the gun in her temple and said he was gonna shoot her. She was so brave!"

Figure 20: Rec park where Bobbie was kidnapped

LaVerne let the phone drop from her hand. Her jaw hung loose and the tears flowed down her cheeks and dropped on the receiver which lay in her lap. Mrs. Wilde reached over and picked it up.

"Good Gawd a'mighty, Dan, Speak to me! It's your Ma! Is that girl alright???????"

"Hi, Maw! Everything's alright now! Bobbie is fine. She' s just a little nervous. ALL the reporters and police and that awful man! Mr. Hudson's here and he's taking over. We were kidnapped, Ma! Mr. Hudson says he'll bring us home. But right now, we have to go look at some mug books or something like that. Don't worry, I can take care of myself."

"Boo.. hooooooooo.... Ohhhhhhhhhhhhl Thank Gawd! They's alright!" Violet hung up the phone and buried her head in her chenille robe sobbing her heart out.

"It's all over now. The children are safe and sound. They'll be home soon. Our prayers have been answered." LaVerne had regained control of herself.

———————————— ❧ ❧ ————————————

When LaVerne and Lola arrived at Riverby, the sun was doing push-ups behind the ridge. The morning was fresh and clean and sweet. A mountain warbler sat on a limb of the largest Bing cherry tree and sang out the good news. LaVerne breathed a private word of thanksgiving to the Lord for delivering her child safely from a night of horror.

"LaVerne, there's a police car! And a car full of…. of reporters! Look it says press on that sticker, and there's a man with a camera." Lola jogged her sister back to reality.

Mam-maw, Beck and Norma had formed a solid phalanx across the front steps of the old house.

"Shhhhhhhh! Quiet You'll wake up the whole house." Beck was trying to corral the hub-bub. 'This is a very respectable Guest House and there are people resting here. We simply can't have you here! Now go away. Go away!"

Norma was trembling. The police! Here! Please Dear God. She thought. Let Claude sleep and not hear this commotion and come outside that tearoom door. I must not allow myself to look at the tearoom. It might give him away.

Beck ran to Lola's car. "Sister are you all right? The reporters told us everything. Bless their little hearts, what a terrible experience."

"Come on ladies, we just want a picture of Miss Hedges. Don't you have one in the family album? Just a bathing suit picture. That'll do nicely. We' return it to you." The cameraman was pursuing Mam-maw.

"Hold on thar! Hold on! What's the commotion? Jeffie, I overslept!" Grandy slammed through the front door buttoning up his trousers." Good Granny alive, the sun's up! Jeffie what in tarnation is going on?"

"Sir, we're from the Asheville Citizen and……"

"Jes leave my paper in the box by the road, you didn't have to deliver it personal. I'm a gonna write another letter to your editor, if'n you don't giet off'n my property!" Grandy couldn't quite grasp the situation.

Beck, Lola and LaVerne climbed the front steps wearily,

"Beckie, Verne, Lola? Where you been. Tain't hardly daylight, what y'all doing up?" He turned to the reporters who still held their ground. "Git off'n my property, I says I seen who yone paper took up fer in the last election and if you don't git off'n my porch, I'm a gonna git my gun."

The reporters withdrew to their cars and drove off.

"Who'er you?" Grandy addressed the stare highway patrolman who stood back to let the reporters through. "The law? Good Grannie Alice, what's going on here Claude's not here!"

"Claude, who? Sir. I'm patrolman Snyder. Your granddaughter was kidnapped last night by North Carolina's public enemy number one. He is wanted for killing a highway patrolman, armed robbery, assault and now… kidnapping. I have just received word on my car radio and was told to advice you that Miss Lola LaVerne Hedges and Mr. Daniel Wilde are now under the protection of and in the custody of the High Point Police. They will be held there for questioning. They have not been harmed in any way. Her uncle, a Mr. Hudson, is with them. I just came out here to give you the good news. Thank you and good morning." He saluted Grandy and drove away.

"Somebody, help me, I feel faint." Beck and Lola rushed to LaVerne and eased her into a rocker. Mam-maw sat down heavily next to her. Grandy snatched up the paper from the top step and began fanning first LaVerne and then his Jeffie.

"You'll be all right directly. Them rascally Republicans is enough to give the swoons and vapors to a strong bodied man… much less a refined woman." Grandy refolded the paper to make a larger fan.

"Dang nab it! One of them fellas left a copy of this morning's paper and here I am a fannin' with it", He stopped fanning and looked at the front page. The headlines read.

## "SIXTEEN-YEAR-OLD BEAUTY AND LOCAL BOY KIDNAPPED BY PUBLIC ENEMY 1!"

"How dare they put double banner headlines in the paper!" Beck exploded.
"It doesn't matter now." LaVerne sighed. "You girls look after Mama. I'm all right. I must look a fright though. I'll go wash my face under the pump and put on a clean fresh dress. It's time to start breakfast. All forty hungry guests will be down here any minute now."

# Chapter 25

# Expression Lesson

The news broke at breakfast. All of Riverby, when they answered the breakfast bell, had either seen the morning paper or had heard snatches of the night's event.

After breakfast, LaVerne took her second cup of coffee to Mam-maw's room and called Delilah to come in for a conference.

"I have turned the menu for the noon meal over to Miss Mabel and the older girls but I'm depending on you to see it through.

"For tonight's dinner, take several of those hams from the smokehouse and par-boil them so they won't be dry. Then skin them and score them and glaze them. Make cracklings out of the skin and make crackling cornbread to go along with the dinner. In the water where you have par-boiled the hams, simmer some green beans and potatoes. Cook some okra too and serve them with butter and salt. Get Mose to check with Grandy and bring up enough corn on the cob to serve everyone. I'll come in late in the afternoon and make cold slaw. Also, get out some of those home-canned pickled peaches and watermelon pickles to go along side. For dessert make that good apple roll dessert you are so good at. Don't disturb me unless the stove blows up. I'm going to sleep until Miss Bobbie comes home."

"Yas'm, don't you worry none. I'll handle everything. You jus get yo'self a good sleep." Delilah shuffled out.

When Mam-maw came in later on in the morning to take a nap, LaVerne was sound asleep. Beck had driven over to the Wilde's to pick up her boys. Flossie had already awakened Hy, Mabes and La out in her guest house and told them the news. Then she had driven them as fast as possible back to Riverby.

The girls reported it was the most perilous ride of their lives. "And you all worry when we ride with our teenage dates."

Lola strolled about the house checking on the flower arrangements and changed the sheets in the Medallion room for Homer to use when he arrived with Bobbie. Finally, she lay down and drifted off to sleep.

At two o'clock in the afternoon, Homer and Bobbie arrived at Riverby. The cheers from the front lawn and the front porch awakened the nappers and everyone gathered around to see with their own eyes if Bobbie was really all in one piece.

"No time for questioning, now." LaVerne insisted as she drew Bobbie inside the house. I'm putting this child to bed."

"Lola! Where's Lola?" Homer wanted to know. "I've been up since daybreak, been to the Police Station, had to fight reporters and THEN I had to drive all the way here and NO WIFE."

"Calm yourself, Homer. I'm right here. Come inside. I have a cool milk shake made up for you with an egg in it and your covers turned down." Lola steered him up the stairs.

Grandy roused himself from his hammock. He had been sleeping with his hat over his eyes. The rascally newspaper lay in a wadded-up heap beneath him.

--------------------- ❧ ❧ ---------------------

"What's the racket? Reporters back here again?"

"What's the noise all about? Can't a tired man get some rest at his own home?"

"Afternoon, Papa." Claude greeted Grandy by putting his arm around Grandy's shoulder and giving him an affectionate slap on the back.

"Claude! Did you sleep good? I left you some coffee next to your bed last night. Have you had your breakfast? And lunch? I'll rout them girls out to cook you up some ham and grits. Let me look at you boy."

Claude looked great. Actually, he had been up since very early in the morning. He had heard the commotion from the reporters and police when they arrived at dawn but he had remained hidden in the Tearoom until they left. After he had watched Norma leave for her early shift at the mill, he had secretly taken a raw dip in the river. When he returned to the Tearoom, he found clean clothes laid out for him. Wondering, he quickly put them on. Shortly, Leon entered the little room with a plate piled high with eggs, sausage, grits, toast, strawberry jam and his other hand held a small pot of coffee.

"Come in, son, come in." Greeted Claude effusively.

"Thanks for the clothes…. and thank goodness for breakfast I could eat a horse. You don't happen to have a 'hair of the dog' on you, do you? I could use it. Oh well, Delilah's strong black coffee will do just as well… It almost floats the spoon,"

He rubbed his hands together and poured out a steaming cupful and drank it right down. While Claude wolfed down his food, he sized up Leon.

"Well, what damage did I do last night? Have I been here just one night? Who all did I insult? Seems to me I remember a lot of people on the porch…. Is the house full? And for evermore, what were the police and reporters doing here this morning? Gave your old man quite a start, let me tell you. The Blanks females were holding them off like a solid line of tanks. You should have seen Papa with those reporters. We should have had a movie of lt."

"Samson picked you up in Pack's Square and delivered you c.o.d. at the front door singing hymns and in front of the biggest load of boarders we have ever had up here. Bobbie and Dan Wilde managed to get themselves kidnaped last night. Mam-maw, Mom and your sisters were up all night long. Mom went to work at the mill this morning but Mr. MacFadyen had already heard the news and do you know he made her take the day off to rest? Even drove her home himself. That shows you what they think of Mom."

"Leon, your mother is true and faithful to the end of time. Got a smoke on you, Leon?" Claude swished the last of the coffee around in his cup and swallowed it with a gulp. His hand shook only slightly as Leon struck a kitchen match and held it to the cigarette, he had purloined Mr. Claude.

"Shall I go tell Mom that you're up? She's setting her hair. Maybe I should tell Mam-maw or somebody. Most all of them are asleep."

"Let's let sleeping dogs lie for a while. I want to stretch out again for a few minutes and then I might just mosey on up to the Village and see some of my friends."

"I wouldn't do that if I was you…. Dad. Why don't you lie back down and later on I'll bring out Grandy's razor and shaving soap and shave you? You'd like that, wouldn't you?"

———————————— ❧ ❧ ————————————

"Beck, you look rested from your nap." Gloria Parkerson greeted Rebekah as she appeared in the kitchen to get a glass of iced tea.

"Gloria! What are you up to? Mary Ann, what are you doing out there on the porch peeling potatoes?"

Gloria laughed as she looked up from the gigantic bowl of cold slaw she was making. "Since Mary Ann and I are almost completely packed up in order to leave first thing in the morning, we sent back word that we'd be in charge of dinner tonight. We decided we'd been off kitchen duty long enough this summer and we are having a wonderful time. Mary Ann is thrilled," she lowered her voice, "and is getting ready to help Delilah with making the dessert. I want you to know she cleaned and snapped all the string beans for tonight and has peeled apples and potatoes and I don't know what all. Not only that, but she insisted that Bobbie and your sister take her room for the rest of the day. Bobbie has been in a tub submerged up to her eyebrows in soapsuds and has shampooed her hair twice. Mrs. Hedges is actually lying down on Mary Ann's bed and she can talk back and forth to Bobbie in the bathroom. Rebekah, Mary Ann has walked the pipe at last."

"What do you say we fix up the dining room for buffet style tonight? Mose can carve the hams as people come through the line, Delilah can dish up the vegetables, Mary Ann can serve dessert, I can serve my cold slaw and Norma can make the coffee and serve it."

"I'll carve the hams. I have an announcement to make at dinnertime. Gloria, I want you and your family and Mary Ann and hers to spend Christmas with the children and myself in the Delta. Please say you will. And thank you, for everything."

———————————— ❧ ❧ ————————————

"Bobbie, are you sure you're all right?" LaVerne still felt anxious about her daughter. "Maybe you should have a medical examination."

"He didn't lay a finger on me. I'm fine, but Mother he was so dirty! But that long nap and wonderful bath put me back in shape." Bobbie sat cross-legged on the bed with her slip on and with a huge bath towel wrapped around her wet head. Mary Ann had given her permission to use anything in her room. Bobbie was carefully applying nail polish to her nails from the Cutex kit in front of her.

"I just want to make sure. Your father will be here most any time now. I feel so responsible and I was so worried."

"Mother, I'm untouched, I promise. I am genuinely sorry I caused you so much worry and anxiety. On that trip last night, my whole life seemed to flash in front of my eyes. I realized how mean and ugly I've been this summer. I don't know what has been wrong with me. I tried and I just don't know. But I'll change, just wait and see."

"I think you owe apologies to many people, Bobbie. If things don't go to please you, you want to get even. If someone gets in your way, you want to run roughshod over them. You must take time with people. Get to know them. Be loving and patient. Think not of yourself but of others."

Bobbie held up her left hand and admired the precision of her manicure. "I promise, I will. You're going to see a new me from now on." She attempted to close the conversation. Her mother had been singing this theme song all summer and it sounded like the needle was stuck.

"I'll tell you what, Muz. Suppose I stand up in front of all of Riverby after supper and thank ever one for being so nice and helping out last night. I could even fill then in on some of the details of my experience...."

"Bobbie, that's a splendid idea! Right after dessert we'll ask everyone to remain seated. Don't forget to thank Mrs. Parkerson and Mrs. Thompson." LaVerne was dumbfounded that Bobbie wanted to apologize to any one! And thank everyone Hallelujah, Bobbie was a changed girl and overnight. It just goes to show you that you trust in the Lord.

Bobbie started on a pedicure. She was smiling sweetly to herself. Bet a cookie La will let me wear her white dress with the red poppies on it. Wonder what kind of perfume Mrs. Thompson has?

She was already planning what she would say.

----------------- ❧ ❧ -----------------

The buffet line was moving right along. As Beck served up the ham, she told each person, "We have persuaded Bobbie to tell everyone her whole dreadful experience of last night, so keep your seat after dessert."

After the dishes had been cleared away, Norma made her way from table to table replenishing the coffee cups.

Bobbie appeared in the doorway with her mother. Bobbie certainly didn't look as if she had endured a night of horror. Her blond wavy hair was shining clean and bright. She wore a white dress with red poppies on it and in her hand she carried a pink rosebud corsage. A wave of applause greeted her and she smiled and blew kisses to the crowded dining room.

LaVerne was misty-eyed but rested looking as she made her way to the kitchen door. "Delilah, Mose, just stack the dishes for now. Come on in the dining room and listen to Miss Bobbie's story."

All the family children sat tailor-fashion on the floor while the family grown-ups took their seats with the guests. Bobbie made her way without hesitation toward the sideboard.

Arriving at her destination, she leaned against the cool marble top and laid her corsage on it. The mirror reflected her blond hair with the waves cascading down her back. She held up her left hand for silence and began in a tremulous voice.

"You'll never know how wonderful it is to be back and all in one piece. Last night, when we sped past this house with all my dear ones in it, I truly was frightened and wondered if I'd ever see any of you again."

LaVerne dabbed her eyes.

"First, I want ALL the family to know that you didn't lose a daughter, sister, niece or cousin to Dan Wilde. And you, dear guests, didn't lose a waitress. We did NOT get married." She held up her left hand again to show the absence of a ring. It seems I did lose something, though....

Her aunts leaned forward in their chairs.

"My green culots. She pointed to Betts who lounged against the center post wearing the culots pinned at the waist with a big safety pin.

A ripple of laughter went through the crowd.

"l received this lovely pink corsage from Dan Wilde a little while ago." She placed the corsage away from her red poppy dress.

The crowd seemed to lean forward as she launched into her story with a strong voice.

"Dan and I left the skating rink promptly at ten thirty in order to get back home by eleven. Just as we got into the car a mean and desperate looking and dirty man poked a cold steel revolver in my side and ordered me to move over. Of course, we were helpless to resist and had to obey. He acted like a maniac and I was scared we were the victims of a mental patient. Later he told me that he had robbed a concession stand of a hundred dollars and that he was desperate to get out of there.

"He had been hiding out in the mountains for many days and was starved. The bullet wound on the side of his face was oozing for want of medical attention. You all know by now after reading the papers, that last week he shot and killed that highway patrolman and in the exchange of gun-fire, he had been grazed by a bullet.

"He told us right away that he wouldn't take us out of the state because he didn't want the F.B.I. on his trail but, of course, Dan and I didn't know where he would take us and whether he would leave us alive or, or…. dead."

LaVerne gave a wrench to her knotted handkerchief.

"He knew the roads so well that going down Old Fort Mountain he would say, 'Slow down Buddy for this next curve. It has a dangerous hairpin twist to it.' Then around another curve he would order Dan to go fifty miles an hour because he knew the road would be straight as an arrow on the other side.

"As the evening, or rather I should say, the long dark night progressed, I began to relax. He sensed this and said, 'Aren't you frightened?' I replied that I wasn't now but that I would feel better if he would take that gun away from my ribs."

"Oh NO!" The women in the dining room cried out.

"I studied his profile, hoping that if he didn't kill me, I would be able to identify him later on… if I got the chance. At one point, he dropped a book of matches on the floor and I surreptitiously picked them up and put them in my purse to turn over to the police for finger prints

"That WAS clever," the dining room murmured.

"After another hour or, so, I lost track of time of this speeding madness, we heard a police siren and I was so relieved I was certain the police were coming to our rescue. But the criminal mind we were dealing with had other plans. Dan was ordered off the highway and down a hidden country lane into the darkness. As the siren grew closer and closer this madman jammed the gun against my head and ordered Dan to turn off the lights and for us not to make a sound. For the first time in my life, I fainted." Her voice faltered.

"How horrible for the poor child!" The dining room was stunned.

"It was about this point, that Dan seemed to give up all hope. He wasn't making any sense and, no wonder, for he had been doing all that wild driving. All he could think about was George's car. He kept pleading with the man not to damage the car or dirty up the upholstery. Well, Mr. Scarface told Dan that he had picked us out from the rest of the mob at the Park because of that car: He had carefully checked several cars on that lot and had chosen George's because it was new, had good tires and a full tank of gas and he knew an Oldsmobile could take off like a shot, if necessary and the maroon color was dark enough not to attract attention. And, by the way, as Mother and I were having supper on our trays in the room, word was sent to us along with the corsage that George got his car back and without a scratch! The car had been found abandoned three blocks from the Police Station. The KILLER is still at large!"

"I'm so relieved," beamed LaVerne, still thinking of the car.

"Well, nothing else unusual happened until we approached Thomasville. Without a word of warning, he directed Dan to stop at the next traffic light and pull over to the curb. Then he ordered us out. He pointed to a dirty looking hotel on the main street and told us to go in, register as man and wife, go to our room and not make any calls until six o' clock in the morning. He threatened us and told us we'd be watched by his buddies,"

A gasp came from her aunts.

"The irony of fate about all this was that a Police car was right next to us! Waiting for the green light! My thoughts were running wild. Should I shout and scream for attention? Would he shoot us? Would the police come to our aid immediately? I knew there must be a price on his head. Maybe we could collect a reward! But then I had been so relieved that he hadn't held us for ransom I knew mother couldn't get up the money…."

LaVerne had her handkerchief over both eyes.

"I was grateful for that," Bobbie continued.

The dining room stole a glance at LaVerne and sadly shook their heads.

"We did as we had been told. We registered in the hotel, after watching the police drive off and watching our "friend" drive off in the opposite direction. But we did NOT go to our room…. after all, we didn't have a chaperone."

Bobbie looked at her aunts. They nodded in agreement.

"We sat in the lobby behind some potted palms and waited for the time to pass. Even though he had told us that his cronies would be secretly watching us, we saw no one and at five o'clock Dan put the call in to the Police. You all know the rest. We were taken to the High Point Police Headquarters where we called our mothers. We were questioned and asked to look at mug books and both of us picked out Jo Wilson. He's North Carolina's public enemy number one.

"The reporters came and were taking pictures of us and hearing our story when Uncle Huddy came in. It was kind of exciting at that point because a reporter had posed me on the Captain's desk with a police hat on my head and I had my legs crossed and well, the next thing I knew, I had been jerked off the desk and whopped on my fan….er, spanked with the police hat and then Uncle Huddy whipped out his mashie and hit a reporter with it and kicked a camera out of another one's hand." Bobbie giggled, "I think the police were glad to see us leave."

The dining room began to buzz with conversation.

"I think it's dreadful how the press tries to take advantage of innocent people," Lola huffed.

"Now, Frank, sit down," Jeffie laid a restraining hand on Grandy, "Homer didn't let them take any pictures of Bobbie with her legs crossed."

Out on the side porch and crouched beneath the dining room windows, two men made motions to each other and quietly began to sneak back to their car parked down by the Bing cherry trees.

"I'll file my story as soon as we get back to the paper. Man, that was better than an interview. What a scoop this'll be!"

"You're lucky to get your story. I didn't dare try for any pictures," said the other man disgruntledly as he swung his heavy camera into the back seat of the car. "We might as well head on back."

Bobbie held up her hand for attention. "Now I want to thank you all. First, Uncle Huddy for bringing us home." She walked to his chair and gave him a kiss. Homer cleared his throat and fidgeted in his chair.

Continuing through the dining room, Bobbie kissed each person as she went. Her gesture brought a smile of approval from her mother.

"thanks to Mrs. Parkerson for helping with the dinner. And to Mrs. Thompson for the use of her room and tub and gorgeous perfume.... hope you didn't mind......

"To Mam-maw....... for many, many secret reasons.

"To Grandy....... Bobbie swallowed hard before kissing his cheek.

"To my mother. Because I love her very, very much." LaVerne's face was contorted with pain and pleasure.

"To my wonderful aunts, for all they did. And to all the rest of you, dear family and guests, I am at your service."

"Maybe she doesn't, need Expression Lessons," Lola whispered to Beck.

As Bobbie left the dining room blowing kisses to each and all, she ran right into her Uncle Claude blocking the doorway.

"I want a word with you, young lady."

Bobbie suddenly realized Claude had seen her whole performance. Their blue eyes met in mutual understanding.

# Chapter 26

# "They'll Be Back"

"Now I know why they call it Labor Day," complained Hy as she shouted down the empty upstairs hallway to La and Mabes and Bobbie who were busy stripping the rooms in their assigned wings of Riverby.

"Just be glad this is the last day of labor for us. Anyway, it's kind of fun, and sad, too, to think that all the guests have finally gone," answered Mabes as she gave one final check to the Parkerson's rooms and closed the doors. By nine o clock that Monday morning, the last guests had paid their bills and after many fond farewells, had packed up their cars and driven out of the driveway toward home.

Lola had quickly issued her last orders for the summer:

"Step lively now! Girls! Strip the beds down, take down the curtains in each room. Shake the rugs and mop the floors. Don't forget to check the closets and dresser drawers for anything the guests might have left behind. Boys! Be sure all the upstairs windows are closed and locked and then close and latch the outside shutters securely. Drain the fish pond and transfer the gold fish to the big tank in the dining room. LaVerne! Rebekah! Are you going to sit on the porch all morning and drink coffee? You know you have to check the pantry and finish your packing. If we work hard, we can all be out of here by afternoon. I'm going now and take care of winterizing my cottage."

"Sister, what are we going to do all winter long without the Major General telling us what to do?" Beck laughed sarcastically as she watched Lola leave the porch and head for the cottage.

"Don't be critical, Beck. Lola has been my driving force this summer. I never would have made it without her help. I know I have the most wonderful sisters in the world. You've been so sweet and thoughtful to me this summer." LaVerne put her hand on Beck's. "Come on Beck, let's go get our duties attended to. Lola is right, we must finish up and get on the road."

"Well, I admire Lola more than I let on. Do you know that she has made arrangements to pay the taxes on Riverby for the year? And has paid the subscription on the Asheville Citizen through next summer? But, if she gives me one more order today, I won't be responsible for my actions."

LaVerne and Beck continued to laugh as they made their way into the kitchen.

"Let's get down to business, Sister, what's the food situation? There are dozens of home canned vegetables and preserves in the pantry. The smokehouse is in good shape and I have left an order with Miss Lou to send over some bacon and sausage after hog killing time. Grandy's garden will still be coming in until after the frost. Oh yes, I also made arrangements with Mrs. Wilde for milk. Charles and Leon will pick it up on their way home from school in the afternoons."

"Beck, you think of everything!" LaVerne called from the back of the pantry. "Oh, we're in fine shape in here. There's almost a full barrel of flour back here, over twenty pounds of coffee, half a keg of salt, plenty of sugar and lard. Papa said he would get the boys to help him with the root cellar." LaVerne closed the pantry door.

"Be careful now boys! Don't bruise them potatoes. One gets bruised, it'll rot and next thing you know they'll all be wasted," Grandy directed.

"Do you want the sweet potatoes and turnips and onions back in this corner?" Asked Tom Jr.

"Yep, that'll do. Now you boys finish up there and get up on the Tearoom roof and turn those apple slices over. They should be near 'bout ready to bring in. "

"What about those baskets of fresh apples we brought down from the orchard?" Jaybo wanted to know.

"They goes in that little green room upstairs. Just put 'em down easy on the floor up there. They'll keep for a long time."

"I always wondered what made that room smell go good." Bill remembered the sweet aroma from the little room.

"Grandy, I gotta go now. I promised Mam-maw I'd help her in her flower garden," Sonny ran off without being dismissed. Instead of going to the garden, he headed for the cave. Mam-maw stood in her garden with Martha Lee and Betty.

"Don't you worry about the water freezing in the bird bath, Miss Betts, Martha and I will take care of that when the time comes. We want the birds to keep coming here. They'll need a drink of water for weeks yet. Now, let me see, want you girls to help me re-pot some of these geraniums and ferns and hens and chickens from these urns. We can bring them into the house for the winter and it will be a blessing to look at them blooming when the cold winds blow down from Ole Hickory and bring the snow."

"Betts, I wish you could stay here all winter long. You know, Mother and I are going to move down to the Thompson's room and there'd be plenty of room for you, too. We'll have a private bathroom and Mam-maw and Grandy are right across the hall and Charles and Leon won't bother us cause they sleep in the Medallion room all winter. They don't mind sleeping upstairs by themselves but I'd get, lonesome up there with all those empty rooms closed up."

"It would be fun to be here with you, but I've got to go back to Arkansas and see my friends. And school will be starting soon. I know what we can do. Let's keep a diary and say, once a week or once a month, we can exchange them and keep up with each other." Betts had her hands cupped to scoop up the rich loam to add to the geranium she was potting. "I'm sure going to miss you, Marth." She kept her head down.

"I want you girls to work on that Snowball quilt this winter, like I showed you how to do. If you are real good and keep piecing on it, you might get enough squares to make two quilts and next summer you can help me quilt them." Mam-maw tried to ease the pain of parting for the girls.

"It won't be too lonesome for me," Martha tried to reassure herself, "Aunt Lola is letting me take piano and voice lessons from that new music teacher in the village. Maybe by next summer I'll be able to sing some opera pieces."

Mam-maw suddenly seemed to grow tired. "You girls finish up here and bring the pots to the dining room and water the plants. I want to go check on my yarn and stocking clips and burlap. We're going to need some new rugs by next summer and I want to see if I have plenty of scraps to work with. Don't forget, Betts, you have to help your mother finish packing so don't dawdle."

Lola bustled into the parlor room with a vase of flowers in each hand. This should just about do it, there's a vase of flowers on each table and I made an arrangement on the big round table in the dining room. Beck, where are you going to put your apples?"

Beck had just entered with a large wooden bowl of red Staymens which she had polished.

"I'll put them here by the radio. Good, I see Harold Jr. laid a fire in the fireplace. Did he finish stacking a good supply of wood on the side porch?"

LaVerne answered with a "Mmmm" as she plumped up the pillows in the chairs and dusted off the tables. She straightened the magazines and gave a final once over to the room. She wanted it to look cozy and inviting. The winter would be long and hard and her parents would spend many days here, days of solitude.

"Everything seems to be in good shape. We'd better get our families together and finish packing." Lola moved out of the room and yodeled for the children.

"Are you sure you wrote down the directions, exactly right?" La asked Hy.

"You just remember how to turn the heel like Mam-maw taught you to do and I'll remember how to turn the toe. I think knitting will be fun and think how impressed some certain young High Point men will be to be getting hand-made knitted socks from debs! We shouldn't have any trouble since Mam-maw taught us both how to cast on stitches. I'm glad you got the hang of the heel; I never could seem to catch on how to do it." Hy jammed one more sweater into her already over-crowded suit case and sat on the lid to close it.

"Girls! Stop your gabbing and get these things out to the car. Homer has been warming up the Franklin for thirty minutes and blowing that klaxon. Sonny! You most positively cannot take that silver basketball home."

"Aw, Ma, it's not as big as a basketball. This is my tinfoil collection. I've saved all summer long and kept this hidden behind a big rock in the cave and I want to take it home to show my friends. I can send this away someplace and get a big prize for it…."

"You positively cannot take that THING home." Lola closed the conversation.

Beck was on the sleeping porch surrounded by suit cases and boxes and hampers and children.

"Bill, I will not drive all the way to Mississippi with a frog. I don't care how many contests it won this summer I will have enough to do keeping the car in the middle of the road and slapping at jumping children. You cannot take that frog. That's final. Tom Jr., what are you throwing?"

"If you won't let me take my seventy-nine buckeyes back to Mississippi, I'm going to throw them all back in the river. Next summer I'm going to go down by the bridge and see if I can find them. But," he warned as he threw another one into the swirling rapids, "I'm keeping a dozen of them, right here in my pocket. Boy! My pitching arm has really improved this summer. Look, I can hit the pipe!"

"Jay," Beck called loudly, "get up here and get your overalls off. Call Sis and get her up here right now."

Jaybo and Sis arrived up the back stairs just at that moment.

"I've been packing myself a lunch, Mama. I'm already hungry and you're taking all day to pack. Come on! Let's get on the road." Jaybo had a large red checkered Riverby napkin tied by the corners. It contained three sandwiches made with salt rising bread, an apple and a piece of cake.

Sis hid the tiny flower pot that had an acorn buried in it. "Just think, I'll be sitting in an oak tree by Christmas." She forgot herself and spoke out loud.

"Last call for Anvil Brand overalls and inner tube sandals!" Harold Jr. called as he checked each family group. "I'm under instructions to pack them all away." He had his arms loaded.

"Where is Mabes?" LaVerne wanted to know. We've got to close these suitcases and valises so your father can load up the Studebaker. "What are you packing there, Bobbie? We have run out of suitcases. Now don't put in anything else."

"These won't take up much room. They're my press clippings about the kidnaping. Do you think I made the front page of the Arkansas Gazette?

"I sincerely hope not," her mother replied.

"I'm not taking anything home, Muz," said Betts. "Bobbie can have my packing room for her papers. I'm leaving something here. I'm going to give Martha Lee my ring." She reluctantly placed the Kresses ring on her pillow.

"Some present. It's tarnished and the band looks like it's almost broken to me."

"Lola LaVerne Hedges! You behave yourself!" Harold Sr. called out Bobbies hated name in a loud voice.

Mabes quietly closed the door of Mam-maw's room and stood briefly outside the door. On Mam-maw's pillow and under the black shawl, Mabes had left a folder. Inside it were fourteen separate pencil sketches of each of Jeffie's grandchildren.

Mabel looked at the sketch in her hand. It was a profile sketch of Mam-maw. She was sitting in her rocker with her green eyeshade on and knitting. The ball of yarn was on the floor next to her feet clad in her carpet slippers. Something about the sketch disturbed her but she wasn't quite sure what it was.

"It looks just like Mam-maw," she said with her critical eye. She started to tear up. "No, I'll frame it and give it to Muz for Christmas. This looks just exactly like Mam-maw." But she still felt disturbed.

"Last call for trunks, suitcases, hampers, boxes, bags, children and mothers! Charles and Leon tried to be gay as they loaded up the cars out front.

Harold Sr. tied the last grip onto the luggage rack of the Studebaker and his four children climbed into the old Touring Car and claimed their seats.

Homer sounded his klaxon once again for Lola. "Lola! Let's get going. What do you want with this old dead stick? I'm not riding all the way back to High Point with a dead stick."

"That's not a dead stick, that's my Flowering Dog-wood tree that Papa gave me. It's the State flower and I think it was very thoughtful of Papa to dig it up for me. It'll grow just fine. All it needs is some mulch around the roots and it'll thrive. Just wait and see.

Beck slapped at the fighting children in the LaSalle. "I said to move over. Mama gave me this ham and I'm going to take it home with me. "Double up back there and put it on the floor. Jay! Take that sandwich out of your mouth and be helpful. Everybody quiet down, "I'll be back in a minute."

"Sister, you not only look neat in that black suit of Rebekah's, you look like a fashion plate," Lola admired LaVerne's appearance

"Harold says we'll stop off in Asheville long enough for me to go to Bon Marche's and I can get some decent shoes and a pocket book to complete my ensemble. I don't even mind not having a hat." she laughed. She was beginning to feel like a school girl.

"Hold on, daughter," Mam-maw called. "I have a present for you from Tizzie." Mam-maw brought out a handsome black straw hat and handed it to LaVerne.

"I think I'm going to cry."

"Don't take on, daughter. Tizzie styled this specially for you and left it in my care. This was in thanks for the room and board while she was here visiting. I've been saving it, for the right moment and I think this is it."

"Sister, you look like a million dollars! "Beck complimented truthfully,

"Everybody is loaded up! We'd better start off or we'll have to spend another night here and make up all those beds again," Lola warned. "Where's Papa? I want to tell him goodbye."

"You should know by now that Frank never tells anybody goodbye. If I know him, he's in his garden. Wave to him as you go by. Good bye everybody! Be sweet! I love you!" Mam-maw went out to the front lawn as the cars started up.

"I'd better go in the house and see if anybody left anything," Charles said and dashed into the house

"Come on little kitty, let's go upstairs and you can help me make a Snowball quilt. Where are you going Leon?" Martha wanted to know, with a catch in her voice.

"Down to the river."

The three cars left the driveway and turned onto the highway. The Studebaker preceded the LaSalle toward Asheville. Beck had to go back for one more embrace from her mother before starting up the LaSalle. Homer steered the Franklin over the Swannanoa River bridge, toward Black Mountain.

They were all waving a final goodbye to Mam-maw. Grandy had waved his hoe from the garden as the cars rolled past him.

Sonny, sitting on the ball of foil called out, "There's Leon! He's walking the pipe."

The Studebaker was gaining speed as it crested the rise in the highway near the curve that would take them out of sight of Riverby.

"I'm still waving but I can't see Mam-maw anymore," said Betts.

LaVerne settled back against the upholstery. "I'll just think for three days I don't have a thing to do but sit here and watch the scenery. I will eat other people's cooking for three days and won't have a dish to wash. "She brushed a speck of dust off the front of her dress and adjusted the buttons on her blouse. When she withdrew her hand, she laid it along the top of the door of the Touring Car. A mountain breeze picked up the scrap of paper concealed in her hand and blew it away from the car. LaVerne knew she wouldn't be needing her railway passes.

"Keep waving, children," Beck instructed as she tried to see the road through her tears.

"We are! We are! Mam-maw's almost out of sight. Look, she's still waving to us! Now she's going back to the porch."

"I bet she's going to start rocking," Sis said. "Mam-maw was holding up the earth, the sky, the clouds and the mountains."

Jeffie slowly, heavily and tiredly climbed the steps to the porch and looked at the empty rockers. She sat down in her favorite rocker and looked across to the mountains. They were still there sitting proudly and looking back at her.

She adjusted her eyeshade and reached down into her sewing bag and brought, up a piece of burlap and spread it across her knees. The word "WELCOME" was penciled across the backing. She brought out her yarn and crochet hook and began her work.

"I want to have this ready for next summer, Ole Hickory, they'll all be back. Yes, there'll be another summer......."

Ole Hickory didn't answer.

# Addendum – The Same Running Stream

M. Miriam Hedges (a.k.a. Mabes in the Riverby Inn manuscript) independently wrote a lengthy unpublished family history addressed to her two grandsons entitled, *The Same Running Stream*. Naturally, her book includes the history of her mother's family, Lydia LaVerne Blanks. *The Same Running Stream* expands the Riverby Inn book with additional background stories starting with Jeffie's father and mother, James and Prudence Gill, and ending with chapters on Riverby Inn. Relevant excerpts from The Same Running Stream are included here as an addendum with permission from T. Crocker, Miriam's son.

# Prudence and James Gill

(Excerpted from Chapter 2: Westward Ho)

It was along the Massard Prairie that my great-grandparents, Prudence and James Gill, followed what might have been a Bison trace. Their trip had begun in

Virginia, from Prudence's father's plantation, then through the width of Tennessee where they stopped to visit relatives. As they entered Arkansas, they drove straight southwest. Somehow, having missed the Arkansas River Trail, they found themselves in unknown country following an overgrown trail. Along the way they passed a lone sentinel mountain in the center of the prairie, a quirk of nature, for it looked like a large "potato hill." Off in the distance they could make out the Fourche Mountains, a low range resembling clouds on the horizon. After assessing their situation, the Gills decided to continue along the trail which led them due west. As they rode on, it was noticed that the lush prairie grasses were obliterating the trail. Having passed many bleached skeletons en-route, they reasoned that the herd had diminished through slaughter.

Just the same, being young and adventurous, they rode on toward the new territory which beckoned them. Prudence and James Gill were not alone. Their entourage consisted of their own wagon piled high with wedding gifts, and a large Conestoga wagon packed with supplies. The latter was driven by their slave, a wedding present from Prudence's father. Suddenly leaving the intense heat of the prairie, they entered a land of low rolling hills which appeared to be the gateway to Paradise. The country became spectacular. Turkey and quail drummed in the underbrush, while clouds of brilliant green Carolina parakeets swept overhead. The plaintive calls of mourning doves could be heard in the distant woods. Surrounding them were sloughs left by the spring rains, on which water fowl skimmed the surfaces. Impressed by the variety of water birds, they were unaware their location was directly under the Great American Flyway of water fowl. Penetrating deeper into the tree line, the trace led them through a circus of darting wild life. Woodchucks and rabbits raced under the wagon wheels which were already crushing wild flowers.

The sight was too much, causing James to leap down from the wagon to scoop up a clod of earth for tasting. A man of the land, he smiled at Prudence saying: "Marly--wonderful rich loam." Enthralled to find themselves in this storehouse of wonders, they chose to pitch camp on the spot. Actual facts have been lost in time as to why the young Gill couple decided to leave the comfortable lives of their youth and go west. We do know that their close cousins, the Burrows, had already moved to Arkansas. These men were educators and sought to establish schools and churches in the wild territory. Others migrating into the Frontier were seeking fertile and inexpensive land where they could make their mark economically, socially, and politically. The latter promised positions yet unfilled. It is likely that the Burrow men influenced the Gills to remain in Arkansas. The Territory was lawless for many years to come, bonding those of social and economic status.

Kinships spread outside immediate family ties--where cousins married cousins. Close friends were absorbed into complicated kinships. Even in my childhood days, everyone was referred to as "Aunt," "Uncle," or "Cousin" So-and-So. Families were large in this period of history, with Arkansas leading the country in birthrate. Our ancestors spread their genes generously through families of from ten to fourteen children. Women died young, leaving their husbands to remarry and father second families. With the Hoppers and Gills merging with the Burrow and Blanks families, my maternal heritage was established.

Perhaps it was that first night camping under a star pocked sky that the Gills decided to remain where they were forever. They chose to claim the land straddling both Yell and Perry counties and to call it "Nimrod." The choice of this name may have stemmed from two sources. One being the chance on that first night or "beginning," that they read from the book of Genesis. The passage 10:8-10 speaks of Noah's great grandson: "Like Nimrod, a mighty hunter before the Lord." The safety of the "Ark" may have suggested its tie with the safety of their future in ARKansas. The other possibility may have sprung from Prudence's ancestor, Phillipe Burrow, who came to America from France in 1799 and named his son Nimrod Burrow. The surname must have been Anglicized from Bureau. Nevertheless, the choice of "Nimrod" endures on Arkansas maps. Possibly the largest artificial lake in the state is called Lake Nimrod.[1011]

*Portion of property homesteaded by the Gills (left). Looking south to the Fourche La Fave River (below) and the hills of the Ouachita National Forest.*

*Figure 21: Nimrod property looking South*

*Figure 22: Fourche La Fave River*

General Taylor enjoyed quoting Davy Crockett who spent time in Arkansas: "I don't understand Arkansas. It is remarkable there are so many leading men, and so few followers." After claiming their land, the Gills set about building their homestead. During this period, they lived in a one room dwelling made of logs and wattle, with a lean-to for their servant This little building was destined to be the chicken house at a later date. A spring was enclosed for their water supply, trees cleared to sunlight the garden spot, and plans made for future expansion. A gardener, Prudence took pride in her fruit trees, berries and wild flowers, all transplanted with care. She was a collector of herbs and was knowledgeable in their medical uses. In three years, the new house was built, and "Nimrod" emerged as a comfortable and impressive estate.

Prudence Hopper Gill was the adored only child of a Virginia tobacco planter living in Halifax County, Virginia. Being of the landed gentry, her father was also a slave holder. He was considered to be a kindly man with his neighbors calling him Grandfather Hopper. It has been said by my grandmother that he never sat down to a meal without sending his manservant to the public road ringing a large handbell.

This was to stop wayfarers to pause for rest, and to share his board. When his adored daughter and her bridegroom revealed to him their intention of moving west, Grandfather Hopper was inconsolable. Finally, after becoming resigned to his loss, he took charge of outfitting two supply wagons for their trip. At the same time, he signed over one of his most trusted slaves as a gift. When time came for the painful parting, he placed his Masonic ring on Prudence's finger, and followed it with a significant handclasp. This ring had never left his finger before but both his daughter and he knew that it was for protection. Thus, the young couple left Halifax in tears, but in full equipage.

Until the outbreak of the Civil War, Prudence and James led happy and resourceful lives developing their property. With the new house containing adequate rooms, they enjoyed strolling about their property in gratitude for their good fortune. They were unaware that the Fourche Mountains, off in the distance, held a fate which would erase their Utopia forever. First, James was called away into service with the Confederate Army. Being a Tennessean, he served in Company D, Regiment 44, in the Infantry of that state. This service was to last for four years. During his absence, Prudence remained alone with her father's slave. They busied themselves from dawn to dusk with projects James had outlined. Even in a bone-tired state, Prudence found it difficult to endure her isolation.

At the close of the war a bedraggled James returned home. He was without injury, but suffered from malnutrition. As his strength returned, he picked up on unfinished plans for his claim. They had decided to clear land for a small orchard at the foot of the Fourche range. James was not alone in his projects, for Prudence, feeling the loss of his four years away, had started their family. She was then five months pregnant. On that fateful morning, James packed his gear for the work on the orchard site. Ecstatic over becoming a father, he would not hear to taking his slave along for help- preferring to leave him at home with Prudence. Feeling better physically and in happy spirits, he rode off tipping his old Confederate cap at a rakish angle.

It was an unusually warm day, leaving Prudence weary as the afternoon wore on. She sent the servant to clean the hen house, while she retired for a nap. Sleeping for an undetermined length of time, she was startled awake by the sound of pounding horses' hooves. Quickly looking through her bedroom windows, she saw five wild men churning their horses over her flower beds. With whoops and yells they dismounted and forced their way into her house. Meeting them face-to-face struck terror to her heart, for they were filthy and crude. All wore long beards and matted hair to their shoulders. Hooped earrings pierced their ears, and their sneers revealed missing teeth. Their plundering began with each man grabbing whatever pleased his fancy. The kitchen was devastated, for they removed every scrap of food in sight. By then, Prudence realized that they were the "Bushwhackers," an evil spinoff from Quantrell's gang whose den was in the Fourche Mountains. Frozen in terror, Prudence watched as they left as quickly as they had come. By some miracle, the young pregnant woman was left unharmed except for the cruel parting remark made by one of them. As he mounted his horse, he placed a Confederate cap on the tip of his gun. Spinning it around, he called back as though in great favor: "Ye can find the body of that man o' yourn up on the mountain."

It was growing dark when Prudence gathered her senses. The servant was standing beside her wringing his hands. "O Lord, Mis Prue, I had to hide 'cause I was so scairt." As numb as she was, Prudence gathered up the Bible, a lantern, and a quilt, and ordered the servant to hitch up the wagon. The two terrified souls then left in the darkness to search for the body of James Gill. Their progress was slow on the rugged trail, since they stopped to swing the lantern in all directions. Complete stops were made to examine the gullies. Finally, in the clearing of the new orchard, they found James Gill's body. He had been shot in the back, his boots removed, and his pockets turned out. Gently lifting his body, they wrapped it in the quilt and placed it in the wagon. Prudence held her husband's head in her lap for his return home. As they slowly made their way in the darkness toward Nimrod, the servant became aware of a luminous light filling the Heavens in front of them. Thinking the Lord had sent them an omen, he pointed it out to the young widow.

As the wagon came closer, Prudence knew the Bushwhackers had returned to set a raging fire to her property. Nimrod was burning to the ground. Toward dawn in the smoking rubble, James Gill was buried on a slope where he often sat. Prudence read from the Bible on her knees, as she watched a lone naked chicken pecking through the debris. All its feathers had been burnt off. We lose the servant at this time. He was never heard from again. It is possible he went for help and was ambushed by the Bushwhackers - or, that being free, he deserted the side of his mistress. Dazed, Prudence wandered about trying to decide what to do. The horses were gone, there was no roof overhead, and nothing to eat. Exhausted, she slept in the wagon, with her child moving inside her. She awoke with the determination to survive and to save her baby. Prudence Gill started walking. I have been told that before my brother's death, he located the site of James Gill's grave on the Nimrod property.

The young pregnant woman lived on berries and herbs as she made her way for help. Having many miles ahead before reaching the Burrows family, she showed her Masonic ring to the few who shared her road. Through the Masonic code she was given help until she eventually reached a Burrow homestead in Perryville, Arkansas. It was here that my grandmother was born posthumously. James Gill, expecting a longed-for son, had selected the name for his unborn child. Prudence named her baby according to his wishes—Jefferson Lee Gill. After regaining her health and spirits, Prudence took her baby girl back to her father's house in Halifax. It became a protracted visit, for she knew her father would delight in the company of his little blonde granddaughter. Too, there was another reason for a change of scenery.

Prudence needed to escape the attentions of a certain Mr. Wilson, a friend of Isham Burrow. Very few widows or widowers were left to grieve alone during this time. Most of them remarried

Figure 23: Road likely walked by Prudence

promptly. The Burrow men were active in match-making, and had brought attention to Prudence's tragic experiences. After 1840, the territorial ambition of large families was at its peak. The settlement of these people was very much a part of the Arkansas development and security. After sorting out her devotion to James Gill, Prudence decided to marry Mr. Wilson. She returned to Arkansas with little Jeffie. We know nothing of Mr. Wilson, not even his first name, but the wedding took place. In a year or so, Prudence gave birth to a baby boy, much younger than Jeffie. Mr. Wilson lived for only a few years after his marriage to Prudence. She devoted the rest of her life to her children and died when Jeffie was fourteen years old. With his daughter preceding him in death, Grandfather Hopper drew up a new will. At the reading, it revealed two things: Jeffie was his sole heir, and he had named Hansel Burrow as her guardian. Hansel Burrow was a close relative, much younger than Hopper. As a little girl, I accompanied my mother to meet her half-uncle, who was on his deathbed. There was a striking resemblance between him and his half-sister, Jeffie.

He was known to possess business acumen and was a man to look up to. His name was well-known in Carroll County, Tennessee, where he lived with his second wife and their young children. His first wife had been Frances E. Gill, a possible relative of James Gill who had died childless. His second marriage brought royal blood into his line through the Howard family. On all accounts Hansel Burrow appeared well qualified to serve as Jeffie's guardian. This branch of the Burrow family was a large one. Hansel was one of thirteen children. His sister, Rebecca Miriam, was the mother of my grandfather, Francis Marion Blanks. It was, however, a brother, Isham Lafayette, who distinguished himself as an educator and a churchman. With Arkansas's limited educational facilities, the Reverend Isham Burrow made a name for himself in the field of education. He became known for his high standards of leadership in the underdeveloped territory. A pioneer Methodist, Isham Burrow became the presiding elder after graduating from the Bethel and Andrew Colleges. He was transferred to the Arkansas Conference in 1869, where he found that schools of high grade were much needed. He chose Altus, as the name imparts, for his lofty project. Only two log cabins were on the land he purchased in 1875. After erecting a small house for his family, he built a two-story frame schoolhouse. It was called the "Central Collegiate Institute," but was later named the "Hiram and Lydia School" when it was developed into an academy for young ladies. It was here that my grandmother Jefferson Lee was educated. With the success of the academy, Isham Lafayette Burrow went on to establish Hendricks College.

As a teenager, Jeffie came into the ownership of a fine chestnut mare. The willowy blonde girl created a picture on her mount. Dressed in her Reseda green riding habit, which fit without a wrinkle, Jeffie caught all eyes. The tight jacket was fastened with black frog closings, and her wrap-around skirt touched the ground when she was mounted. Her blonde hair was confined in a black net snood, over which she wore a tricorn hat plumed to the side. Her boots and saddle were the color of her chestnut mare and waxed to perfection. Jeffie, as other ladies of her day, rode side-saddle - a beautiful but dangerous sport. With only one knee gripping the pummel for leverage, safety was tentative. Long skirts were often death traps since they caught on fences, or became caught under the horse itself. Jeffie was considered to be an excellent horsewoman, and there is no report of a mishap. Two generations of children and grandchildren enjoyed dressing up in her riding habit. It withstood the years, providing pleasure to all its wearers. To us children, it was only a costume, but to our grandmother, it was the talisman of the life she once knew.

As a young carefree girl, Jeffie's life was soon to be changed when her guardian, Hansel Burrow, sent her off to boarding school. To her dismay, Jeffie arrived at the Hiram and Lydia Academy to find her roommate to be a full-blooded Cherokee Indian girl with shocking habits. For a long time Jeffie felt frightened of her, but gradually became her friend. It was during a visit back with Hansel's family, that Jeffie was to be introduced to Francis Marion Blanks (who was named for the Swamp Fox). Their romance blossomed into marriage, where she found happiness and a fruitful life. Although she owned the land of "Nimrod," she never returned to the Eden her parents so treasured. Instead, she and Frank Blanks created in time, a place where their children and grandchildren would come to treasure as another Eden.

# Jeffie and Frank

(Excerpted from Chapter 6)

Being typical of her time, Jeffie studied subjects that were expected of young ladies of her background: Latin, French, and music. Years ago, she gave me a well-worn volume of Shakespeare as a token of her school days. Never a serious student, Jeffie would laugh and say, "All I learned at school was to play the piano and to take snuff with my Indian friend." After taking over the protection of Jeffie, Hansel Burrow began to prosper. At this point he decided the time had come to make his move. Inviting Jeffie back to Tennessee for a visit, he took up the subject of her business affairs. She was told that it wasn't comely for a young girl of her breeding to see to business - after all, it was man's work Hansel then suggested buying her out lock, stock and barrel. Young and naive. Jeffie agreed to his officer. The settlement was a pittance of her real worth. Through her acres of rich "bottom" land, Hansel and his family lived well indeed for several generations.

The Burrow family is a fascinating study in that they brought French blood into our lineage. Phillipe Burrow came to America from France in 1774. A French scholar has suggested the original name must have been "Burreau." The name was certainly Anglicized. The Burrows were prolific breeders. Most of them produced from twelve to fourteen children. Not only productive, the Burrows were of handsome stock and genial ways. They possessed a quiet demeanor, being sophisticated and quite sure of themselves. Selective in attitude, they appeared beyond reproach, leading less endowed family members to look up to them.

Hansel's second daughter, Mabel, was a beautiful girl of impeccable carriage. In maturity she became my mother's paragon. At a fashionable wedding, Hansel gave his daughter in marriage to handsome Albert Black, a cotton broker by trade. A fine Tudor mansion was built for them in Fort Smith. Located high on a hill it looked across several acres of modest bungalows, one of which was to be our future home.

From this Olympian setting the beautiful blonde woman dispensed kindness to those less fortunate family members. With my mother, LaVerne, as her dablure, we were often recipients of her largesse. My parents' wedding took place in her gracious drawing room, as harp notes rippled over the gathering from her music salon. From all reports it was a beautiful occasion and one not to be forgotten by my mother. In appreciation she determined to name her first-born daughter "Mabel" after her. Being that child, I suffered years of best behavior and the wearing of the exquisite handmade underwear Mabel Black dressed me in.

(The latter was usually snagged when she raised my skirts to check). When I came of age, I chose to be known as Miriam, which is my middle name in honor of my great-grandmother Miriam Burrow.

A happy future did present itself when Jeffie visited Hansel, for it concurred with the arrival of Miriam Burrow Blanks, and her two grown sons, Francis Marion and Hiram Abif- the latter always being called "Biff." Visits were protracted in those days and the guests stayed on. Hansel's sister, Miriam, was a recent widow, and he wished to introduce his good friend John Bryant to her. Romance filled the air for both Blanks boys were smitten with Jeffie, as was Mr. Bryant with Miriam. It was Francis Marion, the quiet one, who stole Jeme's affection. A wedding date was set, soon to be followed by the marriage of Miriam to Mr. Bryant

With the two weddings over, Jeffie and Frank set up housekeeping in Trezevant, Tennessee, a community populated by their kinspeople. (In remembering their honeymoon, Jeffie took delight in telling how she frustrated her bridegroom by wearing tightly laced corsets under her nightdress). Life in Trezevant was a happy time, with much visiting back and forth with the "double" cousins their marriage brought about

Figure 24: LaVerne, Frank, Jeffie, and Lola

In a short time two little daughters were born to Jeffie and Frank Lola and LaVerne, only ten months apart in age. Lola was the serious one with grown-up manners, while LaVerne was sassy and often misbehaved. Jeffie dressed them as twins, which misled people.

My mother often spoke of her grandmother, Miriam, whom she adored. She also lived in Trezevant, and spent much time with her pretty little granddaughters. All through her lifetime my mother referred to her childhood in Trezevant with nostalgia. Seeking a higher income, Frank Blanks moved his family to Jackson, Tennessee, where he entered the mercantile business. The two girls were enrolled in school, where they made high marks. With the girls thus occupied, Jeffie increased the family income by creating ladies' hats. Frank sold them in his mercantile store with great success. When the girls reached the age of fourteen and fifteen, Claude, their only son, was born. When the girls were eighteen and nineteen years of age, Jeffie surprised the family with the birth of a third daughter, Rebecca 1

The older girls graduated with honors from the "Female Institute of Jackson," Lola receiving her degree in Music and LaVerne in the Liberal Arts. Both young ladies sought teaching contracts and found them in Paris, Arkansas. Fate playing a hand, they also found their future husbands there. Courtship was a happy time, filled with buggy trips to picnic at Mussel Shoals. There was much game playing and music.

Lola married Homer Tyer Hudson, a tall and quiet man, who was to succeed in the manufacturing business. After their wedding they lived in Huntington, West Virginia, where Homer joined his brother Charlie's venture in producing workingman's clothing. Becoming an immediate success, the brothers moved their factories to North Carolina. Lola and Homer had three children: Hybernia, LaVerne and Homer Jr. The latter was born to them late in life, when the two girls were grown.

LaVerne married Harold Herbert Hedges who was then with the Wells Fargo Company. They remained in Arkansas, living in Scranton, Hot Springs and Fort Smith. Their marriage was blessed with four children - Harold Jr., Mabel Miriam, Lola LaVerne, and Elizabeth Lee.

Claude, Jeffie and Frank's only son, was a restless young man who seemed unable to find himself. His drinking brought distress to his family members. When sober, Claude had a winning personality which brought forgiveness many times after his lapses. He married a winsome and pretty young woman, Norma Beale, who gave him two sons, Charles and Leon. Martha, their baby daughter, was born later in North Carolina. These three children brought joy into Frank and Jeffie's lives as they did to other family members.

Rebecca was a sunny little girl with blonde curls and a cheerful outlook on life. This disposition followed her into maturity. While teaching "Expression" at the age of eighteen in Anguilla, Mississippi, she met Thomas Walter Fields, a plantation owner. Tom Fields was much older than Rebecca. After remaining a bachelor for some years, he longed for a family. When he met the young and vivacious teacher, he decided to change his life through marriage. His decision was a happy one for both Rebecca and Tom Fields, for they produced three sons and a daughter- Harris Jessie, Thomas Walter Jr., William Cleveland and Frances. An indulgent husband and father, Tom lavished them with love and much of this world's goods.

These families are the players in our growing up days - especially during our summers. The three Blanks sisters were devoted to one another and visited frequently, which provided a closeness among their children. This unique family relationship was furthered by Jeffie and Frank.

─────────────── ❧ ❦ ───────────────

Our grandfather, Francis Marion Blanks, was named after the Swamp Fox, Francis Marion. His grandchildren called him "Grandie." He was not an easy man to know. Basically quiet, except when riled, he could often be seen gazing off into the distance, a prisoner of his own thoughts. Grandie was a physically arresting man standing over six feet two inches tall. His height was emphasized by his ram-rod carriage. The span of his hand was awesome, and his shoes were number twelve in size.

Upon entering a room, he had the habit of hesitating at the door with the left side of his face averted from the room. This presented a clean-cut profile. Slowly, he would turn his face forward exposing the defect on the left side of his face. From birth he had carried a keratinous growth covering his eye. If medical advancement had been fifty years earlier, the defect would have been removed. It is possible this condition covered a perfect eye. Grandie was sensitive about his disfigurement, which must have contributed to his manner. There was compensation, which is often the case, in the power of his right eye. It was steel blue in color and as penetrating as a laser beam. He missed nothing. Jeffie Gill was a cheerful woman whose interests were with people. She was always a popular woman wherever she was - giving, always giving, to others. Her days were filled with vignettes of activity - children sitting about her hooking rugs or knitting - following her sturdy strides up a mountainside - or sitting at her dinner table feasting on chicken and dumplings.

Though evening scenes were of talent nights, or game playing. Her parlor resembled a gaming place in Monte Carlo with bridge tables set up for action. Everyone loved the woman they called "Mamaw."

———————————— ❧ ❧ ————————————

Jeffie and Frank left Jackson to enter the hotel business. Their choice was Houston, Mississippi, a railroad town known at the time for its transient population. They purchased "The Houston Hotel," a large square red brick building. Our visits to them in this hotel can never be forgotten. As children we thought it was enormous, and being offspring of the owners brought on a sense of embarrassed pride. The spacious lobby looked up three floors to a multicolored skylight When the sun was out, flashing lights patterned the Brussels carpet paving the first floor. Two balconies wove their way around the lobby, with a grand staircase leading up to them. One can still recall the sense of dizziness felt when looking over these railings from the top level. Of course, we were admonished with strict orders never to do so.

Leading off the balconies radiated bedrooms of various sizes, all furnished with giant beds decorated in a harvest of carved fruit. Terror struck our souls when put to bed at night, since these appendages cast gruesome shadows. There were matching washstands, also carved, which presented the necessary tools for ablution - washbowl and pitcher. These were usually of ironstone china, but the bridal suite sported hand painted ones of violets. Chamber pots to match were discreetly hidden behind the doors of the washstands.

Mornings brought on a burst of housekeeping as bellboys and maids shuttled back and forth on the grand staircase exchanging the linen and chamber pots. Hotel keeping was not an easy life in a small-town shy of running water.

There were a few "guests" who lived in the hotel the year round. Most were widows and spinsters who had seen better days. Somewhat spoiled, they demanded attention. Living with our grandparents in the hotel were Claude's wife and her two little boys, Charles and Leon. Leon was just a toddler and he enjoyed climbing up on the dining room tables to purloin sugar cubes. Charles spent most of his time playing out back in the servants' compound. These were small brick houses covered with exotic vines called "Passion Plant" There were several little black boys his age with whom he enjoyed playing "train".

Because of the railroads, there was a constant flow of overnight visitors waiting to make their connections. The dining room attracted well-to- do locals with its exceptional food, and the fact that there was nothing whatsoever to do in Houston, Mississippi. One year-round guest, and the children's favorite, was Judge Roane. We liked him most of all, for we thought he was Santa Claus. Orator that he was, he wore his snow-white hair sweeping to his shoulders. It passed his great beard on the way. Being plump of body and merry of face, he furthered his striking appearance by wearing a white linen suit His double-breasted vest was resplendent in gold chains and dangling fobs. He allowed us to listen to his gold watch. This always brought uncontrollable laughter from his deep insides. We adored him, for he shook like a bowl full of jelly.

Jeffie was like the cruise director on an ocean liner, playing chatelaine of the Houston Hotel. She saw to all the details of keeping the widows and spinsters happy, and cheering the traffic of "drummers" who came and went A night owl, she provided music and games each evening. One might say she was ever mindful of the needs of others. Jeffie possessed an artistic flare which was expressed in the dining room one Christmas. The tables were set in white damask cloths with a mirror plateau in the center of each. Tiny trees made from real evergreens formed a forest around the mirrors. Along the brink of each mirror stood little stags and does enjoying their reflections. This scene was as though they were refreshing themselves at a beautiful lake. It was a charming concept

Filled with success over his hotel investment. Grandie decided to branch out. He opened a movie house. Purchasing two brick buildings side by side, he had a large rectangular window cut in the common wall, thus uniting the two structures. One side was for white people and the other side was for black people. The screen was on the "white" side, of course, but the viewing was adequate from the other side. Although this arrangement was crude, it must be remembered as a step in the right direction. Until then, the black people of Houston had to provide their own amusement

In front of the movie screen was a player piano to accompany the films. Grandie enlisted the help of his eldest grandchild, my brother Harold, to provide the music. He was ten years old at the time. His plump little legs barely reached the pedals, but he worked hard at his job. His careful instructions were to pump fast and hard during the exciting scenes, and to slow down for the romantic ones. He was barely to pump during the death scenes. There were times where the piano made no sound at all, for Harold would be so caught up in the plot he would forget to work the pedals. Reality would jerk him back into action, causing the piano to race in confused speed. During this time, he would glance back at the projection booth to see if Grandie had noticed the hiatus. The last thing the poor little fellow wanted was an outdone Grandie.

---- ❧ ❦ ----

One day panic overtook the Houston Hotel for word had come that Grandie's cousin E. W. Grove was stopping by for a visit. Another member of the Burrow family, E. W. had concocted a chill tonic remedy which had made him rich and famous. There was a frantic scurrying about to shore things up for his visit After being given a tour of the hotel, E. W. cleared his throat to give a travelogue on the merits of Western North Carolina, where he had built the famous Grove Park Inn. The comparison between the Houston Hotel and the Grove Park Inn left much to be desired. E. WC s speech wound up urging Frank to "sell out" and "move up" to where the "future is." He should be wise - liquidate, and invest in Asheville property.

# Riverby Place

(Excerpted from Chapter 12)

Lola and Grandie occupied the front seat of the Franklin touring car as it swept past the turnoff for Oteen. Ahead of them lay Alexander Mountain with the highway encircling it. Coming around the bend they had a clear view of their destination - across the valley sat a rambling white house in comfortable affiliation with the dark mountains behind it. Leaning forward in his seat for a closer look, Grandie thought it might serve well as the setting for a picture postcard.

Turning into the white gravel driveway leading up to the house, Grandie and Lola made their way through stanchions of matched junipers. These sentinels were the remnants of a professional landscaping plan lost in time. A shawl of large shade trees cloaked the premises leaving the house centered in an innocent meadow dusted with Queen Anne's Lace. This site called "Riverby Place," with its deep porches draped with Virginia creeper, seemed to face the world with a homey look.

Back in Asheville, the real estate broker explained the origin of the property:

"Mr. Blanks, this spacious tract was purchased as a site for a rest home. After the house was built it was never used as such. Now vacant for some years, the heirs are anxious to settle the estate. In that most buyers have considered it too large for a family dwelling, it is now on the market for a song."

With these encouraging words, the keys were turned over for an inspection trip. Lola and Grandie lost no time in getting on the highway leading toward Black Mountain.

After parking the chocolate brown Franklin in front of the house, they stood for some moments studying the large double doors sunk back into the deep shadows of the porch. Mounting the front steps, Grandie took out the keys and opened the heavy doors.

The inspection trip lasted for some hours - upstairs, downstairs, and all around the grounds. Everywhere they looked they found drawbacks. The whole place needed painting, inside and out. The kitchen held a vast coal stove and an outmoded water pump over the sink. There was no electricity, and even worse, only one bathroom to serve fourteen bedrooms!

While viewing the grounds, it was decided that the property's assets outweighed the asking price - and besides this factor, Frank Blanks had fallen in love with the place. Without further hesitation, Lola and

Grandie returned to Asheville to "dicker" over the asking price. The agent lowered his figure to accommodate electricity, and the deal was made. Plans went into effect to start the renovation.

———————— ❧ ❧ ————————

Although the gabled house presented a serene facade, there was excitement in its rear view. The house clung to an escarpment of large boulders, some of which had tumbled into the ravine cut by the Swannanoa River eons back in time. This rushing stream was a powerful force of sound and fury. Its abyss was lush with primal growth - wild cherry, dogwood, balsam, and coves of mountain laurel. Overhead great swags of muscadine vines provided swings like circus riggings. It was a noisy setting with the rushing stream playing basso profundo to the bird flute calls high in the treetops. River mists clung close to shore with nodding ferns, while in the shallows a nidus of bullfrogs tended tadpoles waiting out their metamorphic cycle. Shafts of sunlight lit patches of siliceous sand where orange spotted turtles burrowed in glint. The fast currents of the river were alive with water snakes holding their heads up as periscopes of defense.

It was a wild Eden harking back from generations of activity. This Galapagos-like Riverby Place was to become the delight of city children who responded to its siren call. It was here that Frank Blanks' grandchildren became the spiritual kinsmen of the Down River People.

# FOR SALE

This beautiful summer hotel of 23 rooms and 36 acres of land, suitable for summer home sites or garden farms, located in the heart of Western North Carolina, at Swannanoa, N. C., a noted summer home and health resort section. This property borders Swannanoa river on one side and the paved highway from Asheville to Black Mountain runs through the center. The Southern R. R. on the opposite side parallel. The hotel is in a nice grove as you can see from the above photo, and is surrounded with mountain scenery. It has running water piped from a mountain spring, with hot and cold water in kitchen and bath room. For further information and price, write or come to see us.

## Canton Real Estate Co.

Phone 291, Canton, N. C.
Or E. J. Randolph, Phone 91, Asheville, N. C.

*Figure 25: Riverby Place Real Estate Ad July 24, 1921*

Grandie paid little heed to female judgment while proceeding in his own way with improvements. He became cantankerous with workmen over costs and the quality of supplies. Finally, with the electricity installed and additional plumbing in place, Grandie turned his thoughts toward the grounds.

A croquet court was added, extra rocking chairs were put on the porch and hammocks were hung from low tree branches. Grandie then had the backside of the meadow plowed up for a spacious vegetable garden. The garden was enclosed with a high anchor fence to ward off raiding ruminants and dishonest humans. Grandie alone had access to the weighty gate which was opened only by the key dangling from his belt.

In keeping with the big white house, a flock of Leghorn chickens were set loose in the lower meadow, where they pecked out grasshoppers. Later, Grandie dammed up a quiet pond from the River to provide space for his white Peking ducks.

This paddling pond attracted wild geese and a stray Aylesbury. One of the drakes fell in love with my grandmother and followed her everywhere. She called him "Chatter," for he conversed with her nonstop.

One unexplained extravagance on Grandie's part was the special order of two fine white Collie dogs from President Coolidge's kennels. This purchase disgruntled the distaff side of the family who thought fabric for cretonne curtains was a higher priority. All was forgiven, however, as they watched the beautiful dogs rollicking in the Queen Anne's lace. They did complete the picture postcard.

With the additional porch rocking chairs, the sunsets of the Smoky Mountains became an evening feature. The viewing was magnificent, with streaks of color slashing the skies. When nightfall claimed our hill, a canopy of stars hovered over the valley. Off in the distance of the mountains the faint tinkle of cow bells could be heard. Moonlit nights echoed with the moaning of coonhounds high in the mountains, with the occasional bedlam when they were off on a hunt

But the heartthrob of Riverby Place was the big brass handbell used to summon the scattered populace to meals or for rare events. Its toll meant business. Children took turns ringing it as a sort of honorarium for good deeds. Echoing through the valley, it brought everyone to home plate regardless of duties.

The opening party at Biltmore House could not have been met with greater enthusiasm than when, on that hot day of 1922, Jeffie's and Frank's descendants arrived at Riverby's door. The serene atmosphere gave way to excitement as grandchildren fought over the porch rocking chairs, and later, over the assignment of rooms.

It soon became clear that a figure of authority should step in to monitor this opinionated household. Grandie considered the house to be the domain of women, and he appointed his eldest daughter, Lola, as "the keeper of the castle." Dubbed the "Major General," she issued orders in keeping with her title.

"Pick up the mail. Fetch the firewood. Gather six bouquets of wild flowers. Set the tables." And, before electricity, "Polish the lamp chimneys." Reluctant moans could be heard following the Major General's orders, but in time "esprit de corp" won out. We came to enjoy our serfdom, even down to shelling peas for dinner.

The Major General created domains for her sisters by fitting them into their niches of talent. My mother, LaVerne, planned the menus and oversaw the food preparation. Beck, the youngest, and always pregnant, was given the choice job of "flower arranger." She kept drifts of wild flowers throughout the house. Norma, Claude's wife, kept tabs on the napery, counting mountains of linens to be taken to the mountain laundress. This left Lola as purchasing agent and drill sergeant

Even with all hands-on deck, it soon became clear that additional help must be sought Such help was found in the person of Ora, who was a superb cook. After fixing up a small cottage on the grounds, Grandie arranged for Ora's transportation from South Carolina. She loved her one room retreat and collapsed there between meals. Not only was Ora a marvelous cook, she was also a temperamental one. Under death threats we were cautioned to tread lightly in her presence. This was a stringent discipline for our cousins, Charles and Leon, for Ora was terrified of snakes and it was a great temptation for them to leave a few specimens about. We toed the mark on being considerate of Ora, for the thought of being deprived of her hot biscuits struck terror to our stomachs. Everyone catered to this light-skinned woman, including Grandie. He kept her supplied with the South Carolina clay she relished. She ate it like candy.

Not too long after Ora's arrival a houseman came into our lives. His name was Mose. A strapping young black man, Mose charmed everyone with his dazzling smile. His chores were wide of range, from plucking chickens to breaking up the rock fights we children got into. Croquet mallets were also on his list, for we had also found them useful as weapons. The rest of the time Mose spent following the Major General around, lifting heavy objects, and waxing the floors. There were also times when Mose wasn't around at all.

Mose's absences were never explained to us until a taxi, usually bearing an out of state license plate, would pull up in the driveway. The door would open from behind the driver, and Mose would back out supporting a worse for wear Claude. In silence Grandie would unpocket a roll of bills and pay the driver off, as Jeffie put her arms around her son and gently led him into the sanctum of her heart and home. After a few days of doting care, Claude would recover from his lapse and join the family circle to entertain us with his witty tales of travel. His visits were brief - but there was always the next time.

It was during this first summer that our grandmother, Jeffie, became known to the grandchildren as "Mamaw." The slender figure of her youth had given way to comfortable overweight. Her soft body offered surcease to painful ear infections, hurt feelings, and on occasion, contagious diseases. With reassuring hands, she stroked away our childhood ills. Blessed with a happy nature she dispelled unpleasant circumstances. Mamaw had a rosy outlook,

Her loving care was not confined to the family clan, for her largess extended to friends who sought her ministrations. Some would remain in her care for several days before facing the world again. Mamaw attracted the love lorn and children. She simply drew people to her with groups forming at her feet. Whenever she sat down her hands were busy with needlework and it was she who brought craftsmanship into our lives.

One summer she taught both boys and girls how to crochet We made "beanies" of colorful yarns which we wore in happy unisex. She also organized a "pottery factory" on the river rocks, for we had discovered deposits of kaolin clay washed in by an icy cold mountain brook. This infusion was as smooth as pumice and a pleasure to collect Its source was hidden away among ferns and yellow fringed orchids, which were tangled with an orange parasite vine known as "the Love Vine." This secret place also held another phenomenon. Dragonflies in peacock colors claimed it for their breeding ground, and sailed on their iridescent wings in and out of our private grotto.

After collecting our clay, we created vases, bowls, and cups and left them to dry out on the hot boulders. This activity inspired a treasure hunt for interesting rocks, bits of glass, and a few shells, which were pressed into our creations with some artistic effect Mamaw then suggested a "craft show" for the grown-ups to enjoy.

A larger project came our way when, in a moment of madness, our grandmother suggested we decorate our own bedrooms. She provided a small allowance for each child at Mr. Pendleton's store. This was a cave of riches to us, for everything, it seemed, was displayed in this general merchandise paradise. We busied ourselves with paint and yards of cheap fabric - all trying to outdo the other in garishness. My room was done up in a nightmare of chartreuse and orchid, a combination to upset any stomach. The other rooms were just as frightening, but we were too happy to notice.

And so it was with our grandmother. We never went to bed at night without an exciting agenda for the next day. There were hikes up the mountainside to gather apples from Grandie's orchard. These were converted into cider in the press on the back porch - gallons of it. Ora created apple butter and cobblers with our leftovers. We not only fought each other over running the cider press, but scores of bees joined in the melee. The process required one to crank and another to swat away the winged helpers.

We collected butterfly specimens from the country road and meadows. An extensive growth of bright orange "chiggerweed" attracted orange Monarchs and yellow Swallowtails. Grandie's garden patch contained droves of pale-yellow cabbage flies, and at night the moonvine draping the porch lured wonderful Luna moths.

We pressed wild flowers into charming botanicals which were frequently pasted onto old copies of the "Asheville Citizen" newspaper. Later, a display was arranged in the big front hall which came to resemble a wing in the Smithsonian Institute's Museum of Natural History. As our skills developed, we turned our energies to hooking rugs and making chair pads, even creating our own dyes.

Organized sports activities came in the late afternoons: softball, croquet, and kick-the-can. Nighttime fell early in the valley, often finding us warding off the competition of thousands of fireflies. Immediately after dinner everyone retired to the parlor for card games. After the card tables were set up, the parlor became the site of lively competition. The youngest children played "Old Maid" or "Rook," but by the time they reached the age of eight, they were placed at Bridge tables, with Eli Culbertson breathing down their necks. Bridge was Mamaw's game of games. She was an expert player and the receiver of remarkable hands. She became our tutor at early ages - with very strict rules.

A vivid memory remains of this extraordinary woman who gave individual time to her grandchildren. It seemed her purpose was to encourage us in our own ways and to help us excel at them. Immediately after lunch, those of us old enough to skip naps were invited one by one into her parlor where she closed the big sliding doors for privacy. This room became the sanctuary to unburden one's soul. If our moods were sullen, Mamaw would sit at her piano striking chords of doom until we fell to the floor in laughter. Other times we devoted ourselves to truth sessions to relieve our tensions.

—————————— ❧ ❧ ——————————

Saturday nights were "prime time" at Riverby Place. It was set aside for Talent Night All day there was an ambience of show business going on - setting up the outdoor stage, trying on costumes, and rehearsing. Everyone was expected to perform with an act, even the babies. I smile to remember two-year-old Sonny Hudson dressed as Charlie Chaplin with moustache and cane. His wobbly gait brought on hysterical laughter.

With us older children, Talent Night was serious business for competition ran high. We were out to do our best Two costume bags stuffed with discarded loot were at the ready. Mamaw's riding habit was among the lot as were Prudence Gill's long black lace mitts. Bits of silks and velvets added glamour to one's choice, as did a few tarnished bits of jewelry.

To the side of the house lay a gentle knoll which formed our stage. A huge and spreading cedar tree was the backdrop. A small grove of dogwood trees provided a dressing room of some privacy. A bonfire was set up near the stage nestled in a pile of rocks for safety. We kept its woodpile up during the week Before showtime, each child provided his own long stick for marshmallow roasting in the live embers. Apple cider was set out in jugs beside a mountain basket filled with apples which glowed in the firelight

The porch chairs were brought down to form a circle around the fire. These were for grown-ups only. Until our turns came about, the children sat on blankets to enjoy a full view of the "stage."

One Talent Night shall remain with me through infamy. It was our very first one, and I must have been going on fourteen. Entranced by a review on the dancer Isadora Duncan, I became her most avid fan. For days I had studied the article about her in the "Mentor Magazine" where she was posed in gossamer veils in Greek attitudes. This kinship of spirit directed me to show off my terpsichorean interest on Talent Night

My choice was a poor one for my two beautiful and older cousins, Hy and La, were going to perform a dancing duet from their instructor back in High Point. Instead of costuming themselves from the ragbags, they had brought along Tarleton tutus.

Despite my utter lack of training, I confided in Mamaw of my great desire to dance in the Duncan genre. Perhaps alarmed over my choice, she suggested immediate rehearsals on my part Working hard in the seclusion of the parlor, she supported my made-up dance routine with her rendition of "Anitra's Dance" from the Pere Gynt Suite. I think she secretly enjoyed these sessions and I recall the deep choppy chords which accompanied my starts and stops. Caught up in the music I let myself go in abandoned choreography, which found me in less than graceful attitudes. As a conclusion I had my heart set on a dizzying twirl followed by a collapse to the floor in artistic supplication.

After rifling through the costume bags, I came across two chiffon scarfs and a net curtain. After draping myself and after a quick glance in the mirror, I decided my act was ready for an audience.

Music for Talent Night depended on an old crank style Victrola. Like magic, Mamaw had found a record of Pere Gynt Suite in her friend Mrs. Hunter's collection. It was lent to us - and, oh delight - it was full orchestra!

Everything looked promising for show night until I learned that my brother Harold had been appointed the "soundman." This caused unease on my part.

A full moon came across the sky that night as the hounds wailed through the valley. Our collies took up their call of loneliness until they were quieted. My act was soon to follow. My eighty-pound frame shook with fright as I hid behind a clump of arborvitae. Patting my Dutch bob into place, I steadied myself for the first bars of Anitra's Dance. With a loud squawk, the Victrola went into action, and I plunged myself onstage. For a moment I hesitated in classic pose before going into the dance routine. My veils were floating with the breezes when Harold's voice overlaid the music. "Ladies and gentlemen," he intoned, "introducing Wild Mag the Trapper's Bride!"

Of course, this brought the house down and me with it I left the stage humiliated to the core. Back again behind the bushes I refused all overtures to continue my dance. Instead, I sat there planning how to get back at Judas - my own brother - and I did four years later. And now, with a step ahead in time, I shall tell you of my revenge.

Harold, by then, was a student at the University of Arkansas and a member of the Kappa Alpha Fraternity. He was more than caught up in collegiate affairs. Quite full of himself, he called Mother long distance one night to ask if he might bring a "brother" home for the weekend. "He is a great person, Mother, running for the President of the Student Body, and Captain of the tennis team. In fact, he is the 'Man of the Hour.'"

Of course, Mother said "certainly" as she would have had Harold said he was bringing "Jack the Ripper' home for the weekend. The house underwent a thorough cleaning in preparation for Harold's distinguished guest. A turkey was stuffed and baked, shortcake made, and our Studebaker touring car polished. It was parked out front of the house shining in chromium splendor for the "bachelor pursuits" Mother had envisioned.

Now, a few years had passed since my Duncan days, adding a few pounds in needed places on my slim frame. In that I was sixteen years old, Mother allowed silk stockings and a touch of Tangee lipstick on my pouting lips. Wanting to look my best, I slipped into my red dress with flirty flounces, and made a dash for the dining room.

Arriving a minute late, I was out of breath with heaving chest when I sat down. This caused Mother to frown - a signal to calm myself. I did so by keeping my eyes glued to my plate. When I did take a look, across from me sat the "Man of the Hour" and looking every inch of it.

The conversation during dinner was all about the Kappa Alpha fraternity and its merits. This brought on an occasional clearing of my father's throat for he had visited the chapter house one weekend. It seemed every time I looked up the M.O.T.H. was staring at me. As the meal progressed his interest in me became obvious. Right then and there over Mother's strawberry shortcake he asked permission to invite me to the Homecoming Weekend. This greatly anticipated event was why in the first place anyone ever wanted to attend college. No one short of Ginger Rogers or Lana Turner was ever asked as a date! Whoever rated an invitation was expected to be "drop dead" material.

Color rose to Mother's face as she considered his request: "Why I think your invitation is lovely, and it will be a nice experience for Mabel - yes, I shall consider it" Harold was stunned into silence. When he pushed back his plate of partially eaten shortcake, we knew he felt sick.

The weekend sped by with a silent Harold at the wheel of the Studebaker as he drove M.O.T.H. and me about town. It was a whirl for me, but a big bore for Harold. The moral of this story is that "Wild Mags" can grow up and enjoy revenge. I did attend the Homecoming Weekend and had a glorious time with the stag line. M.O.T.H. saw to that - and he did bring about a close relationship between Harold and me for the rest of our lives. I was no longer a kid sister, but a member of Harold's peer group.

---

Back at Riverby four years earlier, Grandie's garden thrived in startling production. He had a specimen harvest of wide variety. Two Jersey cows were now grazing in the meadow and below the barn he had set up a pigsty. The latter was abolished soon after Jeffie learned of it. Also, under Grandie's providence was a storehouse on the back porch where staples were kept under lock and key. It reeked of flour, molasses, salt, dried fruit, smoked hams, and bacon. Of course, there were other mingling odors escaping its keyhole depending on what the Asheville wholesale market had to offer. Across from the old cistern, which had been sealed off for safety, stood an elaborate old cider press. To its side was the creamery department where rich Jersey milk was churned into pounds of sweet butter.

Grandie's keys rattled and clanked as he attended to business - like a sommelier, he was in charge of supplies. Very often the rattle of his keys was a Godsend, for one had time to duck out of his path.

Providing food for this household was no simple matter - counting his children, grandchildren, and visiting friends, we were at least twenty at the table very often more than that. The family alone remained at Riverby for three months during the summer, and on occasion, extended their visits. I can only remember my grandfather as a provider extraordinaire, a shepherd tending his flocks.

I can also remember the twinkle in his one good eye so often missed by some, He was a quiet man except on cold rainy mornings when he would rout everyone out of bed in the dark with: "Time to get up! Rise and shine!" Moans could be heard down the hall as he rapped on bedroom doors.

Frank Blanks suffered no fools, and certainly stood for none in his household.

If a grandchild was "uppity," a thump on his head sent him spinning. Meals were expected to be on time, and he was tight with his cash.

Meals were always looked forward to at Riverby Place for everyone was starved from the cool mountain air. The large brass handbell first gave a warning ring. Ten minutes later it meant business. It could be heard for miles around and we gathered from all directions. The children were expected to be washed and neat before entering the room for grace.

We erred on this rule once when the Swannanoa River was in flood stage. An all-night deluge had left the river with plunging currents churning over the boulders. We were ecstatic with our water sport of jumping in upriver and being tossed about in the maelstrom. As dangerous as it was, for some reason we were allowed to risk life and limb that day. As we shot into the madness, we entered a curve that sent us bobbing like corks down new made currents. Gasping for breath in the icy waters, we felt as though we were special gifts carried downstream to the Atlantic Ocean.

Being loathe to leave the exhilaration of that day we ran late for the lunch bell. Our bodies were skinned and bruised, and our hair uncombed. Soaking wet we were dripping in the rags left from our bathing suits. Without thinking we slipped into the dining room. Grandie pushed back his chair at the head of the table and ordered us to line up against the wall where he gave each of us a sound thump on the head. We were then sent to our rooms to think things over. We left the room in disgrace, but it was the sight of Ora's hot biscuits going to waste that hurt us the most. To this day, however, most of us have a penchant for being on time.

———————————— ❧ ❦ ————————————

After the storm episode, Grandie read in the Asheville Citizen about a child drowned while swimming in a river. He created a beach for us, hoping to calm our activities. Having enjoyed a "swimming hole" as a boy in Tennessee, he blasted a part of the river upstream. After clearing away a few trees and underbrush, several loads of sand were spread on the embankment. At first, we enjoyed sunbathing and a cool dip, but after the novelty wore off, we were back in the currents again. We prayed for rain so we could swim on the wild side.

The river was our summer life from dawn to dusk, and what a miracle it was that we suffered no injuries. There were no broken bones or snakebites from all the climbing over rocks and scaling trees. We did suffer through bouts of poison ivy and bee stings. Running barefoot most of the time, our minor injuries dealt with cuts and stone bruises.

We led a happy and healthful life - plenty of exercise with a wide range of fresh produce to eat. Ora's crusty hot biscuits encouraged the use of fresh churned butter and mountain honey. Another great favorite was Mamaw's tureen of chicken and dumplings, which was served with carrots and baby peas. When the corn came in, it was center stage piled high on platters. Ora's fruit cobblers, made from our apples, cherries, and the juicy blackberries picked by the gallon on the country road, completed our feasts. Jersey clotted cream was passed for dolloping on these delicacies.

The ebony sideboard filled one side of the dining room. Like a great ship bedecked for a cruise, its shelves boasted pound cakes, coconut cakes, and our favorite, jam cake. The sideboard's gingerbread ornament hid secret drawers and a linen press. In passing, one noticed it was marked with age and the good smells of a life well-lived.

On very special occasions we made ice cream in a vast old freezer. It was quite a job turning the crank, for it held the weight of two gallons. Lotus cream was handed down from Prudence Hopper's cookbook. A Virginia delicacy, it was filled with egg yolks, heavy cream, sugar and lemon juice - manna from heaven.

We were not allowed to drink coffee, but we did so by a sneak arrangement of following Grandie's early cups left on the stove. He was generous in his brewing, leaving the big pot half full. We discovered this resource at the time he leased out the barn to a construction crew. They were building the large blanket factory in the village of Swannanoa and needed somewhere to store their equipment and mules. In making friends with the hostler, we were allowed to ride the mules to the construction site. Of course, for this we had to be up at the crack of dawn. But, considering this exciting equestrian sport, we rose from our warm beds to enjoy it. Grandie's leftover coffee opened our eyes for the ride.

After meeting the early train for the mail and newspapers, we returned home by the country road following the river. That put us back just in time to join the others at breakfast Norma had invented her own brand of cereal made from roasted cornmeal. It was hearty and tasty. After a steaming bowl of this mush slaved with cream, we partook of scrambled eggs, escalloped apples, and bacon. Again, Ora's biscuits filled in with selections of jams and jellies. There was plenty of milk to  drink, but from time to time we were served sassafras tea as a tonic. Thus, we were fortified for our long wait until lunchtime.

———————————— ❧ ❧ ————————————

Mamaw was a night owl. Grandie was a lark. After dinner when the card tables were being set up Grandie always left our company for bed. Mamaw, on the other hand, was the last one to retire. She made her rounds every night to see if everyone was tucked in and that the fires had been banked. She slept late in the mornings with her head done up in a turban to keep out the noise. She never ate breakfast with us.

It was the habit of the Blanks sisters to retire for naps following lunch. This rest period took place in a first-floor bedroom reserved for the ritual. It was a spacious room with two double beds and a private bath. Here they would talk, laugh a lot, and finally doze off. It was also the setting for playing "beauty parlor." With the help of us teenagers, facials were given and strange coiffures. Once in a while their cousin, Jeff Newbill, would come in from Asheville to add to the hen party. Jeff was a woman of the world, dressed to the nines, with a reservoir of naughty tales. The young were often exited from the room, leaving the Blanks sisters and their cousin laved with cold cream around their wide eyes.

During this period, Riverby Place was quiet with the little children napping. The older children always sought Mamaw out who took her siesta in a big rocking chair on the shady porch. She always settled herself with handwork.

One afternoon in this setting, Grandie was dozing at the far end of the porch. His favorite straight chair was propped at an angle, and his derby hat tilted to shade his face. Leon, our winsome cousin, and full of the devil, was seen slithering across the porch toward Grandie. We held our breaths as to what he was up to. We watched as he very slowly unhooked a key from our grandfather's big keychain. Shivers shot down our spines over the risk he was taking. Finally, with a grin Leon held the loose key high over his head and beckoned for us to follow. Very quietly we all slipped off the porch and tailed Leon toward the back of the house. He was headed for the storeroom.

A few nights before we had discussed putting on a midnight feast with the storehouse supplies as our goals Working in haste Leon unlatched the door in a big squeak. Grandie stirred in his sleep. When we were breathing again, we tiptoed into the treasure trove and started looting the shelves - peanut butter jars, crackers, sardine cans, pecans, and dried fruits. We then made a quick getaway.

Basking in our success we gave no thought to the storehouse key Leon had pocketed. The feast went on at midnight with loud whispers, giggles, and noshing. The next morning when we went in for breakfast, Grandie was blocking the door with outstretched palms. Without a word Leon dropped the key into his hand. As a reaction, Grandie's palm became a hard fist Everyone was silent during breakfast. The quietness was ominous. Still nothing was said. However, the light dawned by noontime, for there were no cakes set out on the sideboard - a void which lasted for a solid week. What joy we felt when once again the sideboard displayed its riches.

— ❧ ❧ —

A most poignant Grandie story deals with the birth of a calf. Bessie, one of the Jerseys, had been missing for several days in her part of the meadow. Out of the blue Grandie stood up at dinner to make an announcement.

"Under no circumstances," he told us, were we to visit the barn and disturb Bessie. She was expected at any time to deliver her calf. This was the first time we had heard of the blessed event.

"I will be going to the barn in a few minutes to help Bessie bring her baby into the world, and she must not be frightened or distracted while I do so." With this ultimatum Grandie left the dining room and started down the hill toward the barn. Dusk was just settling, and he carried a lantern held high over his head. Once he looked back at the house and shook his head. Like a safari, the grandchildren were following him quietly as mice. The troop was made up of children from various age groups - the tiny tots were in their sleepers. On reaching the barn we silently climbed the ladder looking to the hayloft and stretched out in the straw. On our stomachs we had a clear view of a restless Bessie thrashing about in her stall Grandie had hung his lantern high on a post beside her.

We watched as Grandie rolled his sleeves up to his armpits, then scrubbed them down in a bucket of water. The scent of Octagon soap floated up to us, as he carefully dried his arms and hands on a clean towel. The younger children fell asleep during our long vigil, but the rest of us waited out the time with our grandfather. Suddenly, Bessie began to bawl and raised her weight to a standing position. We watched as Grandie inserted one arm inside the cow, quickly followed by his other one. With great strength he pulled out a neat little package shedding its wrappings. We saw wiggling - then a tiny cry reached our ears. Smiling from ear to ear, and playing to the gallery, Grandie held the newborn calf high over his head for our inspection. It was beautiful. It was adorable. Returning the calf quickly back to Bessie, we watched as she licked off and nursed her pretty bull. While this was going on Frank Blanks finished his duties in animal husbandry then washed himself off and rolled down his sleeves. Picking up the lantern he led the way back up the hill for his followers, as the Pied Piper of Hamlin. The miracle of that birth in the night was an unforgettable experience for all of us. It was also a gift from our grandfather.

—————————————— ❧ ❧ ——————————————

By our third summer at Riverby, we had come to know our neighbors and to show interest in community affairs. Jeffie felt that the time had come to host a fund-raising event for the benefit of Buncombe County. She gathered her daughters about her to make plans. An auction sale was decided upon to benefit the depressed conditions of the mountaineers living high above us in the Great Smoky range. Many were at the point of starving, living in rags and ignorance.

Once the auction idea was launched, everyone went into action. The spacious dining room would be used along with chairs borrowed from the churches. The entire community was to collect goods to be auctioned off - and they did. Piles of crafts were brought in: baskets, hooked rugs, quilts, handwoven yardage from the woolen weavers, jars of home-canned pickles, pottery, naive paintings from the art colonies and even a coonhound puppy. With weekly announcements from the church pulpits, enthusiasm ran high.

As the date neared, plans were made for simple refreshments, and the big sideboard was cleared for display purposes. It was during this time Mamaw put forth the idea of a wonderful door prize - Riverby's gift to the effort. It should be a generous one, in fact eye catching - or even mouthwatering, she said. With these factors there was no need to look further. It should be a huge mountain woven basket filled with the bounty of Grandie's garden!

This proved to be the most difficult task of the entire affair, for a ruse had to be set up to gain entry into Grandie's horn of plenty.

"Now Papa," the Major General cleared her throat, "the time has come for us to prepare for the winter. Yes, we need to put up a few jars of fruit and vegetables. It is canning time."

This preparation for the lean months ahead caught Grandie's fancy and he rather reluctantly turned over his keys to his daughter. Racing through the garden, the sisters went berserk in choosing the finest specimens on vine and bush. Variety was important for their masterpiece; nothing was overlooked by -these blue-ribbon winners of Garden Clubs.

By late afternoon the masterpiece was finished filling a vast handmade clothes hamper. Displayed at a tilt in front of the black sideboard, the Dutch master painter, Ambrosius Bosschaert the Elder, would have been pleased with the Blanks sisters' work.

The auction went off with heartwarming success with lively bidding and money rolling in. Everyone seemed to enjoy himself. Even Grandie who was feeling his oats playing the host was smiling. When asked to draw the number for the door prize, Grandie stepped forward with panache. Using his derby hat for the ticket stubs, he stirred and shook the receipts vigorously. People leaned forward in their seats, for everyone had an eye out or the great bonanza. Charles and Leon struggled under the basket's weight as they carried it around the room for better viewing. It then came to rest at Brandies feet for the breathless moment of drawing.

Grandie withdrew a stub from his hat and called out the number. There was no response. Not a soul answered. After this embarrassing pause Mamaw called out, "Frank, did you draw a number?" Reaching into his watch pocket Grandie pulled out a ticket and read off the number. It matched the one in his other hand. Frank Blanks had won his own door prize!

After the laughter died down, and another number was drawn, Grandie became apprised of his garden betrayal. The next morning the kitchen was piled with produce. As he entered bringing in even more supplies he announced sarcastically to the room, "It's canning time and I expect these shelves to be filled with jars by the end of the week."

Many events took place in Riverby's early days. The older children were entering their teens and new babies were arriving. Distant cousins came to visit along with close friends. As we grew older our interests changed, bringing on day trips to Chimney Rock, Montreat, Old Craggy and Mount Mitchell. And there were our shopping trips to Asheville.

A typical Asheville day meant a visit to the Bon Marche department store for sewing materials for our handwork - then to a bookstore to buy stationery supplies. After a wonderful lunch at the S&W Cafeteria, we would walk over to Pack Square to attend a matinee. Once we saw Douglas Fairbanks in "The Black Pirates" His daring-do acrobatics brought on similar attempts when we arrived home My major highlight on an Asheville trip was attending a production of the Dennis-Shawn Dancers. I loved the "Blue Danube" number, when the corp de ballet was undulating under a huge blue silk covered stage. As the music rose the dancers revealed themselves one by one until they caught up the beautiful cloth and sailed it to the ceiling. There it billowed, as we gasped in wonder.

Ted Shawn was an idol for teenagers. Dressed as a young Indian chief with a headdress that touched the floor, his oiled muscles flexed and glistened in the fast lights. He was a handsome young man with a superb physique. That afternoon I gave serious thought to taking off for "Jacob's Pillow."

With the matinees over we would meet Aunt Lola at her parked Franklin. (This car was renewed every two years, but always in the same chocolate brown color). Our last stop was to pick up Grandie at the wholesale market - we usually found him standing knee deep in cartons of foodstuffs.

We always enjoyed our trips to Asheville, but were ready for home when the time came. We knew the "left behinds" would be waiting to hear about our day of adventures. As the Franklin made its way up Riverby's drive, the children would be waiting to hop onto the running boards or cling to the spare tire on the back. When the car came to a stop for unloading, eager hands reached for the hard candy we threw out as consolation prizes.

# Riverby Inn

(Excerpted from Chapter 12, Part II)

The increasing number of grandchildren and constant flow of houseguests began to bring financial stress to Riverby Place. An aging Jeffie and Frank began to feel their years and deserved, we thought, winters in a softer climate. Such respite was found in Lake Wales, Florida, where, with the sun at their backs, they could enjoy the concerts of the Bok Tower. When all factors were taken into account, it seemed urgent to plan for the survival of our grandparents, and for that of our summer place, Riverby. A family conference was called, the fruition of which was the idea to convert the spacious house into an inn. And so, with thought and some regret, Riverby Place became Riverby Inn.

The splendid new highways weaving across western North Carolina opened up scenic wonders to streams of motorists who came to take in the mountain air. The route from Asheville to Mount Mitchell went through Black Mountain and circumscribed the Riverby property. With Pisgah National Forest, the Vanderbilt Estate, Chimney Rock and various other landmarks within easy reach, the success of Riverby as an inn seemed assured. The future looked rosy.

Giddy with excitement over the transformation, the Blanks sisters plunged headlong into plans. As a stepping stone they renovated an old building at the rear of the house as a Tea Room. Perched over the ravine, its wide screened porch offered full purchase to the tumbling river below. After fresh paint and a few minor changes, small tables were set up to be "napped" in pastel linens. Each morning a cadre of children was sent out to collect wild flowers for the centerpieces. These trips into the fields and along the country road brought back a charming variety—yellow orchids, chiggerweed, daisies, and ferns. Queen Anne's Lace was always available from the front meadow. Keeping the bouquets fresh was always a chore, for wild flowers wilt very quickly - and it fell to me to see to them.

Time and stress went into the menu planning for artistic variety was the Tea Room coda. One specialty was a salad plate in which a cucumber canoe floated amid nasturtium leaves resembling lily pads. The canoe carried a cargo of herbage tossed with a piquant salad dressing. Several nasturtium blossoms completed the picture in case the hungry were brave enough to eat them. There were other innovative attempts at haute cuisine which left my poor mother with trembling fingers as she arranged the displays. Norma was her helper behind the scenes in this steamy atmosphere of anxiety.

My two pretty cousins, Hy and La, were the reluctant but designated waitresses decked out in pastel uniforms from their father's factory back in High Point. To de-commercialize the standard effect, organdy aprons were matched up to the pastel colors, with a crisp bowknot over their derrieres.

The Major General was self-appointed as maître d'hôtel greeting the guests and passing on orders. Beck, who seemed to remain in a constant of pregnancy, was spared heavy duties. She was responsible for writing out the daily menus. Her backhand script was distinguished, but lacked in spelling dependability. The Major General served as the editor.

Mose, the houseman, was called from the Inn to fill in on missions of procurement and to help wash the dishes. It was soon discovered the Tea Room was overstaffed for its patronage.

Just before the grand opening, the beloved old sign of "Riverby Place" came down to make room for the new one of "Riverby Inn." The sign had been commissioned at Black Mountain College where craftsmen met in summer sessions. It contained a silhouette stagecoach travelling with urgency toward the entrance of Riverby. Rather foreboding, the stagecoach looked as if it had just made a hasty escape from the pages of "Wuthering Heights", Directly below the new sign was another jingling out:

Figure 26: Riverby Inn Sign

"Stop in and Rest at the Robin's Nest Tea Room"

On opening day, a car pulled up from the state of New Jersey. It was transporting a group of noisy women in search of a "light lunch." The Tea Room staff was thrown into a panic of preparation. After being seated cordially by the Major General, the women ordered cocktails which were not to be forthcoming. To cover their thirst, they whipped out cigarette holders and began to smoke. The two waitresses stood stiff in their tracks, for they had only seen such brazen behavior in John Held drawings. As billows of smoke floated through the screens, the cries of the wildlife below could be heard scattering in alarm.

The Major General was also frozen in her tracks with her eyes glued on the diners. Without turning she snapped her fingers behind her back for immediate service. The orders were filled with uncommon speed. Just as soon the check was settled the group made a hasty exit. "Southern hospitality" must have been their topic en route home.

As the days wore on there was little attendance for meals in the Tea Room. It soon became obvious that no one really wished to "stop in and rest at a Robin's Nest." The painterly vision of the Blanks sisters came to a sad and unprofitable end.

In the meantime, the Inn itself was bursting at the seams with overnight tourists. The wide veranda overlooking the valley was irresistible as it lured automobiles into the driveway. Once near the house, the tantalizing odors from Ora's kitchen assured registration.

It became evident that extra bedroom space would increase profits. Someone came up with the concept of converting the Tea Room into a teenage dormitory. After a hasty trip into Asheville for cots and blankets, the deed was done. The screened in porch took on a new look which was that of a tuberculosis sanitorium at Sarnac Lakes. It was into this bleak setting the teenagers were displaced - boys at one end and girls at the other.

After giving up our snug rooms in the big house we nearly froze to death sleeping in the open. The river's icy drafts crept in around us. These icy currents also carried strange night noises, which were terrifying. Comfort was sought from whispering to each other throughout the night. Assurance was high on our list. It was on such a night that the grizzly bear visited Riverby.

Just before dawn we heard sniffing sounds about our screens. Holding our breaths for an eternity, loud noises finally came to us from the big house. The porch chairs were being tumbled about and a fearful odor followed the commotion - a feral one. Sitting straight up in our cots we shook in terror. It soon became urgent for us to assess our peril, by wrapping ourselves in blankets and looking outside the Inn.

To our enormous relief, there, in the first light of day, stood Grandie taking aim at the biggest bear ever. With shotgun in position he hesitated before pulling the trigger. The bear stood up on its hind legs and pawed the air with great claws. Snarling at our grandfather, the animal exposed cuspid teeth of mean size. Having heard tales of how difficult it is to kill a bear; we were horrified over Grandie's safety.

Frank Blanks, the protector of his domain, cut quite a figure in his bravery. Dressed in the habit of his sleep, he wore baggy white long johns and enormous carpet slippers. His Derby hat was tilted over his blind eye. The volley from his shot shook the valley in waves like thunder. After the blast we opened our eyes expecting the bear to be flat on the ground. Instead, we saw it disappear though the bushes leading to the river. Feeling let down that Grandie did not take out in hot pursuit, he later told us to never follow a wounded bear. The next day we found pools of blood along the riverbank. In the village a rumor spread that a dead bear had been found up river with its face blown off.

Of course, Frank Blanks was furious over not finishing the intruder off with panache, but he seemed even angrier at the absence of our two guard dogs, Jack and Binx. "Out night owling after Mr. Penland's ugly old hound bitch!" he spat out. Our sleepless nights in the Tea Room became chronic after the bear's visit.

Before explaining about Jack and Binx, I must report that our two beautiful white Collies left our world within weeks of each other. They were delicate from inbreeding and unable to stand the rigors of mountain life. To console our loss, we pictured them in the great meadow of the sky romping about in Queen Anne's Lace for we felt Heaven would have it so.

In their stead two strange dogs came our way - Jack and Binx, neither of whom had a family tree. Jack just wandered in one day looking the worse for wear. He was of such appearance tracing his lineage was impossible. The dog's white coat was covered in black and liver colored spots which afforded him complete camouflage when resting in sunlight and shadow. Guests were often startled on autumn strolls, when he would rear up from a pile of leaves underfoot

Binx was passed on to us as perhaps partial payment on the tiny apartment attached to the Tea Room. It had been occupied for some weeks by "Miss Dolly" and her ailing husband, a middle-aged couple down on their luck whom Jeffie had given food and shelter. One night they left Riverby never to be heard from again. They packed up all their belongings except for Binx and drove off into the night Jeffie always considered Binx payment in full.

Binx was a big fellow of shaggy hair which might have served him well as a sheep dog on the Yorkshire Borders. He ranged the property returning home with his matted hair filled with ticks and cockleburs. By the silly grin on his face we knew he must be part Retriever.

There was nothing in common between these two animals except the fact that they both belonged to the canine breed and that they hated each other. The slightest provocation would incite bloody battles between them. Their lethal fights were almost impossible to break up. Buckets of water were thrown against their fury, and often golf clubs or croquet mallets were put into use. Nothing worked.  After exhausting themselves, they would limp from their battleground and seek refuge under the porch.

As individuals they were loyal mascots, especially on our hiking trips up the mountain. They protected us from rattlesnakes and skunks - running ahead and barking incessantly.

---

After being ousted from our snug rooms, we came to enjoy the independence of sleeping in our drafty Tea Room. We even forgave our interlopers, the Riverby guests, for causing it all. The worst, however, was yet to come when the dining room rules were changed.

Because of the crowds, two seatings were necessary at meal time. The family was served first while the sun was still high in the sky. The guests enjoyed a later seating. Furthermore, we discovered a discrepancy in the menus. Once when finishing our chicken hash, we saw large platters of roast beef and Yorkshire pudding being served up for the guests. It took a longer time for us to forgive this act of inequality.

The evening card games underwent noticeable improvements for several of our visitors were "masters." Jeffie was in her heyday and left off her teaching sessions with us children. This came as a great relief for most of us played our cards without thinking and hated the rules.

Talent nights improved remarkably - to the point of posing a threat to Broadway. Gifted actors and singers emerged from the Riverby ledger. We even dared a male quartet and a struggling chorus line. A few of these people became so caught up in the Inn's activities that reservations were extended. The Morrisons from Cajun country forgot Louisiana and remained for the entire summer. They extended their reservations for several coming years. Bob was the overseer for "Clovely Plantation," a large British Spread in the nation's Sugar Cane Bayous. Doris, his wife, was a charming woman, as were their three pretty little girls. They felt they belonged to Riverby and we felt they belonged to us.

We dreaded departure time. Parents would find themselves forced to drag their children to their cars kicking and screaming in emotional goodbyes. They would finally pack them in along with the luggage. No one wanted to go home. We all shed tears at the sight of forlorn little faces staring from back car windows as they slipped out of the driveway. When they disappeared around Alexander Mountain, we felt the busy hive of Riverby was left with empty cells.

A significant change took place when Aunt Lola, the Major General, erected a guest cottage on the grounds. This was for her husband, Homer Hudson, whom we called "Huddy." Homer was a spoiled and difficult man who demanded every attention in his successful financial life. Everyone and everything made him nervous which resulted in a constant clearing of his throat. In his palatial house back in High Point, separate quarters were set up for him away from his family. The informality at Riverby Inn almost finished him off. His visits there became less frequent - and more prolonged. Lola, his doting wife, realized she must take action especially in the interest of their little son, whom we called "Sonny." Born late in his parents' lives, and with two teenaged sisters, this little fellow lived as a grown-up and spoke as one. Lola, in a great effort, sought to develop a closer relationship with him and his father.

To Lola's great relief the new cottage brought Huddy around. Tucked back near the river, it was some distance from the Inn. Quite private, it might have served well as a CIA safehouse since its only company were the bullfrogs thrumping in the river. In time, Huddy emerged for a little social exchange at the Inn, where he met fellow golfers. Arranging games at the Grove Park Inn, the foursomes arose early each week for their eighteen holes. Huddy was impressive in his plus fours, cap and argyle socks. A tall man, he carried his clothes well. In the meantime, little Sonny shared a project they developed together. It was called the "B-Nanny" a small self-propelled car which gave Sonny great pleasure.

With financial success in his pockets, Huddy, with his brother Charlie, was testing the market with their "bibless" overalls. Made of durable denim, it was destined to become a public sensation. They did very well with their factory orders; however, it was the California firm owned by Levi Strauss that cornered the market with the product called "blue jeans" or "Levi's."

One weekend in generous spirit, Huddy arrived with his Franklin car laden with bolts of cloth - an excess inventory from his factory. Everyone was delighted with such a bonanza. The sisters immediately started converting the goods into slip covers and bed spreads. Having a nice choice in colors, they overlooked a bolt of homely "tobacco cloth" which went unspoken for. I requested a few yards to "work with." After a time at the Lake Eden Camp for Girls with Hy and La, I was chosen to move on up in the world by attending the Scholar Gypsy Camp. Perched high on a mountaintop it encouraged the arts. In this rarefied atmosphere outstanding professors from Eastern schools held classes in their own fields of commitment. In belonging to the Scholar Gypsy thesis, one became a different being, and I shall be forever grateful for the generosity of my sponsor, E. W. Grove, the founder. Here one could explore the garden of the mind while indulging in a celebration of life. To me, it was the best possible of all worlds when I was fifteen.

Our days began at sunrise where we met on the dance platform extending over Lake Eden below. The stillness of the hour left the lake a mirror reflecting the mountains about it. The setting was exhilarating and one was moved to dance. Our instructors assigned themes to follow such as "seaweed swaying under water," "a bird in flight," "tides crashing against the shore" - and once, "dodging taxis on Rue de le Prix." Dressed only in gossamer shifts, we were free to transport ourselves. After most of the summer had passed, we learned something else. Our maneuvers had stirred the carnal instincts of the boys' camp below us. They watched us through binoculars and bet on favorites.

Following dancing we returned to the main studio for breakfast, a cheerful time. Dressed by then in Scholar Gypsy garments, we were ready to pursue the arts of our interest These costumes were tattered and torn, both tops and bottoms, with leaf impressions transferred from leaving them out in all sorts of weather. They were very high fashion, but extremely comfortable for most activities. In two pieces, the pants came to the knee, with a tabard worn at the top - perfect for life in the woods where we painted, composed, and day dreamed. I loved my life at the Scholar Gypsy and longed to pass some of it on to the children at Riverby Inn. That is why I needed the unclaimed tobacco cloth.

Hy and La helped me cut and shape the vagabond suits. We ragged the hems and left them to weather on the river rocks. Using sweet gum leaves as transfers, our results were sensational. We dressed boys and girls alike - all resembling poverty-stricken Peter Pans. Our hearts were wrung by the youngest children who as little urchins might have stepped on stage in Les Miserables. Shoes were impossible with these costumes, thus all went barefoot That is, until Charles and Leon invented flippers made from cast off inner tubes.

These creations flopped with every step. Cut much longer than the foot, they were a challenge to the wearer in climbing steps. To do so, the toes were pointed outward in a blue footed fashion giving the impression that the wearer was not all there.

Riverby Inn was at its peak season. The busy mothers were frantic for time, thus leaving the care of little ones to teenagers. Parental care was missing. All went well until the day we took the vagabonds to visit the turtle cave. This was a secret place across the country road looking out over the Penland cornfield. Our wonderful discovery was hidden in an embankment secluded by a dense grove of sumac trees. Here, a prolific family of orange spotted turtles resided. As we played with the turtles, we heard the double-engined freight train struggling around Bear Mountain on the far side of the cornfield. As the train labored up-grade with its heavy load, it suddenly whistled in alarm. This brought us out of hiding just in time to see the train roll backwards and derail into Mr. Penland's cornfield. Boxcars were on their sides and in numbers. Flippers and all, we dashed through the cornrows with the humane mission of saving anyone who might be injured. Instead, we found a cargo of golden-brown tobacco leaves surrounding us.

"Finders keepers - losers weepers" was the chant as we gathered up armloads of rich cured tobacco fronds. Afraid of being caught, we made a hasty retreat back to the cave.

Turtle racing was put aside as we established a tobacco factory. When stacks of rolled up cheroots had exhausted our supply, we sat back to contemplate what to do next. Try them out, of course. Leon, our hotspur, made a mad dash to the house for matches.

The little children watched as we sat puffing away crouched like Indians. The ceremony was short lived, for we began to turn green. Crawling out of the cave we barely made it to our Tea Room cots. A horrified Mother and Norma stuck their heads into the sick bay. La rallied long enough to assure them we had only eaten green apples. They left believing her lie.

After a few hours our stomach problems were over, but a crueler fate awaited us during the night We awoke with frantic itching and water blisters all 30ver our bodies. Dr. Krutcher had to be called from Black Mountain to attend to us. He diagnosed our ordeal as severe poison ivy exposure. The poor man had no way of knowing that our afternoon had been spent in a verdant nest of poison sumac. After smearing us with Octagon soap and calamine lotion, Dr. Krutcher suggested we remain dressed as we were until our vagabond suits could be burned. With that, he left us writhing on our cots in agony.

The Fields boys were in the worst shape. Their heads were swollen double in size and their eyes were only slits. Hearing of our condition, the Major General came by. Covering her eyes in horror she issued strict orders that we were to stay away from the Inn so the guests could not see us. As we looked from cot to cot we understood perfectly. It was undeniable that we resembled the worst cases in the leper colony of Carville, Louisiana.

Feeling some better the next day, we found the tedium of confinement too hard to take. Some of us were pacing the floor when Charles, peering out the window, said, "Gee whiz. Look at that limousine in the driveway!" As though he had discovered gold, we raced to see for ourselves. It was true. A beautiful dark green Pierce-Arrow car had arrived. The temptation was too great After assuring ourselves that no mention had been made as to staying off the grounds, we crept out the door falling into a Marine landing routine. With quick darts behind bushes we made -it one by one to the arborvitae bushes -flanking the driveway' There we concealed ourselves behind safe foliage.

It was a beautiful automobile - spoke wheels, and discreet chrome trimming. Peeking through the bushes we saw a liveried chauffeur at the wheel. Next to him sat a well-dressed man in a tweed coat and a matching cap. The rear seat held a beautiful woman and a tidy looking nanny. Between them sat a pale little boy straining to look out of the window.

Negotiations were underway between the gentleman and the Major General through the driver's seat Presently the chauffeur left the car and began stacking luggage in neat piles on the Riverby steps. Following his lead, the other occupants stepped out to take deep breaths of the balsam scented air. The little boy was smiling and tugging at his mother's hand when, at this juncture, Jay Fields with swollen head and slits for eyes fell headlong at their feet. The impact on the sharp gravel driveway threw him into spasms of agony. Loyal to the core, the rest of us crept out of hiding to go to his aid.

Surrounded by monsters closing in on her, the woman gasped and quickly stuffed her little boy back into the safety of the car. Her husband joined her. On signal the chauffeur began throwing luggage back into its hold with no waste of time. Jumping into the driver's seat he revved the motor to high velocity. At takeoff, the screech of tires sent gravel flying in all directions. The beautiful Pierce-Arrow lived up to its name, for it split the air in its takeoff down the driveway. This departure was the speediest one in Riverby Inn history.

This dreadful circumstance was never spoken of again, for Jay's father, Tom

Fields, was present He was an indulgent man who spared his children all possible unhappiness. Having waited so long through bachelorhood for his family, everyone respected his doting ways with good humor. Of course, we were delighted that he was on hand.

———————————— ❧ ❧ ————————————

Riverby Inn enjoyed a wide balance of visitors. Some stood out above others. One star was Philip Roach, a handsome man from New Orleans, who had a French wife and little girl called Mimi. Mrs. Roach was an emotional woman given to headaches followed by periods of malaise. There were times when she would become hysterical and keep to her room. Philip Roach kept out of her way by taking little Mimi and the rest of us on hair-raising adventures.

A bellwether, Mr. Roach was often referred to as the Pied Piper of Riverby, for an entourage of children trailed behind him. His daring do and talent for games kept us all spellbound. A treasure hunt sent our blood pounding to the bursting point There were times when he kept us very still to think of serious matters, such as "what is beyond beyond?" He would have us stretched out under the night sky taking in the galaxy. One child became so upset about hurtling into space that the subject was quickly changed to the outlandish thought of landing on the moon.

One day Mr. Roach put us to work building a putting green adjacent to the croquet court A large wasps' nest was suspended on a tree branch above the spot. To test our mettle, Mr. Roach set up a raid to knock the nest down. This was risky business, but with mission accomplished we felt quite good about ourselves. After tin cans were sunk on the putting green, he taught us how to hold our irons. It was his treasure hunts riddled with impossible clues, however, that held our interest the most

These events required preparation in planning including training sessions. We had to be in "shape" for them. This meant early bedtime the night before, which concealed the fact that Philip Roach also enjoyed a rubber of bridge every now and then.

A first aid kit, Mr. Roach insisted, must be carried on the hunt A crash course in bone setting and the dressing of gunshot wounds were other requirements. He explained that knowledge of these matters was important for we were going far afield from Riverby property. We were going to cross the highway and enter the "posted" territory belonging to Mr. Alexander, the owner of Alexander Mountain. We gasped at the thought

Because of the "risk," as he put it, we must drill in the exercise of "keeping low" Marine fashion, in case Mr. Alexander took a shot at us. Delicious thrills went up and down our spines for we had no way of knowing that Mr. Alexander was aiding and abetting the hunt.

The rocking chair group sitting on the porch was to find amusement in watching us cross the highway all hunkered up in secrecy. As we entered the "keep off property," a loud voice bellowed from the hillside: "Are you on my land? No trespassing allowed!!" This proclamation sent us flat on our stomachs until Philip Roach moved us on toward sure death. We consulted our maps for the first clue. This caught us up on the riches ahead, making us forget the threat and to get on with the romance of treasure seeking. Finally, we came to a cornstalk waving a sign which read:

A.    *Continue to keep low.*
B.    *Take 12 paces left.*
C.    *Next clue at the speckled oeufs.*

Of course, Mimi Roach was the only one present who knew what "oeufs" were. The rest of us were satisfied with the discovery of a plover's nest containing a few speckled eggs. The next clue was a gruesome looking Jolly Roger flag- dirty and torn. The raw head had a nasty leer. Thus, the hunt continued in and out of Mr. Alexander's acreage. Our backs were broken from hunching over, but it did not matter a whit We all came upon the "treasure" together for we relied on safety in numbers. The loot was a dozen new golf balls for our putting green. Everyone got a prize from the abandoned birds nest filled with round white eggs marked "Spalding." We returned home happily with our loot

In time Mrs. Roach left her seclusion to join the ladies on the porch. This gave her husband more free-time for the golf games he enjoyed. The Roaches returned to Riverby for several summers for fun and games.

——————————— ✿ ✿ ———————————

One unusually hot morning when gathered at the river, we realized we were not alone. Standing on a rock downstream was an apparition taking a bath. The currents below were foaming with suds. The figure was gaunt, and going through various postures and mannerisms we did not understand. We were mesmerized, but decided the figure was a woman because of the monologue taking place. Falsetto. Suddenly the figure became aware of being watched. Throwing a towel about the nakedness, it stepped forward with a laugh to say "hello." He introduced heinous crime.

After enjoying the hospitality of the house for some days, Jeffie decided it was time for a little "pay back." Besides, the opportunity was too great to let slip by - she asked the psychiatrist to evaluate each of her grandchildren. While Leopold and Loeb languished in their cells, Dr. M turned his craniological expertise on us.

We were taken according to age, the eldest going first We never really knew the outcome of his findings, but there were a few hints. My brother Harold was expected to be a community leader and to enjoy renown as a public speaker. Dr. M met a brick wall with Hy and La, for they were impossible to deal with. They refused to answer his questions. To satisfy his meal ticket, he told Jeffie that he expected them to marry early. As for myself, various art supplies appeared on my bed watercolor paints, reams of paper, and very sharp pencils. Interesting to report, these supplies have never left my life - they are kept in constant supply.

As far as my other cousins are concerned, time and tide seem to have erased the outcome of their evaluations. I do recall Jeffie seemed pleased with the overall results. One day an urgent long distant call came to Dr. M. He was to return to New York immediately. In a few weeks the Asheville Citizen bore headlines on the Leopold-Loeb case. The murder of little Bobby Franks had been avenged and the trial was over. We never heard from Dr. M again.

———————————— ✌ ✎ ————————————

My mother, LaVerne, was considered to be a "blue stocking." She kept up with the changing world as an avid reader which brought her to become an authority on many subjects. Etiquette and childcare caught her attention. Her specialty hovered around the right - and wrongs for young ladies, or so it seemed to me.

Her doctrines were strict at times, and often properly so. I really was not very grown up at the age of fourteen. Nature kept me in the body of a little girl and Mother dressed me accordingly. Children's Vogue was her manual, with an occasional lapse into whatever Madge Evans was wearing. Madge was a beautiful young screen star with bouncy blonde curls. The studios, trying to conceal her true age, dressed her in pleated skirts and midday blouses. She wore patent slippers with straps called "Sis Hopkins," and her straw hat had streamers down the back. I was dressed accordingly, but never really looked like Madge. My hair was in a straight Dutch bob and where Madge filled out her midday blouse, I looked flat chested and consumptive. And so it was, that I was dressed like Madge on the day we stepped off the train in Black Mountain, North Carolina. Aunt Lola and her daughters, Hy and La, were to meet us after a separation of one year. Adoring my cousins, I could scarcely wait for the good times ahead. Mother was holding her new baby, Betts, and I was tugging with four-and-a-half-year-old Bobby who knocked my hat askew, but I straightened it just in time for the reunion.

Aunt Lola was walking toward us, but the girls were not with her. After hugs and kisses we made our way to the parked Franklin car. Standing beside it were two beautiful girls, whom I mistook for Hollywood starlets. They were surrounded by boys. Wearing makeup, short skirts, and spike heel shoes, I thought they were sensational. Then, they broke away from the group and ran toward me with open arms. Hy and La. How could they possibly be the same cousins I knew only a year ago? Then realization set in, and [ was crushed with humiliation over myself. That night I felt worse as a pair of "step ins" flew over my head, and a pair of wispy "bras." We were undressing for bed and there I was, caught like a rat in a trap in a pantywaist and bloomers. Slipping into bed I wiggled out of my disgrace under cover. After a sleepless night I reached a resolve over Mother, the Children's Vogue. and Madge Evans to emerge as a new personality. If I didn't, I should waste away and die of shame over myself.

Raking about for the price of a Tangee Beauty Kit, I finally reached my goal, and ordered one. When it arrived, I hid it in the back of my dresser drawer away from prying eyes. It kept company with a pair of silk stockings, a garter belt, and various items important to my plane Doris Morrison, sensing my frustration, provided me with one of her dresses - a black satin one. Very stylish, I thought, but glory be! It was Hy who saved my life with a pair of her spike heel pumps. They were bright green. Each night I would prance around my room straining the calves of my legs in them, for wearing them required practice.

September. The summer was over and we were returning to Fort Smith, where the new "me" was to emerge. Our railroad passes this time placed us into the luxury of a compartment on the sleeping car. Although we were grateful for this consideration, it was crowded with Mother, the little girls and myself. When the train neared Poteau, Oklahoma, Mother was preoccupied with the minutiae of packing up. I mentioned it would be less crowded if I changed in the public women's room just outside our door. Mother nodded.

My change was a speedy one for it had been rehearsed many times from head to toe. On went the black satin dress, the spike heel shoes, and the Tangee makeup. After a glance in the mirror I decided a touch of color would add to the effect, so I slung a long salmon colored chiffon scarf around my neck. Since Mother had not yet seen my secret collection, I thought it wise to go directly to the observation platform ahead of her. Weaving my way back through the rocking train and challenged by unsteady shoes, I finally stepped out onto the platform. Leaning against the railing in an attitude of relaxed boredom, I allowed my long scarf to trail over the side. Looking back, it is a miracle that the train wheels did not engage it, or I might have met the same fate as my idol, Isadora Duncan, who, while motoring, was choked to death on her long scarf. As was the custom in those days, the trains backed into the stations with a piping noise to let waiting greeters know of its arrival. There were two people waiting to meet us - my father and six-foot Ander Orr. I was thrilled to see Andy, but it seemed to me his Adam's apple had developed alarmingly as it seemed in a state of excitement. I looked at my father who had his head tilted to one side and a pensive smile on his face. He seemed to be staring at me, but suddenly wrapped his arms around me and whispered, "I think you look beautiful. I would never have known you!" Just then, Mother, clutching the little girls in each hand, stepped out to join us. After greeting the reception committee, she turned her attention my way in stunned silence. Without a word she opened her handbag and extracted a folded handkerchief. When it was unfurled, she stepped in front of me and scrubbed my face with it Off went the Tangee, but the taste of it will remain with me forever.

---

Back at Riverby when I was almost seventeen, the older grandchildren were occupied with their own interests. With Hy and La, this dealt with boys and some very attractive ones. I too fell into step with my popular cousins by trying to grow up with them. Our weekends swarmed with boys from High Point, a few from Asheville and one or local citizens. One was Spec Alexander who seemed to know everyone in the state of North Carolina. Spec had red hair, freckles, and wore horn-rimmed glasses - which provided his sobriquet. We had a glorious time dashing around hairpin curves on our way to the movies or to roller skate. It was Spec who introduced me to Frank Shields, the promising tennis player. He dropped by Riverby often, and I felt smitten with him. He was a very handsome young man.

After playing about most of the summer, the Major General thought we were wasting our time. She packed up her daughters and sent them to Europe on the Mauritanian. Left behind, she turned her attention to me by introducing me to the new president of the Swannanoa Bank. Despite her efforts toward higher finance, the romance failed to take off, and it was with some relief that both of us looked elsewhere.

After their grand tour, Hy and La returned to Riverby for the balance of the summer where they felt bored. Not for long, however, for a best-selling author came to stay at Riverby.

A man of the world, from New Orleans, he was married and the father of five children. Along with this history, he was endowed with a charming personality. The serious part of this vignette is that he fell head over heels in love with Hy. This romance shook Riverby to its roots. His intentions were not concealed and Hy was gaga about him. When Aunt Lola realized the situation would not run its course, she sent for her husband, Homer Hudson. Steps were taken by ordering the best-selling author off the premises. His departure left the lovelorn Hy in a state of despair. The entire episode was a bad scene for our usual tranquil setting. Time does heal, however, and before long everything was back to normal.

# Editor's Note

Sometimes a simple thought or idea takes on a life of its own and if you run with it you embark on quite a journey. My "thought" came in the spring of 2018 while immersed in genealogical research. The thought was crystal clear, "I need to help my mom have a greater understanding of her family." Thus, began the plans for a road-trip that would begin in her mother's home town of North Carolina. I prepared all summer of 2018 to familiarize myself with names and places I knew nothing about in preparation for our planned trip in the fall. I had a loose plan that included searching for graves and houses, but I fully expected that we would fill-out our schedule prompted by ideas and impressions along the way. That's exactly what happened in a big way.

We had visited the Outer Banks for fun and were packing-up for the drive west to High Point. I had a thought that I really needed to find a living relative, not just search out graves and landmarks. My dad helped me with a lead to a living cousin; and over breakfast I cold-called Chuck Wood, a first cousin of my mom's. Chuck couldn't have been more kind, gracious, and excited during our call. Within a few minutes, we had a dinner invitation to his home in High Point for that night! Chuck also invited his brother Penn, and so it was like finding two "uncles" I never knew I had. For my mom, it was a wonderful reunion with cousins she hadn't been in contact with since her 20's. Stories flowed about family and places of her past. Penn loves genealogy and he pulled out photos, books, and stories. I was in heaven (I should have been recording it). The food was good, but our real feast was all our new insights and perspective about our ancestors.

And this is how it all started. Penn had a two-volume 568-page manuscript called Riverby Inn! I asked him if I could keep it for the night—a big ask of any genealogist, particularly coming from someone he'd just met that day. He graciously let me borrow the manuscript and I was immediately hooked. It was like watching a mini-series in the 1930's about a family I had never known. I was in love with this family! I felt an instant connection to Mam-maw Jeffie. I love the picture of her and Frank in the beginning of this book. Her sweet smile reflects the loving mother and grandmother that she was. Oh, how she loved and influenced her grandchildren.

I had never really known my grandmother Hy as she died when I was young. My mom's view of Hy was shaped by many difficult years and mom imparted those impressions to me. But in the manuscript, Hy came to life. I met her as a teenager—still young and vulnerable, adventurous and at times rebellious, and not yet shaped by the challenges of adulthood. Even my mom's feelings, as conflicted as they were for her own mother, softened as she saw a side of her mother that she had never known.

I knew in that first late-night reading of the borrowed manuscript that it had power to shape the hearts of an audience that was bigger than just me and my mom. I wanted my children to have it. Were there other cousins that like me had never seen it or heard its stories? Were there others outside the family that could draw inspiration from the rich stories of sometimes messy and sometimes crazy love that fill the pages of Riverby Inn?

I wanted to know about the house that brought them together. I could envision the porch, the river, the yard, but what did it really look like? Pictures bring things to life, make them real and personal. So began a quest to find pictures of the Riverby Inn and the people in the story. I spent the next several months searching for photos. That journey led me to find cousin after cousin all over the country. One cousin might have a piece of information or photo, but most often they led me to another cousin. In many cases,

I introduced cousins that hadn't known each other, some even living in the same city. With each new lead, I discovered that we, the descendants of Frank and Jeffie Blanks, have a wonderful extended family! Everyone has been so kind and helpful.

After three trips to Asheville and many emails and texts I found one of my greatest treasures, Martha Lee. The last living grandchild of Riverby. Martha was born and raised in Swannanoa. The timing was perfect, her children invited me and my mom to her 95th birthday party. Martha's children are as gracious as she is, welcoming these unknown cousins form across the country. I can see why Martha was such a treasure to Mam-maw. It means a lot to me to share the special name sake with her as one of the "Lee's". I have had the privilege of meeting many other cousins along the way. I love and thank all the cousins I've met through this experience! I've thought often of Mam-maw Jeffie and I can almost hear her whisper just how happy she is that her descendants are finding each other.

This journey has been a guided one, as "Betts" said, "with God's help". I started out just to digitize and edit the manuscript. But the ideas of what should be added kept coming. Ideas and items fell into place or popped-up seemingly out of nowhere. One thought that grew was my personal desire to have a painting of the Riverby Inn, to see color and life in the picture. I wanted it for my wall and to share with others, but I was soon convinced it needed to be on the cover of the book. Additionally, on my last trip to Asheville, I came across a post card of an old house and remembered reading something that Frank said to my great-grandmother Lola on seeing the house for the first time, "it would make a nice post card." Soon, the painting of Riverby will be postcard.

This all started as a genealogy quest. Usually, genealogical research leads to data, mostly facts and sometimes if one is lucky to a few stories. It is rare indeed to find so many relatives' memories compiled into one novelesque manuscript. I love Betts' words, "what was once our book is now theirs [ours]." I sincerely hope that publishing this book will be a blessing to the extended Blanks family and a joy to all those outside the family that read it.

This book has come about because of collaboration. The journey is not over. If you have anything to contribute to the family's discovery of our past, please follow the link below to contribute photos or stories about the Blanks extended family or the Riverby Inn in particular.

I'm beyond grateful to my husband Jeff for his overwhelming support and invaluable technical help, he's a great co-editor and without him this project wouldn't be what it is.

Christy Lee Richards

https://www.facebook.com/groups/431462494187962/?ref=share
join the Frank and Jeffie Blanks Family group on fb

# End Notes

[1] Homer Leon Blanks' death was recorded in the Asheville Citizen Times on September 16th, 1960.

## Swannanoa Native Dies In Air Crash

The bodies of Leon Blanks, 33, a native of Swannanoa, and of three of his companions who perished Thursday in the wreckage of a small plane on Costa Rica's Osa Peninsula, were recovered Monday, an Associated Press dispatch from San Jose said.

Found dead in the wreckage with Blanks, were R. D. McDonand, Merrill Hire and George Brundage. Blanks and McDonand were National Airlines pilots, and Hire and Brundage, residents of San Jose. Hire was described as owner of the plane.

Cause of the crash had not been determined.

Blanks was the son of Mrs. Norma Beale Blanks and the late Claude C. Blanks, who resided for many years at Riverby Inn in Swannanoa. The mother is now residing with her daughter, Mrs. William Nickless, in Oak Park, Ill.

Survivors in addition to the mother and daughter include the widow, who lives in Miami, Fla., and a brother, Charles Blanks of Houston, Texas.

Leon Blanks lived in Swannanoa from the time of his birth until about 12 years ago.

[2] GPS coordinates: 35.600158, -82.407401

[3] GPS coordinates: 35.595263,-82.533972

[4] GPS coordinates: 35.595478,-82.554592; Image source: https://dc.lib.unc.edu/cdm/ref/collection/nc_post/id/7820

[5] GPS coordinates: 35.594811,-82.554079

[6] GPS coordinates: 35.607219,-82.413096

[7] The image shown may be the train wreck mentioned in the story. Source: Asheville Citizen Times, December 14, 1933, pg. 14

[8] Claude's dog was covered in an Asheville Citizen Times, September 6, 1930

## Large St. Bernard Dog Center Of Litigation

If a huge St. Bernard dog visitor to Asheville from Mukwonago, Wis., could speak his mind, he probably would give utterance to the statement that "the love of money is the root of all evil."

The dog, purchased from the Berncrest Kennels in the Wisconsin town, came to his present owner, C. F. Blanks, of Swannanoa, with a price upon his head, a matter of $275. Such a price for a dog of blue blood pedigree is not unreasonable and in ordinary cases should not cause any complications. However, when he arrived in custody of the Southeastern Express Company, the dog found his new master waiting with the $275. He also found waiting Miss Alice H. French, who was armed with a warrant of attachment to be served on his canine person. It was then that the legal complications began.

Mr. Blanks paid to the express company the purchase price and charges on his huge pet, and in turn Miss French attached the amount for the $200 which she says represents a debt owed to her by the kennels shipping the animal to Asheville. Satisfied that he had been bought and paid for, the dog went happily home with his master. However, he later turned up in Magistrate C. F. Sumner's court.

Magistrate Sumner, in accordance with the law governing such matters, yesterday deferred action in the case until publication of a warrant of attachment has been made for 30 days. The case will be tried October 4 or 5, provided all parties concerned are ready. In the meantime, the dog is with his master and his price is being held by the express company, pending an outcome of the action. There can be no doubt, it was said, that the dog is the legal property of Mr. Blanks, for he has a receipt from the express company.

The St. Bernard dog is one of the largest ever seen in Asheville. He is several pounds heavier than Jiggs, another of the same species who recently came into prominence over a suit heard by Magistrate Sumner.

[9] The Asheville Citizen Times described the kidnapping in a front-page story on January 28, 1938

Kidnap Victim Identifies Payne

Miss Lola LaVerne Hedges, left, yesterday from the witness stand identified Bill Payne as the man who kidnaped her and a companion from the Asheville Recreation park last August. Dr. J. R. Sevier center is president of Fassifern school at Hendersonville, where Miss Hedges is a student. Mrs. Emma Payne, mother of the defendant now on trial for the murder of a highway patrolman is shown at the extreme right.

## Miss Hedges Describes Her Abduction By Payne

### School Girl Identifies Him As Kidnaper At Murder Trial

A pretty 16-year-old school girl took the stand in Buncombe county superior court here yesterday and told how "Mr Payne" kidnaped her and a companion at the Asheville Recreation park last summer, and forced them at pistol point to drive him to Thomasville.

The witness was Miss Lola LaVerne Hedges, of Fort Smith, Ark. and the "Mr. Payne" she referred to is Bill Payne, on trial for his life in connection with the slaying of a state highway patrolman.

Miss Hedges subpoenaed by the state came here from Hendersonville where she is a student at Fassifern girls' school. She spends the summer with relatives at Swannanoa.

**Kidnaped At Park**

A few days after Patrolman George Penn was slain last August 22, Miss Hedges and a companion, Sam Wolfe, 18, of Swannanoa, visited the Recreation park.

As they were getting in their car shortly after 9 o'clock that evening, a heavily-bearded stranger poked a gun in Miss Hedges ribs and told her to do as he instructed.

Wolfe, at the time was entering the opposite side of the car and the stranger got in and sat down beside the girl.

He kept the gun pressed hard against her side, but told the couple if they did as he told them they would not be harmed.

As the three continued east on the Black Mountain highway and passed within a few hundred feet of Miss Hedges' home the school girl struck a bargain with the desperado.

**Asks Him To Move Gun**

"I would be a lot more comfortable if you would take that gun out of my side," she said.

"Give me your promise you won't try any funny stuff," replied the uninvited passenger, as he removed the gun.

Through the night they traveled stopping for gas and food and proceeding under the stranger's directions.

Shortly after they passed through Thomasville, the shabbily-dressed passenger took the wheel and turned back along the route they had just passed over.

Back at Thomasville he handed Miss Hedges 25 one-dollar bills pointed out to her a hotel, instructed the couple not to spread an alarm for three hours and drove off, assuring them he would telephone shortly telling where he had left their automobile.

Miss Hedges and Wolfe complied with the parting instructions.

**Picks Out Payne's Picture**

At dawn they communicated with their folks at Swannanoa, contacted Thomasville policemen and described their abductor.

"It sounds like Bill Payne," the policemen remarked.

A short time later at High Point police headquarters Miss Hedges and Wolfe selected from twelve pictures the man they said was their kidnaper.

It was a likeness of Bill Payne, and so closely had the 16-year-old school girl studied the features of her captor she was positive he was the man.

Back at home she told of the polite and considerate abductor, and

—(Please Turn To Page Ten)

## GIRL DESCRIBES HER ABDUCTION BY BILL PAYNE

(Continued From Page One)

the courtesy he showed her and Wolfe during the long ride.

"I thought he was a petty thief who had robbed somebody at the Recreation park. He told us he had been living in the woods and hadn't eaten in several days."

**Admitted Kidnaping**

Then on January 3 the notorious Bill Payne was captured by G-men at Sanford. Turned over to Buncombe county authorities to face trial on murder charges. Payne admitted. Sheriff Laurence E. Brown testified on the witness stand yesterday, that he is the man who took Miss Hedges and Wolfe on the midnight ride.

Miss Hedges too identified him yesterday from the witness stand.

Payne sat with his hand in his chin listening, as the pretty blonde school girl told her story. It was the first time he has been called "Mr." in the courtroom here, and spectators laughed.

[10] GPS Coordinates: 34.952272,-93.065746
[11] GPS Coordinates: 34.936388,-93.055492